Garage Virtual Reality

D1611473

Linda Jacobson

SAMS
PUBLISHING

A Division of Prentice Hall Computer Publishing
201 West 103rd Street, Indianapolis, IN 46290

To my grandmothers, Matilda Jacobson and Melitta Mezansky, for teaching me the importance of self-reliance and the value of sharing, and to poets everywhere, because "poetry comprehends all science."—Percy Bysshe Shelley, Defence of Poetry

Copyright © 1994 by Sams Publishing

FIRST EDITION

All rights reserved. No part of this book shall be reproduced, stored in a retrieval system, or transmitted by any means, electronic, mechanical, photocopying, recording, or otherwise, without written permission from the publisher. No patent liability is assumed with respect to the use of the information contained herein. Although every precaution has been taken in the preparation of this book, the publisher and author assume no responsibility for errors or omissions. Neither is any liability assumed for damages resulting from the use of the information contained herein. For information, address Sams Publishing, 201 W. 103rd St., Indianapolis, IN 46290.

International Standard Book Number: 0-672-30270-5

Library of Congress Catalog Card Number: 92-62687

96   95   94   93   4   3   2   1

Interpretation of the printing code: the rightmost double-digit number is the year of the book's printing; the rightmost single-digit, the number of the book's printing. For example, a printing code of 93-1 shows that the first printing of the book occurred in 1993.

Composed in AGaramond, Futura, and MCPdigital by Prentice Hall Computer Publishing

Printed in the United States of America

Trademarks

All terms mentioned in this book that are known to be trademarks or service marks have been appropriately capitalized. Sams Publishing cannot attest to the accuracy of this information. Use of a term in this book should not be regarded as affecting the validity of any trademark or service mark.

PUBLISHER

Richard K. Swadley

ASSOCIATE PUBLISHER

Jordan Gold

ACQUISITIONS MANAGER

Stacy Hiquet

DEVELOPMENT EDITOR

Dean Miller

PRODUCTION EDITOR

Gayle L. Johnson

COPY EDITOR

Mary Inderstrodt

EDITORIAL COORDINATOR

Bill Whitmer

EDITORIAL ASSISTANTS

Sharon Cox
Lynnette Quinn
Tammy Stewart

TECHNICAL REVIEWERS

Randal Walser
Jerry Isdale
Eric Townsend

MARKETING MANAGER

Greg Wiegand

COVER DESIGNER

Jean Bisesi

ILLUSTRATOR

Richard Eberly

DIRECTOR OF PRODUCTION AND MANUFACTURING

Jeff Valler

IMPRINT MANAGER

Kelli Widdifield

BOOK DESIGNER

Michele Laseau

PRODUCTION ANALYST

Mary Beth Wakefield

PROOFREADING/INDEXING COORDINATOR

Joelynn Gifford

GRAPHICS IMAGE SPECIALISTS

Tim Montgomery
Dennis Sheehan
Sue VandeWalle

PRODUCTION

Nick Anderson
Angela Bannan
Diana Bigham
Ayrika Bryant
Lisa Daugherty
Mitzi Gianakos
Sean Medlock
Wendy Ott
Juli Pavey
Angela M. Pozdol
Ryan Rader
Beth Rago
Tonya Simpson
Suzanne Tully
Dennis Wesner
Alyssa Yesh

INDEXER

Jennifer Eberhardt

Overview

Contents

Garage Virtual Reality

Garage Virtual Reality

xiv

Garage Virtual Reality

Acknowledgments

Rounds of applause go to the following people, who contributed much to the process of producing the following pages: Stacy Hiquet of Sams Publishing, for suggesting that I write this book; Gradecki Publishing, *PCVR* magazine, and Joe and Waverly, for their contributions (living up to their belief that "sharing will greatly benefit everyone in the process of getting virtual reality off the drawing boards"); everyone who provided programs, interface designs, schematics, and virtual worlds for the disk and Chapter 8, including Doug Faxon, Joe Gradecki, Mark Koch, Mark Pflaging, and Mark Reaney; my brilliant tech editors Randy Walser, Eric Townsend, and Jerry Isdale; the folks in the sci.virtual-worlds virtual community who responded to inquiries with thoughtful, thorough explanations, especially Mark Reaney, Pete Falco, Jon Blossom, Bill Cockayne, Mark Koch, Dave Stampe, Randy Pausch, Chris Babcock, Chris Hufnagel, and Juri Munkki; Rich Gold and the Xerox PARC library; and David Javelosa of Sega/America for arranging the Sega VR demo.

Thanks, *Wired* magazine, for publishing my "Garage VR" article that led to this book.

Thanks, Karen Nazor, for your astute literary agentry and encouragement.

Thanks, Bean (Tina Blaine), for your editorial advice and for lending a hand (and arm) for the Power Glove photos.

Thanks to all my friends who read parts of this book and provided editorial comments, technical expertise, and constructive criticism.

Thanks, my D'Cückoo family, for providing me with space—both literally and figuratively—to write this book.

Thanks, Kathryn Eberly, for your support, balancing perspectives, motivating commentary, and that Martian Popping Thing.

About the Author

Linda Jacobson was born in Brooklyn, New York, and raised in the Rockaways. She has written about emerging communications and entertainment technologies since 1980, when she graduated from Boston University with a journalism degree. Linda learned how to read schematics and play with computers at her first job as a technical writer for an audio/video synchronization equipment manufacturer. After moving to San Francisco in 1982, Linda launched her journalism career as an editor for the music recording industry magazine *Mix*. In the years following, she helped develop and edit several other publications, including *HyperMedia* (now *NewMedia*), *EQ*, and *Wired*.

Linda's first book, *Cyberarts: Exploring Art and Technology* (Miller Freeman, 1992), is an anthology of essays and articles about the use of digital technologies in the arts.

These days Linda serves as Virtual Worlds Editor for *Wired*, teaches seminars on VR for San Francisco State University's extended education program, and documents inventions for the Xerox PARC computer science lab. She also works with the multimedia techno-arts collective/world funk ensemble D'Cückoo. With her friends Timothy Childs and Peter Rothman, she co-organizes and hosts meetings of VeRGe, the San Francisco Bay-area virtual reality group.

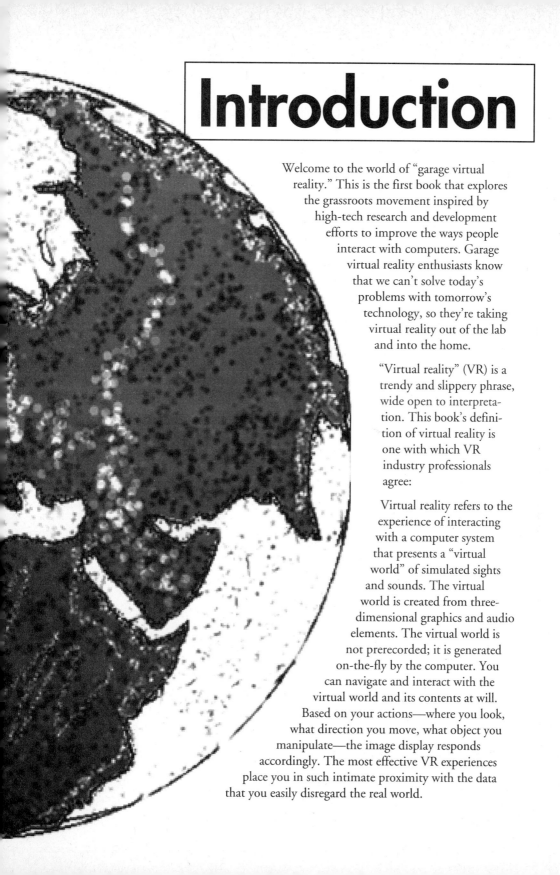

Introduction

Welcome to the world of "garage virtual reality." This is the first book that explores the grassroots movement inspired by high-tech research and development efforts to improve the ways people interact with computers. Garage virtual reality enthusiasts know that we can't solve today's problems with tomorrow's technology, so they're taking virtual reality out of the lab and into the home.

"Virtual reality" (VR) is a trendy and slippery phrase, wide open to interpretation. This book's definition of virtual reality is one with which VR industry professionals agree:

Virtual reality refers to the experience of interacting with a computer system that presents a "virtual world" of simulated sights and sounds. The virtual world is created from three-dimensional graphics and audio elements. The virtual world is not prerecorded; it is generated on-the-fly by the computer. You can navigate and interact with the virtual world and its contents at will. Based on your actions—where you look, what direction you move, what object you manipulate—the image display responds accordingly. The most effective VR experiences place you in such intimate proximity with the data that you easily disregard the real world.

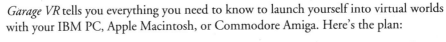

Garage VR tells you everything you need to know to launch yourself into virtual worlds with your IBM PC, Apple Macintosh, or Commodore Amiga. Here's the plan:

Chapter 1, "The Search for 'Tech-Knowledgy,'" takes a look at the time-honored tradition of creating technological innovations at home, in the garage, workshop, or basement. Chapter 2, "Way Back When," provides a brief historical overview of virtual reality and cyberspace. It also lists books and magazines for readers interested in learning more about high-end VR. Chapter 3, "VR Comes in Several Styles," describes the categories of virtual-worlds technologies, or "levels" of VR: immersive VR, simulator VR, projection VR, desktop VR, and garage VR. Chapter 4, "The Engine: Computer Platforms," discusses personal computers in terms of their capabilities to support garage VR exploration.

Chapter 5, "The Windshield: Visual Displays," explores the relatively low-cost 2D and 3D visual output devices that let you display and view virtual worlds. Chapter 6, "The Cockpit: Input Devices," investigates the usual and unusual low-cost input devices that let you control your interactions with virtual worlds. Chapter 7, "The Fuel: Software for Garage VR," describes the software programs, both commercial and freeware, that let you create, explore, and interact with garage VR. It also covers basic concepts of 3D modeling, rendering, stereoscopic imagery, and virtual world-building. Chapter 8, "Hacking for the Trip," helps you set up your garage VR assembly line. This is the "how-to" section for those who want to build interface circuits, head-mounted displays, or stereoscopic viewers; engineer a "virtual handshake"; or analyze garage VR software code.

Chapter 9, "Carpooling: Traveling with Friends on the Data Highways," explains ways to radically enrich your garage VR efforts with the help of a modem, phone line, and telecommunications software. Chapter 10, "Places to Go," suggests several professional and personal uses for your garage VR system. Chapter 11, "The Road Ahead: The Future of Garage VR," examines the future of garage VR. Virtual reality is a relatively new technology; no one can accurately predict its long-term future or its precise economic and cultural significance. Consider another previously newfangled technology: photography. Several decades passed before people developed a full appreciation of its enormous impact.

Appendix A is a reprint of a *CyberEdge Journal* interview with a teenage garage VR enthusiast. Appendix B explains how to download files and programs from remote computer systems on the Internet. Appendix C lists names and addresses of vendors of low-cost VR products. Appendix D lists information resources: reading materials and VR clubs, organizations, and producers of relevant conferences. Appendix E is the garage VR glossary. Appendix F covers the contents of your garage VR "fuel kit"—the disk provided with this book.

Interspersed throughout the book are tour guide profiles that introduce you to some warm-hearted pioneers who have helped put garage VR on the map. All of these tour guides have made significant contributions to the field and eagerly share ideas and resources with others who want to travel the same unpaved paths. All the tour guides possess sharp minds, strong opinions, remarkable energy, old-fashioned *chutzpah,* and the desire to challenge the techno status quo. Like garage VR, all the tour guides are young (at heart, if not by the calendar). Without exception, they're male. I hope this book inspires women to join the "Garage VR Explorers' Club."

Virtual-world builders intend to create and present experiences that occur in reality or only in the imagination, representing ideas that can be manipulated in ways not possible in the real world.

This book attempts to illustrate the experience of building virtual worlds, thereby motivating novices to build some themselves. If more of us bring VR technologies into our homes, we can help create a demand for the hardware and software. In turn, demand can help lower the price of high-tech tools. Then, individuals working on their own can concentrate more on creativity than on the inherent technological limitations of low-end VR.

I also hope this book encourages a sense of community among the geographically dispersed and that it reaches people who feel lonely on their virtual journeys. As garage VR pioneer Bernie Roehl says, "When you're sitting in front of a computer screen for long hours, it's so easy to think, 'I'm the only in the world doing something like this.' I find it really inspiring to talk to people who are interested in VR, because it reminds me that I'm not alone."

You're not alone!

Linda Jacobson
lindaj@well.sf.ca.us
San Francisco, October 1993

The Search for "Tech-Knowledgy"

The Search for "Tech-Knowledgy"

"A good traveler has no fixed plans
and is not intent upon arriving.
A good artist lets his intuition
lead him wherever it wants.
A good scientist has freed himself of concepts
and keeps his mind open to what is."
—Lao-Tzu

We love to know. Our search for knowledge and our quest to learn dates back to the days when our ancestors lived in caves. Long before the word *science* existed, we were scientists—because we needed to survive.

That survival instinct led to the first scientific discoveries: transforming plants and herbs into food and medicine, turning rocks and sticks into tools and weapons, and making animal skins and innards into clothing and shelter. Through observation and experimentation, people crafted ways to boost the quality of their lives.

In those early times, however, people based "scientific" ideas on theories put forth by philosophers and religious leaders. Not until the late 1600s did such scientists as Isaac Newton and Edmond Halley start emphasizing experimentation as a valid method of gaining knowledge of the world and how it works.

A new generation of thinkers began examining the natural world by testing ideas and instruments. Their methods and achievements shaped Western scientific thinking and changed the way people viewed the world. Many fifteenth-century Europeans, for example, thought the sky contained crystal spheres that carried the stars and planets around the earth. Newton's invention of the telescope in 1692 resulted in discoveries that forced people to reject that old notion. This invention in turn altered people's ideas of their own positions in the universe.

New inventions and discoveries continue to change the way we look at the universe. Today, astronomers at Ohio's National Supercomputing Center use three-dimensional graphics software on supercomputers to construct visualizations of the galaxy's complex star fields. They use *virtual reality* (*VR*) devices to "fly around" in the data. Their goal is to understand the structure of the universe. Already the astronomers have witnessed surprises in the data—things they couldn't experience before there was VR—such as the way vast numbers of galaxies clump together in threads, ribbons, and clusters, leaving tremendous voids.

Astronomy is one of many sciences reaping the benefits of VR technologies. Through the construction and exploration of virtual worlds, more scientists in medicine, aerospace, physics, geology, chemistry, genetics, and molecular biology are finding new ways to achieve their diverse objectives.

Likewise, people working in a wide range of other professions are exploring virtual worlds—and, as a result, are enhancing every field of human endeavor:

 Architects use VR to test building designs before they hand out blueprints.

 Pilots soar into cyberspace to learn how to fly without having to take off into real skies.

 Stockbrokers "fly" through fields of financial data to help clients make the right investments.

Engineers and designers don VR goggles and gloves to test the designs of everything from aircraft to cars to furniture.

 Sales and marketing executives admire the potential of engaging their customers with virtual versions of wares.

Entertainment technologists and artists aim to harness VR to affect and enhance the illusory domains of cinema and stage and to shape the future of the video game and the arcade, at home and in public. Theme park designers are gearing up to produce VR rides. Motion picture studios are developing virtual movies in which the audience will interact with the actors.

Meanwhile, scientists and academicians at corporate and educational institutions around the world are devoting long hours to the research and development of virtual-world technologies and techniques.

The exciting and important advances made by these professionals have inspired a new generation of techno-savvy computer users who don't necessarily have access to funding. The professionals can spend company money to buy equipment, and they receive paychecks for their efforts. They represent the "techno-elite." Until recently, they were the ones who defined VR. Their experiences proved that virtual-world travel costs big bucks: a modest, immersive VR workstation system costs at least $20,000. Nonetheless, determined, creative "technoids" across the country are redefining VR by hacking personal-computer-based VR systems for less than $2,500. These people are the garage VR pioneers.

Thinkers and tinkerers, garage VR pioneers devise, craft, and navigate their vehicles of discovery—usually at home, alone, and after finishing work or school for the day. Their minds spew ideas, stoked by the courage of their convictions and the strength of their dedication. They recognize that ideas are worthless until application proves them practical. Working feverishly, compulsively, sometimes obsessively, they turn idea into invention. By designing low-cost, computer-based environments and devices that allow various levels of sensory immersion, they inadvertently contribute to human and scientific progress.

In seeking insights into virtual worlds, the garage VR pioneer blends two quests for knowledge: discovery and invention. Discoverers set their sights on some distant horizon of space or time, and inventors focus sharply on nearby challenges. Discoverers are adventurers who want to explore the world. Inventors are artisans who want to change the world. Discoverer and inventor unite in the soul of the garage VR pioneer.

Changing the world isn't necessarily what motivates the budget-conscious virtual-world explorer. Above all else, the garage VR pioneer wants to participate in—and not merely watch—the development of a technology. The pioneer cherishes the ways VR can enhance one's experience of physical reality and laughs at the suggestion that one needs lots of money to become virtual.

Garage VR represents the most recent pursuit in the grand tradition of American at-home ingenuity. Over the years, everyone's lives have been affected by the accomplishments of inventors who worked quietly on their own, funded by their personal savings or by their parents' savings:

- Samuel Morse wondered whether he could transmit information by "lightning wire." By 1837, he had devised the first electromagnetic telegraph, which sent a message more than 50 feet, from one room to another in his Poughkeepsie, New York, house.

- Charles Goodyear experimented in his kitchen lab for more than four years before his 1839 discovery of vulcanization—how to prevent rubber from getting sticky in the heat and brittle in the cold. (The kitchen wasn't at his house, but in a cottage on the grounds of his home-away-from-home: debtor's prison.)

- A room in his Menlo Park house in rural New Jersey served as Thomas Edison's first invention factory. It was there, in 1877, that he yelled "Halloo!" into a contrivance that played back the shouted word—thus inventing the first phonograph.

- Also in 1877, George Eastman started cooking chemical emulsions on his mother's kitchen stove in Rochester, New York. He was intent on simplifying the process of picture-taking. He made photography foolproof and went on to found Eastman Kodak.

- Behind his Detroit home, Henry Ford spent hours in a work shed. There he built his first automobile, the Quadricycle (so named because of its four bicycle wheels), but it couldn't fit through the door. Armed with an axe, he demolished the work shed's door frame and wall. Then he took his first drive.

- While on vacation in 1903, after watching a frustrated streetcar driver continually stop the vehicle to climb out and swipe frost from the window, Mary Anderson went home to Birmingham, Alabama and penned a patent for the first fan-shaped windshield wiper.

- In 1920, Earl and Josephine Dickson devised the first adhesive sanitary bandage in their kitchen in New Brunswick, New Jersey. Their invention later was purchased and named the Band-Aid by Johnson & Johnson, for whom Earl worked as a cotton buyer.

- In 1938, in the basement of his home in upstate New York, Chester Carlson used a process he dubbed *xerography* (from the Greek *xeros,* meaning "dry," and *graphein,* meaning "to write") to produce an image. He patented the process, which later became the product of a company called Xerox.

Soon after the debut of Intel's first commercial microprocessor in 1971, electronics hobbyists started wiring keyboards, television screens, and microprocessors to primitive microcomputers. Two such technoids were Stephen Wozniak and Steven Jobs. They built small computers in the Jobs family garage in Palo Alto, California. In 1975, the duo launched a company to market the first Apple computer, which was sold in kit form to members of the country's first computing association, the Home-Brew Club.

 In 1981, while still living with his parents in Queens Village, New York, Thomas Zimmerman decided he wanted to conduct "invisible orchestras" playing real music. He also wanted his air-guitar playing to create real sounds. Working in his bedroom, Tom adorned a gardening glove with plastic tubing and $10 worth of LEDs and phototransistors. He wired the glove to his Atari 400 computer. When he waved his gloved hand, the Atari's built-in sound synthesizer made music. This invention was the inspiration for the DataGlove, which Tom later marketed with partner Jaron Lanier under the name VPL Research in Redwood City, California. Figure 1.1 shows Tom with one of his DataGloves.

A few years after Tom sold his share of VPL Research and set up shop as an independent engineer in San Francisco, the mass media started trumpeting the marvels of VR. This technology's celebrity (and the affordability of certain control and output devices for personal computers) gave rise to a new generation of home-based inventors. Hot to cybertrot, these neo-nerds grabbed the VR gauntlet and waltzed it right into their residential workshops. In wired garages across the land, they're revving their reality engines so they can stick their heads and poke their fingers into the kinds of cyberspaces previously inhabitable only by the techno-elite. With the right tools and techniques, they're building virtual worlds. And they're not hocking the house to do it.

Now You Can Join Them

Naturally, you need more than cash. You need time. You need access to electronics supplies. You need tinkerer traits, such as the ability to wield a soldering iron to connect one device to another. You need programming chops to create interactive worlds on your PC. However, you don't need to learn programming to conceive a simple *walk-through,* in which you navigate through a virtual environment but can't interact with various virtual objects in that environment.

Most of all, you need a burning desire—if not to turn your dreams into reality, then to turn your dream *worlds* into virtual reality.

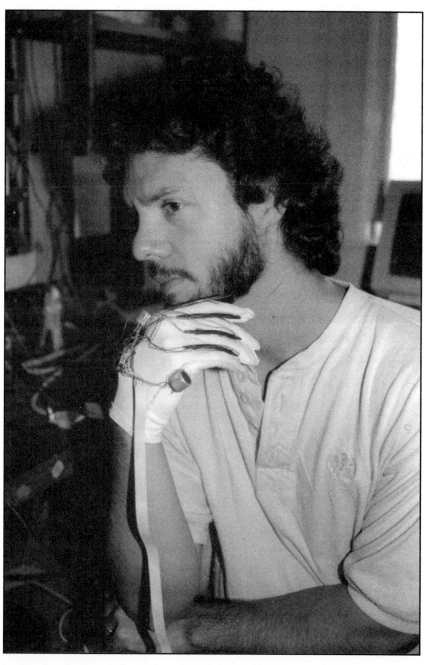

Figure 1.1. *Inventor Tom Zimmerman wearing one of his early DataGloves. Designed in 1985, it worked with the Commodore 64, and it sported ultrasonic position sensors that detected motion in five degrees of freedom. Tom is now working on his PhD at the MIT Media Lab. The glove is retired. (Photo by Linda Jacobson)*

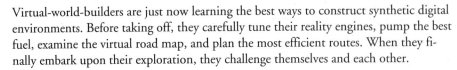

The Search for "Tech-Knowledgy"

Virtual-world-builders are just now learning the best ways to construct synthetic digital environments. Before taking off, they carefully tune their reality engines, pump the best fuel, examine the virtual road map, and plan the most efficient routes. When they finally embark upon their exploration, they challenge themselves and each other.

Garage VR developers are helping to humanize the technology. Because building virtual worlds invariably leads to the sharing of information and experiences with other people, it affects the social and cultural relationships we have in the real world.

Successful inventions offer benefits to society at large. They present ways to improve our chances to survive and thrive. They even generate employment and boast the ability to make economies grow. These are indeed the hallmarks of the inventions created by garage VR pioneers, the people who blend the traits of discoverer and inventor. Perhaps you recognize some of these traits in yourself.

Way Back When

Way Back When

GARAGE VR

To know where you're going, it helps to know where you've been.

The desire to visualize alphanumeric data as an "information place" that we can enter and explore, where there are graphic objects that we can move and manipulate, stems from our yen for more intuitive interaction with data. Most of us use the catch-all term "virtual reality" to describe this approach to dealing with computers. Some people like the term. Others—particularly academicians, researchers, and some software and hardware developers—eschew "virtual reality" because the term is trendy. Its meaning is vague and open to interpretation.

Popularized in the late 1980s, this appellation probably won't remain fashionable for very long. As more people in business, science, education, and entertainment incorporate virtual-world technologies in their work, products and applications that now bear the VR title will blend into the mainstream of computer-based development and engineering. Instead, we'll probably identify the resulting effects: synthetic digital environments, simulated buildings, 3D terrain, full-body immersion, and so on.

A Rose by Any Other Name…

Techno-firms keep coming up with new names for virtual reality, including

Computer-generated artificial worlds

Computer-augmented reality

Synthetic digital environments

Telepresence

Virtual worlds

Artificial reality

Annotated reality

Three-dimensional immersive environments

…and more names crop up every year.

One VR-related term that probably will survive is *cyberspace*. Cyberspace is the place created by the networking of multiple VR systems. Cyberspace also describes the gargantuan information space in which we all operate. Some people say that cyberspace is where you are when you're having a phone conversation. Science fiction author William Gibson coined "cyberspace" in his 1984 book *Neuromancer*. Gibson imagined that all who live by computers will one day commingle in a jointly created virtual world: "mankind's unthinkably complex consensual hallucination, the matrix, cyberspace…."

Virtual reality may seem like science fiction, but it represents the convergence of several nonfiction scientific disciplines, including human-computer interface design, simulation and data visualization, robotics, computer graphics, stereoscopy, and computer-aided design.

Technically speaking, VR's primary ancestor is the simulation industry, which dates back to the flight simulators that the U.S. Air Force started building after World War II. Another predecessor is the entertainment industry. In 1952, a young cinematographer named Mort Heilig saw the first Broadway production of the giant-screen film *This Is Cinerama!* This pivotal encounter led him to invent the Sensorama simulator (see Figure 2.1). Sensorama was a one-person demo unit that combined 3D movies, stereo sound, mechanical vibrations, fan-blown air, and aromas to suggest the potential of what Mort called "experiential cinema." The viewer sat on Sensorama's motorcycle seat, grabbed the handlebars, and peered into Viewmaster-type goggles to enjoy "the ultimate film experience": a multisensory ride through a flower market, the beach, and the streets of Brooklyn. Patented in 1962, Sensorama was based in part on technology that Mort patented in 1960—Stereoscopic Television Apparatus for Individual Use (a TV viewing mask). (See Figure 2.2.) Mort showed Sensorama around the big studios in Los Angeles, but the movie moguls just didn't appreciate the significance of his vision. Instead of inspiring Hollywood, Sensorama wound up as a coin-operated attraction at arcades in the early 1960s.

A few years later, a young engineer named Ivan Sutherland demonstrated to the scientific community the radical notion of using computers for design work. This paved the way for computer graphics, opening the door for hundreds of computer uses. In 1965, Sutherland wrote, "A display connected to a digital computer gives us a chance to gain familiarity with concepts not realizable in the physical world. It is a looking glass into a mathematical wonderland." This perspective led to Sutherland's development of the first fully functional head-mounted display for computer graphics—the helmet that led to today's stereoscopic data goggles. Sutherland went on to cofound Evans & Sutherland, a leading supplier of high-end military simulators.

Stereoscopy—the viewing of objects that appear three-dimensional—dates back to 1832, when Charles Wheatstone invented the stereoscopic viewer. By the end of the nineteenth century, stereo viewers were all the rage. Today, three-dimensional graphics is the field of computer science concerned with representing objects in three dimensions on a two-dimensional screen. Artists use computers to create complex 3D images that can be changed almost instantly to suggest how your view would change as you move around, through, over, or under a scene. The 3D graphics software imbues the image with visual cues that trick the viewer into thinking that he or she is seeing depth, or three dimensions. Yet the image is flat—2D. When viewed in true 3D with stereoscopic devices, the image seems to extend in front of and behind the face of the monitor. Imagine how a product designer uses this technique to visualize and examine every surface and line of an object before creating the real thing.

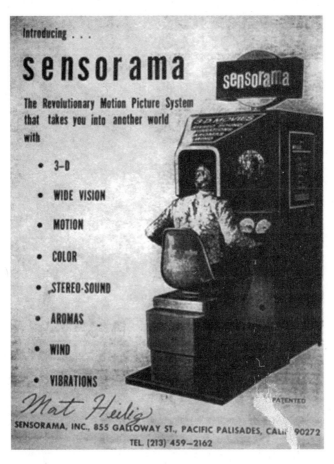

Figure 2.1. A Sensorama flyer.

In virtual reality, 3D imaging imbues virtual objects with substance, imparting a greater sense of "presence" in the virtual world.

Virtual worlds needn't appear three-dimensional to provide an enriching experience. Arts scholar Myron Krueger wasn't concerned with stereoscopy when he coined the term *artificial reality* back in 1970. He was interested in "computer-controlled responsive environments" that approached computers from an aesthetic standpoint. Krueger felt that computer keyboards prevented most people from using computers for artistic expression. So he created Videoplace, an art installation consisting of a computer-controlled video camera and large projection screen. As the user faces the screen, the camera below the screen captures his or her image, which is combined with computer-generated graphics and projected onto the screen. Movements are translated into actions in the two-dimensional graphic scene. The person's image, displayed in colorful silhouette, can lift, push, or toss graphic objects, swing on graphic ropes, and shrink, rotate, or move anywhere on the screen. See Figure 2.3.

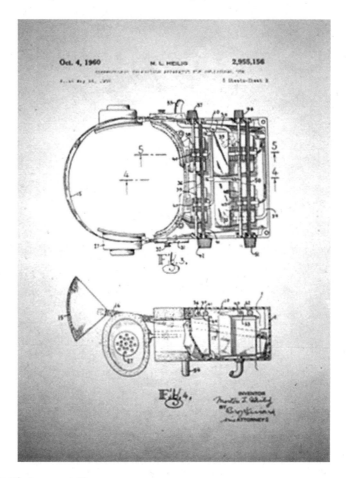

Figure 2.2. *The Stereoscopic Viewer patent.*

Throughout the 1970s, Krueger struggled to find funding for Videoplace. Meanwhile, the federal government was backing other research and development (R&D) projects that played lead roles in VR's history, such as MIT's Moviemap project, which lets the user "travel" through a videotaped version of Aspen by touching parts of the screen. Then there was the U.S. Air Force's SuperCockpit project. Marshalled by Tom Furness at Ohio's Wright-Patterson Air Force base, SuperCockpit came to fruition in 1981 after many years of development. The mock cockpit uses computers and head-mounted displays to depict 3D graphic space through which pilots learn to fly and fight—without taking off into real skies and inflicting real injuries. SuperCockpit was amazingly successful. It cost many millions of dollars, however, and researchers at NASA Ames Research Center in Moffett Field, California decided to develop a more affordable system.

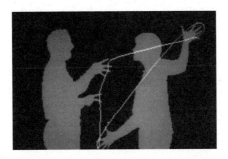

Figure 2.3. Artificial reality, also called projection VR. This is "Cat's Cradle," an art piece from Myron Krueger's Videoplace system. Here, graphic "string" is magically attracted to the fingertips of participants.

NASA's resulting Virtual Interface Environment Workstation—developed mainly for planning space missions—was the first to combine computer graphics, video imaging, three-dimensional sound, voice recognition and synthesis, a head-mounted display (based on video monitors taken from miniature TVs bought at Radio Shack), and a data glove (based on an invention by Tom Zimmerman and Jaron Lanier). That data glove caught the public's eye when it appeared on the cover of *Scientific American* in October of 1987. The realization that NASA's achievements were based on commercially available equipment, and that devices such as data goggles could be built with stock electronic parts, triggered research programs throughout the world

Lanier and Zimmerman went on to form VPL Research, the first VR system supplier. VPL Research proved there was a market for virtual reality. Other organizations, ranging from software firms to large computer corporations, started developing and selling VR products and services. Today, some 65 companies in the U.S., including Fakespace Labs (see Figure 2.4) and Autodesk (see Figure 2.5), are nourishing this burgeoning field. Some sell costly devices, software programs, and complete systems to government agencies, research institutions, and corporations. Others—including some garage VR pioneers—develop affordable tools and applications for home computer owners. Over the next few years, dozens more will join the act.

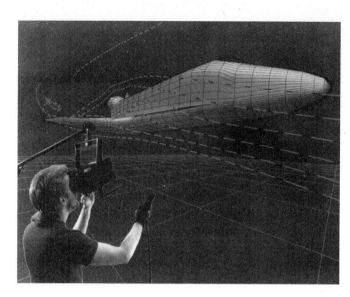

Figure 2.4. *Using the DataGlove and the "BOOM" stereoscopic display by Fakespace Labs of Menlo Park, California, to simplify access to the virtual world—in this case, a visualization of the airflow dynamics of an aircraft wing.*

Figure 2.5. *A virtual world created with Cyberspace Developer's Kit from Autodesk of Sausalito, California. A simple scene such as this might be used by city planners to visualize a skyline in order to predict the effects of a new building before construction begins.*

Garage VR pioneers know it's not easy to create a virtual world. The resulting images don't even come close to resembling the virtual realities running on slick, high-end, multimillion-dollar systems. In fact, garage VR is downright crude. But as one homebrewer put it, "Sure it won't be fast. I don't care. Sure it will have lousy resolution. I don't care. Sure it will be buggy. I don't care!"

What he and other garage VR pioneers do care about is the fact that they're sparking creative breakthroughs, and that they're helping to drive the development of an industry, a market, a communications tool, and an artistic medium.

Postscript

This chapter scratches the surface of virtual reality's deep foundation. If you yearn to learn more about its history, definitions, high-end applications, and leaders in the realms of advanced research, development, and engineering, check out one of the following recommended books or newsletters:

Cyberspace: First Steps, edited by Michael Benedikt (MIT Press). 436 pages, $24.85, 1991.

The authors of this unprecedented collection of scholarly papers include acclaimed writers, academicians, and researchers such as William Gibson, Michael Heim, Allucquere Rosanne Stone, and Meredith Bricken. The contents comprise the proceedings of the first annual International Conference on Cyberspace which took place at the University of Texas in Austin in 1990.

The Metaphysics of Virtual Reality by Michael Heim (Oxford University Press). 200 pages, 1993, $19.95.

This essay collection, bibliography, and glossary views computing from an ontological perspective (*ontology* studies the nature of being). A strong writer, Heim ponders the philosophical problems puzzling VR designers and users, the hazards of living with computers, and the erotic allure of cyberspace.

Cyberarts: Exploring Art and Technology, edited by Linda Jacobson (Miller Freeman). 340 pages, 1992, $22.95.

This oversized paperback contains six sections, including *Music and Sound* (with a section on 3D sound), *Interactive Media,* and *Cyberspace and Virtual Realities* (covering artificial reality, VR status report, the art of building virtual worlds, and more, with chapters by Jaron Lanier, Myron Krueger, Kit Galloway and Sherrie Rabinowitz, Vincent John Vincent, Steve Tice, Brenda Laurel, and Mort Heilig). Explanatory hypertext annotations live in the margins of the same pages as their associated references. This book contains dozens of black-and-white photos and diagrams, plus 16 pages of color artwork.

Artificial Reality II by Myron Krueger (Addison-Wesley). 300 pages, 1991, $24.95.

This hardcover book (an updated version of a 1973 publication) is heartfelt and arts-oriented, focusing primarily on Krueger's pioneering work with Videoplace, Videodesk, and his other installations, all of which predate the debut of so-called "virtual reality." Augmented by many illustrations and photos, Krueger's writing is opinionated and fun to read.

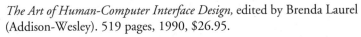

The Art of Human-Computer Interface Design, edited by Brenda Laurel (Addison-Wesley). 519 pages, 1990, $26.95.

Edited by one of VR's most respected and innovative thinkers, this giant paperback includes one section that explores the development and impact of virtual-worlds technology with writings by Scott Fisher (one of the scientists at NASA Ames Research Center who pioneered virtual reality), Nicholas Negroponte of the MIT Media Lab, John Walker of Autodesk, and cyberartist Michael Naimark.

Virtual Reality by Howard Rheingold (Summit Books). 384 pages, 1991, $22.95 (available in hardcover and paperback).

Thought-provoking, far-ranging, and ground-breaking (but not light reading), this was the first book to thoroughly explore VR. It doesn't include illustrations, however. Rheingold is a well-known journalist who edits *Whole Earth Review.*

Virtual Reality: Through the New Looking Glass by Kevin Teixeira and Ken Pimentel (Tab Books). 293 pages, 1992, $22.95.

This paperback is thorough and fairly easy to understand (even though it was authored by an engineer and a computer programmer). It provides many helpful photographs, diagrams, and explanations of how VR technologies work.

CyberEdge Journal

The leading VR industry newsletter, a bimonthly that covers virtual reality and related subjects. $129/year (student discount available). #1 Gate Six Road, Suite G, Sausalito, CA 94965; (415) 331-3343.

PCVR: Virtual Reality and the IBM Personal Computer

Bimonthly magazine dedicated to the garage VR pioneer. Features step-by-step how-to articles for building hardware and software—and includes a disk with software. Past articles cover interfacing an IBM PC to the Mattel Power Glove and Sega liquid crystal display (LCD) shutter glasses, and building 3D sound, head-mounted display, and head-tracking systems. $26/year (back issues, $4.50). PCVR, PO Box 475, Stoughton, WI 53589; (608) 877-0909.

Pix-Elation

Bimonthly

publication of Virtual Reality Alliance of Students & Professionals (VRASP), this is *the* social commentary sheet for the VR community. Also includes serious interviews, articles, and news about events in the VR industry. $15/year for regular membership, $10/year for student membership. VRASP, PO Box 4139, Highland Park, NJ 08904-4139.

Presence: Teleoperators and Virtual Environments

Here's where VR's leading researchers report the results of their inquiries, direct from IBM, JPL, MIT, NASA, UNC, and similar sterling institutions. Explores VR design issues, human cognitive and sensorimotor systems, telerobotics, simulation software, and the impact of "transformed presence" on philosophy, culture, and aesthetics. The most in-depth, insightful source of VR knowledge available. $50/year individual (quarterly), $120/year institution. MIT Press, 55 Hayward St., Cambridge, MA 02142; (617) 253-2889.

Virtual Reality Report

Academic in tone and presentation, this report is published nine times a year ($197/annual subscription) by the same company that produces the annual Virtual Reality industry conferences held on both coasts and in England. Meckler, 11 Ferry Lane West, Westport, CT 06880; (800) 635-5537.

Virtual Reality Systems: Applications Research & Development

Quarterly trade publication that debuted in March of 1993, written by the industry's software and hardware developers and application designers. Invaluable for those who want to keep up with the commercial end of VR. $65/year. VR Systems, 1562 First Ave., #286, New York, NY 10028; (212) 717-1318.

VR Comes in Several Styles

CHAPTER
3

VR Comes in Several Styles

"Tous les genres sont bons hors le genre ennuyeux."
("All styles are good save the tiresome kind.")
—François Voltaire, 1694-1778

How slick and sophisticated is virtual reality today? The quality of a virtual-world expedition relates directly to the type or *style* of VR. The styles of VR differ in the extent to which they immerse your senses in the virtual world. Style selection determines the caliber and complexity of the system hardware and software. That level of sensorial immersion is determined by

 the type of input (control) and output (display) devices used in the VR system

the speed and power of the computer supporting the VR system

In essence, the style of VR that someone chooses for a project depends on the purpose for creating the virtual world in the first place.

Immersive VR: Sticking Your Head in the Virtual World

Immersive VR is the style that generates the most excitement and possesses the most techno-glamour. Fully immersive VR (also called *inclusive VR*) is designed to make you feel as if you exist totally in the virtual world. Cut off from the physical world by a head-mounted display, you see and hear three-dimensional sights and sounds that seem to surround you. You reach out your gloved hand to open doors, scoop up objects, soar through a bit-borne cosmos. Clothe yourself in a data suit, and your whole body enters the picture.

This thrill doesn't come cheap. Research lab-quality, immersive VR systems start at around $25,000 and can reach into the millions. Embarking on high-ticket virtual-world exploration are scientists and engineers at supercomputing centers and aerospace facilities, military personnel in the Air Force and Army, and researchers at university and commercial laboratories—such as those established by pharmaceutical companies or such heavy-duty think-tanks as Silicon Valley's Stanford Research Institute International (SRI). At SRI, for example, the scientists employ immersive VR to develop applications in medicine, education, bioengineering, design and modeling, data visualization, and software development.

Why does immersive VR cost so much? Its components, particularly the input and output devices, represent advanced technologies that require high maintenance and that are not produced in mass quantities. As you learn more about VR, keep in mind those Economics 101 lessons concerning supply and demand; as the marketplace grows and the demand for VR equipment increases, the prices will drop. (We hope.)

The costly components associated with fully immersive VR include the following:

Reality engine: The horsepower required to drive multi-sensory stereoscopic immersion and interactivity comes from an expensive computer system and its internal and external hardware, including image generation boards (graphics subsystems), sound synthesizers and 3D sound processors, computer/video signal converters, and position/orientation trackers. The typical reality engine—sometimes called the *graphics engine*—is a minicomputer or workstation, typically built by Silicon Graphics, Sun Microsystems, or IBM. To process and display separate video images for each eye (thus supporting 3D imagery), the workstation needs two graphics boards. Sometimes the system incorporates two workstations instead, plus an image synchronization system to make sure the left eye's image and right eye's image are issued at precisely the same time.

Head-mounted visual display: Most commercial head-mounted visual displays (HMDs, or goggles) incorporate LCDs and stereo earphones and run in the $6,000-$10,000 range. However, a $3,800 HMD appeared in 1993 (it comes from VRontier Worlds of Stoughton, Wisconsin), as did a $75,000 model that uses fiber optics instead of LCDs (from CAE Electronics of Saint-Laurent, Quebec). The high cost of any HMD is due to its position-sensing input technology, the corresponding computational requirements, and the special optics required to provide a wide field of view with the HMD's relatively small LCDs. Acknowledging the head-mount's heavy, cumbersome, strap-it-on design (the reason they're also called helmets), manufacturers are thinking smaller and lighter. Their goal is to develop powerful visual displays that are as easy and convenient to wear as eyeglasses. Figure 3.1 shows a Liquid Image HMD.

Figure 3.1. One type of immersive VR system, based on the MRG2 Head-Mounted Display manufactured by Liquid Image Corporation of Winnipeg, Manitoba. Note the stereo audio headphones.

Figure 3.2 shows a CAE Electronics HMD. This was made by CAE Electronics for the U.S. Army Research Institute. A visual display system, coupled with large, bright CRT projectors with fiber-optic cable, the FOHMD, according to CAE, is "attractive for remote sensing and remote presence, where the FOHMD can place the operator of a reconnaissance robot 'in the vehicle.' By controlling the reconnaissance cameras by operator head motion, and allowing the operator to fly or drive the vehicle while looking around himself naturally with head motions, the FOHMD will give the operator the feeling of direct presence in the vehicle. This will result in better vehicle control, and enhance the capability of the operator to hug the terrain, exploit cover, and perform evasive maneuvers…. The stereo[scopic] ability of the helmet can also be exploited for remote telemanipulation, such as underwater salvage, space station assembly, or nuclear reactor repair."

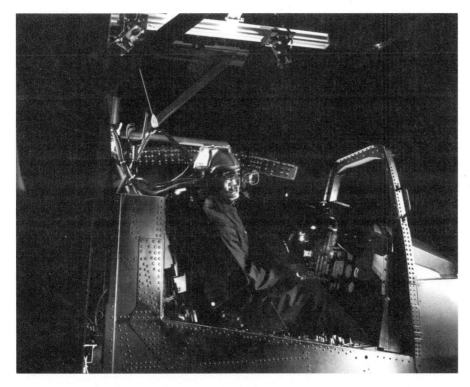

Figure 3.2. An immersive VR system based on the Fiber-Optic Helmet Mounted Display (FOHMD).

3D modeling and world-building software: A virtual world consists of discrete three-dimensional objects and entities; entities include—but are not limited to—points of view, lighting sources, and sound channels. This virtual world requires a simulation manager: software that controls objects and runs the simulation itself. The virtual world also needs device support: software to drive the input and output devices that let you enter, navigate, and interact with the simulated environment.

Virtual-world creation begins with the design of 3D objects. Some high-end world-building programs can import 3D graphics constructed in common file formats, whereas some provide internal modeling capability. The most powerful VR development programs support interactive creation of 3D objects right inside the virtual world.

A 3D graphics program, such as the high-end industry standard—AutoCAD from Autodesk—lets you display 3D objects (*models*) on a computer screen from any angle and position. Say you're creating a virtual world based on a cuckoo clock. You can display the computer model of the clock as seen from the front, the sides, the bottom, or even from the perspective of the cuckoo. In virtual reality, you want interactive 3D graphics to change your perspective of the clock in near *real time*. (It's near real time because a slight lag occurs between the time you issue the command to move your viewpoint and the time the resulting image is displayed.) This gives the impression that you're manipulating a real cuckoo clock. Buying the modeling software to do this requires deep pockets; the cost for a relatively straightforward 3D graphics program for workstations can run as high as $15,000.

After the objects are created and imbued with visual and auditory characteristics— color, texture, lighting, sound effects, and so on—they receive their behavioral characteristics. The objects are programmed to move, drop, fly, bounce, light up, make music, or otherwise react to input from the associated input devices. Some virtual-world technologists code these routines from scratch. Others employ predeveloped routines, or *libraries*, sold as world-building software packages and designed for people who possess programming skills. The price for commercial software for building worlds, such as WorldToolKit by Sense8, starts at around $3,500.

3D (or 6DOF) input devices: These devices let you navigate and interact with the virtual world. They operate in free space ("3D") and measure six degrees of freedom (6DOF): x-, y-, and z-axes relate to motion direction; pitch, roll, and yaw relate to rotation direction. The Deluxe Device du Jour is the wired glove, the descendant of the one invented in Tom Zimmerman's bedroom (with offspring made legendary by VPL Research). The DataGlove is now marketed by Greenleaf Systems of Palo Alto, California.

A company called Virtual Technologies of Stanford, California sells a similar device called the CyberGlove. While wearing the glove, you make simple gestures to communicate with the computer and interact with virtual objects. Want to pick up a virtual pail? Extend your gloved hand *into* the graphic version of the pail, make a fist, and both your real and virtual hand move up—as does the pail. Fiber-optic sensors lining the glove measure how much you bend each finger and tell the computer to render your graphic hand accordingly. Working in conjunction with the fiber optics is a position-tracking sensor in the glove, which reports your hand's position and orientation to the computer. Such VR gloves cost thousands of dollars. Body suits lined with fiber optics and position sensors cost as much as a luxury automobile, and they are custom-made.

Less expensive (and correspondingly less immersive) 6DOF input gadgets exist in the form of wands, mouse devices, joysticks, and forceballs. There is a debate about whether gloveless interfaces support the illusion of immersion as much as wired clothing does.

These days, you can assemble a professional immersive VR system for "only" $20,000. That would get you an Intel i486-based 50MHz PC stocked with two SPEA Fire graphics boards (one per eye for the stereoscopic effect), computer-to-video signal conversion equipment for translating RGB computer images to NTSC video output, a head-mounted display (HMD) by Virtual Research of Santa Clara, California, position-tracking sensors from Logitech of Fremont, California, a SpaceBall 6DOF input device from SpaceBall Technologies of Lowell, Massachusetts, and Sense8 WorldToolKit software. Put them all together, and you have a system that provides a frame rate fast enough to create a decent illusion.

Not all immersive VR worlds appear equally real, which is a result of the type of engine, input/output devices, and software chosen to build the system. For example, the virtual battle zones portrayed in the military and aerospace training systems (driven by super-computers) appear eerily genuine. The graphics in the goggle-equipped Virtuality arcade games resemble cartoons. Driven by Commodore Amiga computers and custom graphics boards, and distributed in the U.S. by Horizon Entertainment of St. Louis, Missouri, various Virtuality game centers reside in shopping malls across the country. Figure 3.3 shows one such Virtuality system.

Figure 3.3. The Virtuality system from W Industries.

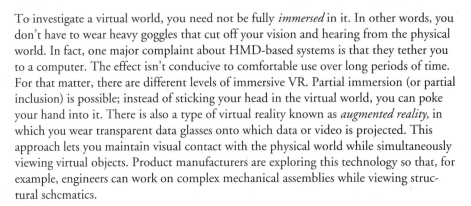

VR Comes in Several Styles

To investigate a virtual world, you need not be fully *immersed* in it. In other words, you don't have to wear heavy goggles that cut off your vision and hearing from the physical world. In fact, one major complaint about HMD-based systems is that they tether you to a computer. The effect isn't conducive to comfortable use over long periods of time. For that matter, there are different levels of immersive VR. Partial immersion (or partial inclusion) is possible; instead of sticking your head in the virtual world, you can poke your hand into it. There is also a type of virtual reality known as *augmented reality,* in which you wear transparent data glasses onto which data or video is projected. This approach lets you maintain visual contact with the physical world while simultaneously viewing virtual objects. Product manufacturers are exploring this technology so that, for example, engineers can work on complex mechanical assemblies while viewing structural schematics.

These varied approaches explain why people can apply the umbrella term VR to many different types of computer-based simulation systems. In general, people agree that in addition to immersive VR, the other styles of virtual reality supported by such systems are simulation VR, projection VR, and desktop VR, from which garage VR stems.

Simulation VR: Climbing Inside the Virtual World

Simulation virtual reality represents the oldest type of VR system, because it originated with the flight simulators developed by the military after World War II. Today, million-dollar military tank and flight simulators continue to place soldiers and pilots inside realistic virtual worlds. Similar simulators help teach highway police officers how to engage in high-speed chases. Figure 3.4 shows such a simulator, the Mobile Operations Simulator by AGC Simulation Products, an offshoot of Atari Game Systems (in Milpitas, California). The system is designed to teach driving and decision-making skills to law enforcement officers. Each networkable $60,000 unit features five 25-inch viewing screens that provide a 215-degree panoramic view. The simulator includes standard vehicle controls with tactile and audio feedback. According to AGC literature, "All objects contained in the synthesized universe are represented as three-dimensional, solid objects which can be viewed from any angle, such as when driving around to the rear of a building. Any impact with a solid object will result in a collision…. If the wheels encounter a bump in the road, the forces of the bump transmitted through the steering linkage are simulated by a proportional jolt in the steering wheel."

Basically, simulation VR places you inside a physical mock-up of a vehicle that you control. Inside this cabin (known as a cab or pod), video screens or computer monitors provide your windows to a two-dimensional, albeit realistic, virtual world. You're not encumbered by cables extending from goggles or gloves, and you can interact with realistic physical controls. The cabs can be networked easily, allowing several people to participate in the same virtual world. Because the simulation VR system doesn't process stereo images or usually compute updated images in response to position-tracking, the graphics look much smoother, crisper, and faster than those in most commercial immersive VR systems. The virtual landscapes presented by the military and police simulators boast incredible photorealism.

Figure 3.4. *A simulation VR system: the Mobile Operations Simulator by AGC Simulation Products.*

The entertainment industry can thank Mort Heilig for launching a trend with his Sensorama Simulator. You can experience a modern-day simulator when you visit a Virtual World Entertainment Center. The first such site, originally called BattleTech Center, opened in a Chicago shopping mall in 1991. By the end of 1993, Virtual World Centers will have opened in New York, Los Angeles, San Diego, and the San Francisco Bay Area. More will appear in the next few years.

At the Virtual World Center in Chicago, it costs about $7 to enter a networked simulation of thirty-first century humanoid fighting machines, dubbed BattleMechs. After a training session with uniformed BattleTech officers, you climb into your Mech, a slick-looking enclosed pod containing a fighter-plane seat, control-laden dashboard, and two color display screens. You wage a 10-minute war against other players driving other Mechs, and you talk to your teammates by microphone. Team members cooperate to accomplish a mission. You pit your skills against those of other people, not a computer.

VR Comes in Several Styles

As with immersive virtual reality, the BattleTech system doesn't limit your actions to preprogrammed paths; it lets you hide behind trees, duck under rocks, and scramble into buildings. In this type of simulator VR, full immersion is replaced by illusion and supported by the physical and the computer-generated environments. The Virtual World Center's entire design supports the illusion of being in a place far, far away from a shopping mall.

Behind BattleTech is a complex network of PCs. All programming, engineering, and artwork emanates from within Virtual World Entertainment headquarters. Concealed inside each pod are five custom Texas Instruments- and Motorola-based computers that handle game and simulation code, I/O, graphics, and sound. Five speakers in the cockpit pump out 12 independent channels of sound effects. The pods' on-screen graphics show accurate renderings of the virtual world, including light sources and 3D perspectives. To optimize power, the pods' display system doesn't redraw each Mech during game play. Instead, it selects and flashes an appropriate image from a collection of Mech pictures. Outside the pods, a souped-up Macintosh Quadra on the network serves as the Operator's Station. Players poke its touchscreen before game play to customize their adventure. At the end of the game, players receive a printout of their actions and watch a Quadra-driven display of the game—physical validations of their virtual experience.

The Virtual World Centers sport the ambience of a Victorian explorer's club: Jules Verne meets *Bladerunner*. The player climbs into one of the Center's many streamlined pods, closes its door, presses a button in the cockpit, and "takes off" into a virtual world. Then, the cockpit morphs into whatever form it must take to suit the chosen world—either a Mech for BattleTech or a Martian cruiser for the racing and exploration game Red Planet.

By 1996, 30 Virtual World Centers will open in Japan. All centers here and abroad eventually will be networked, so Americans and Japanese can challenge each other—*telegame*—in the same virtual world. It won't be long before kids start cheering each other in intercity tournaments, and maybe even in globally televised Virtual World Series games.

Companies other than Virtual World Entertainment are developing plans to open other kinds of simulator VR centers in theme parks and public spaces around the world—perhaps one in a shopping mall near you.

Projection VR, Artificial Reality: Watching an Image of Yourself in the Virtual World

This category of virtual reality owes its existence to Myron Krueger, the interactive computer artist who pioneered full-body participation in computer-defined aesthetic experiences. In the 1970s, he devised a way to use custom computers. He projected live video and graphic images onto a large screen that provided a large window onto a virtual world. He coined the term *artificial reality* to describe the kind of environment created by his system, which could be experienced without wearing or even using input devices.

In 1973, Krueger wrote, "An artificial reality perceives a participant's action in terms of the body's relationship to a graphic world, and generates responses that maintain the illusion that his or her actions are taking place within that world." Then and now, projection VR shows you an electronically generated image of yourself that you control by moving around the control space. Your video image can be projected into a scene created by computer graphics. It also can appear inside a video-based scene or a landscape containing both video imagery and computer graphics. Either way, you physically stand *outside* the virtual world, but communicate with virtual characters or objects *inside* it.

Krueger's most recent version of this approach is called Videoplace. The Videoplace exhibition is funded by the National Endowment for the Arts and the National Science Foundation. It travels to museums, galleries, and conferences throughout North America, Europe, and Japan. The public is invited to experience Videoplace at its home base in the Connecticut State Museum of Natural History in Storrs, Connecticut.

A projection VR system such as Videoplace provides groups of people with a good view of a virtual world. That's why this style of VR now serves as an attention-getting promotional tool at conferences and trade shows, as an educational tool in museums, and as a source of fun and folly in the entertainment arena. The most popular projection VR today is the Vivid Group's Mandala artificial reality system.

The Mandala system is the realization of a vision shared by artist Vincent John Vincent and computer programmer Francis MacDougall, both of Toronto, Ontario. In 1984, they developed a system that enables people to dance, play, make music, create visual art, and communicate within a computer-based world. Then they formed a company, Vivid Group, to market Mandala, which was introduced in 1986 as a commercial product for sale or rent. The Mandala Virtual Reality System employs a video camera as the interface between a person and a personal computer. A basic Mandala system costs about $8,000 and includes a Commodore Amiga 2500HD computer and monitor, color video camera, video digitizer, RGB-to-NTSC video gear, sound synthesizer, authoring software, and sample Mandala worlds. According to the folks at Vivid Group, Mandala for the Apple Macintosh is in the works. Until recently, they refrained from Mac development, because the original Macintosh II couldn't handle real-time video adequately. Figure 3.5 shows an image captured by the Mandala system. This artificial world is part of the interactive PC-based Mandala installation at the National Hockey League's Hockey Hall of Fame in Toronto, Ontario. At the installation, you stand in front of a large blue screen. Your image is captured by video camera, then combined with computer graphics and video imagery output on a large monitor—so you can play goalie and keep the other team from scoring.

Figure 3.5. *A projection VR system: Mandala, created by the Vivid Group.*

The Vivid Group also offers IBM PC-based Mandala systems. They handle all the production for the PC in-house and sell specific, contracted productions on a custom basis. The system costs $36,000; production costs vary.

You might be able to experience a Mandala system at nightclubs and large public dances (also known as *raves*), particularly in major cities such as Los Angeles, San Francisco, New York, Austin, and Washington, DC. You can watch kids cavort in Mandala worlds on the Nickelodeon cable channel on the game show *Nick Arcade*. You also might get the chance to witness the slickest Mandala world yet—in the Star Trek exhibit developed by Paramount Pictures with the Vivid Group. This exhibit, featuring a Virtual Reality Transporter Experience, took off in 1993 on a three-year tour of science museums around the country. The holodeck simulator is scheduled to land in Denver from February through April of 1994, in Pittsburgh from June through December of 1994, in Tampa from February through August of 1995, and in Dallas from October through December of 1995.

Garage VR, Desktop VR, Homebrew VR: Now You Can Afford It

People who didn't possess the cash, real estate, or other capabilities to develop immersive, projection, or simulation virtual realities came up with the category of *garage VR:* the low-cost method of interacting with virtual worlds using a standard personal computer.

Actually, people in the VR industry apply the *desktop VR* moniker to a more expensive route to virtual-world-building; this type incorporates a UNIX workstation, $2,000 stereoscopic LCD shutter glasses and forceball input devices, and relatively costly software packages such as the Sense8 WorldToolKit or the Autodesk Cyberspace Developer Kit. Sun Microsystems recently developed its own Sun Virtual Holographic Workstation, including a Hitachi stereo monitor, StereoGraphics CrystalEyes stereoscopic glasses (see Figure 3.6), Logitech 3D mouse, and transmitter—all based on a SPARCstation 2GT. Starting at $46,000 (a price that Sun expects will come down), this system is intended for industrial design and manufacturing applications. Figure 3.7 shows the 3D mouse by Logitech. Popular for use in desktop VR applications in business and industry, this mouse can operate in standard fashion and in 3D mode for interaction with a virtual world. Besides the mouse, the system includes transmitting and receiving devices to track the mouse's position and orientation as the user moves it through the air.

Figure 3.6. *Desktop VR: A 3D data visualization application using CrystalEyes stereoscopic glasses by StereoGraphics Corp. of San Rafael, California.*

Garage or "homebrew" VR, on the other hand, applies to resourceful do-it-yourselfers who want to explore virtual worlds—no matter how crude or rudimentary those worlds are. "Garage" generally constitutes a total cost for the system that doesn't reach beyond $2,500, including the *reality engine.* This engine is a computer with the horsepower to handle the graphics and real-time interaction, such as an IBM PC-compatible (with an

80386, '486 processor, and VGA board), a Commodore Amiga, or an Apple Macintosh. The graphics capabilities of these ordinary computers run 3D imagery at a speed once associated with $100,000 workstations.

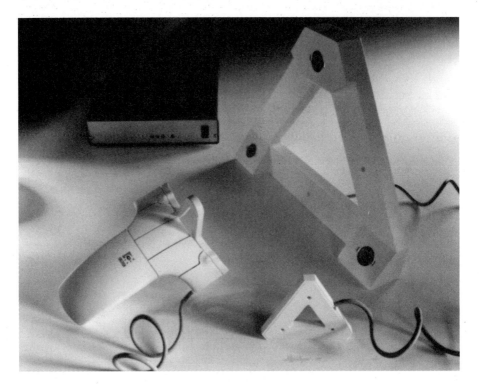

Figure 3.7. *The 3D mouse by Logitech.*

The *windshield* of the garage VR system (its output device—its window into the virtual world) can be a standard computer monitor. For partial immersion in the virtual world, you can use the type of stereoscopic shutter glasses originally developed for video games. (They support the depth illusion so well that it doesn't matter if they look kind of dorky.) More complete immersion, garage-style, has been developed by some truly committed hackers; one VR hobbyist built a stereo head-mounted display using two Sony camcorder monitors, driven by a Mac II with two video boards.

The *cockpit* (or steering wheel and dashboard in a garage VR system—its input devices) can consist of simply a keyboard and a mouse. Or you can control your position and viewpoint within the virtual world by manipulating a joystick, forceball, or 3D mouse. You also can take the Power Glove route. Introduced in 1991 and discontinued shortly thereafter, Mattel's Power Glove for 8-bit Nintendo game systems made a big splash with programmers who connected the Glove to their PCs. In doing so, they could control graphic scenes and music synthesizers.

When you add position-tracking devices to your system, the computer can track your head movements while providing a 2D or 3D picture. Then, your virtual perspective shifts accordingly as you swing your head.

The fuel for the garage VR system—the software to create, render, and display the scenery—can be acquired for free or for a fraction of the cost of the high-octane stuff. Some software packages provide the capability to create a *walk-through* (or *fly-through*), which is computer animation that lets you control, in real time, your viewpoint in a virtual world. Ideally, the garage VR fuel lets you do a number of things. You might build a virtual world that contains many graphic objects, walk through the world in real time, define the objects by giving them attributes (characteristics such as color, sound, and weight), define how one object can affect another, and interact with the world by grabbing and moving those objects. Some relatively low-cost VR development tools offer 3D graphics tools for people who don't know programming languages. These packages provide graphical user interfaces (GUIs) that are mouse- and menu-driven.

Whatever fuel runs the system, garage VR graphics look choppy and move slowly. In fact, the slickest-budget VR scenery consists of monochrome wireframes. Yet, the point of garage VR is not to achieve gorgeous images—and those engaged in such garage pursuits don't bemoan the lack of image quality. The point is that anyone with a decent home computer now has a way to enter, navigate, and interact with simple real-time virtual worlds.

PUTTING VR ON THE MAP

Randy Pausch

PROFILE

1

RANDY PAUSCH:
"Virtual Reality on $5 a Day"

Way back in 1990, interactive VR systems cost big bucks. To experience VR, you had to visit a sophisticated research lab. Then, along came a young computer scientist who showed the real world that traveling to a virtual world need not break the bank. He published his research results in the proceedings of the 1991 Human Factors in Computer Systems Conference (presented by the Association for Computing Machinery's special-interest group on computer-human interaction). In doing so, he inspired a generation of do-it-yourselfers to explore the brave new realm of low-cost VR.

"Driven by our desire to expose numerous people to the new medium, we developed our low-cost virtual environment system with the hopes of making the technology more accessible to a greater number of people. Our challenge is to provide productive access to the technology. In the best of all worlds, computer scientists would provide tools to allow artists to express their creativity freely without the need for advanced programming skills. However, since the technology is young and fragile, close collaboration with programmers is still necessary."

Today, Randy Pausch is an associate professor in the Department of Computer Science at the University of Virginia in Charlottesville. Since the publication of the following paper, Randy has continued to research and develop interactive VR systems and research their effects on participants. In 1993, he co-wrote two more pioneering research papers: "User Study Comparing Head-Mounted and Stationary Displays" and "A Software Architecture for the Rapid Prototyping of Virtual Environments." Both papers were

(Photo courtesy of Randy Pausch)

submitted to the October 1993 Symposium on Research Frontiers in Virtual Reality, presented by the Institute of Electrical And Electronics Engineers.

Virtual Reality on Five Dollars a Day

by Randy Pausch

Computer Science Department
University of Virginia
Thornton Hall
Charlottesville, VA 22903
E-mail: pausch@virginia.edu

As appeared in Proceedings of the ACM SIGCHI Human Factors in Computer Systems Conference, (New Orleans, Louisiana, April 28-May 2, 1991).

©1991 Association for Computing Machinery. Reprinted by permission.

Abstract

Virtual reality systems using head-mounted displays and glove input are gaining popularity, but their cost prohibits widespread use. We have developed a system using an 80386 IBM-PC, a Polhemus 3Space Isotrak, two Reflection Technology Private Eye displays, and a Mattel Power Glove. For less than $5,000, we have created an effective vehicle for developing interaction techniques in virtual reality. Our system displays monochrome wire frames of objects with a spatial resolution of 720 by 280, the highest resolution head-mounted system published to date. We have confirmed findings by other researchers that low-latency interaction is significantly more important than high-quality graphics or stereoscopy. We have also found it useful to display reference objects to our user, specifically a ground plane for reference and a vehicle containing the user.

KEYWORDS: Virtual reality, head-mounted display, glove input, computer graphics, teleoperation, speech recognition, hand gesturing, three-dimensional interaction.

Introduction

Virtual reality systems are currently gaining popularity, but the cost of the underlying hardware has limited research in the field. With any new technology, there is an early period where informal observations are made and large breakthroughs are possible. We believe that the best way to speed up this process with head-mounted display/Glove input systems is to provide low-cost versions of the technology so larger numbers of researchers may use it. We have developed a complete virtual reality system for less than $5,000, or less than five dollars per day if amortized over a three-year period. We built the system because we had an immediate need and also to show that virtual reality research can be done without expensive hardware.

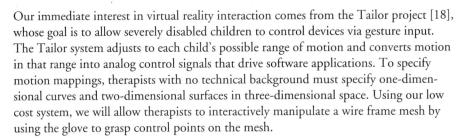

Putting VR on the Map
Randy Pausch

Our immediate interest in virtual reality interaction comes from the Tailor project [18], whose goal is to allow severely disabled children to control devices via gesture input. The Tailor system adjusts to each child's possible range of motion and converts motion in that range into analog control signals that drive software applications. To specify motion mappings, therapists with no technical background must specify one-dimensional curves and two-dimensional surfaces in three-dimensional space. Using our low cost system, we will allow therapists to interactively manipulate a wire frame mesh by using the glove to grasp control points on the mesh.

Our system provides 720 by 280 spatial resolution and weighs six ounces, making it higher resolution and lower weight than head-mounted displays previously reported in the literature. In this paper, we present several design observations made after experience with our system. Our first observation is that increasing spatial resolution does not greatly improve the quality of the system. We typically decrease our resolution to increase our rendering speed. We also observe that stereoscopy is not critical, and that reference objects, such as a ground plane and a virtual vehicle are extremely helpful to the user.

System Description

The main processor for our system is a 2.5 MIP, 20 MHz, '386-based IBM-PC compatible with 640K of RAM, an 80387 floating point co-processor, and MS-DOS. Our head-mounted display uses a combination of two Private Eye displays manufactured by Reflection Technology, Inc. [1]. The Private Eye is a 1.2 by 1.3 by 3.5-inch device weighing 2.5 ounces. Its 1 inch-square monochrome display surface has a resolution of 720 horizontal by 280 vertical red pixels against a black background. Optics between the user's eye and the display surface make the image appear to be one to three feet wide, "floating" several feet away.

The Private Eye is implemented with a vertical column of 280 red LEDs, manufactured as a unit to pack them as densely as possible. To fill the entire visual display area, the LEDs are switched on and off rapidly as a vibrating mirror rotates through the 720 different vertical columns of the display, as shown in Figure P1.1. The Private Eye can "shadow" a standard CGA display with resolution of either 640 by 200 or 320 by 200 pixels, or it can be accessed by a library which supports a spatial resolution of 720 by 280 resolution. The library allows the painting of text and bitmaps, but does not support graphics primitives such as lines; therefore, we use the device by shadowing a CGA display.

Reflection Technologies is marketing the Private Eye primarily as a "hands-busy" display [*the user straps the Private Eye onto their head, with the display extending down in front of their eyes*]. The user can look down into the display without obstructing normal vision. We mount[ed] two Private Eyes underneath a baseball cap [*see photo of Randy*]. We have also used sunglasses with leather sides to shield the user from peripheral distractions. Our head-mounted display can either be stereoscopic or biocular (each eye receives the same picture).

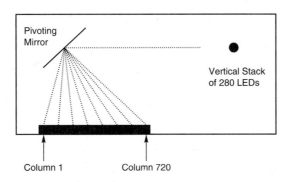

Figure P1.1. *Private Eye design, top view.*

We use a Polhemus 3Space Isotrak [20] to track the position and orientation of the user's head. The Isotrak senses changes in a magnetic field and reports three spatial (*x, y, z*) and three angular (yaw, pitch, roll) coordinates 60 times each second. Our system uses the Mattel Power Glove as an input device for position and gesture information. The glove is manufactured by Mattel, Inc., under licence from Abrams-Gentile Entertainment, Inc. (AGE). The Power Glove is provided to retail stores at a wholesale cost of $62 and is sold at a retail cost ranging between $70-100. Although Mattel does not release unit sales figures, they report that in 1989, the Power Glove generated over forty million dollars in revenue, implying that over half a million gloves were sold that year.

Early glove research was conducted at VPL Research, Inc., the manufacturers of the DataGlove [23,27]. The DataGlove uses fiber optics to determine finger bend and a Polhemus tracker to determine hand position. Neither of these technologies could be mass produced easily, so the Power Glove uses variable resistance material for finger bend, and ultrasonics for hand position.

The Power Glove is marketed as a peripheral for the Nintendo Entertainment System. To thwart rival toy manufacturers, the data stream between the Power Glove and the main Nintendo unit is encrypted. When the Power Glove was originally introduced, it was rumored that dozens of research groups across the country began working on decrypting this data stream, and that several groups actually broke the code. An article appeared in *Byte* magazine describing how to attach the glove as a serial device, but only allowed the Glove to emulate a joystick-type input device [6]. Rather than engaging in cryptography, we phoned Chris Gentile at AGE and described our research goals. He allowed us to sign a non-disclosure agreement and within days sent us a decrypting device that allows us to use the glove as a serial device communicating over an RS232 line. AGE and VPL Research have recently announced the VPL/AGE Power Glove Education Support Program [26] and plan to provide a low-cost glove with five degrees of freedom for between $150-200.

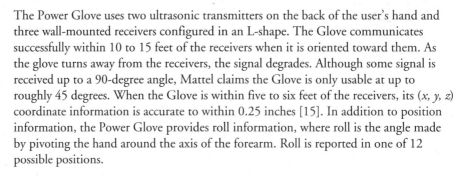

The Power Glove uses two ultrasonic transmitters on the back of the user's hand and three wall-mounted receivers configured in an L-shape. The Glove communicates successfully within 10 to 15 feet of the receivers when it is oriented toward them. As the glove turns away from the receivers, the signal degrades. Although some signal is received up to a 90-degree angle, Mattel claims the Glove is only usable at up to roughly 45 degrees. When the Glove is within five to six feet of the receivers, its (x, y, z) coordinate information is accurate to within 0.25 inches [15]. In addition to position information, the Power Glove provides roll information, where roll is the angle made by pivoting the hand around the axis of the forearm. Roll is reported in one of 12 possible positions.

Finger bend is determined from the varying resistance through materials running the length of the finger. The user's thumb, index, middle, and ring finger bend are each reported as a two-bit integer. This four-position granularity is significantly less than the resolution provided by the VPL DataGlove, but most of the gestures used in previously published virtual reality systems can be supported with only two bits per finger [2,8,11,25].

The only hardware we plan to add to our system is for voice input. Several small vocabulary, speaker-dependent input devices exist for the PC, all costing several hundred dollars. Once this is added, many of the commands currently given by hand gesture will be replaced by voice input.

All software for our system is locally developed in ANSI-standard C [12]. We have a simple version of PHIGS [10] and are using a locally developed user interface toolkit [17]. Our low-level graphics and input handling packages have been widely ported and allow our students to develop applications on Suns, Macintoshes, or PCs before running them on the machine equipped with the head-mounted display. We are currently developing a three-dimensional, Glove-based object editor.

Although fast enough to be used, the limiting factor of our system's performance is the speed of line scan conversion. We draw monochrome wire frame objects, but are limited by the hardware's ability to draw lines. The hardware can render 500 vectors per second (of random orientation and length), but our CPU can execute the floating point viewing transformations for 3,500 vectors per second. In practice, we tend to use scenes with roughly 50 lines and we sustain a rate of seven frames per second. High-performance scan-conversion boards currently exist, which would substantially improve our rendering capabilities, and we expect their price to drop substantially in the coming year.

The major limitation of our system's usability is the lag of the Polhemus Isotrak. Other researchers using the Isotrak have also reported this problem; no one has precisely documented its duration, but it is within 150 and 250 milliseconds [9]. Ascension Technology, Inc. recently announced the Bird, a $5,000 competitor to the Polhemus Isotrak with a lag of only 24 milliseconds [21].

The existing system, when augmented with voice, will still cost less than $5,000 in hardware ($750 for each eye, $3,000 for the head tracker, $80 for the Power Glove, and about $400 for the voice input). For less than the cost of a high resolution color monitor, we have added the I/O devices to support a complete virtual reality system.

Research Observations

Fred Brooks [5] has commented that:

> "A major issue perplexes and bedevils the computer-human interface community—the tension between narrow truths proved convincingly by statistically sound experiments, and broad 'truths,' generally applicable, but supported only by possibly unrepresentative observations."

Brooks distinguishes between findings, observations, and rules-of-thumb, and states that we should provide results in all three categories, as appropriate. Most research presented to date in virtual reality is either what Brooks calls observations or rules-of-thumb, and we continue in this vein, stating our experience:

The quality of the graphics is not as important as the interaction latency.

If we had to choose between them, we would prefer to decrease our tracking lag than increase our graphics capabilities. Although we have much greater spatial resolution than other head-mounted displays, this does not seem to significantly improve the quality of our system. Our experience confirms what has been discovered at VPL Research and NASA Ames Research Center: if the display is driven by user head motion, users can tolerate low display resolution, but notice lag in the 200-millisecond range.

Stereoscopy is not essential.

Users of biocular and monocular (one eye covered with a patch) versions of our system could maneuver and interact with objects in the environment. Since a straightforward implementation of stereo viewing slows down graphics by a factor of two or doubles the hardware cost, it is not always an appropriate use of resources.

A ground plane is extremely useful.

Non-head-mounted virtual worlds sometimes introduce a ground plane to provide orientation [3,22]. In expensive head-mounted systems, the floor is usually implicitly included as a shaded polygon. We found the need in our system to include an artificial ground plane for reference, drawn as a rectangular grid of either lines or dots.

Display the limits of the "vehicle" to the user.

In virtual reality, a user's movement is always constrained by the physical world. In most systems this manifests with the user straining an umbilical cord. Even in systems with no umbilical and infinite range trackers, this problem will still exist. Unless the user is in the middle of a large, open space, the real world will limit the user's motions. In the VIEW system [7,8], a waist-level hexagon displays the range of the tracker, but is part of the world scene and does not move as the user flies. We treat the user as always residing in a "vehicle" [24]. The vehicle for a Polhemus is roughly a 10-foot hemisphere. If the user wishes to view an object within the range of the vehicle, he may walk over to it, thereby changing his own location within the vehicle. If, however, the user wishes to grab an object not currently in the vehicle, he must first fly the vehicle until the desired object is within the vehicle, as shown in Figure P1.2. Note that the user may be simultaneously moving within the vehicle and changing the vehicle's position in the virtual world, although in practice our users do not combine these operations. For small vehicles it is probably appropriate to always display their bounds, but for larger vehicles it may be better to show their bounds only when users are near the edges.

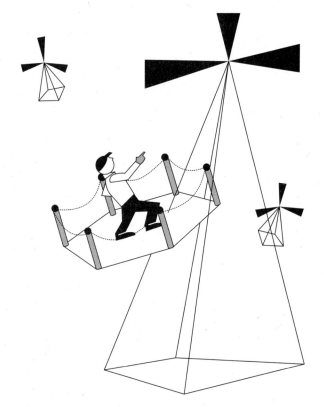

Figure P1.2. *Displaying the vehicle to the user.*

Future Work

Adding voice input will allow us to experiment with a model we have developed to support object selection via simultaneous voice and gesture input. We have already built a prototype of this selection model using a display screen in combination with voice and gesture input and will attempt to repeat those results using a head-mounted display [19].

We also will be addressing the registration problem, or the correct matching of real and synthetic objects. Until force-feedback technology improves from its current state [14,16], Glove-based systems will have to use real-world objects as tactile and force feedback to the user for some tasks. For example, one could perform a virtual version of the popular magic trick "cups and balls" by moving real cups on a real table, but having arbitrary virtual objects appear under the cups. The graphics for the cups, which can be grasped and moved, must closely correspond to the real-world cups. By attaching trackers to real-world objects, we will study how closely the visual image must match reality to avoid user dissatisfaction. A second approach to this problem is to use the Private Eye as a heads up display, wearing it over only one eye and allowing the user to correlate the real-world and synthetic graphics.

We are currently pursuing support to create a laboratory with between 10 and 20 low-cost virtual reality stations. By providing reasonable access to an entire graduate or undergraduate class, we suspect we may quickly develop a large number of new interaction techniques. Jaron Lanier has commented that in virtual reality, "creativity is the only thing of value" [13]. A good way to spark creative breakthroughs is to increase the number of people actively using the technology. We are also exploring the possibility of creating a self-contained, portable system based on a lap-top machine.

Conclusions

The field of virtual reality research is in its infancy and will benefit greatly from putting the technology into as many researchers' hands as possible. The virtual reality systems previously described in the literature cost more than most researchers can afford. We have shown that for less than $5,000, or five dollars per day over three years, researchers can use a head-mounted display with glove and voice input. Our system has a higher spatial resolution than any previous system and is significantly lighter than previous systems [4,7]. For glove input, the Power Glove has provided excellent spatial accuracy and usable finger bend data. Based on experience with our system, we have found that interaction latency is significantly more important than display resolution or stereoscopy, and that the user can greatly benefit from the display of reference objects, such as a ground plane and a virtual vehicle.

Putting VR on the Map
Randy Pausch

Acknowledgements

This work could not have proceeded without the help we received from Chris Gentile of AGE. Novak of Mattel, Inc. also provided assistance with an early draft of the paper. We would also like to thank Ronald Williams, Pramod Dwivedi, Larry Ferber, Rich Gossweiler, and Chris Long at the University of Virginia for their help.

References

1. Becker, A., Design Case Study: Private Eye, Information Display, March, 1990.

2. Blanchard, C., Burgess, S., Harvill, Y., Lanier, J., and Lasko, A., Reality Built for Two: A Virtual Reality Tool," ACM SIGGRAPH 1990 Symposium on Interactive 3D Graphics, March, 1990.

3. Brett, C., Pieper, S., and Zeltzer, D., "Putting It All Together: An Integrated Package for Viewing and Editing 3D Microworlds," Proceedings of the 4th Usenix Computer Graphics Workshop, October, 1987.

4. Brooks, F., "Walkthrough—A Dynamic Graphics System for Simulating Virtual Buildings," Proceedings of the 1986 ACM Workshop on Interactive Graphics, October, 1986, 9-21.

5. Brooks, F., "Grasping Reality Through Illusion: Interactive Graphics Serving Science," Proceedings of the ACM SIGCHI Human Factors in Computer Systems Conference, Washington, D.C., May 17, 1988, 1-11.

6. Eglowstein, H., "Reach Out and Touch Your Data," *Byte,* July 1990, 283-290.

7. Fisher, S.,McGreevy, M.,Humphries, J., and Robinett, M., "Virtual Environment Display System," Proceedings of the 1986 ACM Workshop on Interactive Graphics, October, 1986, 77-87.

8. Fisher, S., "The AMES Virtual Environment Workstation (VIEW)," SIGGRAPH '89 Course #29 Notes, August, 1989 (included a videotape).

9. Fisher, S., Personal Communication (electronic mail), Crystal River Engineering, Inc., September 28, 1990.

10. Foley, J., van Dam, A., Feiner, S., and Hughes, J., *Computer Graphics, Principles and Practices,* Addison-Wesley, 1990.

11. Kaufman, A., Yagel, R. and Bakalash, R., "Direct Interaction with a 3D Volumetric Environment," ACM SIGGRAPH 1990 Symposium on Interactive 3D Graphics, March, 1990.

12. Kelley, A. and Pohl, I., *A Book on C,* Second Edition, Benjamin/ Cummings Publishing Company, Inc., 1990.

13. Lanier, J., Plenary Address on Virtual Reality, Proceedings of UIST: The Annual ACM SIGGRAPH Symposium on User Interface Software and Technology, November, 1989.

14. Ming, O., Pique, M., Hughes, J., and Brooks, F., "Force Display Performs Better than Visual Display in a Simple 6-D Docking Task," IEEE Robotics and Automation Conference, May, 1989.

15. Novak, Personal Communication (telephone call), January 3, 1991.

16. Ouh-young, M., Pique, M., Hughes, J., Srinivasan, N., and Brooks, F., "Using a Manipulator For Force Display in Molecular Docking," IEEE Robotics and Automation Conference 3 (April, 1988), 1824-1829.

17. Pausch, R., "A Tutorial for SUIT, the Simple User Interface Toolkit, Technical Report Tech. Rep.-90-29," University of Virginia Computer Science Department, September 1, 1990.

18. Pausch, R., and Williams, R. Tailor, "Creating Custom User Interfaces Based on Gesture," Proceedings of UIST: the Annual ACM SIGGRAPH Symposium on User Interface Software and Technology, October, 1990, 123-134.

19. Pausch, R., and Gossweiler, R., "UserVerse: Application-Independent Object Selection Using Inaccurate Multi-Modal Input," in Multimedia and Multimodal User Interface Design, edited M. Blattner and R. Dannenberg, Addison-Wesley, 1991.

20. Rabb, F., Blood, E., Steiner, R., and. Jones, H., "Magnetic Position and Orientation Tracking System," IEEE Transaction on Aerospace and Electronic Systems, 15, 5 (September, 1979), 709-718.

21. Scully, J., Personal Communication (letter), Ascension Technology, Inc., PO Box 527, Burlington, VT 05402 (802) 655-7879, June 27, 1990.

22. Sturman, D., Pieper, S., and Zeltzer, D., "Hands-on Interaction With Virtual Environments," Proceedings of UIST: the Annual ACM SIGGRAPH Symposium on User Interface Software and Technology, November, 1989.

23. VPL Research, DataGlove Model 2 Users Manual, Inc., 1987.

24. Ware, C., and Osborne, S., "Exploration and Virtual Camera Control in Virtual Three Dimensional Environments," ACM SIGGRAPH 1990 Symposium on Interactive 3D Graphics, March, 1990.

25. Weimer, D., and Ganapathy, S., "A Synthetic Visual Environment with Hand Gesturing and Voice Input," Proceedings of the ACM SIGCHI Human Factors in Computer Systems Conference, April, 1989, 235-240.

26. Zachary, G., and Gentile, C., Personal Communication (letter), VPL Research, Inc., July 18, 1990. VPL/AGE Power Glove Support Program, VPL Research, Inc.

Putting VR on the Map
Randy Pausch

27. Zimmerman, T., Lanier, J., Blanchard, C., Bryson, S., and Harvill, Y., A Hand Gesture Interface Device, Graphics Interface '87, May, 1987, 189-192.

This work was supported in part by the National Science Foundation, the Science Applications International Corporation, the Virginia Engineering Foundation, the Virginia Center for Innovative Technology, and the United Cerebral Palsy Foundation.

The Engine

Computer Platforms

CHAPTER

4

The Engine
Computer Platforms

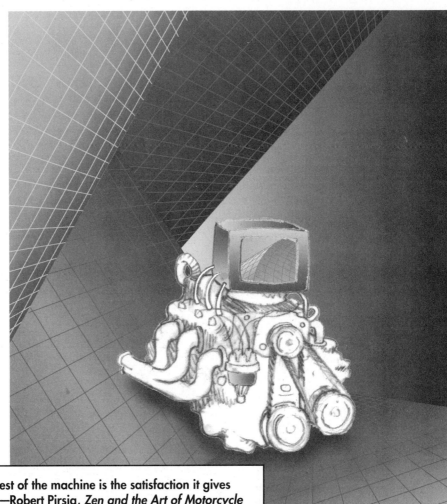

"The test of the machine is the satisfaction it gives you."—Robert Pirsig, *Zen and the Art of Motorcycle Maintenance*

R. Eberly '93

UNIVAC I (Universal Automatic Computer) was the first computer intended for business use. Built in 1951, it took up as much floor space as an industrial washing machine. Those who looked with awe upon UNIVAC might have scoffed at the notion that before long, a far more mighty machine would fit easily atop a writing desk.

In UNIVAC's time, few would have guessed that 40 years later computers also would be available in a wide selection of sizes and styles. Today's byte-machine shopper can choose a supercomputer, minisupercomputer, minicomputer (also called a workstation), or microcomputer (the beloved personal computer).

"Beloved" is not hyperbole. Many computer owners literally cherish their machines. Perhaps you too rely on your system more than you rely on your relatives. Maybe you call your computer by name or adorn it with decorations. Maybe you scold your computer when it misbehaves—uh, malfunctions. Whatever, chances are good that if you own or borrowed this book, there's a special computer in your life and you're wondering if it can serve as a virtual-worlds machine—*reality engine* to VR cognoscenti.

To do its job as reality engine (or *deck* in science-fiction jargon), the computer processes and outputs interactive three-dimensional simulations, or virtual worlds. These worlds—or more accurately, the objects they comprise—exist as models in the form of an alphanumeric database stored in computer memory. The computer makes continuous calculations to display the models in visual form; this process provides the foundation for the *simulation*. The simulation is interactive, because it responds to your actions: you can pick up or otherwise manipulate objects in it and control your position and viewpoint. Performing as a reality engine, the computer executes the simulation and also handles the participant's interface to the simulated world. When you consider the tasks this machine must handle, it's important to separate the simulation from the interface.

The reality engine in a typical commercial or research-level immersive VR system is a heavy-duty workstation. To send simulation data to the system's head-mounted display, the engine pumps out the virtual world image one frame at a time, similar to the way film and video work. The more powerful the engine, the more quickly it can display the sequence of frames. The faster the frames are displayed, the more convincing the simulation.

The physical dimensions of a modern workstation resemble those of a personal computer: it can sit comfortably upon a desktop, although it needs room for the ample 19-inch monitor typical of workstations. However, a workstation possesses more elaborate circuitry than a personal computer. That's because workstation computing involves extremely complex mathematical calculations. Workstation computing also typically involves a link into a local area network; that way, each workstation user can share files and resources in the extensive data banks that support many businesses, universities, and similar information-dependent organizations. A workstation usually is not a personal data repository for one individual. Likewise, the cost of a workstation doesn't suit the budget of a typical individual: starting at five figures, some workstation prices reach into the $100,000 range.

On the VR fast track, most drivers covet machines made by Silicon Graphics, Inc. of Mountain View, California, a company that specializes in three-dimensional visual computing systems and software for industry and business needs. SGi's Reality-Engine™ is the graphics-rendering subsystem that performs at scorching speeds. RealityEngine works with the SGi Iris Power Series of graphics workstations.

SGi and another high-end engine builder, Sun Microsystems (also based in Mountain View, California), recently introduced or are about to unveil UNIX machines that they consider to be in the IBM PC price range. SGi's $5,000-and-up Indy system holds great appeal for computer graphics devotees. Likewise, Sun's $4,200 Classic computer and $8,000 accelerated LX model each pack a wallop for a relatively small investment. You can bet these systems will make inroads on the field of professional VR. Meanwhile, comparably priced, extensively configured PCs boast so much horsepower and graphics capabilities that they perform better and cost much less than older workstations. That's why businesses now employ top-of-the-line PCs to support computer-aided design applications, 3D modeling, and virtual-world-building.

The average personal-computerist, however, owns a considerably less expensive engine. You don't need sizzling workstations and macho PCs to venture into virtual reality. If you own a standard IBM PC or a PC clone, an Apple Macintosh, or a Commodore Amiga, several options exist that let you create and explore your own synthetic digital environments.

When weighing these options, remember that your computer is nothing more than a tool. Whether wielding a computer, power drill, food processor, or sewing machine, you're converting *raw material* into a *product* by using a *device* that *performs a process.* Raw material is something that can be described and measured in precise terms. In the computer domain, raw material consists of facts, or data. With this material, the computer generates a product known as information. This results from the computer's process of relating many isolated facts to each other. It's up to you to determine the specifics of the process.

Any garage VR endeavor requires a detailed examination of the tools at hand. You must decide what product you want to produce—the information contained in your virtual world. What raw material will you need to obtain that information? What kinds of input and output devices will you need to help perform the process? This chapter, and subsequent ones, help you answer these questions. They help you determine the procedures by which you'll collect the data, put it in your engine, process it, output it, and ideally, enjoy it.

Before deciding what virtual worlds you want to visit and how you will create and explore them, you need to consider the reality engine's three distinguishing features—

speed, capacity and versatility. These attributes determine which virtual worlds you'll visit and how you will get there.

Engine Requirements for Garage VR

One day we might be able to sit at home and simultaneously visit virtual worlds that look almost as richly textured and multidimensional as the real one. Today, however, we must make do with the cartoonish imagery characteristic of garage VR. That isn't necessarily a barrier to enriching experience. VR industry studies have shown that people will gladly sacrifice image quality for higher speeds at which they can move through the virtual world (that is, the rate at which image updates occur) and the ability to interact with objects in the world. (Figure 4.1 shows a sample garage VR system.)

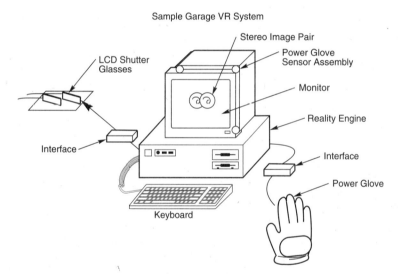

Figure 4.1. *A sample garage VR system.*

Your ability to move through and interact with a virtual world relies on the reality engine's ability to process and display real-time graphics. These tasks require intense mathematical calculations. Therefore:

 Your computer should have a relatively high-power main processor chip (CPU). World-building software relies primarily on the CPU to calculate and render images at a speed that convinces you that you're interacting with the virtual environment, not the computer.

 The faster your computer runs and the more memory it can address, the more adept it will be at supporting virtual-world exploration. Nevertheless, the speed at which your computer displays a virtual world (typically between two and 50 frames per second) is only as fast as the slowest part of the chain. Any bottleneck in any part of the process affects the results. One such limiting factor might be the data path between the CPU and the video card.

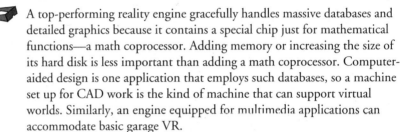

A top-performing reality engine gracefully handles massive databases and detailed graphics because it contains a special chip just for mathematical functions—a math coprocessor. Adding memory or increasing the size of its hard disk is less important than adding a math coprocessor. Computer-aided design is one application that employs such databases, so a machine set up for CAD work is the kind of machine that can support virtual worlds. Similarly, an engine equipped for multimedia applications can accommodate basic garage VR.

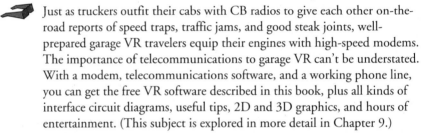

Just as truckers outfit their cabs with CB radios to give each other on-the-road reports of speed traps, traffic jams, and good steak joints, well-prepared garage VR travelers equip their engines with high-speed modems. The importance of telecommunications to garage VR can't be understated. With a modem, telecommunications software, and a working phone line, you can get the free VR software described in this book, plus all kinds of interface circuit diagrams, useful tips, 2D and 3D graphics, and hours of entertainment. (This subject is explored in more detail in Chapter 9.)

In the virtual world, silence is not golden. People enjoy a better perceptual experience in the virtual world (and the real world, for that matter) when they can hear things as well as see them. At this stage in VR's development—even at the high end of the scale—a virtual world that presents a combination of mid-resolution graphics and sound is more effective than a virtual world of higher resolution graphics and no sound.

Engine Performance

Let's look at how specific engines suit garage VR applications. (Figure 4.2 shows a diagram of the reality engine.) The following material is organized by computer brand, but even if you own one type, reading about the others will enhance your understanding of the reality engine's role.

If you don't own a computer, but you want to explore your own low-budget virtual worlds, this information should help you choose the most satisfying machine. The following paragraphs don't provide everything you need to know about the PC, Macintosh, and Amiga, however. To learn more, visit a reliable computer store and also check out some books and magazines that cover each computer.

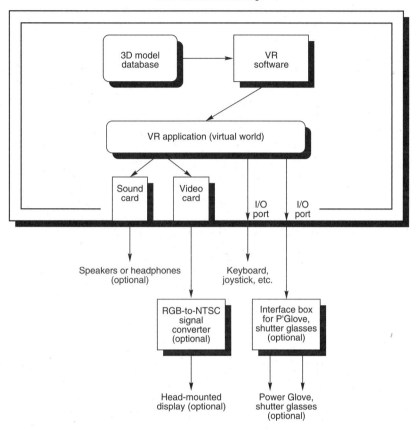

Figure 4.2. *The reality engine—IBM-PC, Macintosh, and Amiga.*

NOTE

As you read, remember that technology evolves ever so rapidly. By the time you see these words, some of the machines and products mentioned here will be surpassed by more powerful wares. The technology (including brands, models, capabilities, performance, and price) will change—but the concepts, objectives, and philosophies will remain the same.

The IBM PC and Compatible Engines

The PC is the engine of choice for most garage VR endeavors. Millions of PCs perch on desks in dens, bedrooms, and garages across the nation. Many companies sell different products for those PCs, so PC owners can choose from the greatest variety of sound and graphics boards, input/output (I/O) devices, free software and demos, and books and magazines tailored to their needs. (Indeed, the disk that comes with this book is for IBM-style PCs.) PC owners also enjoy the greatest extent of support in cyberspace, the domain of computer networking where people with PCs share their VR experiences, opinions, and public-domain software.

What Model of PC is Best for Garage VR?

You won't get very far on the older machines—those based on the Intel 80286 chips and even older 8088 CPUs. They move at a tortoise pace compared with today's models. Most VR software won't work with such systems. These CGA computers don't have much video memory, so they can't switch video frame buffers, a task necessary for stereoscopic (3D) applications. You need something newer, faster, more roomy, and more colorful—a display system sporting at least 256 colors at 320x200 resolution. Now that PC product lines are multiplying like rabbits, and their offspring cost less than ever before (especially with the advent of Intel's precipitous Pentium chip), getting access to the right PC engine should be a cinch.

One suitable model of PC is built around the Intel 80386 CPU, first used in the Compaq DeskPro in 1986. Since then, millions of personal computers have been built around the '386 chip.

Other than the chip, an adequate PC engine is equipped with at least four megabytes of RAM, a math coprocessor, and a VGA board driving a 13-inch color monitor. If the PC runs at 25MHz, with four megs of extended memory (RAM above the 1M mark), and its hard drive has several free megs of space, it will take you to most places in the garage VR domain.

Maybe your '386 computer doesn't have a math coprocessor. It's easy to upgrade and the addition isn't costly (street value of a decent coprocessor is about $90). You just pop the chip into the empty socket that's included in virtually all '386 PCs. This numbers-lovin' gizmo enhances the speed and power of garage VR and CAD applications. In fact, finer CAD programs (and VR packages) require a math coprocessor. Even programs that don't demand a coprocessor will receive a dramatic boost in performance when they encounter it.

Virtual worlds look even better on PCs equipped with 80486 CPU technology. These systems cost only a bit more than '386-based machines. PCs built around this chip represent the current standard in personal computing—and in garage VR.

Selecting a model from the '486 family is like taking a multiple-choice test: (a) SX, (b) DX, or (c) DX2? For garage VR purposes, the right answers are (b) and (c), because the

DX and DX2 chips each include a built-in math coprocessor. The SX doesn't. The DX chips come in speeds up to 66MHz (that's one hot machine), while the SX tops out at 33MHz. The CPU's speed affects rendering performance; faster CPUs mean faster graphics, limited only by the system's video card.

A '486 engine running at 33MHz with eight megs of RAM, a 200MB hard drive, 14-inch color monitor, and a Super VGA (SVGA) card costs about $2,000 and easily accommodates world-building software and VR-style I/O devices (with a bit of device-driver programming). It also presents smooth, crisp graphics (1024x768-pixel resolution in 16-color mode). Keep in mind, however, that working at this high resolution isn't always the best route for viewing virtual worlds. The greater the resolution, the more pixels on-screen. The more pixels on-screen, the greater the tax on overall performance, because the chip must process a heavier load of pixels.

You even can upgrade your '486 to further boost its ability to run graphics, modeling, and programming applications. Intel's OverDrive Processor, for example, is a single, standardized chip that accelerates math performance and memory management. It's not cheap (mail order prices run about $500), but it boosts '486 DX or SX system performance by 70 percent. It increases 16/20MHz 486SX chips to 40MHz, and it doubles the speed of 33MHz 486SX/DX machines.

The PC shuttles data to and from the CPU and memory while it loads data from disk and squirts images onto the monitor. Here's where the width of the input/output bus affects the PC throughput. The different bus types are the original ISA, the wider EISA, and the standardized VL-Bus (*local bus*), which provides higher speed connection than EISA. The use of a VL-Bus greatly increases data throughput, a primary consideration in virtual-world exploration.

Graphics on the PC

The reality engine's video card (also called *graphics adapter* or *display adapter*) converts data from digital bits into an analog signal that is transmitted over a bus to the monitor. The monitor translates the signal to create images on its screen.

Depending on what type of chip it uses, the video card has either a frame buffer, accelerator, or programmable coprocessor design. The frame buffer approach is the oldest, simplest, slowest, and least expensive. It limits graphics performance, because it requires more exchange of data with the CPU than accelerators and coprocessors do. Programmable coprocessor cards cost the most, but are adjustable for the special device drivers used in high-end CAD, video production, and true-color photorealistic imaging. Prices for accelerator cards generally fall between those of frame buffers and coprocessors. Dedicated to handling video functions and processing, an accelerator card removes a big load from the CPU. This card costs a few hundred dollars and represents the best choice for the graphics involved in garage VR, which at this point doesn't involve lifelike images.

If you entertain notions of using a head-mounted display, you'll need to route the video card's output signal to it. Most video cards support digital RGB monitors, whereas head-mounted displays use analog NTSC signals. RGB monitors show much sharper images than those on NTSC-format video displays. (The NTSC method eliminates color detail and limits color intensity to prevent distortion during signal transmission.) Therefore, the system requires some type of RGB-to-NTSC video conversion circuit to accommodate the head-mounted display. In addition, if you intend to generate stereoscopic virtual worlds, you need a way for the system to project simultaneous image pairs. These options are discussed later in this book.

Sound on the PC

Introduced by IBM in 1981, the first PC emitted one sound: a cold little beep that let the user know an operation was completed or that he or she had made a mistake. In 1987, a company called Ad Lib debuted the first sound card for the PC, allowing it to output rich, complex sounds, far more evocative than that old beep tone. Today's PCs can emanate the sounds of a Baroque orchestra or a Florida swamp. Audio can play an integral part in virtual worlds, helping to heighten the illusion through virtual objects that speak, issue sound effects, and play music.

A sound card installs inside the PC and improves the quality of the PC's sound output, similar to how the PC's video card improves the display of images and text. Naturally, the audio software you use must be compatible with the specific card. For the PC to benefit most from the enhanced sound quality, the sound card should be connected to a power amplifier and speakers or headphones. If you want to record voices and sounds that aren't generated electronically, you need a microphone and a sound card that can accept microphone input.

If you don't want to clutter your desktop with speakers and amplifier, check out the Twin Sound "slip-in" desktop stereo system by Sound Minds Technology. It installs inside the PC's 5 1/4-inch disk drive bay, works with all sound boards, and outputs stereo sound from built-in speakers. It includes left/right volume controls, headphone jack, and an input connector for microphone or CD audio.

These days, Ad Lib's current PC sound card, the Ad Lib Gold, faces solid competition, including Creative Labs' Sound Blaster Deluxe and Pro Deluxe, Media Vision's Pro Audio Spectrum, Logitech's SoundMan, and Advanced Gravis UltraSound, each costing less than $150.

Some PC sound cards also work directly with external digital music equipment, interconnected through the standard protocol, Musical Instrument Digital Interface (MIDI). MIDI is the bridge between computers and digital musical instruments. With the right MIDI hardware and software, a personal computer can serve as a complete digital audio recording and production system. With MIDI gear and a sound card, you can create great-sounding, CD-quality digitized sound files and MIDI files for output to external, or *outboard,* sound-making devices.

All PC sound cards support stereo sound. To truly enhance your virtual worlds, you'll want to create the illusion of three-dimensional sound. Two companies—Crystal River Engineering and Focal Point—produce PC sound cards that process and output binaural audio specifically for VR applications. Not cheap, they each go for almost $2,000. Focal Point, however, recently joined forces with Advanced Gravis to produce UltraSound Max, a 3D sound card that costs less than $200. Chapter 6 explores its use.

Apple Macintosh Engines

How ironic. The machine that introduced personal computer owners to the graphical user interface now lacks significant support from VR technology developers.

This drought appears even more surprising when you consider that just a few years ago, the de facto industry standard for real-time VR simulation programming was Body Electric, a Macintosh package developed by VPL Research. Priced at $2,500, Body Electric worked in conjunction with the 3D modeling software for virtual-world design, Swivel 3D (developed by VPL Research, now sold by Macromedia). A promotional video produced in 1987 for the VPL DataGlove prominently featured a little Mac Plus running the glove software. VPL Research continues to sell Body Electric, now in version 3.5, for high-end VR programming on the Mac.

Why haven't more developers supported Macintosh-based VR? One reason concerns the number of Mac owners relative to PC owners: while the installed base of Macs grew to ten million since the machine's introduction in 1984, the number of PC Windows users soared to 22 million since operating system supplier Microsoft started doing Windows 3.0 in 1990. Today, Microsoft sells 1 to 1.5 million copies of Windows every month. Here the Mac-lessness of garage VR results from Apple Computer's view of the Mac, that its ROM chips and operating system are no-trespassing territory (an attitude similar to Sony's view of its Beta videotape technology, which resulted in Sony's loss of market leadership to the lower-quality VHS format). This means there has been no torrent of Mac clones. Only one platform can support the Macintosh desktop interface, and that belongs to Apple. However, in the summer of 1993, Apple Computer started the process of unlocking the gate to their technology, which means we will see Mac clones.

Another reason we don't see many Mac reality engines in garage VR today is that a Macintosh generally costs much more than a comparably equipped PC clone or Commodore Amiga. The Mac Quadra, a veritable workstation, is a luxury model that just doesn't fit the image of the self-reliant, do-it-yourself Radio Shacker.

Nevertheless, people with less powerful Macs are using their modems to acquire the freeware demo programs available for fooling around with elementary garage VR. Meanwhile, a cornucopia of 3D design programs (including one that supports real-time walkthroughs of simulated environments) portend the near-future availability of world-building applications. And despite the current dearth of Mac VR software, people have been devising homemade interface circuits for hooking up garage VR devices. Low-cost commercial products also are available for accomplishing that feat.

Macintosh computers come in a variety of models, all gifted with that famous plug-and-play capability. Device interfaces, that are optional on other personal computers, are standard on the Mac, including built-in display circuitry, local area networking capability, and serial ports for output devices, standardized SCSI connectors for high-speed data transfer, and the Apple Desktop Bus (ADB) port for input devices. It's a snap to add most Apple-sanctioned peripherals to the Mac; you just plug them in. You don't have to reconfigure the system or perform the setup procedures sometimes required with PC add-ons.

All Macs use Motorola MC68000-series chips for their CPUs. Newer Macs employ the 68030 or 68040; the former runs at speeds of 20MHz, 25MHz, and 33MHz, whereas the '040 clocks in at 25MHz and 33MHz, depending on the model. As is the case with the PC, 3D design and modeling benefits from the fastest Macs, and most 3D design packages require a Mac with a math coprocessor. The Mac IIsi and IIci, for example, each contain an MC68882 coprocessor as a standard feature.

In 1990, VPL Research based its Macintosh VR design/control workstation on a IIfx model with eight megs of RAM, an 80MB hard drive, a color monitor, a 24-bit color video card, a serial expansion card containing four serial ports, an ethernet card, and an analog-to-digital signal converter. Since then, Apple Computer has brought out several more advanced Macs, including $10,000 systems designed for corporate and research applications (the Quadra) and $1,000 systems intended for family use (the Classic and LC series).

Today's ideal Mac reality engine has a 13-inch color monitor, six to eight megs of RAM (more is better), System 7.1 for enhanced memory access, and the aforementioned math coprocessor (although most of the free VR-style software doesn't require the math chip). If your Mac contains four or less megs of RAM, it's easy to add more. Older Macs—the Plus, SE, and SE/30—can't support garage VR. You need the type of Mac that is built on the '030 or '040 chip and provides at least two serial ports, SCSI, ADB, NuBus card support, and video output. (If you want to connect an input device or interface box, it needs either a serial port or ADB connector). A NuBus card lets you accelerate graphics rendering and capture video clips. However, none of these programs needs a special graphics accelerator card, or any more VRAM (*video RAM*—memory that contains a copy of what you see on-screen) than comes with the Macintosh's standard innards. Also, none of the free, low-end Mac VR programs require much hard disk space.

As is true for every kind of reality engine, the faster the Mac runs, the better its virtual worlds look. You can upgrade your 25MHz '030 Mac IIsi or IIci with a 68040 CPU accelerator, which brings its speed up to 33MHz. The $200 Mac IIsi NuBus Adapter Card contains the Motorola 68882 math coprocessor for speeding up graphics. Some accelerator cards include memory cache circuitry for improved performance; cache cards also are available separately, priced at about $300. For a comprehensive guide to upgrading every Macintosh model, refer to the June 1993 issue of *Macworld* magazine.

Shopping for a new model? The LC III is great for small offices and home use, and it suits garage VR because it lists for about $1,300 (street prices are lower), uses the '030, and can use virtual memory (which lets you work with multiple applications without the added RAM they normally would require). People have saved big bucks by buying an LC III over a comparably configured IIsi. With the addition of an accelerator card, it outperforms the IIsi. Without the accelerator card, it still runs twice as fast as its predecessor, the LC II, but unlike the LC II, it can be upgraded with a math coprocessor.

For $400 more than the LC III's retail price, the Centris 610 with its '040 chip serves as a solid 3D design system. Twice as fast as the IIci, it has built-in video support for all Apple displays, as well as RGB or VGA signal output—important for those who are considering future compatibility with head-mounted displays.

Once again, you can count on a good multimedia computer performing VR tasks well. The Mac is the original multimedia machine. If your Mac system supports QuickTime in style, it will serve you well on the road to virtual worlds.

If you're interested in buying a new Mac, keep an eye out for Apple Computer's upcoming product lines. The Macintosh III family is on its way to market, as are Apple machines that incorporate the PowerPC, a muscle-bound CPU based on IBM's RS/6000 RISC chip.

Graphics on the Macintosh

The Macintosh is renowned for its crisp, clear graphics display that is designed to support the desktop interface. It looks much better than any PC-style VGA monitor. However, choosing a Mac's specific display hardware—the monitor and the optional video card—can be an overwhelming task. The tubes that support Macintosh monitors come in many different sizes, from 12-inch to 22-inch. The larger the monitor, the larger the image, but remember that higher-resolution displays (which comprise a greater number of pixels) tax the system's overall performance.

Some Mac models have built-in circuitry that lets you simply plug in and drive a color monitor. For example, the Mac IIsi contains video circuits for connecting a monitor. The older Mac IIx doesn't have built-in video, but it does have six expansion slots, so you can stuff one with a video display card. The Mac IIcx doesn't offer built-in video either. It provides three NuBus expansion slots.

Your needs and budget will determine your choice of monitor and its resolution, screen size, and color-handling capability. For about $350, you can buy a 14-inch color display based on a Sony Trinitron tube, showing thousands of colors. If you shop around, you can find a better deal. (Also, many new Macintoshes are SVGA-ready,

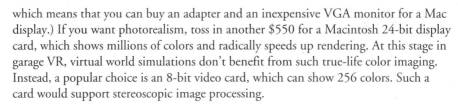

which means that you can buy an adapter and an inexpensive VGA monitor for a Mac display.) If you want photorealism, toss in another $550 for a Macintosh 24-bit display card, which shows millions of colors and radically speeds up rendering. At this stage in garage VR, virtual world simulations don't benefit from such true-life color imaging. Instead, a popular choice is an 8-bit video card, which can show 256 colors. Such a card would support stereoscopic image processing.

When you don't use an add-on video card, you sap system memory for your graphic needs while virtual world-viewing. The Mac has to devote 320K of its total memory to video RAM, storage that is then unavailable to your simulation and interface software. A plug-in video card still hogs some memory to store each current screen, but it brings its own RAM to the party. That's much better for garage VR than using a Mac's internal video support.

A graphics card is mandatory if you want to build your own head-mounted display or use stereoscopic glasses with the Macintosh.

Sound on the Macintosh

The Macintosh was the first personal computer that came standard with a digital-to-analog converter (*DAC*) for playing digitized sounds, supporting a relatively sophisticated audio system. This converter converts digital data to analog electrical signals that can be output over loudspeakers or headphones.

An older Mac—Plus, SE, SE/30, LC, Mac II, IIx, IIcx, or IIfx—doesn't have built-in sound synthesis capabilities; it relies on its CPU and a special sound chip to support the playback of standard, 8-bit digitized sounds. To produce higher quality sounds, these Macs needed special software that could emulate a sound synthesizer or sampler, plus the necessary interface hardware. Extremely processor-intensive, this type of software requires extra attention from the Mac's CPU. When that chip must simultaneously handle real-time graphics and emulate a synthesizer, it splits its attention between the two chores. This slows down overall performance.

The newer Macs' sound-processing capabilities include creating sounds, recording and playback, and even compression/expansion of stored sounds. The Mac's built-in synthesizer can create basic beeps or orchestral flourishes. To take advantage of this, application developers need to know the ins and outs of the Mac's Sound Manager, a collection of routines for including sounds with software applications.

Newer Macs, such as the LC II and III, IIsi, and Centris, come equipped with sound input hardware (including microphone) and driver software to record sounds.

Like the PC, the Mac accepts the addition of sound cards that enhance its music-making capabilities. These sound cards work directly with external digital music equipment, interconnected with a MIDI interface box. When it first started producing 3D audio systems for the desktop, the company Focal Point used the Macintosh computer with a modified Digidesign Audiomedia sound card to support 3D audio applications. This configuration cost almost $1,500, however.

Many thorough, readily available books and magazines tackle the use of the Macintosh in sound and music systems.

Commodore Amiga Engines

The Commodore Amiga scores high in versatility and its ability to support artistic pursuits—and it's priced just right for garage VR. Some claim it's unmatched in multimedia potential. Offering real-time playback of full-screen animation and video, stereo audio, and a true multitasking operating system, the Commodore Amiga is the machine of choice for budget-conscious videographers, musicians, graphic artists, multimedia producers, and techno-savvy hobbyists. Garage VR programmer Eric Townsend calls his Amiga "an experimenter's computer." He compares it to a foreign car: "You can buy a Nova or Chevette—or you can buy a Volkswagen Beetle. You don't buy a VW Bug if you need a reliable form of transportation, one that you can buy parts for on every corner. You buy it because it looks funky. That's how Amiga owners are. Sure, they can buy a Mac or PC, but they don't want the same thing as everyone else. They want a multitasking machine. They want a machine that can switch between graphic desktop interface and command line interface. Some computer geeks like that, because they say, 'It has windows and graphics, but if I get pissed off at it, I can just type code!'"

Even though 4.4 million Amiga computers have been sold around the world since the machine's debut in 1985, no Amiga software developer has designed a real-time, interactive simulation program for commercial distribution. Nonetheless, Amiga owners can feed upon a smorgasbord of 3D graphics programs, including reasonably priced software and a cornucopia of shareware and freeware. A company called Ixion, Inc. offers VR Slingshot, a multiplayer Amiga game that supports stereoscopic (3D) shutter glasses. Such Amiga-ready glasses are sold by two companies, Haitex and MegageM, and come with supporting software for creating 3D images. The popular artificial reality system seen on TV and at nightclubs, Vivid Group's Mandala, runs on the Amiga, as do two quasi-VR programs, Domark's Virtual Reality Studio and VRLI's Vistapro.

The Amiga's serial and parallel ports provide interface paths for controlling garage VR devices such as the Mattel Power Glove. In cyberspace, you can find free software to control those interfaces. People who hitch Power Gloves to Amigas are the type who enjoy programming and seek the rewards of Glove-hacking, a time-consuming task.

Another reason for the Amiga's popularity among technoids is its multitasking capabilities. (The IBM PC and Macintosh let you switch tasks, moving back and forth between different programs, but multiple programs can't operate at the same time.) To take advantage of programs that run simultaneously, you need a method to synchronize them and handle communications among them. The Amiga lets you achieve this with an interapplication language called ARexx (built into the AmigaDOS operating system, versions 2.0 and later). Eric Townsend says, "Imagine if you could have your MIDI music sequencer program running at the same time as your 3D graphics eye candy and the sequencer was sending data to the eye candy as well as to the synthesizers. My insides go all squishy at the thought."

Amiga models include the discontinued A500, A600 ($250-$350 depending on configuration), discontinued A1000, A2000 (about $600), and A3000 (about $1,000, with five megs of RAM and 105MB hard drive). The A1200 and A4000 are the newest models; they boast better graphics than their predecessors. The A1200 goes for about $550. Mail-order prices for the spiffy A4000 start at $1,700. Like Macintosh computers, Amigas rely on Motorola 68000-series CPUs. The A1200 uses the '020, whereas the A3000 runs on the '030. The A4000 comes with an '030 or '040, depending on your budget.

In the Amiga domain, *modular* is the operative word. First, you purchase the base computer (CPU box and keyboard), then add a color monitor (starting at about $250), hard drive, maybe a printer, perhaps a video adapter, and so on. Even the base computer comes in different configurations. You can order an A4000 with a 68030 processor and the standard four megs of RAM with 120MB disk drive for less than $1,800, for example. Or, you can buy it decked out with an '040 chip, six megs of RAM, a math coprocessor, and a hefty hard drive for about $2,500.

If you want to connect a Power Glove to the Amiga to control your own 3D worlds, an A500 or A2000 with three megs of RAM and hard drive will suffice. You can spruce up an old A1000 to the 2.5 megs of RAM and 20MB hard drive needed for rudimentary garage VR play. High-performance 3D modeling programs, however, require an engine with a 68020 CPU, math coprocessor, hard drive, and at least three megs of RAM (10 megs is optimum). The garage VR enthusiast will tool around in style with an A3000 (25MHz '030 CPU), 14 megs of RAM, a 300MB hard drive, and a 15-inch VGA monitor.

Thanks to the Amiga's modularity and the appeal it holds for hobbyists, a vast range of customizing options exist. There are low-cost widgets that let you use A2000 cards in an A500, adapters that let you add more serial ports to A600 and A1200 models, math coprocessors to add muscle to graphics performance, internal chips for fattening RAM, and accelerator cards with '030 and '040 CPUs to rev up slower engines. There are also boxes that enable the A1000 and other grizzled Amigas to run with newer versions of AmigaDOS, and an endless parade of accessories from designer mice to compilers and hardware/software emulation for PCs and Macs.

It's too bad that all these choices render one model of Amiga incompatible with another. If you get your mitts on Power Glove software that works on an A2000, it'll probably choke on the A3000. When garage VR experimenter Chris Hufnagel first

attempted the Power Glove interface with his A3000, he used a direct connection to the serial port. "Unfortunately, I tried to use software with libraries that were designed and compiled for the Amiga 500/2000," Chris says. "Since the programmers didn't take into account that people with faster processors might use the libraries, it was as reliable on my Amiga 3000 as a three-dollar bill. I had to develop custom code for my VR applications."

Using other low-cost VR input devices, such as the Global 3D controller, also requires some clever hacking. This need for techno-creativity arises from a lack of vendor-supplied device drivers. The Amiga sports all the input and output ports found on every other personal computer, yet hardware and software developers aren't writing the kinds of drivers needed for VR, because most view the Amiga as a game machine or a video production tool.

Graphics on the Amiga

People who describe the Amiga as a game system or video studio-in-a-box know from whence they speak. The Amiga is a great graphics engine, especially because (unlike the PC) it features a standardized graphics environment.

The standard Amiga monitor can display a new screen at a rate of one image every tenth of a second. The current standard monitor is the $250 Amiga 1084. Standard Amiga resolution (on the newer machines) is 752x480 pixels with 256 colors, but you can buy a 17-inch color monitor that displays 1024x768 resolution for less than $1,000.

The Amiga 1000 provides a low-quality, color NTSC composite video output, whereas the 500 and 2000 each output a low-quality, black-and-white composite signal. The A3000 provides normal Amiga RGB output. The A4000 offers two color display outputs: RGB and composite VGA. The RGB ports output sharp, accurate images. The composite output matches NTSC resolution and is used for sending signal out to videotape, for example, or to a head-mounted display.

The Amiga boasts several different graphics modes, but to maximize 3D rendering and animation performance, you still want to increase the Amiga's RAM. As mentioned, many vendors offer chips that you pop into your Amiga to accomplish this. And, as the real power of 3D modeling comes in higher resolutions with millions of colors, most Amiga owners invest in display adapters (video cards). Many types exist, with varying features, running from $100 to more than $5,000 (most prices fall in the under-$500 range), and many rely on the Amiga's own '020, '030, or '040 for its processor. Superior 3D rendering demands a good-quality monitor, better than the 15kHz display in the Amiga 1084. It's better if you can find a flicker-free, 31kHz RGB device (keeping in mind that you still need NTSC/VGA output for any head-mounted display). In addition, many European developers have recently brought out video cards with built-in rendering hardware.

The Amiga's flexible, well-documented graphics hardware simplifies the task of stereoscopic animation. If you want 3D imagery, you need special NTSC switching/buffering circuitry—an adapter that runs the stereoscopic glasses. One company markets such an item, as well as the glasses: a $225 stereoscopic viewing system called StereoPro, by MegageM. It works with any Amiga graphics and rendering program that can display stereoscopic images. The StereoPro LCD viewing glasses plug directly into the StereoPro interface, which plugs into the #2 joystick/mouse port on any Amiga and uses the Amiga's internal timing circuit to synchronize the glasses.

Many Amiga owners, especially graphics enthusiasts, subscribe to *Amazing Computing* and/or its sibling publication, *AC's Tech/Amiga.* The latter comes with a floppy disk and offers how-to articles (such as how to build a SCSI interface or how to add Amiga graphics to Super8 film and transfer it all to video tape), programming tutorials, graphics tips, and so on.

Sound on the Amiga

Evern since the Amiga debuted with its built-in, digital sound synthesis skills, many home studio owners have sworn by the Commodore-approved approach to music production. A decent selection of electronic music software and hardware products for the Amiga platform exist, including low-cost digital sound cards and MIDI interface boxes. Inexpensive software packages for music composition, performance, notation, and sequencing on the Amiga are marketed by Dr. T's Music Software, Blue Ribbon Bakery, and Microillusions. If you're interested in this area, check out the magazines *Keyboard* and *Amazing Computing.*

The Amiga's dual-sound, four-voice outputs can pump out stereo audio for direct hook-up to an amplifier and stereo speakers, but no research and development in 3D sound on the Amiga has resulted in related products or shareware software—yet. In the meantime, a few music-loving, garage VR programmers are experimenting with using the Power Glove to control Amiga-generated sound.

Potential Engines

Three announcements issued in 1993 concern newly minted machines that won't appear in stores until after this book's publication. Nonetheless, the information distributed about these products provides reason enough to consider their potential role in garage VR pursuits.

Commodore Amiga CD32: In July of 1993, Commodore Business Machines outlined its plan to compete as a heavyweight in the video-game arena. This company announced its impending introduction of the Amiga CD32, a 32-bit CD-based machine that employs a 14MHz Motorola 68020 chip and Commodore's custom Advanced Graphic Architecture (AGA) chips—the same graphics engines used in Amiga computers. This system relies on the graphics-chip pair and an audio subsystem (helped along by hardware accelerators) to enhance performance, whereas the main CPU deals with everything else. Its CD-ROM drive can serve as an electronic game machine, movie box, and standard CD music player.

Described as providing "arcade-quality performance," the Amiga CD32 screen display can render seven million pixels per second, showing up to 256,000 colors per frame, chosen from a palette of more than 16 million. The system can't support texture-mapping, an important facet of virtual-world design, but it costs only about $400. Accompanied by about 70 game titles, it is scheduled to appear in stores in late 1993 in Europe (where Commodore earns 90 percent of its profits). The U.S. launch happens a few months later.

Commodore also announced its intention to provide an add-on computer module that will enable the CD32 to serve as a full-blown Amiga computer.

The Atari/IBM Jaguar: In the spring of 1993, IBM and one-time video-game king Atari made a surprising announcement. These two companies joined forces to unleash the Jaguar, an interactive multimedia entertainment console based on custom chips, including a 64-bit RISC processor. The PR people say we'll find the $200 Jaguar in department and electronics stores in 1994. The Jaguar's first software titles come on cartridge, like Nintendo and Sega games. Atari developed the Jaguar; IBM manufactures and markets it—their first mass-market consumer product. A reported work-in-progress is a Jaguar compact disc player that will play regular CDs and Kodak PhotoCDs. It will cost about $200.

The Jaguar is based on Atari's 64-bit RISC processor and custom digital signal processors. The Jaguar's video display chooses its colors from a palette holding millions of hues, driven by a rendering engine that can manipulate shaded, 3D polygons (the building blocks used to create virtual objects) in a real-time simulation. Other features that intrigue VR aficionados include real-time texture mapping and video effects. All this means that the machine will support simulations of people and vehicles far more realistic than the graphics offered in cartridge-based, 16-bit video game systems.

The Jaguar's audio system employs a custom, dedicated, high-speed digital signal processing chip. The result is CD-quality stereo sound. In addition, the box will use a digital signal processing port for connection to digital audio peripherals, presumably such equipment as audio CD players and MIDI setups.

Atari includes an expansion port in the Jaguar to accommodate connection to cable and telephone networks in the not-too-distant future, when we'll be able to download interactive programming through our cable TV and phone lines. A key player in developing this part of the plan is the Time Warner media/entertainment conglomerate, the second largest cable operator in the United States and owners of a 25 percent stake in Atari.

We'll have to wait and see whether software companies will support the Jaguar. Atari is wagering that they will. It points out that the Jaguar's graphics performance is

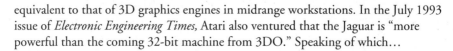

equivalent to that of 3D graphics engines in midrange workstations. In the July 1993 issue of *Electronic Engineering Times,* Atari also ventured that the Jaguar is "more powerful than the coming 32-bit machine from 3DO." Speaking of which…

The 3DO Company: The ballyhooed 3DO is a company and a technology backed by industrial powerhouses such as Matsushita (the world's largest manufacturer of consumer electronics and the parent company of Panasonic, Quasar, Technics, and MCA), communications giant AT&T, Time Warner, and Electronic Arts (founded by the same guy who started 3DO, Trip Hawkins).

Some of 3DO's architects were involved in the design of the Commodore Amiga; Trip Hawkins was involved in the launch of some important Apple Computer products, including the LaserWriter. The first 3DO machine, made by Panasonic and priced at $700, beckons 1993 Christmas shoppers.

This San Mateo, California company hopes its technology will become an international standard as pervasive as VHS video. Instead of manufacturing and marketing products, however, 3DO created a licensing program to let manufacturers do that. Within several months of the company's debut, more than 300 companies expressed interest in producing 3DO hardware and software (including Domark, a company that markets a low-end virtual-world-building package). The first hardware product is a Panasonic's FZ-1 REAL 3DO Interactive Multiplayer (see Figure 4.3), a CD-based interactive multimedia system that attaches to color TVs and stereo equipment. It comes with a hand-held control pad that can link to seven other control pads at the same time. The control pad includes a headphone jack and volume control. The multiplayer also handles standard audio CDs and Kodak PhotoCDs.

More 3DO hardware is scheduled to appear in 1994 from Sanyo Electric Company (another multiplayer) and from AT&T, which plans to build a network version of the multiplayer so that "3DOwners" can access interactive programming services over phone lines.

Some 3DO features that look promising for simple VR include a powerful graphics animation processor and 640x480 pixel resolution—processing over 50,000,000 pixels each second—with about 16,000,000 colors for photorealism and 3D, texture-mapped, polygon-filled graphics. For comparison, most video game systems offer 16-bit animation processing of one million pixels per second and 256 colors. For speedy data access and transfer, there's a 32-bit RISC CPU. Offering full-screen video playback at 30 frames per second, the multiplayer reads compressed video data off a CD-ROM, decompresses the imagery, and displays it on-screen. The resulting picture is smooth, free of flicker, and capable of realistic visuals and simulations.

Another attractive 3DO feature is a digital signal-processing chip that provides CD-quality sound and incorporates a "3D audio imaging" technique. Software developers can use it to localize effects and music, giving the impression over headphones that sounds emanate not only from your left and right, but from above, below, and in front of you.

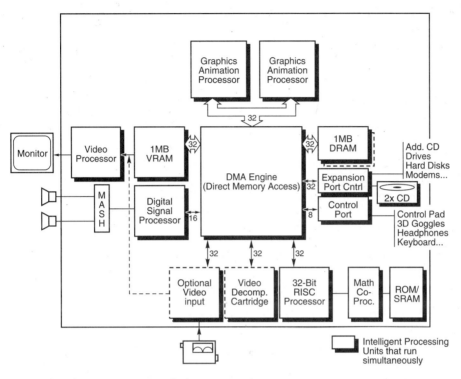

Figure 4.3. *The 3DO Interactive Multiplayer: system architecture.*

Development of 3DO titles takes place on a Macintosh Quadra or IIvx working in conjunction with the 3DO development system. The box connects to the Mac on one end and a TV on the other end. Development kits also are available for PCs. 3DO offers its licensed software publishers an authoring toolkit for creating titles. Some of the tools include 2D animation and imaging, 3D modeling, and Macromedia Director, Macromedia MacroModel, and Macromedia Three-D development packages. These tools let the programmer define moving light sources, texture mapping, and other cool effects that contribute to the 3D illusion when you change "camera angle" using the remote control. A key selling point of this toolkit is that it allows people who don't have extensive programming chops to develop 3DO software titles. Developers also can check out free materials from the 3DO Content Library, a storehouse of clip art and texture effects, music and sound effects, photos, and film footage.

Although the first crop of 3DO titles includes quasi-traditional games, interactive reference libraries, and educational software, out soon will be realistic sports and flight simulations that come somewhat close to resembling VR, supporting immersion, navigation, and manipulation. Because 3DO technology boasts open architecture, dozens of hardware manufacturers are concentrating on building fancy add-ons that will plug into the multiplayer's expansion port. First among these will be 3D shutter glasses for partial visual immersion in the software scene.

The 3DO multiplayer, Atari Jaguar, and Commodore Amiga CD32 each run off prerecorded media—CDs or cartridges. This approach precludes any real-time updating of images that the system could provide in response to some type of position-tracker that would sense your head or hand movements. The 3DO and Jaguar control units do let you change your viewpoint in a graphic scene with a joystick-type device, so interactive walk-throughs will be possible, drawing from the speed, realism, and responsiveness inherent in these new systems. With the addition—and maybe some clever hacking—of low-cost input and output devices, these young upstarts might bring some computing and image manipulation powers to the VR garage.

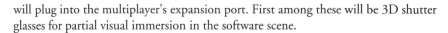

A Primer on Engine Performance

Every year, high-tech factories roll out new computers that offer faster, cooler, and more efficient performance than their predecessors. At the core of each computer is its central processing unit (CPU), the chip that processes and calculates all the data bits and bytes. The traffic cop of computer circuit byways, the CPU directs the flow of program instructions and data. The larger the chip's "model" number (for example, 68030 versus 68040; 80386 versus 80486), the faster it runs, and the more memory it can handle. A chip also is categorized by how many bits it can handle simultaneously. An 8-bit processor handles eight bits (one byte) at a time. A 32-bit chip, naturally, processes four times that many.

Exactly how fast this vital processor works is determined by its clock speed, measured in megahertz frequencies (millions of cycles per second), such as 16MHz or 24 MHz. A higher clock speed, however, doesn't necessarily mean the computer system as a whole runs that fast. Slower components in the system require the processor to wait around for them. The term *system throughput* generally applies to a computer's overall performance of operations, taking into account input and output (I/O) operations, memory speeds, and the time it takes to write to (record data on) disk.

Most CPUs represent Complex Instruction Set Chip (CISC) technology. Newer RISC-based computers rely on a chip design invented in the mid-1970s at IBM. Reduced Instruction Set Chip (RISC) operates much faster than CISC. The latter processes myriad complex instructions for many different types of computer operations; RISCs contain smaller instruction "libraries," thus processing fewer instructions and, as a result, run much more quickly.

To help the main CPU operate more efficiently, a computer contains coprocessors that handle special tasks. Typical coprocessors assist with accessing memory and exchanging data with various input and output devices. The video chip controls the system's display. For complex calculations, the CPU usually looks to the math coprocessors. Graphics and CAD programs also depend on math coprocessors, known as FPUs, for floating-point units, which make mincemeat of the biggest number-crunching tasks. Some newer CPUs (80486, 68040) include FPUs.

Equally important as the CPU is the computer's data storage chip, which stashes the raw material for the processor to work on. Humans love to anthropomorphize inanimate objects, so we employ the word "memory" for this storage device. Random Access Memory (RAM) gives the PC breathing room; the more RAM, the larger the program the PC can run. All data in RAM is lost when you switch off the computer. Read-Only Memory (ROM) is the permanent data storage area. RAM and ROM size usually is measured in millions of bytes: megabytes (megs, to the initiated).

In the IBM PC domain, older computers possess "lower" and "upper" memory. Lower memory is the first 640K of RAM; upper memory is everything above 640K. Newer PCs running Windows or other recent operating systems don't require dealing with such memory division. Apple Macintosh and Commodore Amiga computers don't divide their RAM, either.

Most of the electronic components in a computer reside on the *motherboard* (also called the *system board*). The main components include the CPU, coprocessors, ROM (permanent memory storage), slots for RAM memory chips (volatile memory), the power supply, and ports to various I/O devices.

You can install special circuit boards, usually called *cards,* in the computer to enhance its capabilities. One type is the video card, a display adapter installed in one of the computer's option slots. The video card provides the interface to which you connect the monitor. It controls the way the monitor displays text and graphics.

Communication paths, called *buses,* provide the routes for data traveling to and from the CPU, coprocessors, memory, and I/O ports. Bigger (wider) buses can carry more data at once from place to place, and the system as a whole runs faster. Each bus is made up of parallel lines of data pathways, or *interconnects,* ranging from four bits to 64 bits wide. Typical pathways in a bus include the data channel, address channel (transmits the specific location of the data in the computer's memory storage area), and clock or control channel (coordinates timing between all components). The larger the address channel, the more memory that can be accessed. Although theoretically capable of addressing huge amounts of memory, all machines have lower limits based on physical and cost constraints.

How does the computer know that a particular data signal traveling on a bus arrives at its destination? The system uses a clocking technique, employing one bus just to coordinate and synchronize all the others. The clock makes sure that every chunk of data is packaged and stamped for the right delivery time and place.

Two common interfaces for transferring data to and from a computer's storage devices (hard drives, scanners, and so on) are SCSI (pronounced "scuzzy") and IDE. Macintosh and Amiga systems usually use SCSI, and PC systems usually use IDE drivers.

You can shuttle data from one computer to another via a serial port connection, using modems, or through networking, using Ethernet or AppleTalk (which is faster than using a modem).

Two good sources of basic information about computers are *Understanding Computers* by Nathan Shedroff, J. Sterling Hutto, and Ken Fromm (Sybex, 1992) and, for PC users, *Absolute Beginner's Guide to Memory Management* by Mike Miller (Sams Publishing, 1993).

Of the Beginning

The original notion of a portable personal computer challenged established attitudes that considered the computer a large, centralized resource for institutional use. That challenge first was put forth by Alan Kay, one of the computer industry's great innovators. While he was a post-graduate student at the University of Utah in 1968, Kay envisioned a small personal computer, which he called Dynabook, short for Dynamic Reference Book. He later cofounded Xerox Palo Alto Research Center. There, he led a team that invented a prototype personal computer with an interactive graphical user interface. Its display screen presented information with icons, menus, and windows, manipulated by a contraption called a mouse.

Kay wanted to link computer users to a visual environment in which we can harness our innate powers of recognition and interpretation, powers that lead naturally to the kind of abstract reasoning that lets us solve problems on the computer. This goal, not coincidentally, resembles current theories on the *raison d'être* for virtual-world technologies and techniques.

Xerox didn't harvest the fruits of Kay's labors. He later moved on to the position of chief scientist at Atari. Since 1984, however, Kay has been researching interfaces as an esteemed Apple Fellow.

Computer connoisseurs revere Kay's work but debate over who first marketed personal computers in the United States. Not until the mid-1980s did computer shops start hawking graphical user interfaces; however, a decade earlier a company called MITS set the gears in motion. MITS produced the do-it-yourself Altair. In the December 1974 issue of *Popular Electronics*, MITS invited readers to mail-order a $397 kit with which they could build a computer based on Intel's 8080 microprocessor. It came with the BASIC language. To start the Altair, the user had to set its 25 console switches in a cumbersome sequence. Its RAM weighed a whopping 256 bytes— 2,000 times less than today's personal computers. The day after the article appeared, MITS received 200 orders.

In 1977, the first personal computers appeared on store shelves: the Apple II, Commodore PET, and Radio Shack's Tandy TRS-80. International Business Machines entered the

The Engine
Computer Platforms

microcomputing market in 1981 with its trend-setting IBM PC. Three years later, Apple unveiled the Macintosh with the Kay-mandated graphical user interface, mouse, and high-resolution display, an approach that forever changed the way the data-lovin' world interacts with computers.

The first affordable *portable* computer, the Osborne 01, already had hit the market in 1982. Nicknamed the "Volkswagen of Computers," it cost $1,795 including software. The Osborne 01 featured a five-inch screen, full-size keyboard with numeric keypad, two 5 1/4-inch floppy drives, and three output ports (serial, modem, and parallel), all packaged in a case the size of a small sewing machine. It weighed about 25 pounds.

Eleven years later, portions of this book are being written on a portable computer with a nine-inch screen, in a case the size of a notebook, that tips the scale at four pounds.

The Windshield

Visual Displays

CHAPTER 5

The Windshield
Visual Displays

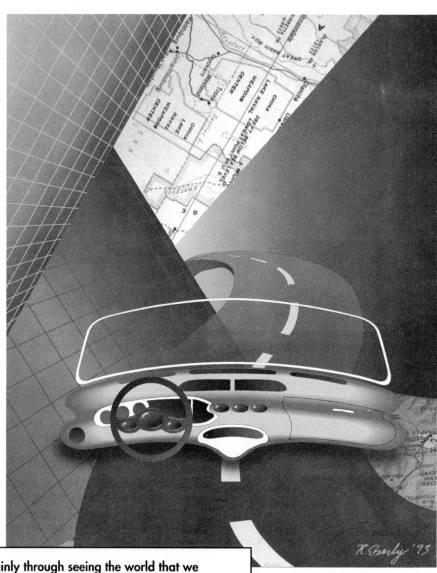

R. Eberly '93

"It is mainly through seeing the world that we appraise and understand it."—Diane Ackerman, *A Natural History of the Senses*

Seeing as how 70 percent of our sense receptors reside in our eyes, we can believe that eyes are "the great monopolists of our senses," as Diane Ackerman states in her book *A Natural History of the Senses* (mandatory reading for virtual-world creators). Compelled by vivid imagery, we seek to provide clear views through our windows onto virtual worlds.

Output device is the tech-term for such a window. Output devices fit into two categories: *displays* and *effectors*. A display can be as plain and simple as the monitor that accompanies your computer—or as sophisticated as a three-dimensional, fully immersive head-mounted display (HMD). An effector embraces the visual display, audio headphones, and external devices such as digital music synthesizers and physical (tactile/force) feedback devices—anything that has an effect on your sense organs.

An array of output devices graces the pages of VR industry publications, but few of these high-end products serve the needs of budget-minded hobbyists. Still, we need to know the distinguishing characteristics of these "windshields" to understand what's possible for garage VR exploration.

The Technology of Head-Mounted Displays

We already know that the goal of the VR creator is to make the participant feel a sense of presence in the virtual world. Immersive applications support this illusion chiefly through the visual output device, one that cuts off your vision from contact with the physical world. This device—the head-mounted display—basically consists of two tiny TV screens and a set of special optics. The optics help you focus on images that aren't much farther from your eyes than the tip of your nose. Optics also increase the image display's field of view (how far in each direction—up and down, left to right—the display extends).

The head-mounted display serves as an *input* device too, because it contains tracking sensors that measure your head's position and orientation, and it transmits that data to the computer. As a result, the computer generates a sequence of images one frame at a time—on-the-fly (in real time, not prerecorded)—so the HMD can show images that correspond to your shifting viewpoint and actions.

When connecting the helmet to the reality engine, you must consider the method of transmitting computer images to the helmet's display screens. As mentioned in Chapter 4, the typical computer generates RGB display signals, while most HMDs employ television components that rely on NTSC signals. If the graphics processor in the reality engine is output directly to the HMD, the chain must include a signal converter between computer output and display input to handle the signal translation. (Some newer HMDs facilitate this process by including RGB input options. And some personal computers can output NTSC signals.)

Immersive VR is most successful in presenting a convincing illusion when the display offers a large field of view, boasts high resolution, displays images at a fast frame rate, and presents stereoscopic imagery. Let's tackle these characteristics individually.

Field of View

The HMD shows a wide image. The measurement for the image's width is expressed in degrees as field of view (FOV). In the real world, if you possess normal vision, your vertical FOV is about 150 degrees of the world around you. (Actually, your eye can deal with 180 degrees up and down, but your eyebrows and cheeks get in the way.) Your horizontal, or lateral, FOV is about 180 degrees, and even greater when you roll your eyeballs to the corners of your eyes.

For sake of comparison, a regular movie screen fills about nine degrees, or five percent, of your horizontal field of view and even less of your vertical FOV when you're seated in the middle of the theater.

As you can imagine, a wide FOV imparts a greater sense of presence or immersion in the virtual world. Thus, VR professionals claim that the *threshold* of immersion begins at about 80-85 degrees FOV in both directions. (In HMDs that provide less than 80 degrees horizontal FOV, it feels like you're viewing the virtual world through a tube.) An HMD, however, needs optics to spread those tiny screen images without distorting them. In the process of magnifying the screens, the optics decrease the perceived image resolution. Therefore, some HMD designers keep their FOV down to about 50 degrees to improve the appearance of the image. Others write software that employs a "pre-distorting process" to correct the distortion induced by the optics.

Let's discuss FOVs of some current high-end HMDs. One HMD out in the field is the Flight Helmet by Virtual Research, which features a horizontal FOV measuring about 100 degrees. The W Industries Visette in the Virtuality arcade game system has a 90-degree FOV. The Leep Systems CyberFace 2 has a 140-degree horizontal FOV, which is relatively wide but is said to induce distortion on the edges as a result. The Liquid Image Corporation's Mirage FOV specs out at about 110 degrees horizontal, as do the RPI Advanced Technology Group's new lightweight HMSI glasses, which boast an 85 degree vertical FOV.

Resolution

Most high-end HMDs use liquid crystal displays to present images. Most color LCDs have a resolution of 360 horizontal by 240 vertical pixels. Three elements—one red, one green, and one blue—make a single pixel. According to my calculator, that means the display shows 28,800 pixels. Compare that to a typical computer screen, which sports hundreds of thousands of pixels, and you'll get an idea of how blocky an HMD image can look—especially when it's just a couple inches from your eyes. Some HMD manufacturers use higher-resolution CRT (cathode ray tube) displays, the kind used in video camera viewfinders. They're black-and-white, but they boast many more pixels than the LCDs, and special filtering techniques have been developed to enable color display in CRT-based helmets.

The Virtual Research Flight Helmet offers a 360x240 resolution, whereas the W Industries Virtuality system's Visette presents a 372x276 resolution. The Leep Systems CyberFace 2 resolution is 479x234, whereas the monoscopic CyberFace 3 resolution is 720x240 (because it doesn't display a pair of stereoscopic images). That's the same resolution supported by the Liquid Image Corporation's Mirage—it too is monoscopic. The small HMSI display from RPI Advanced Technology Group features 412x210 resolution that can optionally increase to 640x480, 1024x768, or even 1280x1024.

LCD and CRT manufacturers are working to create better display technologies with higher resolutions—but they're not the kind of technologies that humble hobbyists can easily afford.

The trade-off with lower pixel resolution is faster image rendering. The grainier the image, the faster the scene can move.

Frame Rate

Frame rate refers to the number of frames per second appearing on the display—the speed of the simulation. In a movie theater, film runs at about 24 frames per second. On TV, video runs about 30 frames per second. Old Saturday-morning cartoons crank out at a rate of about 15 frames per second. In all of these, you can't distinguish between individual frames: they move by in a stream that's perceived as continuous motion. In the land of VR, this frames-per-second (fps) measurement is sometimes expressed as Hz (Hertz, or cycles per second). Professional virtual-world-builders, at this stage of the game, shoot for about 15-22 fps in immersive applications. This is known technically as the *update rate*.

Unlike movies, video, and cartoons, virtual worlds exist in real time. They're not played back from a recording medium. When you wear an HMD equipped with a position-tracker, the computer sends a new image frame to the display each time you move your head or perform an action that affects images, such as when you catch a flying fish. Using data transmitted by the tracker, the computer "senses" your position, calculates it, and sends a corresponding image to the display. The difference in time between your action and the computer's reaction is known as *lag* or *latency* rate. The slower the computer's CPU, the greater the lag. The rate at which the computer display can update a scene is known technically as the *refresh* rate.

Even sophisticated immersive VR systems induce latency in their simulations. This is because of the tracking system's complexity and ensuing data bottlenecks—sometimes as much as a noticeable quarter-second lag (250 milliseconds). The virtual images don't synchronize with your actual movements. Indeed, a lag greater than 100 milliseconds can make some participants feel sick. Even a 50-millisecond lag diminishes that real-time feeling.

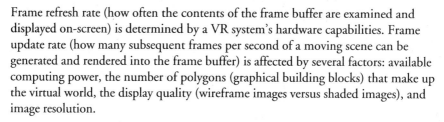

Frame refresh rate (how often the contents of the frame buffer are examined and displayed on-screen) is determined by a VR system's hardware capabilities. Frame update rate (how many subsequent frames per second of a moving scene can be generated and rendered into the frame buffer) is affected by several factors: available computing power, the number of polygons (graphical building blocks) that make up the virtual world, the display quality (wireframe images versus shaded images), and image resolution.

Cruder pictures mean a better frame rate and less lag. The faster the frame rate, the better the real-time effect. Not surprisingly, complex imagery may make the world look better, but it slows down the frame rate and increases the lag.

Stereoscopy

It's easy to confuse the adjectives *3D* and *stereoscopic*. People tend to use the former buzzword when the latter is the correct technical term. Interactive, three-dimensional computer graphics obviously exist on a flat surface in the two-dimensional realm, but they appear to have the dimension of depth. You can rotate interactive 3D graphic objects to see their back surfaces. You can move 3D objects to see what's behind them. Your perspective, as well as such effects as lighting and shadows, are calculated by the computer.

Stereoscopic images technically exist in two dimensions, but they appear to float in space in front of the surface on which they're displayed or projected. It looks like you can reach out and grab them. Stereoscopy applied to 3D graphics can dramatically increase the illusion of presence in a virtual world.

It's a time-honored tradition, stereoscopy. It's embodied in those cardboard eyeglasses with the red and blue plastic lenses (the kind supplied for 3D movies and with 3D comic books). Remember those red plastic ViewMaster gadgets? If you played with one of them when you were a kid, early on you experienced stereoscopic techniques that let people view objects as if they exist in three dimensions. The ViewMaster's predecessor, the classic stereoscope, was invented in Great Britain in 1838. It's an instrument with two eyepieces through which you view a pair of photos, both of the same subject, each taken at a slightly different angle. The two photos are seen as a single picture that apparently exists in three dimensions and that has height, width, and depth.

Stereoscopy plays on the fact that each of your eyes, because of the way they're placed in your face, sees a slightly different image when looking at anything. Your brain merges those two images into one image that appears to have depth and other cues that impart the object's position, distance, and size. (The books on VR that are listed in Appendix D thoroughly explain the science of stereo vision.)

In computer-generated stereoscopic imagery, the amount of *parallax*—the distance between the left image and the right image—determines how close or far away the virtual objects seem to be from the viewer. A smaller parallax, for instance, results in the illusion that the object is far from you.

A head-mounted display presents stereoscopic images by rapidly flashing one image for the left eye, then a slightly different image for the right eye, then the same thing over and over again at such a rapid rate (about 60 times a second per image) that you don't sense the alternations. A plain computer monitor can perform the same task, but to perceive the doubled imagery as stereo and not blurred pictures, you need to wear stereoscopic electronic glasses with rapid-fire shutter lenses that are precisely synchronized with the alternating screen images. More on those in a minute.

Stereoscopy has its drawbacks. A full 10 percent (and as much as 20 percent) of the population can't sense the illusion. Their brains can't properly merge the doubled images, and thus they can't appreciate the 3D effect in an HMD.

Another problem inherent in electronic stereoscopy lies in the technological burden it places on the computer system. Displaying separate pictures for the left and right eye, in most systems, doubles the image processing power required of the reality engine. Some immersive VR technologists deal with this by linking two synchronized reality engines, one to handle each eye's display. Another approach involves doubling the graphics capabilities of a single engine. This costs less than the first solution, but programming chores increase correspondingly. It also tends to decrease the resolution of the display.

Therefore, the need for stereoscopy depends entirely on the application. If the virtual-world experience involves extensive object manipulation and hand/eye coordination, stereoscopy is warranted. However, stereoscopy is less important when the application focuses on architectural or landscape walk-through environments, in which the participant doesn't have much complex interaction with individual, nearby objects. In those types of applications, it's better to trade stereoscopy for higher resolution, faster frame rate, and/or a wider field of view. That's why many immersive VR systems simply take the monoscopic approach.

Sometimes, you can't even tell, in a high-quality, immersive, monoscopic VR simulation, that each eye is seeing the same image. The virtual-world-builder wields other tools in the kit to present a convincing simulation.

Who Says You Need a Helmet?

The various limitations of HMDs have resulted in the development and increasing use of *partial immersion* systems, in which you don't don a head-mounted display, but wear stereoscopic glasses, or simply view the virtual world through a two-dimensional window. This doesn't prevent the ability to shift your viewpoint or interact with the world, or to stick your hand in the virtual world through the use of a wired glove or other input device.

Garage VR experimenters can choose from a few different low-budget routes to reach their virtual destinations:

The most convenient route is provided by the basic monitor. If you're just starting out with garage VR, consider taking a few trial runs with this reliable display. Okay, so maybe it doesn't do stereo. Maybe you'll go without position-tracking for a while. This means you don't need to program low-resolution stereo images, tax your CPU, or contemplate signal conversion. You can harness the monitor's capabilities to generate decent interactive 3D graphics and present a clear, crisp image. You don't deal with cumbersome garb weighing down your neck or perching on your nose.

Rudimentary garage VR experiences, supported by such programs as Virtual Reality Studio, Vistapro, and Virtus WalkThrough (see Chapter 7), work just fine on the monitor of a PC, Macintosh, or Amiga. With programs such as REND386 or VREAM, and some Power Glove reconstruction, you can build a position-tracking, interactive vehicle and view your virtual worlds through a windshield that in normal life is a normal monitor. With a little imagination, you'll achieve virtual immersion.

Seeing in Stereo

When you're ready to deal with stereoscopic graphics and/or partial and full immersion, several routes are available, depending on which reality engine you use.

When it comes to three-dimensional computer graphics and/or stereo imagery, the IBM PC is the leader in the low-budget arena. This is due to the amount of research done in the area, the attendant availability of applicable software, and the proliferation of low-cost graphics programs, adapters, and accelerators. Many textbooks and professional references cover the PC's graphics capabilities. (Recommended books are listed at the end of this chapter and in Appendix D.)

The Amiga comes in second in the stereoscopy support contest, thanks to its high power, low price, versatile frame buffer control, and standardized graphics environment. On top of that, many Amiga models provide NTSC signal output, useful for those brave few who might choose to build an Amiga-compatible head-mounted display.

The Macintosh is great for painting, drawing, and image-processing, but 3D graphics files consume anywhere from about 100K to more than 100 megabytes of hard disk space, require plenty of free RAM, and still sometimes take over a day to render. Driving on the Macintosh toward a stereoscopic landscape will take you over some rough road, especially if your Macintosh isn't a Quadra or a hopped-up IIvx. If you want to coax a stereoscopic, fast-moving image display from a more modest Mac, stick with simple wireframe imagery.

If you're intrigued by the notion of Mac-based immersive VR, consider investing in the new 68040-based Apple Centris 660AV (about $2,500 list) or Quadra 840AV (about $4,500 list); both provide video outputs that satisfy the signal needs of HMDs. And each of these "AV Macs" contains an AT&T 3210 digital signal processor chip, which crunches massive hunks of data in real time and runs its own system software. When it comes to handling graphics, the DSP lets these machines shine.

Whichever reality engine you choose, various ways exist to help it display image pairs so that each eye sees only the appropriate image. First we'll review the simplest and least expensive techniques for seeing in stereo. Then we'll move up to the complex, more costly approaches to viewing virtual worlds.

One basic technique employs polarizers to filter the image pairs. A polarizing lens blocks the light traveling in a horizontal or vertical plane, depending on the lens. The horizontal data for one image is displayed on the screen's upper half, while the vertical data for the same image is shown on the lower half. The data is merged by a beam splitter and viewed with a pair of polarized filter glasses. The beam splitter, which resembles a flat, rectangular sheet of translucent plastic, is mounted in such a way that it's held in place and aligned with the screen display. This approach cuts the screen's vertical resolution in half. Few would call this a VR technique, even those who work in the garage.

A book published by Brady, *True Three-Dimensional Graphics* by Michael Hyman, includes a BASIC program for colored filtering on an IBM PC and instructions for building and using a polarizer filtering system. You probably can find this book in a library that has a good computer book section, such as a university library.

In the colored filter approach, the left and right eye images are displayed in complementary colors, such as red and blue or green. You look at the images through a pair of glasses with corresponding colored lenses (those are the filters), so each eye sees only its respective image. This is the same technique used in 3D comic books. Using a computer paint program or image-processing software, you can draw the basic image, then duplicate it. Then, you place the pair of images side by side on the computer screen, about the same distance apart as the distance between your eyes (about 2.5 inches) and not much larger than about 3 inches high. If the images are farther apart and/or larger, it's tougher to see the 3D effect. When you have your stereo image pair in place, check it out with some colored filter glasses. Actually, the best way to draw and place the images is to shrink them and move them while wearing the glasses until the image achieves its best three-dimensionality.

As you may already know, your eyes tire after long periods of viewing through these funky shades. Naturally, the method won't work with monochrome monitors, because they don't show complementary colors—which also means you can't use full-color images. Finally, your images can't have really good detail because of their small size, and sometimes you see "ghosts" due to the cheapo filters.

Okay, so there are limitations; it's still fun to experiment with this approach.

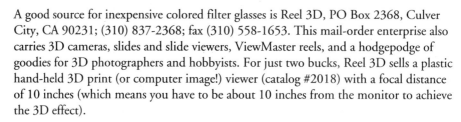

A good source for inexpensive colored filter glasses is Reel 3D, PO Box 2368, Culver City, CA 90231; (310) 837-2368; fax (310) 558-1653. This mail-order enterprise also carries 3D cameras, slides and slide viewers, ViewMaster reels, and a hodgepodge of goodies for 3D photographers and hobbyists. For just two bucks, Reel 3D sells a plastic hand-held 3D print (or computer image!) viewer (catalog #2018) with a focal distance of 10 inches (which means you have to be about 10 inches from the monitor to achieve the 3D effect).

People have long experimented with building low-cost, wide-angle viewers based on fresnel lenses (flat plastic magnifiers), prisms, and mirrors to merge image pairs in a way that supports stereoscopy. The viewer is placed against the monitor's screen and works with software that generates two separate images, one for each eye, side by side on-screen. One such device, which works with the PC, Macintosh, or Amiga, is included in this book: see the section in Chapter 8 titled "How to Build the Virtual Reality Window: A Low-Cost VR Display."

If this simple stereoscopy appeals to you, but you don't want to get into locating supplies and building contraptions, you might want to invest in the relatively low-cost ready-made 3D viewer—the Cyberscope.

Simsalabim Cyberscope Viewing Hood

Introduced in 1993, Simsalabim's $179 Cyberscope (shown in Figure 5.1) transforms the ordinary monitor of a personal computer (IBM PC or clone) into a 3D display. The Cyberscope is a plastic hood-like device that attaches to the front surface of your monitor with Velcro. The viewing end contains two slots, each measuring 5/8-inch by 7/8-inch. The Cyberscope software presents a pair of wireframe images side by side on the PC screen. (You can use the Cyberscope with other types of rendering software, however, to view shaded images.) The Cyberscope's optics reflect, through the slots and onto your eyes, the image pair so that you perceive it as a single, sharp 3D object that appears to float in front of you. The object is about 4 inches wide, and its resolution is determined by your monitor's resolution. You can control the object in real time, using the mouse to rotate it around any axis and move it in different directions. The Cyberscope software works with a standard IBM two-button mouse. It also can handle Micropoint's Z-Mouse, a $250 6DOF controller (discussed in more detail in Chapter 6).

The optics employ four front-surface mirrors, a technique that results in a full-color image with a wide field of view and no haunting by ghostly or flickering images. According to the folks at Simsalabim, here's how it works: The mirrors face the screen in a way that they rotate the left and right images by 90 degrees in opposite directions; the pixels are distributed symmetrically on either side of the screen's center line. Then they're shifted together. To display the letter F, for example, the on-screen images look like this:

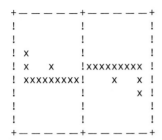

The Cyberscope works with a '386 PC or better with any standard VGA monitor measuring 14 to 17 inches; no adjustments are necessary, and no extra data processing is required to coordinate the left and right image synchronization. Available in fashionable black or white plastic, the hood blocks out ambient light so you can see the 3D image clearly. And its design affords a comfortable, downward viewing angle.

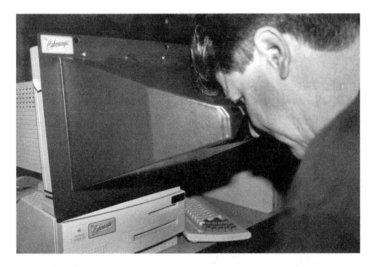

Figure 5.1. *Cyberscope. (Photo by Linda Jacobson)*

When you buy the Cyberscope, you also receive an initialization program and sample software for presenting stereo image pairs. As of this writing, the freebie is CyberSmash, a Pong-like 3D ball game. The newest version of CyberSmash supports the Creative Labs' SoundBlaster PC sound board.

Simsalabim also sells a basic 3D wireframe drawing tool designed for Cyberscope viewing. This $99 package imports raw 3D data and also imports and converts .DXF files—the standard format in 3D design programs.

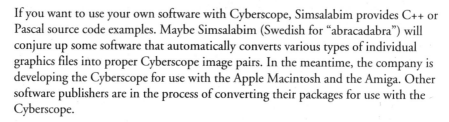

If you want to use your own software with Cyberscope, Simsalabim provides C++ or Pascal source code examples. Maybe Simsalabim (Swedish for "abracadabra") will conjure up some software that automatically converts various types of individual graphics files into proper Cyberscope image pairs. In the meantime, the company is developing the Cyberscope for use with the Apple Macintosh and the Amiga. Other software publishers are in the process of converting their packages for use with the Cyberscope.

You can order the $179 Cyberscope by calling Simsalabim at (800) 3D-TODAY (338-6329). Or, write for a brochure and newsletter: Simsalabim, PO Box 4446, Berkeley, CA 94704.

Stereoscopic Shutter Glasses

Showing two slightly different images on-screen at the same time takes up extra pixel real estate and thereby reduces the resolution of the overall image. A more sophisticated approach to stereoscopy cashes in on the display technique of *field-sequential stereo graphics*. This technique maintains the entire image resolution and doesn't require that you shrink or scale your images. We must dive down to the technical level of electronic image display to help you understand this type of stereoscopy.

Field-sequential, full-frame color video/graphics display techniques have existed since the early days of television. On a cathode ray tube (CRT) monitor—the type used with televisions and most computers—the image, or frame, comprises hundreds of horizontal lines. An electron gun in the back of the CRT scans these lines from top to bottom, starting at the upper-left. It sprays out each individual line across the screen in the form of a narrow stream of electrons—that's the cathode ray. The front of the tube (the screen's inside surface) is coated with phosphors that light up when they're hit by the electrons. The more electrons, the more light. The varying light patterns make up the image on-screen, just as varied colored dots of ink make the photographs reproduced in this book. These light patterns are grouped into small dots called *pixels* that you can see on the display screen. Resolution refers to how many pixels reside in the horizontal and vertical dimensions of the screen, but this depends on the screen size. Two displays containing the same number of pixels but having different sizes will have different resolutions.

As that electron beam shoots across the tube, it "refreshes" the display. Each row of pixels is scanned in a single refresh, which means the beam traces the entire picture at once. The refresh rate, or scan rate, is the rate at which the scanning beam sweeps successive frames of the displayed image. This process typically occurs about 60 times per second, or 60 Hz (better VGA monitors run at 72 Hz). The point at which the gun stops at the bottom and returns to the top of the screen is called the vertical blanking period.

Meanwhile, the frame buffer (the graphics system's display memory) contains the light values of all the pixels at any given time. It supplies this data to the electron beam as it rapidly scans and refreshes the display. When the image changes—when you move a graphic object, for example—the frame buffer is updated and the electron beam sprays the new picture pattern.

In a television, the beam works a bit differently. Here's where the "field-sequential" part comes in. A TV screen is divided into horizontal lines. The electron beam first shoots out the odd-numbered lines (262.5 of them), called the odd field, then shoots out the even-numbered lines (another 262.5), called the even field. The two fields are interlaced or interwoven to make up a single frame of 525 lines, which occurs 30 times each second (30 Hz). A frame contains the total image information of a scene.

You can take a similar field-sequential approach to set up 3D computer-generated graphics for viewing with *stereoscopic glasses.*

Stereoscopic glasses are based on LCD shutters. Think of them as electronic filters. They turn the monitor into a desktop VR system by letting you "see in stereo" as you peer at the computer screen (and they cost significantly less than HMDs). Put on a pair of these glasses and look at a stereoscopic image; it appears to float in front of your face, popping off the surface of the screen. Two or more people can view a single stereoscopic display while wearing LCD shutter glasses.

Here's how these glasses work: Liquid crystal "shutters" are mounted in the lenses of a pair of plastic goggles. The computer controls the electronic shutters, synchronizing them to correspond with alternating left-eye and right-eye versions of an image displayed on the monitor. In other words, the shutters occlude the image from alternating eyes. When the left image appears on-screen, the left lens opens and the right lens closes. When the right image appears, the right lens opens and the left lens closes. Just like those red-and-blue 3D comics, the left and right images are identical, but slightly offset from each other to match the real-life perspective of your left and right eyes.

Inside the glasses, the shutters run at a frequency that coincides with the multiplexed (left/right) sequential field information displayed on the monitor. It's essential to synchronize the alternating shutters with the corresponding alternating screen images. The shutters open and close so quickly that your brain can't detect the activity. Each eye receives separate image information, but the brain is fooled into thinking it's one image.

Shutter glasses need "stereo-ready" signals for the purpose of synchronization. To provide field-sequential stereoscopic graphics, the display rate must at least double its normal speed. It must multiplex the alternating left- and right-eye images so they can be viewed with the glasses as a single stereoscopic image. A standard computer monitor runs at 60 Hz for stereoscopic graphics, so the frame rate is 30 Hz *for each eye.* (Higher-quality SVGA monitors run at 72 Hz, with a 36 Hz frame rate per eye.) These signals are supplied through the graphics cards on personal computers, specially programmed to output alternating left- and right-eye images. (Figure 5.2 shows how LCD shutter glasses work.)

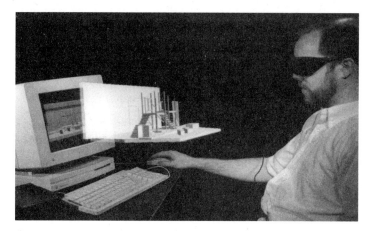

Figure 5.2. *A simulation of how LCD shutter glasses work. (Photo courtesy of Mark Reany)*

Today, the price of a pair of LCD glasses and the accompanying computer interface device runs around $250 or less. Higher-quality systems, such as those sold by StereoGraphics Corporation, operate at a much faster frame rate (120 Hz) and provide a smooth, clear, impressive illusion of depth. These more costly LCD glasses rely on a sync detector and infrared (IR) light transmitter to send out the timing signal to the shutters. They also require special, expensive, multisync (high-frequency) display monitors.

StereoGraphics Corporation, the pioneering developer of wireless shutter glasses (systems start at $1,300), has initiated a stereo image standard for personal computers—a standard that is supported by many 3D graphics-oriented software and hardware companies. StereoGraphics' battery-operated CrystalEyes work with a small wireless transmitter that sits on top of the monitor. It emits synchronized IR signals containing timing information for the shutters. The left and right images appear simultaneously, but the monitor's vertical scan section is "blanked" or "strobed" at twice the normal frequency. The result is one left-image field instantly followed by one right-image field. Unlike less expensive glasses, CrystalEyes are flicker-free because the display frame rate runs at 120 Hz (120 images, or frames, per second), rather than the 60 Hz rate associated with most stereoscopic shutter glasses.

When working with lower-cost 60 Hz shutter glasses, you need a way to communicate the vertical blanking (retrace) signal to the graphics software for synchronization. The software must communicate with a controller that drives the glasses in sync with the display.

You also need a way to quickly switch the computer's frame buffers—to alternate the left and right images so that each eye sees only the proper image and receives 30 of them each second. Graphics programs designed to support LCD shutter glasses will handle this task, which is known as *page flipping.*

If you don't precisely synchronize the images with the shutters, an irksome flicker effect results. Flicker is visible in standard 60 Hz field-sequential systems. That's why people call these devices "flicker glasses." Some complain that the flicker causes headaches. Others say they grow accustomed to the flicker after a few minutes. Two types of flicker come into play: room flicker (created by ambient light) and image flicker (caused by high-luminosity image areas and/or low update rates). When you turn down the lights in the room, you can reduce the appearance of flicker. Fluorescent lighting (which runs at a 60 Hz frequency) is a real flicker-maker, so switch off any of those fixtures in a room where you're using shutter glasses. You also can decrease the flicker effect if you adjust the screen luminosity with your monitor's brightness and contrast controls.

Eliminating flicker also requires experience with 3D graphics programming and such knowledge as how to avoid high-luminosity areas in an image, how to create a large parallax for areas with high contrast, and so on. (Parallax is the distance in viewing angle between the image pairs that make up a virtual object.) To see which combinations yield the best stereoscopic effects, you'll also need to experiment with different colors in your images. Some stereoscopic graphics programs can run at 70 Hz, which reduces flicker.

What kinds of glasses are available for the budget-conscious shopper? For a while, Sega manufactured $50 shutter glasses for the Sega Master video game system, but discontinued production in 1990. Toshiba built the $50 3-Dimension Scope viewer for its 3D camcorder—also discontinued. Many garage VR hobbyists use Sega and Toshiba glasses in conjunction with a homemade RS232 interface circuit (consisting of basic electronic components) for connecting the glasses to a PC's serial port. Some entrepreneurs stocked up on the Sega and Toshiba glasses, and others started manufacturing their own glasses, based on a similar design.

These low-cost glasses rely on the computer's capability to send a pulse (a 5-10 Volt, 400 Hz timing signal) out its serial port to the interface. This pulse causes the glasses to alternately open and close each shutter. Chapter 8 includes directions and diagrams for constructing an inexpensive circuit board that interfaces LCD shutter glasses to your computer. If you want to equip your shutter glasses with position-tracking capabilities, check out the section titled "How to Build a Head-Tracker from a Power Glove" in Chapter 8.

The technique of field-sequential stereo graphics won't work on LCD screens, so it's not applicable to LCD-based head-mounted displays.

Taking the Head-Mounted Display Way

Perhaps you shun shutter glasses. If you have several thousand dollars lying around, you can buy a ready-to-wear head-mounted display, but frankly, the technology changes so rapidly that the helmet will be surpassed by better, less expensive models in a matter of months. Better to spend that money on a graphics accelerator, more RAM, and/or a trip to Tahiti.

If your bank account balance makes you shrug (or cringe), you might consider building your own head-mounted display. Others have walked that path and lived to tell the tale....

Two innovative guys, Mark Pesce and Michael Donahue (who have a VR technology company called Ono-Sendai, based in San Francisco), constructed an HMD for less than $250, not counting the video cameras. They mounted two LCD color televisions and stereo headphones in a rigid framework located around a full-face motorcycle helmet. They wired the TVs and headphones to two video cameras mounted approximately 11 inches, or 300 millimeters, apart (measured from the center of one lens to the center of the other lens), a distance mandated by the size of the cameras. The cameras also were mounted on a rigid frame. Their two fixed lenses then created a 40-degree binocular FOV.

That 300-millimeter distance between the lenses is much larger than the average 65mm distance (about 2.5 inches) between your two eyes. (This distance is called *interocular gap* by VR pros.) Not surprisingly, this difference messed with the stereoscopic effect. Mark explains, "Our perception of binocular parallax, one of the determinants of depth perception, is based upon the constancy of that interocular gap. When inside the virtual world, our sense of depth and focal plane were markedly different than what we normally experience. Objects five meters away were perceived as though they were less than two meters away. Objects closer than one meter could not be fused binocularly. Ideally, the cameras would be able to 'cross' their lenses and fuse the binocular field."

I heard about another hobbyist who spent less than $500 to transform two Citizen 2.7-inch LCD TVs to build a color, monoscopic HMD with approximately a 90-degree horizontal field of view. He housed the LCDs, along with some optics, in a contraption that he could wear on his head. He also incorporated a potentiometer-based head-tracking device. He equipped his reality engine, a PC, with an RGB (VGA)-to-NTSC converter that provided the signals needed to drive the HMD display.

As mentioned earlier, most of the color LCD displays in HMDs have 360x240 resolution. CRT displays—such as the tiny monochrome screens used in viewfinders of hand-held video cameras—boast higher resolution and better contrast than LCDs, and thus attract VR hobbyists. (Tektronix's display products division even sells 1-inch CRTs specifically for HMDs.) The co-creator of REND386, Dave Stampe, built his HMD using 4-inch Sony CRTs, but the device was painfully heavy. An innovator named Dave Lowry built an HMD from two Sony viewfinders. He warned others of its limitations, such as an extremely narrow field of view (about 20 degrees) in an Internet posting: "Get a couple of toilet paper tubes and look through them to simulate this [FOV]. Some people have used telescope eyepieces (very expensive) instead of the simple plastic lens that comes with the viewfinder to get a wider field of view. I'm squeamish about wearing CRTs two inches from my eyeballs for an extended period [due to electromagnetic emission]."

If you intend to build a stereoscopic head-mounted display, your reality engine must be equipped with two graphics cards—one for each eye's image. You can buy special PC-based 3D graphics accelerators designed to take advantage of the stereoscopic rendering capability offered by high-end VR toolkits such as Sense8's WorldToolKit. The SPEA Fire board is the current accelerator of choice in the VR field. At $2,500 per card, however, installing two Fire boards in a single PC is a costly proposition.

(At least one VR company is developing an affordable SVGA card for the PC that would provide two outputs supporting stereoscopic display. It would split the signal by sequentially sampling the image pairs and feeding each side to each eye in sequence. The availability of such a product at a reasonable price—say, under $1,000—would do much to expand the horizons of garage VR hobbyists.)

Naturally, you also can opt to go the monoscopic route, which requires a single standard graphics processor.

And remember, if your HMD has standard video-in connections, you need a box that converts the computer's RGB signals to the HMD's NTSC signals.

Alternatively, you can aim a video camera at your computer screen and send the camera's output directly to the HMD. This method even supports stereoscopy, in Rube Goldberg fashion: set up two computer systems with two monitors, one showing a left-eye image and the other showing a right-eye image. Set up two video cameras. Aim one camera at the left monitor and send its output signal to the left-eye input for the HMD. Aim the other camera at the right monitor and send its output signal to the right-eye input for the HMD. (Chapter 8 includes plans for building two types of HMDs.)

You might also consider contacting the do-it-yourself doctor, Robert Suding, who holds a PhD in computer science. He sells step-by-step directions that tell how to convert Casio LCD TVs to head-mounted displays, and how to build low-cost IBM PC clone circuit boards for producing stereoscopic images and for building PC circuit boards for multichannel sound and head-tracking. Issue #9 of the hobbyist 'zine *PCVR* published Dr. Suding's "How To Build an HMD for Under $450." You can order that issue of *PCVR* (see Profile 2) or find out about Dr. Suding's other plans by contacting him directly at SAI, 27107 Richmond Hill Road, Conifer, Colorado 80433; (303) 838-6346.

If you want to build an HMD for use with the Amiga or Macintosh, you still need a good, high-resolution graphics card and the ability to program it. (To achieve double-frame buffering for stereoscopic graphics, you must divide the output of the graphics card.) Peter Falco, a student at Rensselaer Polytechnic Institute in Troy, New York, is building Dr. Suding's HMD from the *PCVR* plans. However, his reality engine is a Macintosh Centris 650 (with two video cards and 8MB of RAM). He has to substitute different NTSC converters for the ones named in the Suding plans: "We're using a 'Display Link' by Display Tech at $489 per eye; one Display Link is needed per graphics card," Pete explains. "Also, that card must be a high-resolution Macintosh video card in order for the Display Link to work. (We are using standard Mac 8/24 video cards, but we're looking into something with a little more kick.) The Display Link takes the output from the video card and converts it to the NTSC signal. We're also using a Radio Shack RF modulator *for each eye.* The RF modulators convert the raw NTSC signals coming out of the Display Tech to something that the television can pick up—usually channel 3 or 4. Frame rates in our pre-Beta version are extremely low: five to 10 fps. But we have paid little attention to them thus far. Our plan is to get everything working first, then worry about speed. However, we are using both double buffering and the vertical retrace manager. We're writing our own software to create virtual worlds."

Pete is working on this project with another RPI student, Jeremy Gentile. Rensselaer's Department of Decision Sciences and Engineering Systems will use the results of their work as a prototype for a more complex VR system intended for concurrent parts design and manufacture of parts. A part will be designed by several engineers working concurrently in a virtual world, and then, at the press of a button, the part will be machined by an automated manufacturing system.

Pete would like to make a version of this application available to the public (with a modem). "I hope to set up a dial-in service, such as Prodigy or CompuServe, where people can call in and be in different worlds on the system, linked with various people. This is a ways off. I believe that the technology is there. I just need to graduate and get funding."

For his HMD, Pete also plans to incorporate the Logitech position-tracking kit to permit head-tracking in the x-, y-, z-, pan, tilt, and roll axes. However, many VR enthusiasts feel that a head-mounted display would do just as well tracking three degrees of freedom (orientation information) instead of all six (orientation plus position information). They argue that you need only provide data for the head's orientation: left and right ("pan," as in shaking your head to say no), up and down ("tilt," as in nodding your head), and roll (as in cocking your head to either side). As the HMD blocks your vision from the physical world, the addition of position-tracking (sensing the head's location in the x-, y-, and z-axes) tempts the participant to stand up and sit down, walk back and forth, and otherwise engage in movement that could result in collisions with objects in the real world.

Even without the inclusion of location sensors, the process of building a head-mounted display is extremely time-consuming. Be prepared to spend several hours adjusting the HMD's lens system and tuning the interocular gap. That's not the only problem; if you spend any appreciable time in a space where you can't focus your eyes, you'll get a monstrous headache, and maybe feel nauseous, too. If you a use a video camera to capture screen images and/or you include position-tracking, any attendant lag or latency can induce motion sickness (known as simulator sickness in the VR trade). This occurs even more often when you're driving stereoscopic simulations (another reason to consider monoscopy aided by some clever modeling and rendering techniques).

Another problem with stereoscopic HMDs concerns the beefed-up processing power required to present the pairs of images. All that horsepower applied to the stereo illusion means less juice for image detail and interaction.

Homemade head-mounts are great for immersive VR, but only one person's head can fit in a helmet. That means every virtual world journey must be a solo effort. (Networking isn't possible at this point in garage VR's development, but people are working on it.)

Moreover, the head-mount's resolution typically is lower than a monitor's; the optics increase the image to support a wide field of view, so resolution decreases accordingly.

Finally, some people don't like HMDs because they're intrusive; there's a reason these gizmos are dubbed "face suckers."

(Figure 5.3 shows a homemade head-mounted display.)

Nonetheless, VR hobbyists around the world are eagerly awaiting the appearance of a techno-toy from a major video game company. Developed for the 16-bit Sega Genesis game cartridge system, the Sega VR helmet is an American-made HMD scheduled to hit stores in 1994. Plenty of people who never touched a Genesis game button will buy this product. As one garage VR hobbyist told me, "The first thing we're going to do is hook up an oscilloscope to that helmet and see how we can hack it."

Sega unveiled its VR system with much hoopla at a 1993 consumer electronics convention, where visitors could strap on a prototype version of the product and experience Sega's low-end immersive virtual world. The company claimed that shoppers would be able to buy the system before Christmas 1993. By the end of August '93, Sega confirmed rumors that the product wouldn't hit stores until spring of '94. As of this writing, some industry insiders shrug their shoulders when they hear someone mention Sega VR. A few suggest that Sega will scrap its plans to sell HMDs due to the potential health hazards. Others whisper that Sega intends to produce the system in Japan, based on a prototype of Japanese design, not on one developed by Sega of America. Still others say that we won't see any Sega VR product until the 1994 Christmas season at the earliest.

The details discussed here concern the Sega VR prototype developed by the Japanese game giant's American designers and engineers.

Figure 5.3. *Mark Reany, a VR hobbyist, models his homemade head-mounted display, which he uses in conjunction with the Mattel Power Glove to design theater sets. (Photo courtesy of Mark Reany)*

Retailing for just under $200, the Sega VR helmet immerses players in a full-color stereoscopic version of Genesis games, complete with stereo sound. (Although people call it a "helmet," it's not enclosed. It fits over your head with adjustable straps. See Figure 5.4.) The helmet is packaged with an interface box that plugs into the Genesis box. Control over game action is handled by the standard remote controller that's attached to the Genesis. Most appealing in garage VR terms is the helmet's head-tracking features. Your view of the game changes according to the position of your head in 180-degree horizontal space (yaw) and 45-degree vertical space (pitch).

The connection between the Sega VR interface box and the game system is through a 3-plug cable; one wire carries field-sequential NTCS video signals directly from the game cartridge, another carries the left and right audio signals directly from the game cartridge, and the third carries digital data for tracking and left/right eye imaging (the interface box multiplexes the video signal for stereoscopic display in the helmet).

For the screens, Sega uses the same LCD built into the hand-held Sega Game Gear system. The resulting image is what one might expect for the low cost: low quality. (Remember, this *is* a toy.) I tried a preproduction model in the offices of Sega of America. The first thing I noticed when I put on the helmet was that, in a 3D scene with a narrow FOV, I could practically count each pixel by eye. It took a few minutes of playing the game before I could see beyond the individual pixels and concentrate on the overall picture.

Because game cartridges now provide the Sega VR video signal, one wonders whether Sega's CD game system would provide a higher-quality image in the helmet. The answer is yes, but Sega chose to develop the VR helmet specifically for the cartridge system, because there are some 17 million Genesis owners worldwide—compared with the 750,000 who have Sega CD systems.

Because the game system incorporates a stereo Yamaha FM synthesizer, the Sega VR sound quality is pretty good. Sega developers are looking at the possibility of incorporating spatialized sound in future VR-style games.

The orientation-tracking, in part, is passive electromagnetic technology. Sega's lips are sealed on the secret behind the other section of the tracking system, which was invented and designed for Sega by the VR company Ono-Sendai (and for which a patent is pending; when issued, the patent will tell all). The Sega VR system tracks pitch/roll/yaw orientation, but not x/y/z position, for the user-safety issues mentioned earlier. The tracking sensor is mounted on the front-top end of the helmet. There's a minimal amount of lag time, but it's barely noticeable after your attention is captured by the game's virtual world.

Ergonomically speaking, the Sega VR helmet perches pretty heavily on your head and nose, but its adjustable strap makes for stable wear.

Figure 5.4. *A prototype of the Sega VR head-mounted display for the Genesis game system.*

Although the helmet works with all existing Genesis games, Sega also developed four cartridge games specifically for VR helmet play: when you buy the helmet, you get a flight simulator, Nuclear Rush. Or, plop down $60 to $70 each for Iron Hammer (yet another in a long line of search-and-destroy games), Matrix Runner (an exploratory maze-based mystery), and Outlaw Racing (thrill to the crunching sounds of a 20-car pile-up).

Sega of America continues to develop immersion-oriented software for helmet play. Conscious of the overabundance of testosterone-fueled game titles, Sega says that it has hired a psychologist to help develop games that will interest girls (and, presumably, boys less prone to violence than those who compulsively stab the "fire" buttons on their Genesis controllers).

A product similar to Sega VR, announced during the summer of 1993, is the $220 VictorMaxx head-mounted display, designed to work with both the Sega Genesis and the Nintendo Super NES game systems. This headware features a color monoscopic display and lateral (horizontal) position-tracking, and it is sold with two Genesis games. (Early reports from customers indicate disappointment with the VictorMaxx's performance and suggest that potential home-VR fans hold out for Sega VR.) The manufacturer, VictorMaxx, says it also is developing a $350 version of the HMD for use with the IBM PC.

Like every technology associated with VR, image displays change in the blink of an eye.

Where to Buy Shutter Glasses and PC/Macintosh/Amiga Interfaces

Several companies manufacture and/or sell LCD shutter glasses for the PC and Macintosh platforms, including StereoGraphics of San Rafael, California, and Tektronix of Beaverton, Oregon.

In garage VR, the most common glasses sport the Toshiba or Sega logo, but neither is still in production. People have purchased pairs at toy stores, flea markets, and electronics supply houses that carry new and used equipment. With some shopping around, you can find some too. For instance, people have picked up Sega and Toshiba glasses at All Electronics Corporation in Los Angeles, at Electronic City in Burbank, and at Electronics Etc. in Berkeley, California.

The 3DTV Corporation of San Rafael, California produces a full line of shutter glasses (60 to 120 Hz) and interface boxes for use with PC, Macintosh, and Amiga computers. (See Figures 5.5, 5.6, and 5.7.) Actually, the interfaces work with any computer that has standard serial or parallel ports. Prices range from $150 for a do-it-yourself kit (includes glasses, driver card, wiring diagram, and stereoscopic rendering software) to $350 (glasses, interface box that plugs into the serial or parallel port, and stereoscopic rendering software). 3DTV also stocks a good supply of the original Toshiba shutter glasses, which run up to 90 Hz.

Figure 5.5. *Michael Starks of 3DTV models his Model G (Sega) shutter glasses, which run at up to 120Hz rates. (Photo by Linda Jacobson)*

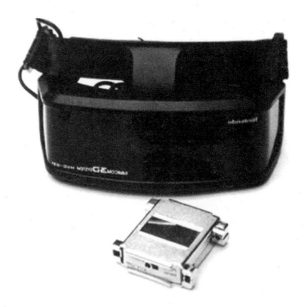

Figure 5.6. *3DTV's $150 Model N (Toshiba) shutter glasses with the PC3D device, an RS232 serial port interface that powers and synchronizes the glasses. These lenses, which are worn with a headband, sport the largest commercially available LCDs—about 1 1/2-inch high by 2 1/2-inch wide per eye.*

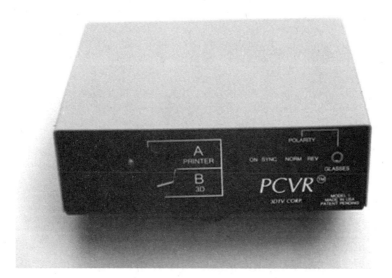

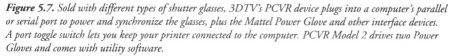

Figure 5.7. Sold with different types of shutter glasses, 3DTV's PCVR device plugs into a computer's parallel or serial port to power and synchronize the glasses, plus the Mattel Power Glove and other interface devices. A port toggle switch lets you keep your printer connected to the computer. PCVR Model 2 drives two Power Gloves and comes with utility software.

3DTV's most recent innovation is a pair of wireless, radio frequency-based shutter glasses. The $250 system employs a small magnetic pickup, which sits on top of the monitor and senses when the display is transmitting each frame. Then, it transmits that information to the wireless glasses. According to the company, this system is immune to the interference problems experienced by infrared-based transmitters.

3DTV was founded in 1989 by inventor and 3D expert Michael Starks. 3DTV's first product was a 3D home TV system, because Michael wants to "bring 3D to the masses." Toward that end, 3DTV also sells stereoscopic video projects, 3D camcorders, 3D VCR systems, and dozens of 3D videotapes. Contact 3DTV for a free catalog.

Another enthusiastic source of 3D and garage VR information is Magic 3-D, a company in Alexander City, Alabama that is run by a dentist named Ray Bolt. The Magic 3-D flyer offers different floppy disks of sample stereoscopic images, supplied with free cardboard 3D glasses and a "VR How-To" booklet. For $30 you receive a three-disk set of images (PC format) and a 3D calendar (with a money-back guarantee if you're not satisfied). Magic 3-D also carries 3DTV's product line.

A company called MegageM, based in southern California, focuses on garage VR gear for the Amiga. Its $225 StereoPro is a 3D stereoscopic graphics viewing system that works with such Amiga graphics and rendering programs as Animatrix Modeler, Vistapro 3.0, and Imagine. The StereoPro LCD shutter glasses plug directly into the StereoPro interface box, which plugs into the Amiga's joystick/mouse port #2. The interface can drive two pairs of glasses. StereoPro comes with a disk of 3D software (including games and sample images), a 3D display program, a program for using the glasses with other IFF/ILBM (Amiga graphics file format) viewer programs, and a developer support library. The package includes instructions for creating stereoscopic images on the Amiga. MegageM also sells 3D VCR videotapes.

A second Amiga-oriented 3D vendor is Haitex Resources in South Carolina. Haitex also produces stereoscopic shutter glasses. The $149 Haitex X-Specs connect to a small interface box that plugs into the #2 joystick/mouse port of any Amiga 1000 or better. The interface supports two pairs of glasses. The X-Specs package comes with software including an arcade game, a molecular modeler, and various utilities, including a device driver for generating stereoscopic pictures from images stored in .IFF file format. This lets you use an Amiga 3D modeling package—such as Byte by Byte's Sculpt 3D, Impulse's Turbo Silver, Incognito's Opticks, or NewTek's DigiPaint—to create and save image pairs as .IFF files, load them into the stereo utility, save them as a stereoscopic file, and check 'em out through the X-Specs. Anther free program lets you define and render 3D objects, positioning light sources and camera angles. The July 1993 issue of *AmigaWorld* includes a how-to article ("1-1=3[D]") about creating stereo images for viewing with X-Specs.

Currently, Haitex is developing a similar stereoscopic viewing system for the PC platform—a time-consuming process because PC owners use so many different types of video cards.

Finally, you can mail-order various LCD shutter glasses, including StereoGraphics and Tektronix products, from the one-stop VR shopping center—Spectrum Dynamics of Houston, Texas. This unique business carries a full line of professional VR equipment. Spectrum Dynamics charges $25 for its catalog, a good reference guide to state-of-the-art VR ware. (It costs so much because the company wants to discourage window-shoppers.)

Haitex Resources
Box 20609
Charleston, SC 29413
(803) 881-7518

MegageM
1903 Adria
Santa Maria, CA 93454
(805) 349-1104
E-mail: 70250.626@compuserve.com

Spectrum Dynamics
2 Greenway Plaza, Suite 640
Houston, TX 77046
(713) 520-5020
E-mail: specdyn@well.sf.ca.us or 70761.1647@compuserve.com

Magic 3-D
PO Box 1377
Alexander City, AL 35010
(205) 329-3767

3DTV
PO Box Q
San Rafael, CA 94913-4316
(415) 479-3516

The National Stereoscopic Association offers memberships and subscriptions to *Stereo World* magazine. Contact

National Stereoscopic Association
PO Box 14801
Columbus, OH 43214

Immersion and Stereoscopy: Hazardous to Your Health?

Researchers who study the effects of viewing stereoscopic images say that our eyes may suffer after long periods of 3D play. They claim that the strain of watching 3D images can disrupt the eye's ability to refocus normally after emerging from a stereoscopic virtual world.

When you watch a seagull snatch a bread crust off a beach blanket and fly away, you focus your eyes based on your actual distance from the bird as it moves. When you watch a stereoscopic virtual version of that gull and its antics, you focus on the monitor even though the virtual bird seems much farther away than a few inches. Although the effects of this phenomenon are not yet fully understood, some researchers believe that the "unnaturalness" of this perception method can cause visual abnormalities. (For that matter, your eyes respond similarly after any activity that changes effective focal or inter-ocular distance, such as bird-watching through binoculars.)

This effect applies mainly to those who spend more than an hour wearing stereoscopic glasses or head-mounted displays. Also, the optical quality of the 3D viewer contributes to the problem. Cheap cardboard-and-cellophane viewers will tire your eyes faster than more expensive viewers will. Some VR proponents argue that proper visual design of the virtual world can help participants avoid this problem.

According to Michael Starks of 3DTV, "The more one uses a display, the easier it gets. But any display will cause fatigue. The more it differs from the brightness, contrast, focus, and convergence demands of the real world, the more fatigue it causes. Also, bad imagery on any display causes more problems, as does bad stereo more than bad mono. People's eyes vary tremendously; the older you get, the harder it gets to view stereo imagery without eye strain. Kids will scream in delight at 3D that sends their parents reeling."

Another health issue that concerns the experts (and our mothers) is any danger from close-up viewing. Due to the relative weakness of any emissions produced by the components, an LCD doesn't emit enough of an electromagnetic field to cause concern. A CRT does. Few VR professionals will wear a CRT-based helmet for longer than an hour. No one else should either.

The third area of health-related interest undergoing much study these days involves motion sickness, or simulator sickness. Symptoms include eyestrain, headache, sweating, dry mouth, disorientation, dizziness, and nausea. Such maladies appear to occur most frequently in immersive VR, when participants view virtual scenes that produce effective experiences of self-motion and they themselves don't physically move, and also when detectable lags take place between head movements and the visual display update in the HMD. These effects can be exacerbated if the participant is under the effects of alcohol, drugs, or medication. Researchers suggest that participants limit their time in fast-moving virtual worlds, and that virtual-world creators should avoid incorporating bizarre or unnerving maneuvers, such as flying backwards or flying rapidly at low altitudes over virtual landscapes.

We'll read and hear more about these matters in the years ahead. Until we know definitive answers, remember this: if you're viewing a virtual world in stereo, blink often. Every once in a while, focus on something that's physically farther away than your monitor. Don't spend more than 30 continuous minutes with your face close to the screen. If your eyes hurt or your head aches, lower your lids and return to the real world.

Reading List: Stereoscopy and Computer Graphics

Banchoff, Thomas F. *Beyond the Third Dimension: Geometry, Computer Graphics and Higher Dimensions*. Scientific American Library, 1990.

Hyman, Michael I. *True Three-Dimensional Graphics*. Brady, 1985.

Lipton, Lenny. *Foundations of the Stereoscopic Cinema*. Van Nostran Rheinhold, 1982.

Okoshi, Takanori. *Three-Dimensional Imaging Techniques*. Academic Press, 1976.

Oliver, Dick, Scott Anderson, et al. *Tricks of the Graphics Gurus*. Sams Publishing, 1993.

Watkins, Christopher D. and Larry Sharp. *Programming in 3 Dimensions: 3-D Graphics, Ray Tracing, and Animation*. M&T Books, 1992.

PUTTING VR ON THE MAP

Joseph D. Gradecki

STOUGHTON, WISCONSIN

PROFILE

2

JOSEPH D. GRADECKI:
"Dedicated to the Low-End User of Virtual Reality"

Drive some 60 miles west from Milwaukee or 15 miles south from the collegiate community of Madison to reach the friendly, hilly hamlet of Stoughton. It's right off Highway 51, which cuts north-south through the center of Wisconsin. Stoughton is farm country; the population is 10,000. When folks gather at the local watering holes, they're as apt to talk about virtual reality as they are to talk about, oh, crops, the weather, or Stoughton Trailers, the region's biggest employer. That's primarily due to the efforts of a new company, VRontier Worlds, which holds VR club meetings at the public library and has been featured in the pages of the Stoughton Hub. *Certainly this burg's city council is the only small-town civic body that has expressed interest in helping to produce a VR festival. One must also assume that Stoughton is the only place where a VR club once set up a PC-based garage VR demo in a convenience store.*

"Low-cost VR is going to drive everything and spawn the VR industry. I see low-cost VR producing the first bulletin board systems that allow you to have actual virtual experiences. Low-cost VR will spawn this because of programs like REND386 that you can get into at the gut level and play with. A garage VR-ist needs to get at the guts of everything. You don't have to spend a lot to play the game."

Joe Gradecki is dedicated to that game. Indeed, he is dedicated to many things: his young family, his job, his spirituality, and his favorite pastimes—skiing, woodworking, and working out. Joe's earnest, open face, framed by longish brown hair, expresses joy when he discusses any of these topics. When doing so, he speaks in italics. Without raising his voice, he seems to *shout*, especially when he talks about his VR applications or Gradecki Publishing. Run by Joe and his wife, Waverly, Gradecki Publishing produces *PCVR*, the bimonthly publication dedicated to "Low-End Users of Virtual Reality."

Joe was born on March 15, 1967 in Litchfield, Illinois, and raised "right smack-dab in the middle of Illinois," in Decatur. He lived there until he was 19. As a teenager, Joe loved programming computers and playing the drums.

Of his early education, Joe says, "Well, school's school. You had to have something *outside* of school, so I got a computer when I was 13—a Sinclair X80. The [Radio Shack] TRS-80 was out, and the first Apple. I couldn't afford those, and I thought the Sinclair was something I could get. I could actually *learn* what people kept talking about. For $200, I could put one on my *desk!* It had graphics—if you could call them graphics. I just did basic stuff with it, little-bitty games, and learned good ol' BASIC."

Through the years Joe progressed from the Sinclair to a Commodore VIC-20, to a Commodore 64, to an Apple II, and, ultimately, to a PC. By the time he owned the PC, he had attended several colleges and earned his Bachelor's degree in computer science at Metropolitan State College in Denver. That was in 1990.

Joe and Waverly met in college and married soon after. They moved to Wyoming to study at the University at Laramie, where Joe earned his Master's degree in computer science. Their son Matthew was born in August of 1992. Nine months later the Gradeckis moved to Stoughton, a move precipitated by phone conversations between Joe and the president of Stoughton's VRontier Worlds, Tom Hayward. Tom had received a sample issue of *PCVR*, and it turned out that he and Joe had some common goals. Tom offered Joe a dream position: VRontier Worlds' director of software research and development.

Joe's first VRontier Worlds project resulted in a game called Mate, a $30 application that enables people to play chess over a phone line. Based on REND386, the game runs on a '386 (or better) PC. You control it with a mouse and a joystick or keyboard arrow keys. Mate features a "three-dimensional representation of a chess board and pieces," Joe explains. "It has a little representation of a head for each player, as well as a hand. You use this hand to pick up and move chess pieces anywhere on the board. When the other person's hand moves, you can see it." To play Mate over a phone line, each opponent needs a modem and the program. Players type in their opponents' phone numbers; Mate automatically dials and connects to their opponents' systems. Both players can interact with the chess pieces at the same time. While playing Mate, they also can send each other text messages.

Joe continues to develop VR applications for VRontier Worlds, programming in C, Pascal, and Assembler. Much of his spare time is devoted to creating software, projects, and articles for *PCVR*. Waverly tweaks his text and tackles all the administrative tasks. Together they produce each issue on a PC and a laser printer in their bedroom. Then they take the master to a printer, who prints 1,000 copies. Joe and Waverly mail several hundred copies to bookstores, newsstands, and subscribers in 19 countries. They store a few hundred copies of each bimonthly issue for samples and to fill back-order requests.

This dedication to documenting affordable VR took root early in 1992 while Joe was a full-time graduate student. "I palled around with two friends, Steve and Sean Casey. One night—probably at one or two in the morning—they whipped out [Howard] Rheingold's book [*Virtual Reality*] and said, 'Hey, Joe, have you seen this?' I looked through it, while they got me psyched on all kinds of different things we could do with it, telling me about all the money we could make. I was glowing. And that was it.

"We were net hackers," Joe continues. "We went out on the net and just went *crazy* trying to find stuff. And we stumbled upon a site that had some VR stuff related to the Sega shutter glasses and the Power Glove. We got that, ran out and bought two Power Gloves, and we hacked them all together.

"But there was no software to use them. REND386 wasn't out yet, so I hacked some code, the same code that's in the first and second issues of *PCVR*. Really crappy by today's standards, but we got a virtual hand on-screen. I got hooked. Then I decided to create a handshaking program that allowed two Power Gloves over two PCs on the Internet to shake hands. *No* one had done anything like that yet. Sean and Steve Casey had a glove, and I had a glove, and we would sit in the school lab till all hours, hacking out this code in C. I had to learn network communication on the Internet level: I had to learn about Internet addresses, gateways, all that stuff.

"Sean and Steve were on one machine, I was on another, and we were able to move our Power Gloves at the same time so the hands on the screen got close enough so we could shake hands. Very crude, but it worked. We had these little wireframe hands that didn't look real good; they weren't in color, but they had perspective and moved just like they should and *yeah*, it was pretty good!"

Shortly thereafter, Joe and the Casey brothers sat around shooting the VR breeze one night, Joe recalls, "and, being spiritual like I am, the idea for *PCVR* was 'given' to me. It just appeared, and I knew what it was. The idea was to gather all this loose information for the net, put my glove code in somewhere, and go from there. That was going to be the foundation of the magazine. The majority of this information was aimed at building VR equipment yourself. I created two issues in a week."

At that time Joe and Waverly were living off student loans. They discussed Joe's idea, and Joe suggested, "Let's tell people on the net about it and charge $3 for a trial issue."

That trial issue—Volume 1, Issue 1—came out in April of 1992. This 28-page, black-and-white, no-frills 'zine was created with a '386 PC clone, HP LaserJet IIIP, Windows 3.1, Word for Windows, and CorelDRAW. Gracing the cover was a simple line drawing of an open hand holding a 3D-rendered ball in its palm. The cover text read: "Interfacing the Power Glove," "Creating a Virtual Hand," and "Graphics Code— What's Available?" (See Figure P2.1.) Definitely a low-budget endeavor, devoid of slick graphics or layout, and sprinkled with typos, *PCVR* epitomized this message: You can do it yourself and you don't need big bucks.

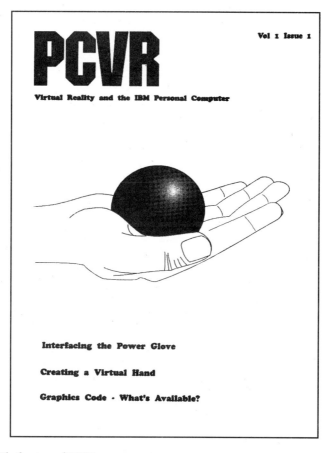

PCVR

Vol 1 Issue 1

Virtual Reality and the IBM Personal Computer

Interfacing the Power Glove

Creating a Virtual Hand

Graphics Code - What's Available?

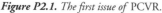

Figure P2.1. *The first issue of* PCVR.

About 25 people each sent $3 for a copy. Joe and Waverly then decided to offer subscriptions and "see what happened," Joe says. "We figured that, if just five subscriptions came in, we would continue with the magazine. If five people wanted to read it, that was good enough for me. We got 15 right off the bat."

Between the Gradeckis' classes and studying, Gradecki Publishing tackled the chore of producing a bimonthly publication. Joe knew exactly what the first six issues would contain. "I basically covered every major hardware topic, except in Issue 4, which was on REND386. I tried to create something that everybody could use."

The first three issues presented information mostly gleaned from the nets. But in Issue 3, Joe also started a "Build Your Own Head Mount" series. "I had never even *seen* a head mount!" Joe laughs. "I didn't know what it was supposed to *look* like! And it's evident in those articles, because I made a big push for stereo, and I've since learned that stereo really is not needed."

Putting VR on the Map
Joseph D. Gradecki

In the following issue, Joe wrote about his error. "I wanted to tell people not to be afraid to make a mistake, because this technology is so new that mistakes are going to happen, and we need to learn from them."

Although the first two issues were printed by a quick-copy service, Issues 3 through 6 were run directly off the Gradeckis' HP LaserJet printer, then hand-bound. By Issue 6, more than 100 subscribers had signed on. For Issue 7, Joe and Waverly decided that glossy, professionally bound copies were in order. "For what we needed then—about 300 copies—printing would cost about $1,600," Joe says. "We couldn't afford that. Then divine inspiration came in again when somebody suggested that I look into purchasing my own offset press. We bought one, put it in a warehouse, and for Issues 7 through 9 we created our own master plates and offset-printed the copies on glossy paper. But starting with Issue 10, we took it to a professional printer."

Then, as now, Joe and Waverly pour all subscription revenues right back into the business. They're considering a company reorganization and the pursuit of paid advertising. They also intend to broaden *PCVR*'s base. Joe wants to change the original subtitle, "Virtual Reality and the IBM Personal Computer," to "Virtual Reality and the Low-End User," or something to that effect. "And we want to stay technical, yet back off a bit, for all the people who will never build the stuff we're talking about but want to know what's going on."

The driving force behind *PCVR,* Joe says, is his and Waverly's spirituality. "I work full-time, I've got a son, I'm writing a book—all of which doesn't leave a lot of room—so I rely on my spirituality to guide me when I create those issues. A lot of people are depending on them. I want to give them *real* material, not just stuff duplicated from the net. I want to be honest and true with it. That guides us. Everything we do with this business is based on spiritually being told to do it or by us praying about it and getting the answer."

When asked why VR intrigues him, Joe answers, "Because I am a software developer, I get to create worlds. Not that I want to play God, because I don't, but there's probably nothing anybody can request that I could not create on one platform or another in one form or another. *Any* experience can be created in virtual reality."

When asked to describe his dream virtual experience, Joe laughs, then says—almost to himself—"We-e-l-lll, keep it clean! I would like to have the ability to *realistically* play in a band in front of virtual people and have them clap in the appropriate places. The ability to play different kinds of music and instantly switch between them, and to switch audiences—all while I'm playing the drums—and I'll be able to *feel* that I'm hitting the drums. That's the *ultimate.* But that's a long way away."

The first few virtual experiences that Joe presented in *PCVR* focused on using the Mattel Power Glove. "Today," Joe says, "I know the location of every single existing Power Glove at every Toys 'R' Us. Only about six regions had them. The stores in New York, the Midwest, and all but one store in California are wiped out of their supply. I personally wiped out two states alone, Wyoming and Colorado. And I'm *glad* they're

getting wiped out. Everybody wants to know where they can get a Power Glove, and I'm afraid that if some people can't find one, their interest [in VR] will go. If we can get all the Power Gloves out and something like the Global 3-D controller comes in, then we get a good foundation to work on. The Glove hurts after using it a while. [Its representation on-screen] tends to jump all over the place. The Glove is a great tool for teaching about virtual reality, but people seem to like that 3-D controller better because it lets them do more to manipulate the environment. They don't have to use the glove in one hand and the joystick in the other."

Indeed, Joe probably won't use the glove in future applications. "The whole idea of the Glove was to manipulate the hand," he explains. "With the Mate software, you can do everything with the mouse that you can with a Power Glove: x-, y-, z-axis control, grip, and ungrip. You move the mouse behind the chess piece, and you know you're close to it because the back of the hand turns blue. You press the mouse button to grip the piece, pick it up, and drag it and let go of the mouse button to ungrip. That drops the piece where you want it. "

In November of 1992, Joe sent an e-mail message in which he wrote, "Everybody gets all excited about hooking up the Sega glasses and Power Glove, only to be disappointed when they find out that there are no applications. At *PCVR* we are trying to change that. First we introduced a simple 3D racquetball game that uses the glasses and Glove. We will be releasing a fighter jet game in the near future…. Most of the activity in the garage VR area has to do with world-creating. I feel that world-building is a waste of time. We need to be developing real-world applications. Unless we can show that VR has real use at the PC level, this technology will remain stuck in research labs."

Today Joe continues to expound upon the notion that VR applications are more important than virtual worlds. "A world is a simple walkthrough. A walkthrough is *not* virtual reality," he states. "All those worlds people have created are neat, but nobody has ever shown me a real good use for a world. For instance, you can go into one of those VREAM demos and pick up a cereal box and move it around. Well, what does that *do?* It doesn't do *anything*. It doesn't show at all what can be done with this technology! And there's so much money waiting to be spent on this technology if we can just show people how to use it. That's why I'm feverishly writing applications that people can really *use*."

Joe created one such application for *PCVR*'s exhibit at a virtual reality industry convention in May of 1993. The experience taught him a valuable lesson. "We showed a simple shoot-'em-up demo that ran in REND386. People would sit down and try it, and they would say, 'That was great, but it's another one of these shoot-up things, just like everybody else's.' To me, that was like, oh, *slap*. If I'd written a demo that was not a shoot-'em-up game, it would have been *incredible!* And in the time I took to create the application for [that exhibit], I could have created something better. A post office guy there said to me, 'I'd really like something that would let me teach my people about angry customers.' I could have *done* something like that. It would have *blown people away!*"

Putting VR on the Map
Joseph D. Gradecki

Tour Guide's Toolbox

Engine: IBM PC clone 486/50, built from a kit

Monitor: color 13-inch NEC, VGA

Modem: US Robotics 14.4

Primary hardware and software: Sega glasses, Global Devices 3-D controller, REND386, homemade boom-mounted tracker, 3D sound capabilities

Music to code by: Van Halen, Damn Yankees

Music to think by: Kenny G, new-age jazz

Total cost: Approximately $1,600

E-mail: `pcvr@fullfeed.com` and `70711.257@compuserve.com`

Gradecki Publishing and *PCVR*

Gradecki Publishing was founded in April of 1992 to publish *PCVR* and provide a common forum for discussing ways to create low-cost VR systems.

According to Gradecki Publishing's mission statement, "*PCVR* intends to bring virtual reality out of science laboratories and into the general computer community. We developed *PCVR* because we saw a tremendous information gap in the VR publications that were currently on the market. We detected a need for a central focusing point for the homebrewist working on or thinking about VR. If we can open VR up to the average person, the marketplace for *PCVR* and other companies will expand tremendously."

Unlike the other VR magazines and journals, which focus primarily on professional and educational VR activities and theoretical information, *PCVR* covers garage VR through editorials, tutorials, do-it-yourself projects using off-the-shelf components, and reviews. ("We do not review high-priced VR equipment that is out of reach for the average person.") Without bandying about the jargon associated with industry journals, *PCVR* runs columns such as "Working with

REND386" and articles that simplify the procedures and materials related to hardware and specific applications, operating systems and environments, and connectivity. To top it off, each issue includes a floppy disk (for PC DOS) that contains all the software discussed in the articles.

PCVR
PO Box 475
Stoughton, WI 53589
Phone/fax: (608) 877-0909
Subscriptions: $26 U.S./Canada, $38 overseas, for six issues
Back issues, $4.50 each U.S./Canada, $6.50 overseas

The
Cockpit

Input Devices

The Cockpit
Input Devices

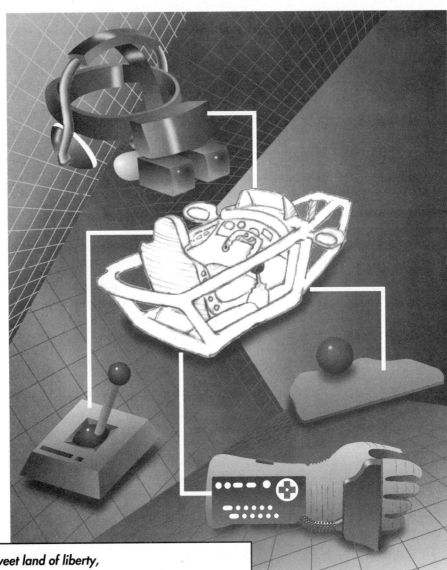

"...Sweet land of liberty,
Of thee I sing....
From every virtual mountain-side
Let six degrees of freedom ring."
—with apologies to Samuel Francis Smith, America
(1831)

When it's time to hit the road, you climb into the driver's seat. You poke your key into the ignition, give it a twist, punch the radio on, release the brake, shift the transmission into drive, grab the steering wheel, step on the gas pedal, and awaaaay you go.

All these actions involve controlling some of the interfaces—the input devices—that let you operate an automobile. Interfaces come between you and any object you want to operate; they represent the interconnection or method of communication between two objects. An interface can exist in hardware or software form. For example, a steering wheel is one interface between driver and car, while the screen design of a word processing program is the interface between the user and the program's functions.

Standard computer hardware interfaces, or input devices, include the keyboard and a pointing device such as a mouse or a trackball. Because one goal of VR is to support a computer-human interface based on our natural, human means of expression, VR systems incorporate some rather exotic input devices for communicating with computers. VR professionals call these input devices sensors or effectors (the latter term also applies to output devices that affect the senses). A sensor may control a viewpoint, whereby movement of the sensor causes a change in perspective in the virtual world such as a shift from looking to the right to looking down. A sensor also may control a graphic object, whereby movement of the sensor causes the on-screen object to move.

Changes in response to manipulation of an input device are called *feedback*. The prevalent forms of feedback are visual feedback (a change in the appearance of something on-screen) and audio feedback (sound effects and music). See Figure 6.1. A more unusual form of feedback is the physical type. Physical feedback transmits pressure, vibration, or other sensory stimuli directly through the input device. Primary forms of physical feedback include *tactile* feedback, which simulates sensation applied to the skin, and *force* feedback, which simulates weight or resistance to motion. Both let you feel the physical effects of making contact with a virtual object, thus increasing your sense of presence in the virtual world. Physical feedback devices are just now entering the domain of garage VR.

A variety of affordable input devices, from standard to exotic, are available to outfit the cockpit of a garage VR system. All are used in conjunction with the keyboard; they don't replace it. For example, you can choose to navigate virtual worlds with a simple controller that normally operates in two dimensions (x-axis and y-axis), such as a mouse, while using the keyboard for z-axis control.

More sophisticated input devices can control data in three dimensions, or with *six degrees of freedom* (6DOF). Each degree applies to a direction of movement. 6DOF refers to a sensor's ability to track six simultaneous directions (or inputs): a combination of spatial *position* (in the x-, y-, and z-axes) and spatial *orientation* (pitch, roll, and yaw). See Figure 6.2.

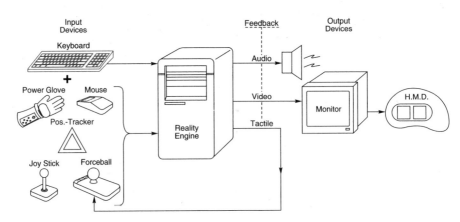

Figure 6.1. *The signal chain of sensors and effectors in a garage VR system.*

Your choice of input device depends on

 your budget

 the kind of interaction you want with your virtual world

the kinds of sensors your system can support

The ability to use a certain input device depends on the availability of a *device driver,* the software program that allows a computer and a peripheral device to work together by controlling their interaction. When you buy a commercial input or output device from an established vendor, you also receive the device drivers appropriate to your computer platform. Garage VR hackers have written their own drivers to support interaction via devices not necessarily created for VR systems.

Old Faithfuls: Keyboard and Company

The most basic cockpit controls, the keyboard and mouse, may not support fast, intuitive interaction with 3D graphics, but they get you on your way. Programs such as Domark's Virtual Reality Studio, VistaPro, and Virtus WalkThrough all work under keyboard or mouse control and even provide keyboard equivalents for joystick functions.

Joysticks provide the kind of control preferred by gamesters and flight-simulator enthusiasts and also can satisfy the needs of basic garage VR exploration. Easy and practical, several low-cost joysticks on the market work with the PC, Amiga, and Macintosh.

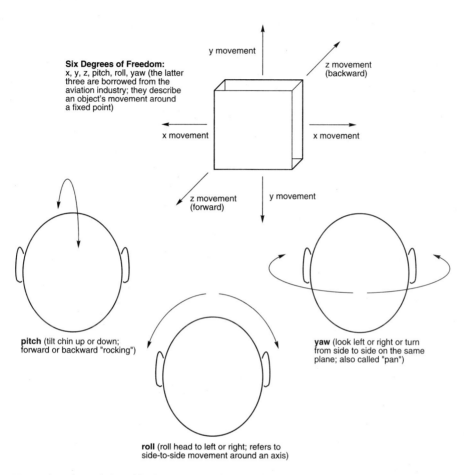

Figure 6.2. *The six degrees of freedom: x, y, z, pitch (tilt), yaw (pan), and roll (rotation).*

Many garage VR hobbyists deploy trackballs to facilitate interaction with virtual worlds. Trackballs offer fast response, a high degree of precision, and the advantage of stationary control, unlike a mouse that you push around on the desktop. When you use a trackball to control the cursor and issue commands, you move your fingers, not your hand and wrist. Figure 6.3 shows one example of a current trackball, the Logitech Trackman for the Macintosh ($99 retail) and the PC ($139 retail). The case fits the curve of your hand; the small trackball is situated to take advantage of your thumb's dexterity. You can customize its three buttons to issue commands. Driver software includes utilities for assigning buttons, creating menus, and setting mouse options.

The Cockpit
Input Devices

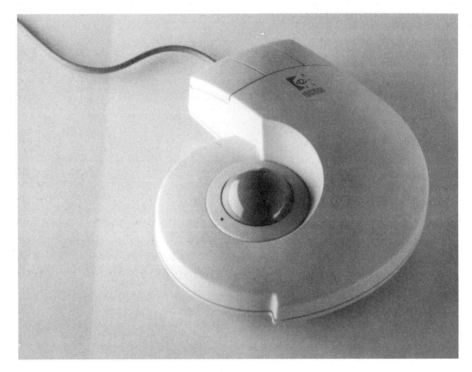

Figure 6.3. *The Logitech Trackman.*

Employing a traditional two-dimensional mouse, joystick, or trackball in conjunction with a keyboard is fine for VR beginners—like riding a bike with training wheels. As you travel further into virtual world exploration, you'll probably want something more versatile.

The Next Step: Take A Test Drive (If You Can)

Every computer fancier knows what it's like to use a mouse. But each kind of 6DOF device takes a radically different approach to your physical interaction with the virtual world. A device's ease of use depends almost entirely upon subjective experience. What you might consider natural and intuitive, your friend might find clumsy and forced. For example, some folks prefer flying through the virtual world with a 6DOF mouse. Others prefer a wired glove. So, before choosing one of these newfangled devices, try it out.

Unfortunately, trying out a device is no easy task. Computer stores don't have VR departments (yet). But you *can* test these gizmos at a virtual reality conference or computer graphics industry exhibition. In several cities around the country, special-interest groups meet to discuss VR technologies and enjoy hands-on demonstrations.

You might be able to try some of these devices at those meetings. See Appendix D, "Information Resources," for a list of some conference organizers and VR groups, or contact the computer graphics department of a nearby university and ask if they know about such conferences, exhibitions, and interest groups.

Also, VR enthusiasts on the Internet or engaged in electronic discussion groups and bulletin boards will gladly answer public queries about their experiences with input devices. So log on!

The Disappearing Keyboard

When industrial, mechanical, and architectural engineers and designers started using workstation-based computer systems for 3D design and manufacturing, their input devices consisted of pressure-sensitive, digitizing drawing tablets; scanners; keyboards; and the traditional mouse. Then along came mouse-like devices that worked in *true* three-dimensional space: six degrees of freedom.

6DOF Mouse Devices

In 1990 a company called SimGraphics Engineering of South Pasadena, California, invented the Flying Mouse, shown in Figure 6.4. It feels and acts like a standard mouse, but when you lift it by the small wings jutting out from its sides, the cursor enters 3D mode. This lets you control a computer scene or object with six degrees of freedom and movement. The 3D cursor mimics your hand movements, letting you grab and move an image in space. SimGraphics engineers trailblazed the route to desktop VR when they thought to combine their Flying Mouse invention with StereoGraphics' CrystalEyes shutter glasses, thus supporting complex manipulation of objects in three dimensions. Customers implemented these systems for computer-aided design and scientific and financial data visualization.

The Flying Mouse was designed for use with workstations and can be made to work with PCs and Macintoshes. An ample software library and sample applications let programmers integrate the Flying Mouse within various applications. At a list price of $5,000, however, it's not the type of device targeted for the typical PC/Mac owner.

Today, a spate of software for 3D graphics and animation on the PC and Macintosh has led to the development of other 6DOF mouse controllers, sold at prices that won't cause a VR hobbyist to run screaming from the room. You can use these devices to rotate an object, change your viewpoint, or adjust a lighting source in the virtual world. They especially suit walk-through and fly-through environments.

One such device is the $250 3D Z-Mouse from Multipoint Technology, a company based in Westford, Massachusetts. The Z-Mouse offers control in six degrees of freedom and can substitute for a regular mouse or trackball. Its black case provides three buttons on top beside a green trackball for x- and y-axis control. A thumbwheel on the side of the case provides z-axis control. When you navigate through a virtual

castle, the Z-Mouse lets you move your position while changing your viewpoint; you could be "walking" through a gallery while looking at the walls on your left and your right, all with fluid, single-handed control. You can change your elevation at the same time.

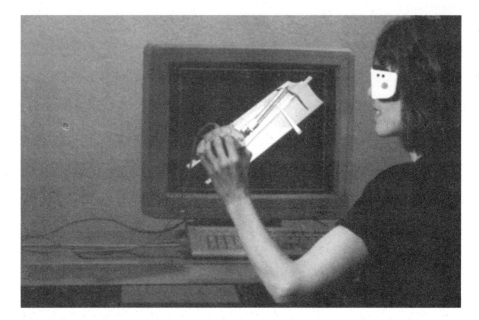

Figure 6.4. *The 6DOF Flying Mouse in action.*

The Z-Mouse plugs into the RS232 serial port on the PC or the Apple Desktop Bus port on the Macintosh. It comes with device drivers for DOS, Windows, and the Macintosh.

The manufacturer hopes that many software developers will start adapting and writing applications to support the 3D mouse. Toward that end, Multipoint sells a $30 Developer's Toolkit (programmer's reference manual, software utility routines, and sample source code for different functions that can be used as templates). As of this writing, the device is so new that Z-Mouse drivers aren't yet available for commercial VR software. That doesn't mean some clever hackers won't find ways to implement the Z-Mouse for controlling their virtual worlds—especially since 6DOF control reduces the amount of code that programmers must write to allow such operations as rotating objects around an axis.

Another new input device is the Logitech CyberMan, which lists for $129. It works with a '386 (or better) PC running DOS 3.3 (or higher) and plugs into a serial port. The three-button mouse rests on a post attached to the base, as pictured in Figure 6.5. You slide the mouse from side to side or forward and backward or pull up and push down on it to change x-, y-, and z-axis position. To change orientation, you pivot the mouse forward and backward (pitch control), twist it left and right (yaw control), and tilt it from side to side (roll control).

Figure 6.5. *Logitech's CyberMan, developed specifically for games and entertainment software, provides limited 6DOF control. It's the ideal low-cost way to control walk-throughs and fly-throughs.*

The CyberMan also vibrates to provide tactile feedback, which can be linked to software events. Inside the CyberMan, a small motor vibrates in response to programmed events in games and virtual worlds. You could program it to pulsate when you're zapped by a giant eel—and even combine the vibrating feedback with *zap*-like sounds.

CyberMan handles all conventional PC mouse functions, but like all the other new input gizmos, it won't work as a 3D controller unless software publishers adapt programs for it. Several 3D games are supplied with the CyberMan, and some software game developers are adapting titles for CyberMan control.

Forceballs

A forceball (also called a torqueball) provides another way to control virtual objects with six degrees of freedom. A billiard-size, stationary ball is mounted on the end of a

short stem emerging from a ramp-like, contoured base on which you rest your arm. The rubber-coated ball senses such forces as pushing, squeezing, twisting, and pulling and translates these movements into corresponding changes to the virtual world, either by manipulating images or changing perspective. The base also contains a set of programmable pushbuttons so you can issue commands without moving your hand to the keyboard.

A forceball isn't very squishy—it doesn't have much give—but it can transmit signals proportionate to how hard you hold it or what direction you push or pull it. For example, you pull up on the ball to fly upward in the virtual world, press forward on it to propel your virtual viewpoint forward, and press the ball to the right or left to move to the right or left. When you pull back on the ball, your position moves accordingly. To change viewpoint, you twist the ball just as you would turn your head to look in a certain direction.

Among the first of these odd-looking controllers was the SpaceBall, introduced in 1990 by Spaceball Technologies (then known as Spatial Systems) of Billerica, Massachusetts. Its current incarnation, Model 2003, provides control of virtual worlds in hundreds of professional VR and 3D graphics systems driven by UNIX engines. The SpaceBall's design, features, versatility, and software result in a $1,600 price tag, which puts it out of the affordable range for garage VR exploration.

In the northern California town of Granite Bay, a few engineers founded Global Devices to build on their belief in affordable VR. Global Devices created a low-cost forceball that emulates the SpaceBall but works with the IBM PC. (See Figure 6.6.) Debuting late in 1992 at the almost unbelievably low price of $250, the Global 3D controller tantalized many VR professionals. Among its appealing features include the capability for software developers to program applications in which the ball provides tactile feedback in the form of vibration. The newest version of the Global controller offers 16 levels of constant vibrating response and 16 levels of vibrating impulse feedback. The Global controller is easy to use, plugs into the serial port, and comes with drivers for use with VREAM and other commercial world-building software packages. (It works with any software program that includes a SpaceBall driver.)

As of this writing, Global Devices had completed negotiations with an unnamed, large computer hardware manufacturer that was going to take over production of the controller. The resulting product, which should hit the market in early 1994, boasts better performance, a sleek design, and an even lower price tag: street price should hover around $100. Developments such as this can do much to close the gap between the "techno-haves" and the "techno-have nots."

Wands and Other 6DOF Pointing Devices

Another type of 6DOF input device is a hand-held wand. Resembling an oversized joystick that you hold up in the air, this is the sort of controller used in the Virtuality game arcade system.

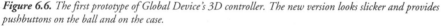

Figure 6.6. The first prototype of Global Device's 3D controller. The new version looks slicker and provides pushbuttons on the ball and on the case.

While the concept might seem like an inexpensive method of virtual world control, its manifestation isn't what most home VR hobbyists consider affordable. For instance, the Cricket by Digital Image Design of New York City is a wand that you can grip easily and naturally. You press its front trigger button to point or to choose objects. You push the thumb button in back for navigation and other types of input selection. The programmable Cricket also provides tactile feedback in the form of vibration. It also lists for $3,200, not including the position-tracking sensors necessary for its operation.

In the summer of 1993, Immersion Human Interface Corporation of Palo Alto, California, announced its development of a different kind of 6DOF input device. The Immersion Probe, shown in Figure 6.7, is a pen-like stylus mounted on the end of a small, lightweight assembly of mechanical linkages, resembling a miniature version of the jointed assemblies that support desk lamps and copy stands. You hold the stylus like a pencil and move it around to send position and orientation data to the computer.

The Probe's assembly bears the weight of the stylus, an approach said to enhance manual control and reduce fatigue; you don't have to hold your hand and arm in the air, as is required for some other 6DOF devices. The assembly provides programmable physical resistance, which can enhance the virtual world experience. Since you hold the Probe the same way you hold a pencil, some people might find using the Probe more natural than flying a mouse or twisting a torqueball. As its location-tracking is mechanical, it provides good accuracy and resolution, and you don't have to worry about the interference problems that plague ultrasonic and magnetic trackers. The Probe is self-calibrating, so you don't have to run a setup routine to get it going. It plugs into a PC's RS232 serial port and runs off an external power supply.

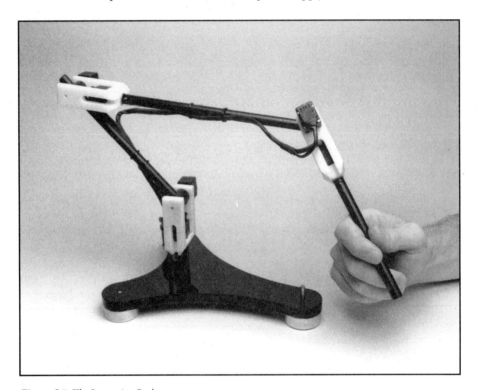

Figure 6.7. *The Immersion Probe.*

The Probe-IC costs $1,085, while the Probe-IX (which offers better resolution) lists for $1,500. To create Probe drivers for integration within applications, software writers can buy the $139 developer's programming library.

Another new type of PC pointer is the $999 Space Controller, produced by Logitech (see Figure 6.8). Logitech developed it for CAD, simulation, and desktop VR applications. About the size of the Logitech TrackMan, the Space Controller consists of a base containing nine programmable pushbuttons and a round, flat, spring-mounted puck about three inches in diameter. You push, press, and twist the rubber-coated puck to provide the computer with precise motion and/or position data. You can set up the two rows of buttons for object selection and other operations, such as assigning them to pan or zoom functions, switching into standard mouse mode, or changing baud rate and

tone generation. The Space Controller's three operating modes are standard 2D (x- and y-axes), dominant coordinates, and all-out 6DOF. You also can map its functions to the different degrees of motion; you might map pan, for example, to the x-axis, and zoom to the y-axis. The Space Controller also issues a beep that programmers can implement to provide audio feedback in their virtual worlds.

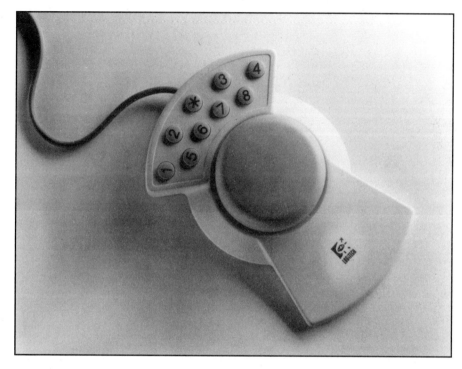

Figure 6.8. *The Logitech Space Controller.*

The Space Controller's tracking capabilities are based on optical technology. Its data report rate ranges from 3.3 to 160 samples per second, depending on operating mode. It runs on power supplied through its connection to the PC's serial port. Like the Global 3D Controller, it works with any software program that supports the SpaceBall.

Digital Gloves

People all over the world are waving their hands at their computers in attempts to interact with data like they interact with objects in the real world. Many feel that the digital glove is *the* VR input device. It permits direct, intuitive movement and object manipulation. Besides, there is something appealing about seeing a graphic representation of your hand move in synchrony with your real hand.

VPL Research described its original DataGlove as a "hand gesture interface device." That's because the glove performs as a gesture-recognition system that monitors finger movement and hand position. The system translates the hand and finger activity into electronic signals that the computer uses for purposes of position-tracking and input control.

VPL's famous fashion accessory is an $8,000 lycra glove that envelops a web of fiber-optic cables between two thin layers of cloth. The cables run the length of each finger and double back. At one end of each cable is an infrared light-emitting diode (LED); at the other end is a phototransistor. Flexing a finger changes the amount of light traveling through the cable. The phototransistor converts the light into an electrical signal. Both ends of the cables attach to a tiny interface board that translates the signals into computer-readable data.

(I heard about a VR hacker named Dave Lowry who built a "DataFinger" from an infrared LED and a phototransistor he purchased at Radio Shack. He also bought an inexpensive fiber-optic cable and attached the LED to one end and the transistor to the other end. He scratched the exterior surface of the cable so that light would escape when he bent it. When powered by 5 volts and bent over a knuckle joint, the signal at the phototransistor varied by two or three volts and affected the on-screen appearance of a virtual finger. Total cost: $5.)

The DataGlove spawned the Mattel Power Glove. Thanks to the hackers of the world, one advantage of the Power Glove over other 3D devices is the existence of many programs that let the Glove work with VR software.

Genesis of the Mattel Power Glove

In 1984, inventor Tom Zimmerman started working with Jaron Lanier and Steve Bryson to build wired gloves. They formed VPL Research and won their first contract from NASA Ames Research Center. A few years later, Tom designed and built a low-cost glove prototype that could be used with video games. He also designed and built its ultrasonic position-tracking system.

NOTE

In 1985, Tom received U.S. Patent 4,542,291 for his invention, the Optical Flex Sensor. In 1991, a U.S. patent was assigned to VPL Research, concerning use of a glove as an input device: U.S. Patent 4,988,981, "Computer Data Entry and Manipulation Apparatus and Method," invented by Thomas G. Zimmerman and Jaron Z. Lanier. Because of these patents, other people haven't been developing similar controllers.

VPL licensed that prototype design to a New York company, Abrams-Gentile Entertainment (AGE), which in turn licensed it to the Mattel toy company. Working with AGE, Mattel used Tom's prototype as the basis for the Power Glove, a controller for the Nintendo Entertainment System. VPL didn't reserve the right to review Mattel's adaptation of the prototype. Nintendo, however, had final approval of the Glove's design.

Programmer and inventor Rich Gold served as Mattel's design manager for the Power Glove. In the 1992 anthology *Cyberarts: Exploring Art and Technology,* he wrote, "We developed the Power Glove in six hectic months of 7-day weeks, working 14 hours a day in a small, converted warehouse. At that time, the VPL DataGlove sold for $8,000. When introduced, the Power Glove retailed for about $80. Of course it can't do everything that the DataGlove can; it's not supposed to. Nevertheless, the Power Glove—which debuted just before Christmas in 1989—was the first 'virtual reality' consumer product…[and] undoubtedly is the most complex toy interface ever designed."

The finished Mattel Power Glove could track a game player's hand movements in the x-, y-, and z-axes as well as the positions of four fingers (the pinky was "cost reduced-out," as they say in the toy business). It provided a set of buttons on a control panel situated on top of the wrist. It came in two sizes, large and medium, for righties only. When you bought a new Power Glove, you also received a cotton liner for the Glove, a black plastic sensor assembly, a color poster, an instruction book, and a program guide.

Mattel wanted the Power Glove to support every Nintendo cartridge game, all 150 of them. Rich's design team had to convert all the Power Glove motions into standard Nintendo game control signals. They achieved this by creating 14 different programs, or user interface metaphors, that let the Glove serve as a direct substitute for a Nintendo control pad. Kids worked the Glove according to one of these metaphors, depending on the type of game being played. For example, they used the boxing metaphor for fighter games, throwing punches and blocks with the gloved hand. They used the driving metaphor for racing games, holding out a gloved hand as if holding a steering wheel that could turn left and right.

According to Rich, the Power Glove design team was more intrigued by the Glove's raw data mode. More sophisticated than an interface metaphor, this operating mode provided the Nintendo system with precise information about the Glove's status. Any game created for use with the raw data mode could provide extremely accurate data to drive an on-screen representation of the Glove in a way that could impart a sense of "presence" in the game. Unfortunately, only one game worked with the raw data mode: SuperGloveBall, which wasn't introduced until the 1990 Christmas season. (At that time, the Mattel team was working on a home VR system complete with head-mounted display, which would have retailed for under $600, but they dropped their plans to manufacture it.)

After manufacturing about 1.3 million Power Gloves, Mattel discontinued production of the Power Glove and SuperGloveBall in 1991. The toy giant cited financial reasons. Mattel couldn't sell enough Power Gloves to make the venture worthwhile. Kids used the Glove to control games that weren't designed for Glove control and were underwhelmed by the results. The Glove emulated the Nintendo control pad, but the system had to track and translate hand gestures, which caused the Glove's response time to be longer than the control pad's. Also, the Glove's weight and material were uncomfortable. Instead of bragging about the Power Glove, convincing friends to buy it, kids believed it was their fault they weren't "good" at it and tossed the things into their closets, or wore the futuristic black-and-gray gloves when they rode their bicycles.

Then, some older siblings, the ones who were into computers, grabbed the gauntlet and initiated the process of hacking the glove into a controller for computer games and music programs.

NOTE

The Power Glove's box included a slip of paper containing a warning: "...With practice you'll be able to use the Power Glove and feel more a part of the action than ever before. But in the beginning it's going to feel strange...so don't expect to be able to play perfectly the first time out. Take the TIME to study the instruction booklet and make the EFFORT to practice." One wonders whether the average 11-year-old took the time and made the effort to even read the warning.

Today a Power Glove is as good as currency. A while back my father bought two Power Gloves for $30 apiece (new, but in battered boxes) at a Toys 'R' Us in Brooklyn. He shipped them to me in San Francisco. I gave one of them to a Berkeley space scientist in exchange for a ride to Los Angeles.

How the Power Glove Works

The Power Glove responds in four degrees of freedom: x-axis (left and right), y-axis (up and down), z-axis (toward and away from the screen), and rotation (roll), each to about a 1/4-inch resolution. The x-, y-, and z-axes are known collectively as "3-space." Roll is reported as one of 12 possible positions.

Overall hand motion is detected via ultrasonics (frequencies of sound waves above the range audible to human ears—that is, above 20,000 Hz). Two emitters are mounted in a small box at the base of the Glove's knuckles, as pictured in Figure 6.9. Three sensors are built into the L-shaped sensing assembly, which typically mounts on top of the monitor. The Glove also contains a flexible circuit board, based on a microprocessor that analyzes the hand motions and performs the data conversion for them.

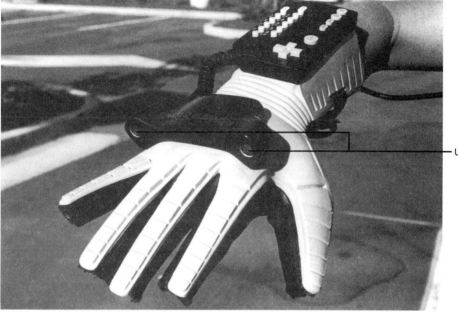

— Ultrasonic Emitters

Figure 6.9. *A view of the Power Glove that shows the knuckle emitters. (Photo by Linda Jacobson)*

Inside the Glove, bend sensors detect individual finger motion. In place of fancy fiber optics to measure finger bend, resistive ink is silkscreened onto strips of plastic mylar. One strip is attached, inside the Glove, along the length of each finger. The extent to which a finger is bent changes the electrical resistance of the ink. This lets the computer measure four different positions, or bend levels, for each of four fingers. (The pinky follows the ring finger movement.) Bend level is expressed in terms of degree of flex as one of four integer values:

       0 = fully extended (no change in electrical resistance)

       1 = a little bent

       2 = more bent than straight

       3 = fully bent

The Glove works best when you point it forward, aiming your fingers toward the screen or wherever the sensor assembly is mounted. Its operating range is 3 to 15 feet from the sensor assembly; within six feet, position data is accurate to 1/4 inch. The Glove's effective working angle is 45 degrees off the center axis.

The Cockpit
Input Devices

Attack of the Hackers

About a year before Mattel discontinued Glove production, computer programmers started figuring out how to wire the Glove to their PCs. Glove hack-tivities went into high gear after the computer magazine *Byte* published "Reach Out and Touch Your Data" by Howard Eglowstein in the July 1990 issue. The article provided the details needed to hook the Power Glove to an IBM PC and to decode its Nintendo emulation mode for use with the computer. *Byte* even ran a photograph of a logic analyzer that showed the relationship of the Glove's clock, reset, and data pulses.

The next big challenge was to figure out how to put the Power Glove into raw data mode, known among hackers as *hires mode* (for "high-resolution"). That way the Glove would transmit position coordinates and not just emulate a Nintendo controller (*lores mode*). Accessing hires mode was no simple task because Mattel and Nintendo considered it proprietary information.

Later in 1990, Abrams-Gentile Entertainment (AGE) built a serial interface device for connecting the Glove directly to the PC and sold some of these boxes to universities. The boxes are no longer available and possess "an almost mythical status," according to Eric Townsend, keeper of the Internet glove-list.

One of those AGE boxes did wind up in the hands of Greg Newby, an assistant professor of computer science at the University of Illinois. He was the first to make public the results of his successful efforts to decode hires mode; he posted the details on the Internet in the newsgroup sci.electronics. Around the same time, a hacker in West Germany applied a logic probe to the Glove lines and a digital oscilloscope and learned that hires access simply required transmission of an 8-byte data packet. Other programmers throughout North America followed these discoveries by writing and distributing free code for attaching the Glove to the Amiga and Atari ST computers.

Word spread quickly. Before long, most Glove-lovin' hackers knew that

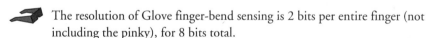 The resolution of Glove finger-bend sensing is 2 bits per entire finger (not including the pinky), for 8 bits total.

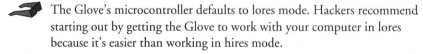 The Glove's microcontroller defaults to lores mode. Hackers recommend starting out by getting the Glove to work with your computer in lores because it's easier than working in hires mode.

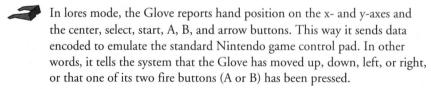 In lores mode, the Glove reports hand position on the x- and y-axes and the center, select, start, A, B, and arrow buttons. This way it sends data encoded to emulate the standard Nintendo game control pad. In other words, it tells the system that the Glove has moved up, down, left, or right, or that one of its two fire buttons (A or B) has been pressed.

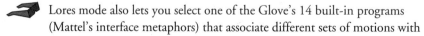 Lores mode also lets you select one of the Glove's 14 built-in programs (Mattel's interface metaphors) that associate different sets of motions with

the Nintendo control pad commands. Each program has its own way of translating finger movements to control the inputs.

In hires mode, the Glove reports the position in 3-space, roll, and configuration of fingers, along with the center, select, start, A, B, and arrow cluster buttons. (These buttons are part of the standard NES controller.)

When in hires mode, the Glove dumps dense data packets for the computer to crunch. You trigger the data lines through its connection to the computer. The Glove device driver sends timed sequences of bits to the Glove. When the Glove receives them, it responds with 12-byte sequences (the data packets) that contain hires data, which in turn trigger the Glove's on-screen representation. Glove drivers, or control code, can be found in various forms on the Internet (see Chapter 7) and on the disk provided with this book.

If you don't buy a commercial interface box, the easiest way to access hires mode is to attach the Power Glove cable to three data pins in your computer's parallel port, which must be bidirectional: the data lines in the port are used to trigger the data lines on the Power Glove. The three types of lines are clock, latch (reset), and data. Hardware for connecting the Glove to the computer is the same for hires or lores mode.

All engines (PC, Macintosh, Amiga) access their parallel ports in different ways. That means Glove control code written for the PC's parallel port, for example, will not automatically adapt to the Amiga's parallel port. You would have to program the Amiga to use that code and do so on a systems level as opposed to a control level. That requires solid programming chops.

Weird Trivia from the Internet's Glove-List

The Power Glove was designed by Chris Gentile (the G in AGE) and someone named Novak at Mattel. If you meet either of them, do whatever it takes to ply their brains for all the information you can get.

The data coming from the Power Glove is not encrypted. Mattel and Nintendo just wouldn't spill the beans on how it works.

The finger sensors were made by Amtec International, 3653 West 1987 South, Salt Lake City, UT 84104; (801) 977-0359. Similar strain gauges can be ordered

from the catalog of Omega Engineering, 1 Omega Dr., Box 2284, Stamford, CT 06906; (800) 826-6342.

 The coolest thing thus far is the original official Power Glove carrying case. It can be found for about $12 (half of what a glove usually costs) at a Toys 'R' Us in the Los Angeles area.

Power Glove Problems (and Some Solutions)

Navigating through virtual worlds with a Power Glove isn't all smooth roads and clear skies. Since Mattel no longer produces the Power Glove, you can't get your money back if you buy a defective unit. There's no one "official" source to call for tips on how to operate the Glove. Keep in mind that thousands of garage VR hobbyists around the world are in the same situation. You can keep in touch with them through telecommunications or by joining a VR user's group such as the Virtual Reality Alliance of Students & Professionals (VRASP). (See Appendix D.)

To register hand position, you must point your knuckles directly at the sensor assembly. Your arm, wrist, and hand grow tired after operating the Glove for a while. The fingers don't bend very easily either. As Mattel designed the Glove for kid-proof playing, it's constructed of tough, heavy rubber and itchy lycra material that don't make for comfortable, long-term use. Its interior lycra material was described by one hacker on the Internet as "a space-age synthetic equivalent of what medieval monks used for shirts." Some hackers have dismantled the Glove and replaced its shell with softer materials.

Inexpensive microphones serve as the Glove's ultrasonic sensors. Some people have experienced difficulty receiving a clean signal from the sensor assembly when it's placed on top of the monitor because sound waves can reflect off the top of the monitor and lose signal strength. One solution to this problem is to hang the assembly on a nearby wall. You can further decrease the reflective signal noise by surrounding the sensor assembly with absorbent material such as a cloth towel or a few anechoic foam pads. Designed for sound recording studios, these pads are sold by professional audio equipment suppliers.

The Glove transmits one degree of orientation movement: roll. You transmit roll data by banking your hand to the left or right, as if your hand is an airplane—in other words, tilting your hand with thumb up and pinky down, or vice versa. (See Figures 6.10 and 6.11.) If you roll your hand while pointing your fingers up or down or toward the left or right, you aim the emitters away from the sensor assembly and thus lose the roll data. Some hackers don't find the roll data at all useful, saying that it causes the Glove's image to jump around and appear choppy.

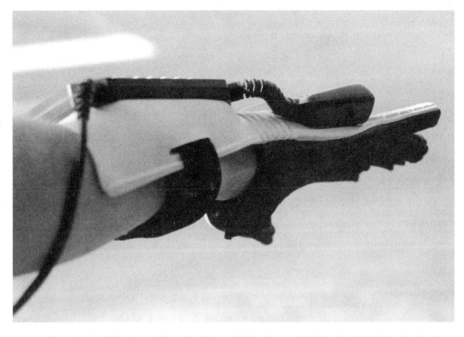

Figure 6.10. A view of the Power Glove that shows roll (banking to the left and right). (Photo by Linda Jacobson)

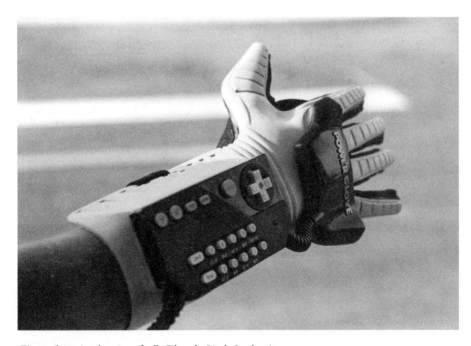

Figure 6.11. Another view of roll. (Photo by Linda Jacobson)

The Power Glove doesn't provide enough resolution accuracy to satisfy some garage VR hobbyists. Because the fingers don't bend too readily, it is difficult to reproduce a desired degree of flex. Even without a glove, few people can easily keep three fingers fully extended, for example, while bending a ring finger just a little. Also, a particular flex value is tough to maintain for a significant length of time. Moving other fingers can affect the flex value of the significant bent finger. For these reasons, some hackers have completely deconstructed the Glove to the finger-bend sensors and successfully used those alone, enabling greater freedom of movement than the stiff Glove allows. After extracting the flex sensors, they build their own hand gesture interface devices based on lightweight cotton gloves and home-built analog-to-digital circuits.

Connecting the Power Glove to a Computer

To transform a Power Glove into a computer input device, you need interface hardware and software that translate Glove data into computer data. You can do one of the following:

 Build your own interface. You need the Glove, a computer with a bidirectional parallel port, and an appropriate parallel port connector. You also need wire-stripping and soldering skills. You fiddle with the end of the Glove cable and solder its cable wires to the proper pins on the computer connector. This book includes instructions for building such an interface; the disk includes glove control software. (Alternatively, you can download public-domain Glove drivers from the Internet. See Chapter 7.)

NOTE

A programmer named Ron Menelli built an interface device similar to the original AGE box and based on the Motorola 68HC11 microcontroller. He has made the schematics and Glove control code available for downloading from the Internet. (See Chapter 9.)

 Buy a commercially available interface box.

We'll explore these avenues in terms of each computer platform.

Interfacing a PC to the Power Glove

To use the Power Glove with a PC and existing Glove control code (programs written in C and C++), you need a '386 PC (minimum) with VGA graphics, a joystick port, and a parallel port.

If you plan to build your own interface box, you'll need to buy some electronic components and connectors. (See Chapter 8.)

Glove control code exists in several forms. For example, VRASP sells Object Glove, a set of programming tools and programs for using the Power Glove with a PC. Essentially a resource library, Object Glove lets C++ programmers add Glove support to existing DOS and Windows 3.1 applications. For more information about Object Glove, refer to Chapter 7.

If you don't want to build your own interface box, commercial devices are available, including those listed in the following sections.

Power Glove Serial Interface

This device was developed by engineering students at the University of Illinois at Champaign-Urbana (UICU). The students started selling the PGSI box in 1993 for $95 apiece assembled.

The PGSI (also called "the Brain box," after one of its developers, Jim Brain) lets you access all the Glove's capabilities with any computer that has a RS232 serial interface. The box performs all the data parsing for you; you need no electronics expertise. It plugs directly into the computer's serial port and uses whatever Glove control code you have. It also lets you connect a pair of Sega-style LCD shutter glasses to the computer.

As the PGSI box doesn't come with a driver for using it with the most popular VR freeware, REND386, getting the PGSI box to work with REND386 requires considerable code hacking and the creation or acquisition of an interrupt-driven serial driver. Cast queries into the Internet to find out more about this or contact the PGSI folks. Keep in mind that the PGSI is marketed by students who have many other things on their minds besides providing PGSI technical support. The box is produced and marketed by the UIUC's Student Chapter of the Association for Computing Machinery, but neither the student chapter nor the national ACM organization is officially affiliated with the project. The ACM Student Chapter at UIUC does not accept responsibility for the PGSI's integrity or operation.

VRASP Yellow Jack-It

Created by Mark Pflaging and sold by VRASP, this new serial interface comes in two versions. The low-end model ($60) supports two Gloves and a set of LCD shutter glasses. The high-end model ($110) supports three Gloves, two joysticks, shutter glasses, and a serial through-port so you can use another serial device when the Yellow Jack-It is not in use. This box also supports the use of one Glove as a head-tracker, such as Doug Faxon's head-tracker, described in Chapter 8. The Yellow Jack-It is supplied with Glove control code for various computer platforms.

Interfacing Macintosh to the Power Glove

Transfinite Gold Brick

Many Macintosh-based VR hobbyists interface their engine with the Power Glove through Transfinite Systems' Gold Brick, a device introduced in 1990. You connect the Glove to the Gold Brick, which connects to the Mac's ADB port. The Gold Brick works best with any Macintosh SE or better running System 6.0.5 (or later versions). It only works with System 7 when you turn off the 32-bit addressing and virtual memory.

Gold Brick Model Two supports the Power Glove and is available in two versions: Model GBC-2 costs $245, and Model GBN-1 costs $169. GBN-1 is a stripped-down version of the $245 box, which provides three status lights, an ADB through-port for attaching other ADB devices, and a software technical manual. In addition, unlike the $169 model, the GBN-2 uses a socketed, single-chip microprocessor that can be replaced with later versions when they become available.

The Gold Brick is supplied with Glove control code, sample demos, and source code. The software lets you define how the Glove sensors are interpreted. It displays a wireframe image of the Glove on-screen, which moves in synchrony with the physical Glove's position and finger-bending (see Figure 6.12). One use for this might be to trigger QuickTime movies. The software was written in MPW C, so if your Macintosh setup doesn't include MPW C, you may have to come up with your own control code. After much difficulty, several hackers (working individually), including Pete Falco at Rensselaer Polytechnic Institute, have ported the position-sensing code into stand-alone THINK C programs.

Transfinite Systems, based in Cambridge, Massachusetts, doesn't have a good track record for customer support. But it does offer a 90-day warranty on parts and a 30-day money-back guarantee.

Pete Falco, the student at Rensselaer Polytech who built his own Macintosh head-mounted display, has created a modification for the Glove Control code, Dr. StrangeGlove, so that it works with the Gold Brick. (See Chapter 7.)

Power Glove Serial Interface

The PGSI box (see the section titled "Power Glove Serial Interface") also works with the Macintosh, but this feat requires a special PGSI-to-Mac adapter. The PGSI vendor at the University of Illinois at Champaign-Urbana sells this adapter for $12.

VRASP Yellow Jack-It

See the earlier section titled "VRASP Yellow Jack-It."

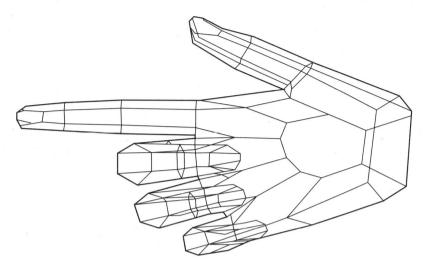

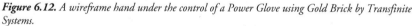

Figure 6.12. A wireframe hand under the control of a Power Glove using Gold Brick by Transfinite Systems.

Build Your Own

You also can build your own interface. Other Glove interfaces to the Macintosh employ the serial port. If you build your own Glove-Macintosh interface, you'll need a Motorola HC11 microprocessor. Directions for building such a device can be downloaded via modem from `ftp.apple.com` in the VR directory under "public." You can grab two sets of instructions: "MacPGlove" and "Dr. StrangeGlove." (See Chapter 7 for details.)

Interfacing Amiga to the Power Glove

Power Glove Serial Interface

The PGSI box (see the earlier section titled "Power Glove Serial Interface") works for the Amiga, too.

VRASP Yellow Jack-It

This new serial interface (see the section titled "VRASP Yellow Jack-It") requires a 9600-baud serial port connection to the computer, which the Amiga can handle. However, you need to supply your own Glove control code.

Build Your Own

In 1990, two programmers named Mike Cargal and Paul King built a cable and wrote a driver to interface the Glove to the Amiga via the mouse port. They published the results of their work, how-to instructions, and code in Volume 1, Issue 1 (1991) of *Amazing Computing's Tech Journal for the Commodore Amiga.* They wrote the code in Modula-2 and gave it shareware status. Because it lets the Glove emulate a mouse, you wave your hand to point at things on-screen.

The do-it-yourself Menelli box will also interface a Power Glove with the Amiga.

To achieve hires Glove action on the Amiga, for the most part you need a compiler and some programming chops. Several public-domain Glove drivers are available for downloading off the nets; you can find most of them in the archives of the glove-list. (See Chapter 9.)

One of the original drivers goes by the filename of GT.LZH, written in Forth by Robert Marsanyi in 1991. The code is set up as a background task that serves as the interface, communicating with other tasks via a set of standardized messages. It works when the Glove is connected to the Amiga's first joystick port.

According to a 1991 post by Robert Marsanyi in a WELL discussion group, "My driver puts the Glove in hires, then responds to messages: 'reset,' if you need to reinitialize the Glove; 'start and stop,' which starts polling the Glove for data and stops it; 'poll,' which does a one-shot 'where-are-you-now' sort of thing; and 'kill,' which shuts the task down. The data is noisy, though, and it does bog the machine down some.

"The GT.LZH driver contains a pre-'compiled' server that sits and spits out Glove events, but you still need some program in the foreground that eats those and does something useful with them," Robert wrote. "I put 'compiled' in quotes because you run it from the shell or Workbench like any compiled program, but it's a Forth target compilation. The Glove needs to be initialized with a special sequence of bytes, and the mechanism for writing data involves flipping bits at a quick clip."

An engineering student, Chris Hufnagel, recently built an interface for his Amiga 3000 and a driver using his SAS/C compiler. When he started out, Chris reports, "At first I used a direct connection to the serial port. Unfortunately I was trying to use Glove control software and libraries that were designed and compiled for the Amiga 500/2000 series. It was as reliable as a three-dollar bill on my Amiga 3000. I then decided to use a Motorola 68HC11 microcontroller to receive the input of the Glove, translate the information, and output it to my serial port, thereby giving a steady, reliable stream at 9600 baud. This made the currently available code more reliable on my 3000, but I was still having timing problems. This led to custom code I developed for my VR application. I programmed my software using mostly C, with parts of assembly code for performance enhancements."

Amiga owners, take note: Other than a few Glove control programs, you won't find much in the way of real-time, interactive VR software. One reason is the incompatibility among Amiga machines. Programmers have written Glove code for the A-500 and A-2000, but as of this writing, no one's coded the A-4000 and A-1200. Yet few Amigaphiles bemoan the lack of rendering and world-building software. Folks have been programming impressive 3D graphics on the Amiga for a while. The existence of an intermediary programming language, ARexx, means that 3D graphics can be set up for Power Glove control. ARexx places ports between the applications. According to Amiga hacker Eric Townsend, "You shove data around these ports. You use something like Deluxe Paint or DPaint 4, which speak ARexx. Then you take a good glove-handling program and simply have that generate control messages for the paint program. Basically you write a filter that takes information from the Glove port and generates ARexx commands for your favorite paint program." By the way, the Amiga version of Vistapro supports ARexx ports.

What to Do After Making the Glove-Computer Connection

1. Try running the Power Glove demo software on the floppy disk included with this book.

2. Use the Power Glove with the applications that support it, such as REND386, described in Chapter 7. Either buy the software or download the freeware via file transfer protocol from Internet sites. (See Chapter 9 for details.)

Where In The World Are You?: Tracking Technologies for Garage VR

Even if you have never experienced virtual reality, you have witnessed basic tracking technology in action. You know those airport and supermarket doors that swing open when you approach? They contain tracking devices that sense your proximity.

In the typical VR system, the tracking technology senses your hand and head position and/or orientation, converts that information into digital form, and sends the data to the computer. The computer uses the data to calculate and render appropriate images in the virtual environment. This is also how your head and hand movements translate to viewpoint-switching and object motion in the virtual world. A position tracker typically joins forces with another input device that lets you select, grab, or otherwise manipulate objects in the virtual world.

A tracking system's performance is described in terms of

 system resolution—the smallest possible change in position that the system can detect, expressed in fractions (decimals) of an inch

 system accuracy—spatial error, or the range within which a reported position is correct, such as ±0.125 inch

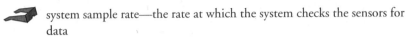

- system sample rate—the rate at which the system checks the sensors for data

- system data rate—the number of positions computed per second

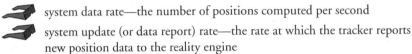

- system update (or data report) rate—the rate at which the tracker reports new position data to the reality engine

- system lag—the length of time between a change in position and the reporting of the new position data. Also called *latency*, this performance characteristic is perhaps the most significant because the results of lag affect the visual appearance of the virtual world.

Most current VR systems employ *active* trackers, which communicate via a two-way signal, using emitters and sensors. The less popular, higher-performance *passive* trackers use a one-way signal, employing sensors only.

Tracking systems are based on different kinds of underlying technology:

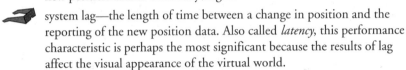

- An *electromagnetic* tracking system generates a magnetic field. This is the most popular and well-established tracking technology in professional VR; it's the kind of tracker used in the W Industries Virtuality arcade game system. It takes up little space and doesn't need to work on line-of-sight. As with all electromagnetic technologies, however, it is sensitive to metals.

- A *mechanical* system is based on a series of linked mechanical assemblies. Potentiometers at each assembly joint measure its relative angle and position.

- *Optical* technology transmits and receives infrared light beams. This expensive, computationally intensive method works only when the sensor and emitter are placed in each other's line of sight.

- An *ultrasonic* (or acoustic) tracker generates inaudible sound frequencies and employs triangulation methods to calculate location. The emitter and sensors must be situated in each other's line of sight.

Several commercial tracking systems are sold for VR users. None is inexpensive, but at this stage of the game, ultrasonic tracking costs the least. They're the sort of trackers used in the Mattel Power Glove and Logitech 6DOF controllers. Each of these ultrasonic tracking systems consists of multiple emitters (transmitters) and sensors (receivers). The emitters output a series of tones so high, even dogs can't hear them. The sensors, essentially tiny microphones, catch these sound waves. The system measures how much time it takes for each sound wave to arrive at each sensor. These measurements are then used to calculate the position and orientation of the emitters.

On the higher end of the "affordable" price range is the Logitech 6DOF controller kit for PC and UNIX engines. It provides desktop VR systems with the least expensive, free-space precision tracking system. The system consists of a 3D Mouse and a 3D Head-Tracker, shown in Figure 6.13. The five-button mouse comes with a small, triangular-shaped sensor that you place on a desk near the mouse. The 3D Head-Tracker includes a triangular device that attaches to LCD shutter glasses or the top of a head-mounted display. It works in conjunction with a small, triangular sensor assembly that usually mounts on top of the monitor.

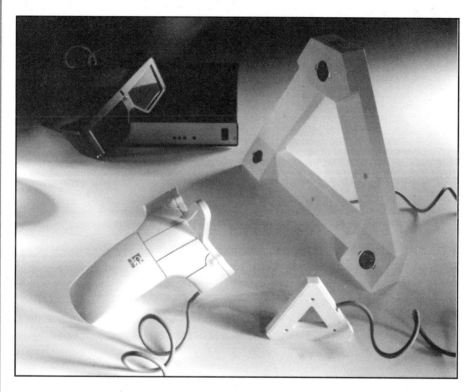

Figure 6.13. *The Logitech 3D Mouse and Head-Tracker.*

The 3D Mouse also doubles as a microphone for sound input. The system comes with a power supply and control unit and plugs into the PC's RS232 connector. According to the company's specifications, lag rate is less than 75 milliseconds, spatial resolution is 1/250 inches, accuracy is 2 percent, and the sampling rate is 50 reports per second.

Logitech sells the 3D Mouse and the 3D Head-Tracker separately for $999 each or together for $2,000 in a kit that also includes a cable so the two trackers can work in synchrony.

On the Power Glove, two emitters are located in a small box mounted at the base of the knuckles. Its three sensors reside in a plastic contraption that Mattel calls the L-bar (see Figure 6.14) that mounts on top of the monitor (see Figure 6.15). For the tracking to work, the Glove must remain pointed at the sensors. The closer the Glove is to the sensors, the higher the tracking accuracy.

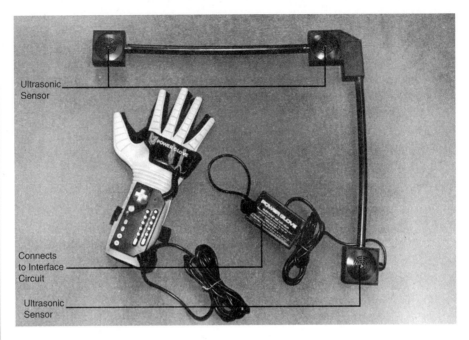

Ultrasonic
Sensor

Connects
to Interface
Circuit

Ultrasonic
Sensor

Figure 6.14. A view of the Power Glove that shows the L-bar sensor assembly. (Photo by Linda Jacobson)

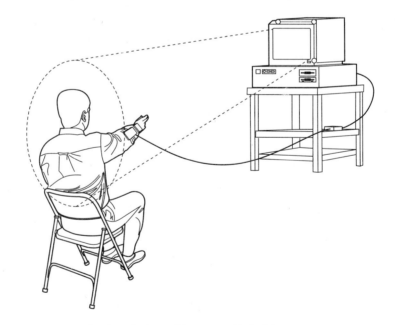

Figure 6.15. A diagram that shows the Power Glove set up with the L-bar.

Ultrasonic tracking systems—especially the Power Glove's—are neither rugged nor robust. They're not extremely accurate. They can be annoyingly unstable. They can induce lag. As this technology depends upon the flight of sound waves, its performance can be affected by anything that gets in their path—including sound waves from other sources such as radio speakers or disk drive fans—and the tracking device must be kept directly in that path. For example, if you try to grab a virtual object by reaching outside the Glove's tracking range (what Mattel calls its "sensing zone"), the Glove's on-screen representation will go out of whack.

Budget-conscious VR hackers like to experiment with different approaches to imbue their systems with location-tracking capabilities. Some try integrating electromagnetic compasses that use flux gate technology. I read about a 2D head-tracker based on potentiometers. Mounted on a headband that you wear, it measures the pan and tilt of the head. Such a device can be fixed—mounted from the ceiling or clamped to the side of your workbench, for example. This device interfaces to the PC through the joystick port.

Some people find it easiest to turn the Power Glove's ultrasonic tracking system into a head-tracker. In fact, one garage VR hobbyist, Doug Faxon, did just that. He graciously provided us with how-to instructions so everyone with a spare Power Glove and some soldering skills can create their own trackers. (See Chapter 8.) Combine your tracker with a Power Glove and a pair of LCD shutter glasses or a homemade HMD, and you have an immersive VR system worth yodeling about.

Another potentially budget-conscious tracking approach that may come into use is based on distributed arrays of multiple sensors. The first commercial implementation of such a system is a video game controller: the $80 Sega Activator, scheduled to hit stores in late 1993. It controls Sega's 16-bit Genesis video games by transforming arm and leg movements into on-screen action. Sold with a power supply and cable, the Activator plugs into the joystick controller port on the Genesis game box. Two Activators can be set up side by side for duets. Figure 6.16 shows Activator control functions.

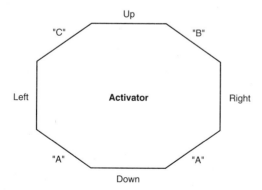

Figure 6.16. *Activator control functions.*

The Cockpit
Input Devices

The Activator comprises a series of flat floor panels that link together like model train tracks, forming an octagon shape about four feet across. Each panel contains an infrared transmitter and receiver. Step inside the octagon and you're surrounded by infrared beams that aim straight up toward the ceiling. You break those beams by throwing out your arms and kicking your feet over the floor panels. The resulting diffusion of IR light translates into different on-screen game actions. When you break two beams simultaneously, you trigger special movements; instead of causing a character to walk forward, you might cause the character to perform a triple somersault. Each beam responds to two levels of control, high and low. Breaking the beam at a low level with a slightly raised foot reflects a different signal back to the receiver than breaking the beam at a high level with an outstretched arm. The Activator works best when you control it barefoot or when you wear white or light-colored socks (without shoes).

The Activator comes with two body-action games, Bounty Hunter and Air Drums, and a manual that explains how to play other games with the Activator. Bounty Hunter is the standard sort of punch-kick-and-kill game. Air Drums is a music-maker that lets you play drum solos with your hands and feet, either in free play or by following patterns. Sega is developing more games specifically for Activator control.

No doubt VR hobbyists will hack the heck out of the Activator, aiming to expand their virtual world control to full-body interaction without donning a megabuck body data suit.

Where to Buy Power Gloves and Interfaces

Mattel manufactured more than 1 million Power Gloves, and a significant portion of those are still available for sale. Some entrepreneurs stockpiled them. You should be able to buy a Glove for between $15 (used) and $50. Don't pay more than $50, however, unless you can't find a Glove anywhere else and you can't live without it. Various sources for Power Gloves and Glove interface boxes and accessories include

 Job-lot warehouses.

 Nintendo game retailers and service centers.

 Vendors of used video games. Even though the products are used, they should be guaranteed to work. They probably won't be in the original packaging and might not include the operating manual and program guide.

 Flea markets. (A friend recently found two used Power Gloves at a flea market in northern California.)

 Kmart Discount Stores.

 Toys 'R' Us stores.

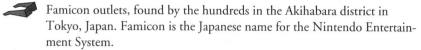Famicon outlets, found by the hundreds in the Akihabara district in Tokyo, Japan. Famicon is the Japanese name for the Nintendo Entertainment System.

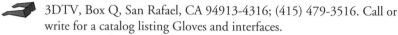3DTV, Box Q, San Rafael, CA 94913-4316; (415) 479-3516. Call or write for a catalog listing Gloves and interfaces.

Funcoland, a mail-order company that specializes in video game equipment. Gloves cost about $15 plus $6 shipping. Call (612) 946-8883.

FringeWare, the bizarro-techno-lover's distribution service. New and used mail-order Power Glove prices depend on availability. "We had several Gloves in stock at something like $42 apiece," says FringeWare's Jon Lebkowsky, "but I wouldn't want to commit to that price, because the next guy with a stockpile might want more or accept less." His partner, Paco Xander Nathan, concurs. "For anything that's out of production, we have to run the broker's gambit: somewhere between 'bid and ask,' depending on availability, plus a slight margin for our time. We've brokered a dozen or two—always getting 'em in and sending 'em back out so quickly. We've got 'secret' sources but now there's more *good* Power Gloves these days that are used than are 'new.' Mattel's production quality wasn't the best. It's not our biggest seller, but we consider it a kind of 'community service' and aren't making much profit off Gloves. Get people using 'em to prime the market for follow-up products, that's my philosophia."

FringeWare also carries Transfinite Systems' Gold Brick for $169 plus $2 shipping in the U.S. FringeWare accepts money orders or checks drawn on U.S. banks. Texas residents must add 8 percent sales tax. Outside the U.S., shipping costs $4. Contact FringeWare for information on other shipping options: FringeWare, PO Box 49921, Austin, TX 78765-9921; (512) 477-1366; e-mail `fringeware@wixer.bga.com`.

VRASP, whose wares include

Power Glove, $45 plus $5 shipping per unit.

Model PGC-1: Single Glove-to-PC Connector, $28 plus $2.50 shipping. Requires PC-compatible computer with bidirectional parallel port, game port, and unmodified Power Glove. You can use a joystick while this connector is attached, but can't use the parallel port for other parallel port devices.

Model PGC-2: Dual Glove-to-PC Connector, $36 plus $2.50 shipping. It's the same as PGC-1, except it allows simultaneous operation of two Gloves.

Power Glove and PGC-1 Connector, $70 plus $5 shipping per set.

Two Power Gloves and PGC-2 Connector, $120 plus $10 shipping per set.

Contact VRASP for information on package deals that include Object Glove software. To order, send check or money order payable to VRASP, PO Box 4139, Highland Park, NJ 08904. Call (908) 463-8787 to inquire about shipping and overseas rates.

 UICU Student Chapter of the Association for Computing Machinery. Mail-order Glove, $45; PGSI box: $95 assembled, $80 kit; 12-volt PGSI power adapter, $12; PGSI coaxial-to-phono plug adapter, $5; PGSI-to-Mac interface, $12. For information about availability and shipping costs and an order form, write to 1304 West Springfield, Room 1225, Urbana, IL 61801, or send e-mail to pgsi@uiuc.edu.

The Radio: Spatialized Sound and Garage VR

Few people would drive cross-country without listening to the radio, CD, or cassette player. Sound enhances our life experiences as a source of entertainment, and even more importantly, as a source of information. Virtual-world-builders employ sound to reinforce the feeling of immersion and presence. In fact, sound effects and music can help compensate for lower-quality graphics in a virtual world.

When you set up your VR system with a computer sound card and a power amplifier for output to speakers or headphones, you're equipped to imbue your virtual worlds with basic sounds. As headphones feed the sounds directly to your brain's acoustic cortex, they provide a more powerful illusion than speakers.

These days you can use your computer to record and play digital audio and MIDI sequences for less than $200. As mentioned in Chapter 4, computer sound cards come in many different forms. Any good sound card contains a synthesizer. Some include a microphone, or microphone jack, along with sound recording software. For example, the SoundBlaster Pro for the PC lets you plug in an inexpensive Radio Shack microphone. Then you can mix voice, music, and sound effects, recording directly off CD or CD-ROM.

A PC sound card essentially deals with two types of sound files: waveform and MIDI data. Waveform files are direct recordings made onto the hard drive from a microphone, tape deck, CD player, or other standard audio signal source. You can play back the files through any sound card for output through headphones or speakers.

Unlike waveform files, MIDI data files don't consume much space on the hard drive. MIDI is the standard protocol used to pass musical information between computers and instruments. MIDI files don't contain the actual sounds that you hear. Instead, they contain terse data such as what note was played, how long it was played, and at what volume. They let you control such sound characteristics as pitch, reverb, and delay, playing back multiple voices (notes) at once. MIDI data is extremely flexible and lets the computer command a multitude of digital music devices. You need a synthesizer to take that data and produce a sound for playback through speakers or headphones.

Some audio-savvy garage VR hobbyists supplement their systems with a CD player or CD-ROM drive to record music and sound effects into the system. CD-ROM drives provide an excellent way to add background ambience to virtual worlds. You must know how to program, however, to instruct your VR application to send messages to the CD-ROM drive, telling it to start and stop playing at certain frame numbers.

This brings up a key limiting factor in sound implementation within virtual worlds: audio playback must occur at a fixed rate. If you slow it down, accelerate it, play it backwards, or stop it, you distort the sound. Any journey into a virtual world, though, involves this type of manipulation of the visual medium—the frame rate is almost always changing as you change your position and viewpoint and interact with virtual objects. Therefore, audio files can not be linked (synchronized) to the frame rate. You have to design sounds so that they are independent of the simulation. This means that the *sounds in virtual worlds must be linked to specific objects and events.* For example, reaching the top of a virtual mountain might trigger the playback of a crowd cheering. In another environment, you might hear the constant sound of dripping water until you turn off a virtual faucet. In a third environment, the chirping of a bird might grow quieter (simulating the Doppler effect) as you move farther from the bird.

Some VR hobbyists enhance their setups with digital music recording and production capabilities. This sort of work space contains a MIDI synthesizer, sequencer or sampling keyboard, and a MIDI interface for feeding the sounds to the engine. The MIDI instrument is preloaded with the sounds for incorporation in the virtual world. Then simple stereo left/right panning is combined with control over the wet/dry balance. ("Wet" refers to a sound that is treated with echo, reverb, or similar effects; "dry" refers to an untreated sound.) A relatively low-cost MIDI-controlled mixer permits independent control of left/right panning and effects-send amount for multiple sound channels. Using a MIDI mixer, sounds essentially can be spatialized using normal stereo panning for horizontal location and by adjusting the volume and the wet/dry balance to control perceived distance. The more distant the sound source, the less direct and more reverberant the sound it emits.

The key word in the preceding paragraph is "spatialized." When we start thinking in terms of spatialization, we start thinking in terms of *three-dimensional* sound, an exciting area of development now accessible from the domain of garage VR.

3D Sound

A standard two-speaker stereo system emits a different mix of sounds from each loudspeaker. This helps clarify the sounds of various elements and also gives the impression that the musicians, singers, and other sound producers are located in different positions in front of you. In other words, stereo conveys a sense of *space*.

When you listen to a 3D sound recording on a stereo system, you hear the sounds as if they were coming from different places all around: above you, below you, beside you, before you, even from some point far off in the distance. Seldom do the sounds seem to

emanate directly from the speakers. When you hear the same recording on headphones, this spatial effect is even more uncanny. Sometimes you can't distinguish the recorded sounds from "real" ones.

Three-dimensional sound recordings are based on an audio manipulation process that lets the recording artist or engineer "place" sounds in space, controlling their direction, distance, and depth, the motion of the sound source, and the overall image's size, stability, consistency, and positioning. Listeners can enjoy the results on garden-variety stereo systems, without adding speakers, special headphones, or fancy sound decoders.

In the studio, when engineers mix various instrument recordings for normal stereo, they spread the musical elements along an imaginary flat line, a horizontal "sound field." That line extends between the two speakers: one at the far left, the other at the far right. The audio mixing console provides an adjustment labeled "pan." While mixing the sounds, the engineer adjusts the pan to place each instrument within the sound field—toward the left, right, or center.

The new 3D sound equipment blurs the flat line of that sound field. While recording or mixing, the engineer uses a 3D sound processor to spread the sound above, below, and beyond the edges of the speakers. This way they place, or *localize,* sounds in the up, down, front, or back positions. This process is also known as *spatialization.*

All 3D sound systems work in different ways but share the same goal: to trick the brain. They fool us into perceiving that the sound is coming from somewhere other than the speakers or headphones. The trick works because of recent advances in computer technology, signal processing, and psychoacoustic research.

Let's focus on psychoacoustics first. Just as we possess stereoscopic vision, we also have stereo hearing. Our two ears are perfectly designed to capture sound. Specifically, they catch sound waves, regular vibrations of air that change the air pressure. The shell-like shape of the outer ear—the pinna—suits it to the job of collecting sound waves from different directions and directing those waves down varying paths through the ear canal. The pinna actually modifies the sound waves, helping the brain determine where the sound came from: front, back, up, or down.

Both ears capture sound waves coming from all directions. The pinnae and the head then superimpose position-dependent sound "cues" on every sound. The brain listens for these cues, which report loudness difference, time/phase difference, and frequency attenuation. *Loudness difference* is what occurs when studio engineers pan sounds to create a conventional stereo image: they make the sound's volume louder in the right speaker or the left. *Time/phase difference* refers to the fact that sound waves don't strike both ears at precisely the same time. *Frequency* refers to the number of times each second that the sound waves hit the ears; *attenuation* means reduction. *Frequency attenuation,* then, is the process by which the ear's shape slightly changes certain frequencies of the sound waves, depending on the direction each wave comes from. Using these three cues, the brain can determine, or *localize,* the exact location of the sound's source.

Let's say you're about to cross a two-way street when suddenly a horn beeps. Without looking for the horn's source, you retreat and wait for the car to pass. The horn's honk reached your left ear before it reached your right ear, which helped you localize the sound and realize that the car was headed at you from the left. Sound travels at around 1,100 feet per second; sounds coming from the left reach the left ear almost a millisecond before they hit the right ear. When the sound does reach the right ear, it seems quieter because of the head's "shadowing" effect. This relates to the time/phase difference mentioned earlier. The difference in wave arrival time, or phase difference, combined with loudness difference, cues your brain as to where the sound originates.

Many other effects result from the shape and placement of our ears, reflections of sound off our shoulders, the distance between our ears, shadowing effects of the head on opposite-side sound waves, and resonances in the outer ear and ear canal. Taken all together, these factors create the *head-related transfer function* (*HRTF*), the scientific term for what happens when our ears scoop up sounds and our brains process those sounds. Each person possesses a unique HRTF, just as each person has a different thumbprint.

Back to 3D sound! For over a century, people interested in sound have been trying to recreate sound in the three dimensions. In the 1880s, they started making *binaural* recordings. Binaural refers to the use of two ears; a binaural recording is a stereo recording made with two microphones that are positioned to emulate the sensitivity and spacing of two ears on the average human head. Sometimes the microphones are even placed on or in the recording engineer's own ears. Preferably, the process involves an artificial or "dummy" head, an odd-looking piece of equipment modeled after a human head and outfitted with a tiny microphone in each ear. Each microphone feeds a separate audio track on the recording tape or other medium. At the listening end, these tracks are fed to separate sides of headphones; sounds captured by the original left microphone are sent to the listener's left ear, while sounds captured by the right microphone go to the right ear.

Different sound equipment manufacturers have each concocted their own recipes for serving 3D over two speakers. Some systems use dummy heads; others, through the miracles of computer science, electronically simulate binaural recording through the application of digital signal processing.

Binaural recording works best on headphones because it recreates the HRTF directly at the listener's ears. That's why an acoustic problem crops up when you listen to a binaural recording over a regular stereo system. The problem is *interaural crosstalk*. Sounds from the left speaker reach your right ear, and sounds from the right speaker reach your left ear, smearing the sonic imagery. On top of that, the size and contents of the room—even its furniture and window and floor coverings—affect the way you hear the sounds issuing from the speakers.

Thanks to computer science, however, the new 3D systems can mimic our auditory system (ears plus brain) by supplementing the binaural process with *transaural* processing. They recreate spatialized sounds for listening over two loudspeakers by preparing specially structured correction signals and applying them to the speakers. Phase information is manipulated to effectively eliminate interaural crosstalk. (*Phase* describes the relative position of two sound waves with respect to one another.)

Okay. Now we know that 3D sound systems artificially duplicate the natural triggers that help our brain localize sound and electronically recreate those effects in real time. These systems provide knobs, joysticks, or similar control devices (sometimes in software form, represented on the computer screen) to allow placement of sounds in the up, down, front, and back positions. They even let you move sounds slowly or rapidly from one direction to another.

A handful of manufacturers produce commercial 3D sound processing systems. Most systems combine loudness difference with either phase difference or frequency attenuation to reproduce the localization cues. Unfortunately, using only two of the three cues results in a less complete sonic "photograph." When a system combines loudness and phase differences, requiring two speakers to provide phase cues for a single sound, the "sweet spot phenomenon" occurs: your head must be situated exactly between the two speakers and within a certain distance from them to accurately decode the cues. Move a few inches in any direction and the effect diminishes. The best results are obtained when the room is fairly dead (acoustically absorbent), especially near the speakers. If you place the speakers too close to a wall, sound reflected off the wall cancels out the phase cues and greatly diminishes the 3D effect.

By using or simulating binaural recording, we can reproduce the ambience of a sound environment. By manipulating and moving sounds in three-dimensional space, we can enhance the overall experience and affect our perception of reality. That's why 3D sound technology intrigues producers of stereo TV broadcasts, video games, theme park attractions, and, naturally, VR applications. As you can imagine, sounds that move realistically in space do much to enhance visual images.

Imagine a virtual world based on the story of Peter Pan. This world includes a virtual alligator, the one that ate the clock. Each time you near the creature, you hear *tick-tock, tick-tock*. The sound comes from the proper direction; if the alligator appears in front of you, you hear the ticking sound in both ears. When you turn your head to the right, you hear the ticking sound more in your left ear.

Or perhaps you're negotiating a virtual world based on a three-dimensional maze. When you approach a dead end, you hear a hissing sound in front of you. When you turn around to head in the opposite direction, the hiss almost seems to come from behind you.

Sound spatializing technology for virtual environments owes its existence to aeronautic and aerospace research. Since the 1980s, scientists at NASA Ames Research Center in Moffett Field, California, have been working on headphone-based 3D sound systems that help people manage information in situations where spatial awareness is important, especially when visual information is limited, or to lessen the visual overload of complex instrumentation. Such systems are designed for use in air traffic control displays in towers and cockpits and for monitoring of robotic activities in outer space situations.

One 3D sound system developed at NASA Ames is now marketed by a northern California company called Crystal River Engineering. It's called the Convolvotron. (*Convolution* refers to the filtering of an input signal by HRTFs.) Consisting of a pair of circuit cards, it installs in a standard IBM-compatible PC. The Convolvotron presents 3D audio signals over headphones to match your head motion and/or the motion of sound sources. As you move your head, the perceived location of the sound source remains constant: when you turn to the left, sound that you first perceived to come from in front of you seems to come from your right. The system costs about $15,000, however, which means that you won't find it enhancing any garage VR systems.

Instead, garage VR hobbyists are talking about some new low-cost, 3D sound circuit cards that pop into a personal computer. (As of this writing, no similar type of spatial processor exists for the Amiga engine.)

In early 1993, Crystal River introduced the $1,800 Beachtron for personal computers, consisting of a circuit board with a synthesizer, recording/playback functions, and software library. The Beachtron lets you spatialize two separate sound sources for binaural presentation over conventional headphones. You can combine up to eight Beachtrons for 16 simultaneous sound sources, and you can record sounds into the PC directly off CD or tape, record live sounds, or create sounds in the computer using the synthesizer software. Like the Convolvotron, the Beachtron works with virtual world-building systems for virtual reality applications.

A similar system comes from Focal Point 3D Audio, a small company based in Niagara Falls, New York. Using Focal Point technology, PC and Macintosh owners can explore CD-quality, 16-bit, 3D sound. It uses a convolution process, incorporating binaural directional information, to turn mono inputs into separate outputs for the left and right ears. Focal Point lets you control and animate the perceived direction, elevation, and distance of each sound channel. You control this process through the Focal Point software or through a MIDI keyboard, sequencer, or other MIDI device. Although the Focal Point system is based on its own sound processor, you also can import sounds from any MIDI sampler or synthesizer. The sounds play back through speakers or headphones. Focal Point also includes mouse and head-tracking support for VR applications and comes with a sample 3D sound application.

Priced at $1,800 per channel, the Macintosh II version of Focal Point includes the Digidesign AudioMedia sound card. For $900, Focal Point 3D Audio will transform your standard AudioMedia cards into 3D sound systems. The PC version of Focal Point costs significantly less, about $1,200. As of this writing, however, the company is negotiating with a major manufacturer to turn over production of the cards. This means that an even less expensive Focal Point PC card will debut some time in 1994, probably priced under $1,000.

In 1993, Focal Point licensed a slimmed-down version of its software to Advanced Gravis, a Canadian company that produces sound cards for the PC platform. In the fall of '93, Advanced Gravis started shipping the 16-bit UltraSound card with Focal Point software. Its list price: $245.

The UltraSound 3D card works on any PC engine running DOS 3.0 or higher. Compatible with software that supports Ad Lib and SoundBlaster cards, it offers synthesis capabilities, 16 stereo channels, and 32 CD-quality voices (notes that can play back simultaneously). It also provides MIDI support in case you want to use standard MIDI files. The card includes a built-in sound sampler, stereo power amplifier, and stereo microphone jack. Its game port can be converted to a MIDI port by adding an adapter, which you can build yourself or buy from Advanced Gravis.

The UltraSound card alone provides 15 panning positions for each voice. With the Focal Point software, the card can import and process a standard waveform file (processing speed depends on the engine). This works best with sounds of short duration; a one-second sound requires about three minutes of processing time. The sound signal is convolved with a predefined set of head-related transfer functions. After processing, the new sound clip file can be played back while you move it around in 3D space in real time. You can localize and interact with up to six simultaneous sounds (two stereo pairs and three mono sources, or one stereo pair and six mono sources). This only works with previously stored sounds; you can't speak into a microphone and simultaneously make your voice seem to swoop around your head.

Advanced Gravis also will sell the Focal Point software separately, for $50, for use with PCs that contain earlier UltraSound cards.

Implementing UltraSound/Focal Point audio in your virtual world requires that you know, in advance, what sounds will appear in your world. Naturally, your engine must provide enough memory to store the Focal Point-processed sound files. Several game vendors brought out new software titles that harness the UltraSound's new spatialization skills, including Doom by Id Software (creators of the VR-style game, Wolfenstein 3D).

Another producer of PC sound cards, Creative Labs, has elevated its $150 SoundBlaster to 3D level. The signal processing chip on every 16-bit SoundBlaster manufactured after October 24, 1993, contains QSound software. This lets the card process waveform files to support real-time sound localization. QSound is a 3D processing system created by Archer Communications, a Canadian company. Introduced in 1990, QSound's early forays made waves in the most exclusive of professional music studios; Madonna and Sting were among the first to release QSound recordings.

Moving from pop stars to computer games, QSound development kits from Creative Labs are now available for free to game developers and VR software publishers. Before long we'll start seeing (and hearing) games and other applications that support SoundBlaster's 3D capabilities. Owners of SoundBlaster cards built before October of

1993 can download the QSound software from Creative Labs' electronic bulletin board (modem (408) 428-6660) or buy the new chip (it pops into a socket on the card) for $46. Seeking developer support, Creative Labs invites programmers who want to create software applications that support the 3D SoundBlaster card to call the company and request a developer's kit.

At this point, the QSound process possesses one drawback of significance to virtual world developers: QSound works only on speakers. Its 3D effect is lost when you listen through headphones. Eventually someone should solve this problem.

Indeed, now's the time to announce a *caveat emptor:* All these new low-cost 3D sound cards are innovative, fun to use, and can enhance your experience of a virtual world. In no way, however, do they produce the kind of precisely spatialized effects that can be created with Crystal River's Convolvotron. They don't even come close to the spaciousness offered by Crystal River's Beachtron or Focal Point's original PC and Mac systems. They *are* affordable, however, and that's significant.

PUTTING VR ON THE MAP

Douglas W. Faxon

PROFILE

3

DOUGLAS W. FAXON:
"Bringing People Together Through Virtual Reality"

One hour's drive north of San Francisco is Santa Rosa, a small city situated in rich fruit, farm, and dairy country. Sonoma County: here, a century ago, mission priests gave neighbors the original grapevine cuttings that blossomed into this glorified wine-producing region. A cruise through its back roads wheels you by Holsteins and horses. Hawks glide over vineyards. In June, the breeze blows through the fields, hot and dry, beneath a cloudless azure sky, past hills not yet scorched their standard summer tan. Santa Rosa is where Luther Burbank settled in 1875 to grow his experimental potatoes and plants; it also was, Believe-It-Or-Not, Ripley's hometown.

"Virtual reality is a tool of self-expression, like music. In the same way that you sculpt air into a presentation that is 'music,' with VR tools you can sculpt a three-dimensional, audio/visual environment that you can show to people and say, 'This is me' or 'This is my concept of something important to me.'"

Passionate about rock and roll, fractals, and the art of M.C. Escher, Doug is a garage VR innovator whose creations prove that a little curiosity and determination can go a long way—and that lack of experience isn't necessarily an obstacle to progress.

In addition to his inspirational virtual worlds, which he shares with us in this book, Doug's accomplishments include a head-tracker, based on parts extracted from the Mattel Power Glove and an interface to virtual worlds that is based on a stairclimber exercise machine.

Doug is a phone technician who lives with his wife Erika and their two cats, Isis and Duffy. Their three-room house is situated behind a barn in western Santa Rosa, well outside city limits. In a tiny back room that doubles as VR lab and music recording studio, Doug explores PC-driven virtual worlds.

Born November 21, 1962, in Santa Monica, California, Doug grew up in the San Fernando Valley. By the time he entered Granada Hills High School, Doug was heavily into playing music—not in the school band, but with a bunch of buddies. Although there was a piano in the Faxon family's living room, Doug starting pounding on drums at age eight. He picked up the guitar when he turned 12. With puberty and a deepening voice came the desire to master bass guitar too.

"I *always* had music going through my head," says Doug. "I joined a non-band: we'd jam our guts out for a weekend and then not see each other for three months. But we were just figuring out how to play the latest Rush song. We weren't real good at it and got tired of copying other people's stuff, so I said, hell, let's write our own stuff. We did that awhile, all straight-ahead rock."

At Granada Hills High, Doug wasn't what you'd call a straight-ahead student. "I was studious, but not much of a conformist. I sure wasn't a jock. Come time for phys-ed class I'd bring out my guitar, sit in the bleachers, and jam by myself. Or I cut school, as much as I could get away with."

Evidently he got away with it: he graduated. Doug then attended a community college for an uneventful two years. At 19, he moved out of his parents' house and moved in with his sister for two years, until she moved to San Diego. Shortly thereafter, Doug came in contact with personal computers. It was not a life-changing encounter. "The first computer I used was Clark's, my roommate. I played adventure games on his Atari 800, then he moved up to IBM PC. He kept saying, 'Doug, Doug, you need to get into computers,' and I would say, 'That's okay, I got my guitar.' I was fascinated by computer games, but I was too busy trying to acquire money to buy music equipment to be interested in getting another expensive hobby."

What he *was* getting was "sick and tired of the L.A. scene." In early 1987, Doug decided to leave southern California, drive to a small Oregon town where he would stay with a friend, and find a home, a job, and, ultimately, himself.

"The day I was preparing my truck and camper shell for living in the trees, my neighbor dropped by. We rapped, we drank beer. Then he said, 'You oughta come down and meet my daughter.'

"'Your daughter? I didn't know you had a daughter.'

"She was visiting him and I figured, why not? But I'd been drinking all day and I was wasted. I decided to sleep it off before I met her, so I took a nap, then went down to his house and introduced myself to her—Erika. It was the first time in my life I felt easy about meeting someone that way, because I figured, I have nothing to lose, I'm moving out of here."

Wouldnchaknowit, Doug and Erika fell in love. He stuck around. Five months later they married, and then honeymooned in the Pacific Northwest. "We tripped around Oregon and Washington, and on the way back down to L.A., we stayed with friends in Sebastapol [a town west of Santa Rosa]. We thought the area was a cool place to live. So we did our resumes on their computer and then we circulated those resumes around here. Another friend knew about this little place for rent out in the boondocks of Santa Rosa. We loved it. We moved here in August 1987."

Thanks to the couple's job skills, both soon found full-time employment. Today, Doug installs and maintains telephone systems. Erika is a department supervisor for a business forms company.

It was Erika who wanted to buy a home computer. "She found a '286 PC with a color monitor and VGA board, back in the days when they were 900 bucks, like early 1989," Doug recalls. "She set it up on her desk in the bedroom and connected a modem to log onto some BBSs. Couple months went by and finally I asked, 'So how do you work this thing?' She sat me down and showed me how to use DOS. The first thing we got into was playing with fractals, 'cause they're so psychedelic and fun. I was fascinated by the idea that you could write an equation and create a work of art."

Doug and Erika experimented for hours with Fractint, the fractal software available free on various BBSs. But when the rainy season hit Sonoma County in the early months of 1990, Doug turned his attention to building and wiring a recording studio in a small room that his landlord added on to the back of the house, behind the bedroom. Erika let Doug move the computer into the studio, where—with the addition of some new software—it served as his sequencer. (A sequencer records and plays electronically generated music via the communications protocol, Musical Instrument Digital Interface.)

Later that year, Doug first learned about virtual reality in the pages of the counterculture magazine *High Frontiers,* which turned into the technoid *Reality Hackers,* which transformed into its current incarnation as the trendy quarterly *Mondo 2000.* Yet the concepts underlying virtual reality were familiar to him: "My inspiration for VR started back when I saw *Tron* and *Brainstorm* in the early '80s. *Brainstorm* was the tantalizing introduction to the idea that people can share experiences with the aid of computer technology. It was beautifully done. Seeing that movie still brings tears to my eyes, because the idea has so much promise. *Tron* was really VR because it introduced the concept of actually getting inside the computer and dealing as an entity with the hardware and software."

Doug's curiosity about VR and computer art motivated him to drive to Pasadena in November of 1991 to attend the second CyberArts International Conference, a gathering of multimedia and VR exhibits and workshops for techno-savvy artists. "I didn't get to try the VR systems because there was too long a waiting line. But I was so hungry to know more. I read about VR wherever I could. Now that I look back on it, I wasn't hooked in at all, 'cause there was so much *more* information about it. I just didn't know where to find it."

Around that time, Doug started logging long hours in cyberspace on CompuServe's computer art and VR forums. He remembers the exact date he "took the final plunge into VR: July 29, 1992. That night, I returned from vacation. In the mail there was a catalog, 'The Best of GO GRAPHICS' from CompuServe. Leafing through it, I noticed some images that reminded me of M.C. Escher. By this point, VR was always floating in the back of mind, and those two thoughts suddenly collided: Escher. VR. Whoa! What a concept! We can *do* this! I'd always wanted to walk around in Escher's stuff, travel through his worlds in 3D, and I realized the technology's here; this is a possibility *now!*"

This idea became Doug's fixation. He consumed piles of books and articles and megabytes of CompuServe postings about computer art and VR. He sent away for VR product brochures and flyers, seeking software he could afford and that would run on a '286 PC, using the keyboard and mouse for input.

"I wound up building my preliminary Escher world with [Domark's] Virtual Reality Studio version 1. I based the world on the book *The World of M.C. Escher.* I envisioned a virtual world based on Escher's 'World of Stairs,' which has a jillion doorways and stairways. 'World of Stairs' would serve as the hub. All its doorways would be portals to other rooms that contained different Escher artworks. After I built 'World of Stairs,' I linked it to other rooms so you could travel through a universe based entirely on Escher's work. The long-term concept is that people will experience it as Escher creatures in a multiparticipant virtual world. They'll enter it using a computer and modem. I envision hundreds of people walking around this maze-like structure; they'll talk with each other using microphones and virtual sound. It will be like a masquerade party where nobody has ties to their real appearance. A flatworm on the ground might really be a cute co-ed from Wisconsin."

Doug used VR Studio's set of basic "building blocks" to create rough approximations of the shapes in Escher's works. "I would look at the Escher picture and copy it by eye. A limitation of VR Studio is that it only lets you assemble 60 objects maximum in each given space, or room. I had to decide what parts of the pictures to omit, which limited the detail. Also, the result is not to scale. There's no texturing, no Escher creatures. It is a very schematic representation, but I was able to model and get across the idea of an Escher space. Given its limitations, VR Studio is the best way for the money to get your feet wet with VR."

For two weeks, Doug devoted every spare moment to building the Escher world. When he reached the point where the world's condition satisfied him, he wanted to upload it to the CompuServe VR forum "so people could see the result of my original idea, which I had posted earlier. But it took me until December to do that, because I worried about legality. Then I thought, ah, screw it, it's not a direct copy of Escher so I can't get in trouble. Besides, I wanted to make a contribution to the forum, because I'd been downloading stuff from it for months."

Then Doug aimed for the big time; he decided to contact the organization that holds Escher copyrights. In February of 1993 he called the Escher book publisher, who directed him to Cordon Art in the Netherlands, which controls the distribution of Escher's work. "Not being a business-minded kind of guy," Doug admits, "I thought maybe they would provide money for a computer system so we could do this right: put together a team of artists, architects, and CAD programmers to create a networked, high-resolution, texture-mapped, multiparticipant VR. I would coordinate and direct the project as technical liaison. At the very least, I wanted permission to use the art."

The woman with whom Doug first spoke told him to mail a letter describing his request. He sent the letter, along with documentation of the program, and a floppy disk containing the self-running file. He didn't hear from them for three weeks. "They had a monochrome 8088 PC in their office so they couldn't run the program and had to find a '286 clone with decent graphics and a 3 1/2-inch disk drive. They saw it, but they told me it was too slow and that they weren't sure how they felt about Escher's work existing in the digital domain. I tried to explain that it wasn't meant to be software for sale, but a network that people could log onto and explore. They didn't understand. She said they would talk about it and let me know. In April of '93, I received a letter, short and sweet, saying, 'We can't give you permission to go ahead with this project. We're currently under contract with a company in Japan that's doing an Escher museum and they're working on an Escher virtual reality film.' I haven't spoken with them since."

Doug intends to continue developing this project—as soon as he learns what that Japanese company is doing.

Several months earlier, Doug had launched another VR Studio project: Gaynor House. Night after night, he dreamed about the place on Gaynor Street in Sepulveda where he grew up. It was just an old tract house built in the 1940s, he says, but a source of many good memories. One morning, when Doug awoke after yet another dream about the house, he thought, "Maybe this is some kind of demon that I need to exorcise. I have the tools, so I'll build a VR Studio version of it."

As Doug was by now familiar with those tools, it took him a week's worth of spare time to re-create his childhood home: a single floor with three bedrooms, living room, family room, bathroom, garage, office, and backyard with pool and deck. He relied not on a book or photos for inspiration, but on mental images. "I had to visualize it from above and from other perspectives to figure out where the walls intersect and how rooms relate to each other. I just went through my memories to remember how things looked and where the furniture was. I remembered, for instance, the time I climbed through the attic from the den to my bedroom to pull speaker wire so I could crank up my Alice Cooper records.

"If I couldn't immediately model a certain room, I had to sit and think about it. Sooner or later, I'd conjure up a memory associated with the spot. For instance, there was a closet in a little hallway between the den and my dad's office. I had to figure out how

its walls corresponded with the other rooms. To visualize that, I went back to a time when we stored all our Halloween stuff on the shelf in this closet, and one time a creepy rubber mask fell on my face and scared the shit out of me. Remembering exactly where I was, and how I felt, helped me conceptualize those walls.

"During the course of re-creating the Gaynor house, I had many memories that I'd forgotten. It turned out to be not only a cool exercise in modeling, but a therapeutic walk-through of my childhood."

After Doug completed the Gaynor House, he sent a disk with the file to his father in Los Angeles (who didn't need to buy VR Studio, because the program creates self-running versions of its files).

"He called me because he was having trouble making it run. I loaded it in my computer and we toured the house together. There we were, both looking at the same thing, only he's in Los Angeles and I'm in Santa Rosa. I'd say, 'Take a left. See that blue thing? That's the door to my bedroom.' When we'd walk into a room, he'd say, 'Wow, I remember this!' Of course, due to the necessarily low amount of detail, my bedroom was the cleanest it's ever been. Then we went into his bedroom and he said, 'Oh. Twin beds. *That's* a symbol of my marriage, isn't it.' In our garage we'd had a big ol' Shopsmith table saw for building forts and soapbox derby cars. I put that in the garage in the Gaynor House. When we walked in there he said, 'There's the Shopsmith! And my old tool box!' Even though each item was very schematic in its representation, he was able to grok exactly what it was."

Doug also sent copies of the Gaynor House to his sister and mother. He asked them if the house was scaled properly and if it felt like they were really there. They said yes, it's accurate, which told Doug that his sense of perspective is accurate—although his sister and mother wished that Doug had included certain pieces of furniture that *they* remembered.

About two months after Doug showed the house to his family, he dreamed about it again, only this time with a twist. "The whole thing went full circle," Doug shrugs. "Now I'm having dreams that I'm walking around the house in virtual reality."

All this time, Doug had been building his worlds using the mouse and keyboard. He had upgraded his '286 PC to a '386, then a '486. He joined the New Jersey-based Virtual Reality Alliance of Students & Professionals (VRASP). Through CompuServe, he met nearby VRASP members, including Calvin "Vinnie" Grier. In early 1993, Doug and Vinnie took a field trip to the University of California at Berkeley to play the student union's Virtuality game system. That was Doug's first experience with immersive VR; his second came a few hours later when Vinnie brought Doug to his office. Vinnie had connected a pair of Toshiba LCD shutter glasses and the Mattel Power Glove to his PC, on which he'd built a few virtual worlds using REND386.

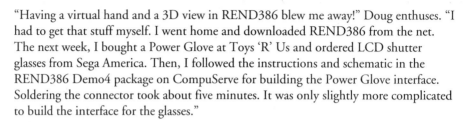

Putting VR on the Map
Douglas W. Faxon

"Having a virtual hand and a 3D view in REND386 blew me away!" Doug enthuses. "I had to get that stuff myself. I went home and downloaded REND386 from the net. The next week, I bought a Power Glove at Toys 'R' Us and ordered LCD shutter glasses from Sega America. Then, I followed the instructions and schematic in the REND386 Demo4 package on CompuServe for building the Power Glove interface. Soldering the connector took about five minutes. It was only slightly more complicated to build the interface for the glasses."

Although Doug enjoys the Power Glove, he admits he "can't use it for everything, which is why I still use the mouse as my main tool. A mouse is a piece of machinery that gets between you and the computer, though. You just slap on the Power Glove and now you have something that tracks every movement of your hand. That to me is a better interface. The best computer/human interfaces are tied intimately to our regular body movements. A head-tracker must be able to really track the way you move your head. I want computer interfaces to be like a second skin. I want a body suit!"

With that idea simmering in the back of his mind, one wet March day Doug had an epiphany. "I'd been playing around with Vistapro, a landscape generator that renders three-dimensional, realistic landscape scenes based upon a topographical map that you can edit. You can create rivers, lakes, waterfalls, clouds, and all kinds of fun stuff. I was using it to create fly-throughs and animations of randomly generated landscapes. I thought it would be cool to actually walk through these scenes in real time. Especially when it's raining outside, and you're going to get all wet and miserable if you go hiking.

"Suddenly I thought, hey, Erika just bought a stairclimber—there's my interface! All I had to do was figure out how to hook it up to my computer. I had to create a modification that would connect the stairclimber to the serial port. The concept is, you're walking on the stairclimber in your living room, only you're seeing a computer-generated landscape. The stairclimber has a servo-controller, so when you encounter an incline, the stairclimber cranks down the valve and makes it harder to walk. When you're walking down a hill or slope, the stairclimber cranks that valve the other way; the software tells the serial port to make it easier to walk on the stairclimber. You build a rule into your software to kick in the servo-motor at certain times."

Doug wrote a letter to Virtual Reality Laboratories, Inc. (VRLI, which makes Vistapro), suggesting that they create a version of Vistapro to work with the stairclimber. He learned that VRLI subcontracts its software programming, and that they're not in a position to work on such a project. Doug intends to secure funding so that he can research and develop a range of computer interfaces for exercise machines. His goal (one of *many*) is to "get enough money to pay VRLI to adapt their software to a computer platform, then make it so Vistapro can render in real time with a head-mount display."

When Doug was working on the stairclimber system, he thought of Mark Pflaging, the East Coast-based VRASP organizer who loves hacking the Power Glove. Doug calls

Mark "the god of the Glove." In late 1992, Mark created a two-glove demo, an interface that lets you see two virtual hands in one virtual world.

Doug recalls, "I thought, if you can have two gloves as inputs, both independently tracked, why not use one of them as a head-tracker? Other people had tried using the Power Glove as a head-tracker and they said it didn't work. I didn't let them stop me. I figured if you can't use the sensor in the Power Glove as a Polhemus-type, six-degree-of-freedom tracker because it has to work on line-of-sight, then you could make it face the screen to create a small cursor. The position of that cursor would determine the view on-screen. Using it in conjunction with another Power Glove, you can touch objects, select them, pick them up, and move them around—a complete VR system that costs less than 150 bucks!"

Doug knew what he wanted to do, but he lacked the programming chops to do it. He wrote down his idea and e-mailed it to Mark, who lives in New Jersey. Mark liked it. He went about adapting his Power Glove/REND386 code to Doug's specifications. Meanwhile, Doug ripped the ultrasonic sensor from a Power Glove and mounted it on the beak of a plastic baseball helmet. After Mark reached a satisfactory point in programming, he would upload a copy of his code to Doug's CompuServe mailbox. Doug would retrieve the code, load it on his system, and try it. Then he would make recommendations to Mark, again through e-mail, on how to improve it.

Working 3,000 miles apart, Doug and Mark created a successful head-tracker. At a VR industry conference in San Jose, California in May of 1993, they demonstrated the head-tracking system in the VRASP exhibit booth. For three days, adults and kids waited in line to don the navy plastic baseball helmet and gray plastic Power Glove, ascend the red plastic stairclimber, and cheerfully interact with Doug's colorful virtual worlds.

"We're still developing the interface," Doug says. "We're including absolute up/down control, so when you tilt your head up, the screen view tilts up a bit. It will be proportional, of course, because you can't look at the sky and still see the screen.

"Also, I put the first head-tracker on the brim of a baseball helmet. I did that so we could maximize its movement from left to right, which would let the sensors track it more easily. But I learned you don't need to place the head-tracker that far from your head. When it's clipped to your glasses, it works just as well. This relates more to its angle rather than to its relative position in space." Figure P3.1 shows this head-tracker.

As you read this, Doug is developing several new VR projects— both hardware and software. He is characteristically blunt about VR today and VR tomorrow: "I'm a dyed-in-the-wool agnostic, so I don't have a problem saying I like to play God. Programs like Fractint, Vistapro, and Virtual Reality Studio let you do that: you can create worlds in the computer that don't exist in reality. They can be beautiful. They can be expressive. They can be emotive.

Figure P3.1. *Doug in his studio, wearing his Power Glove and his head-tracker, which is clipped to the frame of his eyeglasses. Doug is using these devices to control a REND386 scene on the PC. (Photos of Doug Faxon by Linda Jacobson)*

"But right now I spend all my time in those worlds alone. One crucial aspect of improving VR is making it social and participatory through networking. I want other people interacting with me in there. I want to walk around in a maze where the walls shift, where I can meet people to play a game with unpredictable quotients. If you like to hang out in bars or nightclubs, you can save money by drinking at home while meeting people in a virtual lounge. There are movements underway to create net-worked, affordable virtual reality available over modem so more than one participant can exist in the virtual universe at a given time. I see the future of VR as a great place to meet people when you can't get out of the house. So, I want to take VR out of the garage and put it in the living room."

Tour Guide's Toolbox

Stock '486 PC clone with VGA graphics card, 16MB RAM, sound card

15-inch color monitor

500MB external hard drive

Twincom 14.4 fax/modem

Standard keyboard

Logitech Trackman mouse

Mattel Power Glove

Power Glove/serial port interface box, built based on plans included with the REND386 demo program (parts cost approximately $2)

Software: DR-DOS operating system ("I try to stay out of Windows, because it's such a resource sapper; operating in the DOS environment doesn't take 8 megs to load up."), Vistapro 3.03, Virtual Reality Studio 1 and 2, REND386

Music to build worlds by: "Music that's going on in my head. Also, killer guitar masters like Steve Vai and Joe Satriani. The Residents. Progressive bands. I've learned to appreciate all kinds of music, but I'm rock and roll at heart."

Approximate cost of total system: $1,500

E-mail: rzone@well.sf.ca.us and 75720.3413@compuserve.com

GARAGE VR GARAGE VR GARAGE VR

The Universe of M.C. Escher: A 3D Journey
by Douglas W. Faxon

This essay describes a virtual world that Doug first envisioned on July 19, 1992. He wants to make this world a reality by assembling a group of artists and designers to sculpt the space with great precision and detail. If you're intrigued by this idea, contact Doug via e-mail.

The artworks created by Mauritis Cornelis Escher (1898-1972) in many cases flaunt the laws of geometry and perspective in ways that, in earlier days, would have been impractical or impossible to depict in the 3D space in which we live. Within the realm of virtual reality, however, these striking dimensional oddities can be experienced by cyberspace visitors in all their 3D glory from a node on the network near them.

Putting VR on the Map
Douglas W. Faxon

Each visitor will first choose from a menu of Escher's many creatures, assuming the form and limitations of that creature during hir [sic] visit. After a body is chosen, the visitor begins hir journey in the "House of Stairs," an Escher lithograph depicting a large room full of stairways and doorways (hereafter referred to as portals) at various angles to our "ordinary" plane of gravity. The House of Stairs will be the central hub of this universe, providing a sort of "reference point" for lost travelers. In this room, the various gravitational orientations implied in Escher's original work will be simulated by the computer, so that, as a visitor moves through the space, s/he will experience periodic re-orientation of hir personal gravity. The portals at the ends of the walkways will lead to other "rooms," other Escher spaces rendered in 3D for our journey through the astounding and oftentimes startling world of this great artist.

As visitors move through Escher-spaces, they will meet each other's Escher-forms wherever their paths cross, examine and manipulate Escher-objects (i.e., crystals, sculptures, mirror-balls), and experience Escher gravity fields and surface distortions. The more visitors in the universe, the more interactive it becomes, as objects and lifeforms are moved from place to place within the realm. If a visitor's chosen form's limitations prevent entry or exit from a given space due to size or maneuverability, s/he will be provided with an opportunity to exchange identities with one more suitable for the occasion.

The Universe of M.C. Escher will be accessible to anyone with a modem for a monthly subscription fee. Other virtual universes will be added to the system by our design team as time and funding become available. Part fun house, part art museum, and part amusement park, people everywhere will want to experience the Universe of M.C. Escher. With the vastness of Escher's many worlds to choose from, a visitor will probably never encounter the same universe twice. They certainly won't be the same afterwards!

A good reference for viewing Escher's work (the one that I used) is *The World of M.C. Escher,* available at most fine bookstores or through the publisher Harry N. Abrams, Inc. in New York.

The Fuel

Software for Garage VR

CHAPTER
7

The Fuel

Software for Garage VR

Self-serve or full-serve?

R. Eberly '93

You can deck out your reality engine with fancy degrees-of-freedom input and stereo-scopic output gadgets, but it won't go anywhere unless there's fuel in the tank. All that cool hardware is useless without software to create a visualization and present an interactive simulation: the virtual world.

Today's garage VR fancier can choose from three categories of low-cost (or free) software:

1. Power Glove control programs
2. Programs that provide a graphical user interface for relative easy creation of virtual walk-throughs and fly-throughs, with limited or no interaction
3. Dynamic toolkits for serious programmers who want to create fully interactive, immersive worlds

The current software selection, however, doesn't include a VR equivalent to Lotus 1-2-3, Microsoft Word, Aldus PageMaker, or Apple's HyperCard. No software publisher offers an easy programming language for building interactive, immersive virtual worlds. This means that building such a world is an intense, time-consuming experience. You can't just pump the pedal and take off.

Let's say you want to create an interactive virtual world. You need to create the en-vironment and populate it with virtual objects and characters. Toward that end, you build primitive models and modify their appearance so they look realistic. You can use an interactive 3D graphics application to do so; such programs also let you change your viewpoint of the object (rotate it, for instance) or field of view (look at it from near or far) in real time.

Interactive 3D graphics isn't VR, though. A VR application is an animated simulation that lets you define and display a 3D object, alter your viewpoint and field of view, manipulate and interact with the object, and cause the object to affect other objects. That's all possible because VR software lets you imbue objects with behaviors—you can give them physical properties (gravity, elasticity, weight) and program them to trigger some kind of visual, audio, or tactile feedback when a particular event occurs. The VR software also manages the proper sequencing of events across a simulation frame and gives you a way to access various sensors and effectors, including audio output devices.

Less time and effort (and programming chops) are required to create a simple virtual walk-through or fly-through. You might not be able to interact with objects, but you can "walk" or "fly" around the environment in real time, as opposed to viewing a canned, prerecorded playback. For this type of application, you can build a 3D model and use it to make frame-by-frame renderings with light, shadows, and textures. Finally, you can animate the results to create the experience of walking through a structure or other environment.

In both these VR software categories, building a world means you're creating an *application*. Just as a page-layout program is an application that lets you design a newsletter, a VR world is an application that lets you accomplish a task—even if it's as basic as inflating a virtual flat tire with a virtual air pump.

The visualization that enables a virtual world application is a collection of 3D models, technically known as *geometry data,* or simply "geometry." Geometry data consists of coordinate values; in other words, every point in space (every point that makes up a graphic object) can be described in terms of three coordinate values: the values of x, y, and z.

As you can see, an understanding of computer graphics contributes to your ability to create worlds. Likewise, a little programming knowledge goes a long way. If you want to master one of the several versatile VR toolkits, you must know how to construct and edit 3D models, program in C, and handle device interfaces. No matter what fuel you feed your reality engine, you need certain skills to drive.

"The actual creation of *any* kind of VR environment is an adventure in itself," says garage VR pioneer Dave Stampe, who coauthored the public-domain renderer REND386. "The problem is to get tools. To create your own tools, you have to be expert in programming, 3D graphics, matrix algebra, hardware, etc., and a little crazy besides. My REND386 project tries to create the tools, but development is incremental.

"Typically, VR hackers are stymied by the lack of world creation tools (and there's not many hackers who really have *all* their hardware working—most are still at the desktop display stage). Creating objects point by point and placing them in the world by 'guess-and-gosh' is rather frustrating. The situation is improving, but the problem is that good editors (like VREAM) are pretty slow when it comes to actually walking through your world, while fast drawing systems like REND386 have not had enough work done on editing tools. These two functions have to be combined, or you have to get both programs and some way to swap data between them. But the potential is enormous."

In exploring that potential, this book provides an overview of the fuels and tools you need to build virtual worlds. An explanation of how to actually use each program would result in a weighty tome. The goal is to understand the basic components, features, and capabilities of each package and the concepts involved in world-building.

World-Building Nuts and Bolts (in a Nutshell)

Every VR software package employs different tools and techniques to let you design, enter, and interact with a virtual world. Yet most world-building systems share some basic concepts that characterize virtual reality development… concepts that enable developers to create a simulation, an illusion, that feels like another world.

The Universe and Its Objects

Whether your world simulates a playground, factory, supermarket, beach, temple, museum, or concert hall, you've created a *universe* that contains *objects*, also known as entities. (Sense8's WorldToolKit defines *universe* as a collection of linked worlds, and *world* as the active environment portion of a universe simulation.)

Objects are characterized by

Geometry: The shape of the object.

Appearance: The object's size, color, texture, lighting, and shadows, all of which are applied to the object's geometry.

Behavior: The object's reaction(s) to events. Dynamics control interactions between objects, such as collision and gravitational force. Behavior also refers to the sound generated by an object.

An object might be a point of view, which is attached to a sensor. An object might perform a task when the simulation reaches a particular frame. Both of these possibilities concern object behavior.

Objects link to each other using *hierarchies*. In other words, a complex object, such as a cuckoo clock, actually comprises several individually constructed objects, including the enclosure, the clock face, the clock arms, the peaked roof, the little doors, and the cuckoo bird. All those objects must be linked to create one dynamic object that marks time, opens its doors, and sings *cuckoo, cuckoo* at a predetermined moment.

Presentation Techniques

Any object consists of a logically connected set of polygons: multisided, two-dimensional figures—usually triangles.

Once you assemble the polygons into an object's geometry, you render the object, giving it a realistic (or at least distinctive) appearance. Rendering represents the optical phenomena that occur when light interacts with an object's surfaces. It involves color, light sources, and texture. Rendering is performed in wireframe, shaded, or textured modes, using various sources of image data; you might generate shading from within the world-building program, for instance, or import external data files. Texture-mapping, in fact, is a great way to reduce a scene's complexity (polygon count) while producing more detailed views. In some worlds, you'll notice that what *appears* to be a 3D object is really a texture-mapped polygon that rotates to face you whenever you change your point of view.

The presentation process—the use of shading, lighting, and textures, and the determination of field and points of view—is where you can make up for the questionable visual quality that results from the low resolution typical of garage VR—simply by applying abundant artistic imagination.

Virtual-world-builders often borrow techniques from the field of 3D design, in which the experts value psychological *depth cues* that help impart the illusion of three-dimensional space. The most important cues are

Linear perspective: An object's size decreases as the participant's view moves farther from the object. (The farther away your viewpoint, the less detail you can see.)

Motion parallax: When you move your head, you see different parts of an object. You see less if it's far away, and more if it's close.

Overlap: An object covers part of an object that's behind it (also called *occlusion*).

Shading: The intensity of light falling on an object is different for different parts of that object, because of the object's contours. Generally, parts of an object perpendicular to a light source are brightest; those at angles are dimmer. To increase the effect of depth and distance, fade an object's color as the viewpoint moves farther away. Similarly, you can vary an object's opacity to impart the illusion that you're seeing *into* or *through* something.

Shadows: Shadows are caused by an object's placement between a light source and another object.

Dynamics and Feedback

Professional VR world-builders often place more emphasis on the *interaction* between a participant and a virtual environment than on the appearance of the images in that environment.

Interactivity engages the imagination and sparks the all-important "suspension of disbelief" required for a successful VR experience.

This is where you give the world and its objects their attributes, or physical dynamics. What happens when you throw a virtual frisbee? Does it soar off into the distance, maintaining its rigid shape, or does it bend and flop like a flying tortilla before falling to the ground? Other than gravity and weight are physical dynamics that include elasticity, collision detection, and auditory feedback.

Your sensors, or input devices, play a big role here; you can connect them to lights, objects, and viewpoints.

Portals also add to the interactivity quotient. They cause the system to automatically present a new environment when the participant passes through a predetermined portal, or gateway.

Sound creates a powerful sense of presence, whether it's ambient sound, sound effects, music, or voices. Originating from a digitized sound file, algorithm, or external device, such as a CD player or MIDI instrument, sound might play continuously in an environment or appear as a brief snippet triggered by some event. When you script the environment, you specify a time or event at which you want the sound to play.

Consider the acoustic properties of the virtual sound source. If your virtual frisbee hits a virtual wall, it makes a different sound than if it splashes into a virtual fountain. Here's where such effects processing such as reverberation and echo come into play.

If your VR system supports three-dimensional sound, you also must consider whether your sound sources move when you move your viewpoint. Does the sound grow stronger when you face the audible object and grow softer when you turn away? Similarly, consider the pitch-changing nature of the Doppler effect: the growl of a car's muffler gets lower in volume and pitch as the car drives away from you.

Sound also helps impart depth cues; a sound may grow louder as your viewpoint brings you closer to the audible object.

> ### Skimming the Surface
>
> We've only touched on the myriad issues and challenges involved in building worlds. Along with rolling up your sleeves and breaking virtual ground, you can learn some basic techniques of world creation by analyzing the implementations used in VR demos. Cast a critical eye over the demos provided on this book's disk and the demos that are available through the Internet and commercial online services.

3D Modeling

To create VR applications, you need a convenient way of importing and exporting three-dimensional geometries (data describing the spatial attributes of virtual objects), or a way to dynamically create new geometries within the world.

You also can create the 3D models in a modeling program, give them textures that you developed using an image processing or paint program, and import the finished 3D model files into the world-building program.

Modeling is the act of creating three-dimensional objects and scenes. All 3D modeling programs provide the same basic tools and capabilities. These include *primitives* (basic drawing elements such as solid boxes, pyramids, cones, tori, and so on), *snap-to* options (that bring objects into alignment and constrain lines and angles), layers, symbol libraries, and other tools for design.

To create a 3D model, you define the geometrical shape of an object. You define the shape with a process that transforms the coordinate values of any point in *3-space* (x, y, and z) to on-screen coordinates. See Figure 7.1.

Three-dimensional modeling often is based on primitives called *polygons*. The basic building block of virtual objects, a polygon is a flat plane figure with multiple straight sides. (In VR, the polygon typically is a three- or four-sided shape.) When constructing objects based on polygons, you approximate curved shapes by cleverly arranging straight-line segments.

The most popular method for representing an object is the *polygon mesh model*. A cube-shaped object may be a mesh of six square polygons. The cylinder shown in Figure 7.2 consists of eight rectangle polygons for the curved surface and two octagons for the ends.

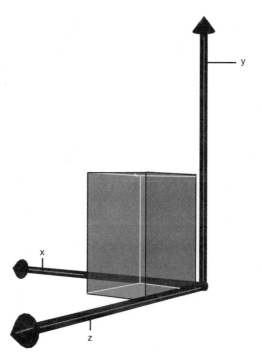

Figure 7.1. *x, y, and z coordinates.*

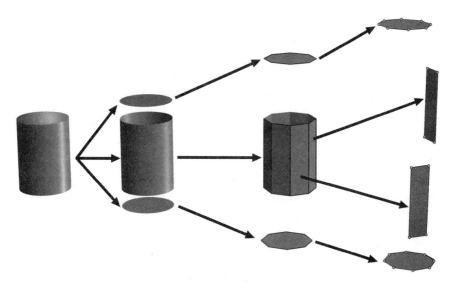

Figure 7.2. *A cylinder consisting of polygonal mesh.*

Some 3D modeling programs combine modeling, rendering, and animation:

Rendering is the process of drawing an image of a 3D model. Textures, light sources, and surfaces can be used to produce lifelike, or at least more realistic, images.

Animation causes objects and lights to move within your field of view. Each scene or frame is played one after another at a rate that makes it look as if things are moving smoothly. In the real-time (not canned) animation characteristic of VR, you can alter the coordinates of your viewpoint.

The modeling and rendering processes can incorporate any of several techniques. The better the technique makes an object look, the more processing time it requires, and the more memory it consumes.

A model generally starts out in life as a wireframe (a basic outline) an object with edges created by line segments. It's transparent, so a wireframe lets you see all the "hidden lines" that make up its edges. The graphics engine can draw wireframes quickly, but a complex 3D scene filled with wireframes is hard to comprehend.

Therefore, a technique (actually, an algorithm) called *hidden line removal* eliminates lines on the wireframe that wouldn't ordinarily be visible when the model is viewed from a particular angle. This makes the object look solid.

Rendering an object treats its surface to create realistic effects. The primary rendering technique for VR is *shading*. In computer graphics, there are two kinds of shading: flat and smooth.

Flat (or constant) *shading* renders each facing polygon by applying a single color value that represents the amount of light interacting with that face. This addition of basic, flat (not highlighted or gradated) color to the object gives it shape and makes it look solid.

Smooth shading, which monopolizes the processor's attention even more than flat shading, also lends more realism. One type of smooth shading is *Gourand shading.* This technique adds shading and lighting effects that give shapes a smooth surface with clear definition and reproduction of the scene's lighting. Gourand shading makes surfaces look as if they reflect light diffusely. Another smooth-shading technique is *Phong shading,* the addition of calculated highlights. Phong shading can be enhanced by shading that gives shapes accurate surface properties, such as wood grain, marble, chocolate, and chrome. Phong-capable programs present the effects of lighting more realistically by adding highlights, blends, shadows, reflections, and transparency.

In the CPU-intensive world of VR, programmers simulate smooth-shading techniques with *texture-mapping,* which lets you apply real or synthetic 2D images to the face of the 3D model. (Usually these 2D images are based on scanned-in photos of wood grain, marble, chocolate, chrome, and similar surface treatments.)

When choosing a 3D modeling program for use with a VR world-builder, some features to look for include

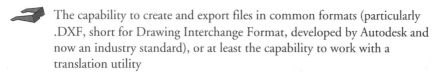 The capability to create and export files in common formats (particularly .DXF, short for Drawing Interchange Format, developed by Autodesk and now an industry standard), or at least the capability to work with a translation utility

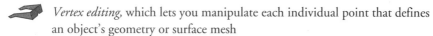 *Vertex editing,* which lets you manipulate each individual point that defines an object's geometry or surface mesh

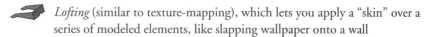 *Lofting* (similar to texture-mapping), which lets you apply a "skin" over a series of modeled elements, like slapping wallpaper onto a wall

 *Spline modeling,* which lets you draw true curved lines

PC modeling: The DOS-based AutoCAD and 3D Studio packages, both by Autodesk, make the "Most Wanted" lists in professional VR development houses. However, they cost thousands of dollars. More appropriate 3D modelers for PC-based VR are the $300 Presidio Software 3D Workshop, $250 DesignCAD, and the $80 Quest NorthCAD Pro. (NorthCAD is sold directly by the Quest Company of Fresno, California, (209) 222-5301.)

VR world-builders who don't want to sculpt their own models can buy ready-made 3D models from a company called Viewpoint (Orem, Utah, (801) 224-2222). You can choose from hundreds of 3D clip models in various graphics formats, in varying degrees of polygonal complexity, and in dozens of categories (anatomy, transportation, toys, and so on). The catalog is free, but the models can cost you anywhere from $50 to $5,000, with an average price of around $400.

Macintosh modeling: There are plenty of 3D graphics programs for the Macintosh, but not many are as versatile and inexpensive as the $300 (retail) Ray Dream Designer. Ideal for garage VR object development, this full-fledged modeling and rendering package imports and exports files in a variety of formats, including .DXF and PICT. It can render a scene with an unlimited number of light sources, and it comes with a library of editable 3D objects and surface properties, including textures.

Amiga modeling: Many Amiga 3D modeling and rendering packages carry garage-friendly price tags. The popular Impulse Imagine retails for about $260 (with solid modeling, texture mapping, and animation), whereas Pixel 3D Pro costs about $170. Some programs cost nothing; one powerful, full-featured rendering package, Rayshade, is a ray-tracing program available on Fred Fish disk #707. Listings of Fred Fish disks appear in *Amazing Computing* (the monthly Amiga magazine) and in *AC's Guide to the Commodore Amiga* (sold by Amiga dealers).

Amiga-Based VR

When deciding which program to buy to create interactive, immersive virtual worlds, Amiga owners don't need to spend much time mulling over their options. In fact, they don't have to spend any time. There *are* no options.

With that in mind, here's a generalization: Amigaphiles are clever people who don't conform to the norm. Ergo, Amigaphiles are the type of computer owners who don't mind getting some data dirt under their fingernails. They'll do whatever it takes to stick their heads and hands in a virtual world.

Chris Hufnagel (chuff@ursula.ee.pdx.edu) represents one such dedicated technoid. An electrical engineering student, Chris owns an Amiga 3000 with 14 megs of RAM, a 300-meg hard drive, a large VGA monitor, and an SAS/C compiler.

"I have always been a graphically oriented person," Chris says. "Numbers are more abstract to me than a Van Gogh painting." With the intention of creating a virtual Van Gogh-like experience to explore, Chris interfaced a Power Glove to his machine, then went about programming his own world-building software. He wrote it mostly in C, sprinkling in some assembly code to enhance the performance.

After creating the development system, Chris started using it to design and display plain vector-based graphics. Then, he moved up to solid vectors. Chris reports, "The worlds I'm creating now are weird, to say the least. I started out with your basic 'town' world: small houses to walk around in, and not much else. Now I'm working on a more 'trippy' world. I've taken a few things from *Alice in Wonderland* and actually include puzzles that need to be solved. I intend to release it as public-domain when I get it finished. I hope that I can integrate my efforts into the real world one day. Somehow, some way. It's all for fun right now."

Amiga owners who balk at assembling custom toolkits may prefer a commercial package, even if it doesn't support immersive (first-person) VR. Tensor Productions' CyberScape does, however, provide the Amiga engine with an affordable style of VR that is relatively easy to develop. The CyberScape authoring system takes the same approach to VR as Myron Krueger (Videoplace artificial reality) and the Vivid Group (Mandala system). You watch yourself visiting a virtual world—made possible by video input to the computer system.

CyberScape is script-based, event-driven authoring software that turns two-dimensional animations into simple virtual worlds. It supports the Power Glove (hires mode), digitized and MIDI sound files, and ARexx events. Its features include collision detection between objects and boundaries and the capability to define such object dynamics as velocity, acceleration, and gravity. You can program objects to trigger events upon contact, including scene transitions, and, for games, keeping score.

This package, which requires a video camera and digitizer, runs at 640x400 screen resolution with 4,096 colors, supporting standard Amiga picture, brush, and animation files.

Priced at $245, CyberScape comes with an object library and some source code (source code licensing is available).

For information, contact

Tensor Productions
819 Gwyne Avenue
Santa Barbara, CA 93111
(805) 683-2165
E-mail: `cshen@bix.com` or `cshen@sbcha0.sbrc.hac.com`

A Checklist of Software Features

Before we delve into the individual package descriptions, here is a checklist of general traits to consider when investigating your software acquisition:

- What kind of application do you want to develop: Power Glove controller, walk-through/fly-through, interactive, or immersive virtual world?
- Does the program present realistic-looking worlds by supporting shaded polygons, texture-mapping, and/or anti-aliasing (the removal of jagged edges—another way to add realism)?
- Does the program require that you specify coordinate values to create objects, or does it provide drawing tools?

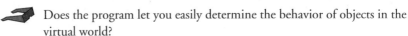 Does the program let you easily determine the behavior of objects in the virtual world?

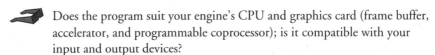 Does the program suit your engine's CPU and graphics card (frame buffer, accelerator, and programmable coprocessor); is it compatible with your input and output devices?

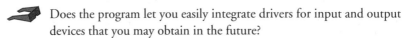 Does the program let you easily integrate drivers for input and output devices that you may obtain in the future?

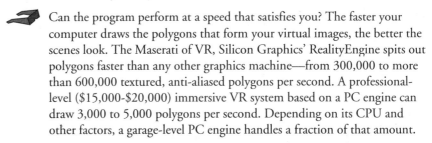 Can the program perform at a speed that satisfies you? The faster your computer draws the polygons that form your virtual images, the better the scenes look. The Maserati of VR, Silicon Graphics' RealityEngine spits out polygons faster than any other graphics machine—from 300,000 to more than 600,000 textured, anti-aliased polygons per second. A professional-level ($15,000-$20,000) immersive VR system based on a PC engine can draw 3,000 to 5,000 polygons per second. Depending on its CPU and other factors, a garage-level PC engine handles a fraction of that amount.

The trade-off for image complexity (number of polygons) is performance (frames per second). As discussed earlier, the fps specification determines the smooth, lag-free appearance of your virtual world. However, the more complex the object you're interacting with, the slower the frame rate. If you're simply zooming around in the middle of a cloudless (virtual) sky, the frame rate soars. Other factors that notch the performance measuring stick are the use of texture-mapping and anti-aliasing, which slow down the speed. So does the presentation of stereoscopic images.

An acceptable frame rate for a low-end, immersive world is about 10 to 12 frames per second. If you divide the polygons-per-second figure by the fps figure, you can figure out how many polygons it takes to build that virtual world. For example, if the PC engine can draw 1,000 polygons each second, and you divide that by 10 fps, you'll get 100 polygons to use in the scene.

As a result, of all these factors (and because hardware systems come in all different configurations), it's tough to give precise performance numbers until you run the software on your own engine.

Garage VR Software Packages

Vistapro 3.0 by Virtual Reality Laboratories, Inc.

Engine requirements: Amiga, Macintosh II, PC (386 or 486 PC with VGA or SVGA card, VESA-compatible, 486/33MHz recommended), DOS 3.0 or better, 4MB RAM (at least 2MB of free extended memory, although more is recommended for handling larger images and landscapes), and a mouse.

Retail price: $80.00 for PC and Macintosh versions; $99.95 for Amiga.

Support for VR-style I/O devices? Yes, stereoscopic shutter glasses.

Support for stereo images? Yes.

Support for interactive sound? No.

Comments: No programming skills are required. Virtual Reality Labs, the publisher of Vistapro, runs a discussion area in the CompuServe Graphics Vendors forum. The disk that comes with this book contains a demo program for the PC.

Source:

> Virtual Reality Laboratories, Inc.
> 2341 Gandor Court
> San Luis Obispo, CA 93401
> (805) 545-8515

Vistapro is a three-dimensional landscape simulation program that lets you create beautifully rendered, animated fly-throughs (see Figure 7.3). You can view them with stereoscopic shutter glasses. Vistapro is not "VR"; you can't interact with virtual objects in it. It doesn't accept input in real time, update viewing angle on a regular basis or render in real time (because of its complexity).

Figure 7.3. A scene from Vistapro.

What it *can* do is render 24-bit landscapes in more than 16 million colors from topological maps based on converted DEM files (Digital Elevation Models created by the U.S. Geological Survey). Nineteen DEM landscapes are included with Vistapro, including Grand Canyon, Yosemite, Mt. Shasta, Olympus Mons on Mars, Japan's Mt. Fuji, and other landscapes. You also can use Vistapro to produce more than *four billion* imaginary landscapes, randomly generated from its fractal algorithms (which can result in scenes that are more interesting than those found on Earth).

Using Vistapro's graphical user interface, first you determine your viewing angle of the scene. After you give it a camera angle and target position, Vistapro renders the elevation contours on a three-dimensional plane. You can put in 3D oaks, pines, palms, cacti, sagebrush, clouds, lakes, streams, snow lines, valleys, and rocks with granite surfaces. You can scale up existing hills into mountains.

Another nifty feature is the capability to add roads, buildings, animals, and so forth by superimposing a .PCX file (the standard IBM PC graphics format) over the landscape.

Those .DEM files that generate images contain coordinate and elevation data at 100-foot increments. Each small .DEM file contains about 65,000 elevation data points and generates 130,000 polygons, whereas a large .DEM file contains about 256,000 data points and generates 512,000 polygons. It supports screen resolutions of up to 1280x1024. On top of that, Vistapro offers blending, texture, and Gourand shading controls to improve the appearance of landscapes.

Vistapro's English-based scripting language enables "transparent" creation of multiple views of a landscape, primarily for animations. Scripts consist of camera and target positions that are landscape-independent; you can use the same script for different landscapes. Script control lets you make changes in a landscape without having to rewrite the script; for example, to change the light source direction, or to see the landscape from different views with and without water, make the appropriate changes and execute the modified script.

The Amiga version supports ARexx and also outputs files that you can convert to .DXF, which you can port into a conversion utility that in turn will convert them to .PLG to run in REND386 on a PC. MegageM's $65 ScapeMaker 3.0 converts Amiga .IFF images, pictures, and logos into landscape files (DEMs) for 3D rendering on VistaPro.

Optional VistaPro "Scape" disks are available for $39 each, with DEMs such as Mars, Yosemite, Kings Canyon National Park, Grand Canyon, San Francisco Bay Area, and Glacier National Park.

VistaPro currently takes up to a half-hour (on a medium-speed engine) to render complicated images. Hopefully, Virtual Reality Labs eventually will give their rendering tool some real-time capabilities.

WalkThrough by Virtus Corporation

Engine requirements: PC ('386 or better, with VGA monitor, 486/33MHz recommended), Microsoft Windows 3.1 or later, and 4MB RAM minimum (8MB or more recommended).

You also need a Macintosh (any model, although Mac II and better are recommended), 2MB RAM or more, System 6.0.4 or later, and a color monitor (recommended).

WalkThrough Pro: Macintosh II or later (68020+), System 6.0.4 or later, 4MB RAM (Mac II Centris/Quadra, System 7.1+, and 8MB+ RAM recommended).

Retail price: $195 for WalkThrough/Mac and WalkThrough/Windows, $395 for WalkThrough Pro, $149 for upgrade to Pro for WalkThrough owners.

Support for VR-style I/O devices? Monitor, mouse, and keyboard support is the rule, but some hackers have hooked up their Power Gloves to their Macs for WalkThrough control.

Support for stereo images? No.

Support for interactive sound? No.

Comments: No programming skills required. Virtus Voyager demo files of prerecorded walk-throughs are available through FTP from `ftp.u.washington.edu`, directory: PUBLIC/VIRTUAL-WORLDS/VIRTUS. Libraries of 3D models are available through America Online ("Industry Connection: Virtus Corporation Models."). Virtus also runs an America Online virtual reality discussion group, with Virtus programmers discussing enhancements in progress. The disk that comes with this book contains demo files.

Source:

> Virtus Corporation
> 117 Edinburgh South, Suite 204
> Cary, NC 27511
> (919) 467-9700
> (800) 847-8871
> E-mail: `virtus@applelink.apple.com` (also on America Online)

Designed in 1990 by Virtus president David Smith, WalkThrough is a 3D modeling and visualization program. Its main purpose is to let the user visualize spatial relationships to support the conceptual development of buildings and structures. Although WalkThrough creates static worlds only, it rates as garage VR because you can "walk through" (using the mouse to change your viewpoint) your virtual environment as you construct it. The model permits on-the-fly alterations, which means you can quickly modify the 3D database and view it from the inside.

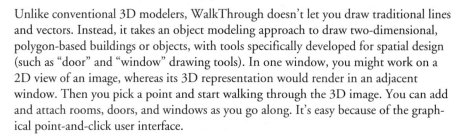

Unlike conventional 3D modelers, WalkThrough doesn't let you draw traditional lines and vectors. Instead, it takes an object modeling approach to draw two-dimensional, polygon-based buildings or objects, with tools specifically developed for spatial design (such as "door" and "window" drawing tools). In one window, you might work on a 2D view of an image, whereas its 3D representation would render in an adjacent window. Then you pick a point and start walking through the 3D image. You can add and attach rooms, doors, and windows as you go along. It's easy because of the graphical point-and-click user interface.

Mark Reaney, who designed the head-mounted display and VR Window (presented in Chapter 8), runs his Mac-based VR system with WalkThrough because "it lets me build a scenic model in a couple of hours and easily modify it as the design process proceeds, checking the work through the VR interface as I go."

Some of WalkThrough's features that make it appealing to CAD and low-end VR users are object modeling tools (which you can customize), flat-shade rendering with transparency effects, color and lighting controls, support for vertex editing, and lofting. Through pull-down windows, you can access preconstructed, architectural clip objects from Virtus' small library of 3D chairs, desks, cabinets, and other furniture and appliances. (After you send in your registration card, Virtus sends you two free "bonus libraries.") You can import and export .DXF and PICT files, plus other types of files for texture-mapping.

One of the "Virtus Rules" states: "Speed and detail are inversely proportional." In other words, running large models slows down the machine. Likewise, transparent and translucent objects and surfaces look good, but they drain processing power.

WalkThrough for Macintosh and WalkThrough for Windows are identical in use, although the PC version comes with a neat cardboard cube that serves as a handy navigation guide. It also helps you understand the relationship between the flat, 2D screen and the 3D "Virtus World."

With WalkThrough Pro, shown in Figures 7.4 and 7.5, you get real-time texture mapping; the program's surface feature libraries give you access to Virtus and other PICT-based graphics for mapping onto 3D surfaces. Virtus supplies libraries containing carpet and other floor and wall textures, plus grass and trees for outdoor scenes. Alternatively, you can create an illustration in a paint- or image-processing program and place that as a texture in your WalkThrough world. WalkThrough Pro moves beyond the static nature of WalkThrough by letting you place QuickTime movies or PICS animations as textures directly into the model.

After you create and save a Macintosh-based WalkThrough world (in the form of a walk-through path), you can turn it into a freely distributable, stand-alone application file by using the optional $99 Virtus Voyager (supplied free with WalkThrough Pro). Then, Mac owners who don't have WalkThrough can simply pop in a disk containing a copy of your Voyager file, click the Play button, and view a prerecorded tour of your world (or even wander around it on their own). All they need is a Mac with System 6.0.4 or better and at least two free megs of RAM.

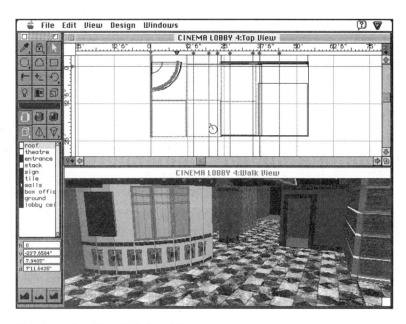

Figure 7.4. *A scene from Virtus Walkthrough Pro.*

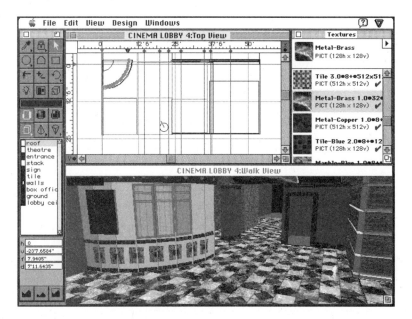

Figure 7.5. *Another scene from Virtus Walkthrough Pro.*

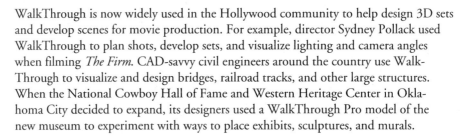

WalkThrough is now widely used in the Hollywood community to help design 3D sets and develop scenes for movie production. For example, director Sydney Pollack used WalkThrough to plan shots, develop sets, and visualize lighting and camera angles when filming *The Firm*. CAD-savvy civil engineers around the country use Walk-Through to visualize and design bridges, railroad tracks, and other large structures. When the National Cowboy Hall of Fame and Western Heritage Center in Oklahoma City decided to expand, its designers used a WalkThrough Pro model of the new museum to experiment with ways to place exhibits, sculptures, and murals.

WalkThrough can do a lot, but it doesn't provide the capability to move or otherwise manipulate its virtual objects. It doesn't support head-mounted displays, stereoscopic imagery, or 6DOF input devices. However, in 1993 Motorola invested a large sum in Virtus. This union may result in products related to interactive, and perhaps immersive, VR. In addition, the Virtus board of directors includes Dr. Frederick Brooks, founder and chairman of the computer science department of the University of North Carolina at Chapel Hill—a major center of VR research and development.

In the meantime, Virtus offers a new $99 software product for people who want to play around with noninteractive walk-throughs and real-time 3D modeling. Virtus VR is available for the Apple Macintosh and the IBM PC ('386 or better, running Microsoft Windows 3.1). The product's name claims VR, but this program doesn't accommodate VR-style input and output devices, doesn't support stereoscopic imagery or interactive sound, and doesn't let you program individual objects to respond to input. Essentially an extremely simplified version of WalkThrough, Virtus VR comes with six precreated 3D "worlds" that you move through in real time using the mouse. (See Figures 7.6 and 7.7.) You can add, modify, and move objects, change colors, and apply textures. Those worlds include the White House (you can rearrange furniture in the Oval Office), the Hindenburg over Paris (*sans* flames), and the Texas motorcade in which JFK was killed. Virtus sells more prepackaged walk-throughs, science fiction in flavor, in the form of optional modules ($65 each). To facilitate the creation of your own 3D scenes, Virtus VR includes sample object libraries.

Virtual Reality Studio by Domark

Engine requirements: Amiga 500/600/2000/3000 with 1MB RAM minimum, PC 286 (or better) with 640K RAM minimum (more is better), 640x480 resolution minimum (runs faster with any Windows accelerator card on 640x480 than without a card on 320x200), mouse, and a joystick is recommended.

Retail price: $90.

Support for VR-style I/O devices? No.

Support for interactive sound? Yes. The PC version supports AdLib sound card and compatibles, Roland LAPC-1 sound card, and PC's built-in "beeper." The Amiga version supports Amiga's built-in sound system.

Figure 7.6. *A scene from Virtus VR.*

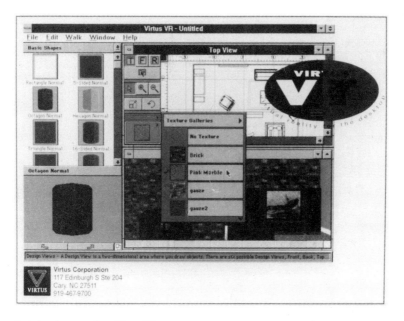

Figure 7.7. *Another scene from Virtus VR.*

Comments: Garage VR floppy disk contains Virtual Reality Studio Version 1.0 for PC.

Source:

> Domark
> 1900 South Norfolk Street
> San Mateo, CA 94403
> (415) 513-8929

Domark, a company based in London, started producing computer games in 1984, then branched into video games. It became a Sega developer in 1991 and set up a U.S. office a year later. Heralded for slick-looking flight and sports simulation games, in 1992 Domark decided to market its in-house games development system as a 3D graphics product. Domark graced it with a user-friendly front end, included access to the scripting language, packaged it as "3D Construction Kit," and expressed surprise when 70,000 copies sold in less than a year.

In the United States, that product was known as "Virtual Reality Studio." Available on today's market, VR Studio Version 2.0—for the price—is a great way to get your VR motor running.

Virtual Reality Studio lets you model and view 3D landscapes and interact with 3D animated objects within those scenes. On even the most humble reality engine, you can whip up dozens of simple objects from a set of basic 2D and 3D building blocks: rectangles, triangles, pyramids, and cubes. (Version 2 added spheres and adjustable "flexicubes," both lacking in Version 1.) Using drop-down menus, you model and render at the same time. Select a cube, place it in the empty world, and stretch it into the shape of a wall or a dance floor. Repeat with other shapes until you construct your object (and link objects into unified groups). Then, you color those objects using the 256-color palette, which you can customize. Only solid shading is supported. You also can make objects invisible. Figure 7.8 shows a scene created using VR Studio.

VR Studio also comes with a library of low-resolution color-clip objects (in the categories of transport, household, garden, city, scenes, and animals) based on bitmaps, including sprites and animation cels.

As you build your world, you maneuver through it and control your viewpoint from a push-button panel, using the keyboard or mouse/joystick combo. Fly-through gateways let you join different virtual worlds, such as caves, spaceships, and amusement park rides.

VR Studio runs at low resolution—640x480 and 16 colors or 320x240 and 256 colors—but that means the scenes flow smoothly and dynamic objects respond quickly to your input.

Figure 7.8. *A scene created using VR Studio.*

For garage VR, the most intriguing feature of VR Studio is its scripting language. Using a language that's a cross between BASIC and assembly language, you can write a control program for each object in your virtual world. The script dictates what happens when your viewpoint or cursor enters a room or touches a door or another object. By writing scripts that specify conditions using an IF/THEN/ELSE structure, you can set an object in motion, score a game, trigger sound effects, or launch into another world. VR Studio's command-line interface appears as a page on which you type the script. That page is associated with a particular object; to simplify the process, each object is assigned an I.D. number upon its creation. Here's an example of one of the many available commands:

```
IF ACTIVATED?
THEN
  INVIS(2)
ENDIF
```

This script causes Object #2 to disappear (become INVISible) when the current object is activated.

After you build, populate, and program your world, you can save a self-running version of it on floppy disk, which you can then give to people who don't own the program—just as Doug Faxon distributed "Gaynor House" to his family (see Profile 3).

When you buy Virtual Reality Studio, you also receive a tutorial videotape and an operation manual. This documentation is sketchy in parts, and it doesn't provide an index, but it wins the prize for the most humorous manual (albeit humor that is veddy, veddy British).

VR Studio isn't without its limitations. Its retail price is low, and so is its image resolution. You can rotate objects at no less than 90-degree angles. You can't build any more than 60 objects in any one environment and you can't render with real-time light shading. Version 2.0 is buggy; when building a world, you should save your work often (especially when nearing the maximum object limit). Some people report trouble with runtime (self-running) modules freezing the system (although that function works well in Version 1.0).

Domark is tackling some of these problems. Virtual Reality Studio version 3.0 will run faster and sport higher resolution and texture-mapping capabilities. Scheduled for release in late 1994, VR Studio 3.0 will run on PC, Atari, *and* Macintosh, and it will retail for less than $200. An enhanced user interface will facilitate world-building, and an open architecture will beckon third-party developers to create various device drivers. A CD-ROM version of the program will carry hundreds of clip worlds and objects. As an official 3DO developer, Domark also is creating a version of VR Studio for the 3DO interactive multiplayer.

With the goal of supporting "true" VR, Domark inked deals with several I/O device manufacturers and plans to write drivers for head-mounted displays and 6DOF input devices. RPI Advanced Technology Group is developing lightweight, monoscopic glasses with position-tracking for viewing and interacting with VR Studio; 3DTV Corp. is creating VR Studio runtime modules that can output stereoscopic imagery. Domark also intends to incorporate drivers that enable VR Studio to import .DXF files and support simple networked VR through a modem.

Object Glove by Mark Pflaging and VRASP

Engine requirements: PC (running DOS or Microsoft Windows, '386 or better).

Retail cost: $40, plus $2.50 shipping and handling (see "Source").

Support for VR-style I/O devices? Yes, Power Glove.

Support for stereo images? No.

Comments: Power Glove Controller. Programming skills are required. (No programming skills are needed to use the demo, however.)

Source:

VRASP catalog #A003 ($40 plus $2.50 shipping) is a package containing "Object Glove" and "Court Jesture" that enables one- or two-Glove access with Borland C++ 3.1. Includes sample applications.

VRASP catalog #A004 ($75 plus $2.50 shipping) contains the Object Glove source code for direct access to the Power Glove, also includes Object Glove/Court Jesture software, sample applications, and documentation.

VRASP catalog #A005 ($2.00 plus $2.50 shipping) is a Glove Demo Disk containing sample Object Glove, Court Jesture, and REND386 Power Glove applications. The REND386 demo supports two Gloves and gesture recognition; you can use glove gestures to fly around in worlds. The Windows demo lets you use the Glove to move a pointer.

The software provided in the VRASP catalog #A005, and the demo programs for Object Glove, can be obtained through anonymous FTP from the REND386 directory of the Internet host site sunee.uwaterloo.ca. The directory path is /pub/glove, and the filename is OBJGLV.EXE. The file also contains directions and pin-outs for constructing Mark Pflaging's Dual-Glove interface (filename: TWOGLOVE.DOC). The file is a self-extracting archive; be sure to transfer using binary mode. After downloading the file to your system, create directories by typing `objglv -d` at the DOS prompt. The archive provides more detail.

On CompuServe, the Cyberforum's VR Workgroup library houses the files O2GLOV.ZIP, OBJGLV.ZIP, DEMO4B.ZIP, and WINGLV.ZIP. OBJGLV.ZIP is the complete demo. The others are slimmed-down versions, provided to reduce download time. O2GLOV contains the DOS demo, WINGLV contains the Windows demo, and DEMO4B contains the REND386 demo. Each file also contains TWOGLOVE.DOC.

Send check or money order payable to VRASP to

> VRASP
> Box 4139
> Highland Park, NJ 08904-4139
> E-mail: `70233.1552@compuserve.com`

Object Glove is an object-oriented driver for a Power Glove interfaced with the PC's parallel port. It is written in C++ for Borland C++ 3.1. Providing access to raw or filtered data straight from the Glove, Object Glove works under DOS and Microsoft Windows and with REND386. Object Glove also supports the use of two Power Gloves simultaneously on one parallel port.

Object Glove is accessible and extensible, offering a simple programming interface that makes it easy to incorporate into other applications. It is interrupt-driven: sampling occurs at regular intervals without requiring attention from the application program. Because it is object-oriented, future improvements to the driver are transparent to the applications that use it. Advanced processing of the Glove's input can be handled by deriving classes from the main driver class.

Supplied with Object Glove, Court Jesture is a gesture recognition system that sends "gesture messages" to applications. It lets you control the computer by defining gestures, then making those gestures with the Glove. It operates in real time, dispensing the gestures (object-oriented) selectively to application objects. Because the gestures actually trigger software events, programmers can interpret gestures in any way. You can group gestures into *sets*; these sets can be activated and deactivated dynamically by the application. When two Gloves are used, you can assign the same or different gestures and gesture sets to each Glove.

The supplied demo program (for DOS and Windows) displays a line drawing of a hand. Based on the movements of the Power Glove, the virtual hand moves around on-screen. In the DOS version, user-defined gestures appear on-screen when they are recognized. You can add or modify gestures by changing a plain text input file; this does not require programming. In the Windows version, you use the Glove as a pointing device, driving the Windows cursor and defining any gesture you want to represent a mouse click. You also can set up gestures to trigger sounds, which play through the Microsoft Windows 3.1 Multimedia Interface (which means the sounds also are user-definable).

There's also a REND386 demo file that shows how you might incorporate Object Glove and Court Jesture for using the Power Glove to control viewpoint and interact with objects in a three-dimensional virtual world.

When you order the programming libraries or source code packages, you also receive about 60 pages of printed documentation.

Dr. StrangeGlove by James Gustave

Engine requirements: Macintosh (uses 384K RAM and 249K hard drive space).

Freeware created and copyrighted by James Gustave (`speth@cats.ucsc.edu`).

Support for VR-style I/O devices? Yes, Power Glove.

Support for stereo images? No.

Comments: Power Glove Controller. No programming skills are required (unless you want to modify the Glove).

Source: FTP from `ftp.apple.com` in the /pub/VR directory.

Dr. StrangeGlove contains all the code required for serial interface connection of Power Glove to the Macintosh. It also displays a small window in which you can use the Glove to toss a ball. Set up for use with the Menelli and PGSI interface boxes, the file includes a .GIF schematic. The Dr. StrangeGlove application is compiled and ready for use. It also includes the complete source code, so you can modify it (great for learning about serial Mac programming).

In the same Apple archive directory that holds Dr. StrangeGlove, you'll find Mac graphics (look in the SpriteWorld demo in the code/ directory).

StrangeGlove GoldBrick is another file in the same directory. Written by Peter Frank Falco, StrangeGlove GoldBrick is a compiled, ready-to-run application that lets Dr. StrangeGlove work with the Transfinite Systems Gold Brick interface box. E-mail Pete for information at `falcop@rpi.edu`.

REND386 by Dave Stampe and Bernie Roehl

Engine requirements: PC, '386 or '486 (DOS) with VGA display (runs faster on a 16-bit card than on an 8-bit card), minimum 540K free memory. This works best on a 486/50MHz engine.

Freeware is copyrighted by Bernie Roehl and Dave Stampe.

Support for VR-style I/O devices? Yes, Power Glove and stereoscopic shutter glasses.

Support for stereo images? Yes.

Support for interactive sound? No.

Comments: Primarily a programmer's tool. Development work requires Turbo C++ 1.00 or above, or Borland C. No programming skill is required to run the demo. Knowledge of 3D geometry data is required to build worlds. Hackers such as Joe Gradecki and Mark Pflaging have developed adjuncts to REND386, implementing ways to use it with various I/O devices on various engines (and they offer those utilities free to the public). Also, many virtual objects and worlds based on REND386 can be downloaded from various Internet sites and CompuServe.

Source: FTP from `sunee.uwaterloo.ca`, directory /pub/rend386. Demo available: /pub/rend386/demo4.zip. The source code and developer's kit are in /pub/rend386/ devel4.zip. Or you can FTP from other Internet sites, electronic mailing lists, and CompuServe Cyberforum (see Chapter 8). A cleaned-up and somewhat enhanced version of the source code is in jirend.zip, available on Compuserve, `sunee`, and other FTP sites. The number 4 in the filenames refers to version 4 of REND386. By the time you read this, Bernie and Dave will have uploaded version 5 and will have almost completed version 6.

According to REND386's creators, "The libraries are available for free; the only reason for making the demo a separate set of files is to give people who aren't interested in writing software a chance to see what can be done on widely available hardware."

To run the demo or to sample virtual worlds (after storing them in your system), at the DOS prompt type `demo4` or `demo4 filename`. The `filename` is the name of the .PLG file, .FIG file, or .WLD file you want to load.

Today's trendiest fuel is REND386. It offers fast, flexible, colorful, stereoscopic graphics on a PC with support for mouse, joystick, keyboard, Power Glove, shutter glasses, and (with a bit of device-driver programming) head-mounted displays. REND386 helps programmers and courageous techno-types get started quickly (and inexpensively) in VR.

This toolkit essentially is a simple, 16-bit, polygon-based program that performs 3D screen rendering. REND386 was written in Turbo C using 386 assembly language, then it was let loose in January of 1992 by Dave Stampe and Bernie Roehl from Ontario's University of Waterloo.

With REND386, you can develop worlds, define surfaces, and assign colors. Its animation feature means you can make objects that bounce and spin, doors that swing open when you approach, and vehicles on which to hitch a ride. The Power Glove interface lets you select, move, and rotate objects in the world. And because REND386 was built for speed, it lets you really experience that real-time virtual feeling.

A REND386 world database consists of three file formats: one for the world, the hardware configuration, and optional loadable device drivers; one for the geometry; and one for hierarchies. To create simple objects in REND386's .PLG file format, you specify the object's polygons and vertices, or coordinates. This is a relatively easy procedure. (The world-building toolkit consists of a text editor and a sketch pad.) The .PLG file format doesn't like complex models, however.

Most folks prefer building 3D objects outside of REND386, using a 3D modeling program. You convert the model from .DFX file format to a .PLG file, then import the file to REND386. Available on the net are software utilities that convert geometries from various file formats (3DS, .DXF, and so on) into .PLG format. An inexpensive program by Quest, NorthCAD Pro 3D, can save a file as a .PLG file, so no conversion is necessary.

Traveling through a REND386 world is easy; you press your keyboard arrow keys to change your point of view and field of view; key combinations provide for x- and y-axes movement. You select and move objects with the mouse, or by pointing and grabbing with a Power Glove. Catching a moving object with the Glove sometimes is challenging and requires patience, if not dexterity.

The speed at which REND386 draws pictures depends on a few variables: the configuration of your hardware (processor type and clock speed), the complexity of the virtual world, and whether the scene is mono- or stereoscopic. For example, one of the sample .PLG demos included with the package is a simple chess piece. It consists of 500 polygons. On a slow 386 machine with a stock VGA, the chess piece can be moved at a rate of 10 fps; on a faster ('486/33MHz) engine with a 24-bit video card, the rate increases to about 26 fps. The fewer the polygons in an object, the faster the frame rate. For example, if a 500-polygon object trots by at 16 fps, a 100-polygon object canters at about 38 fps, and a 20-polygon object gallops at 75 fps.

To achieve the highest possible speed, REND386 comes preconfigured for 320x200, 256-color VGA mode for mouse and joystick control. To handle other resolutions, you need a different driver. Higher screen resolution and/or more colors limits the real-time performance. However, you can add a graphics accelerator to speed things up a bit. Clever hackers have modified REND386 to run on various graphics cards to enable, for example, board pairs and multiple frame buffers for interfacing head-mounted displays.

One such hacker, Jerry Isdale, modified REND386 to add support for the Global Devices 6DOF controller. "In the process of this modification," he says, "I reworked the source to make it compile in Borland C version 3.1 with fewer warnings. I also rearranged the source hierarchy.... I also integrated a Logitech Mouse/Head-Tracker driver that Dave Stampe had written. That driver and the Global controller both required serial interface control code. I modified some from a public-domain C library and used that instead of the code Dave [Stampe] supplied. My version of the code, without Dave's tracker code, is available on CompuServe." This code, jirend.zip, also is available on `sunee.uwaterloo.cd` and `ftp.uwashington.edu`.

As mentioned earlier, REND386 can handle simple stereoscopic scenes. If you specify such parameters as your distance from the screen, REND386 automatically creates the correct left- and right-eye images. Version 5.0 also supports side-by-side images for viewing with fresnel lenses, and it supports multiplexed devices, such as LCD shutter glasses.

Some other hip features of REND386 version 5.0 include the capability to create autonomous objects that move by themselves. It also can sense when your viewpoint comes within boundaries of an object. You can put an invisible border around a virtual steering wheel, for example, and program it so whenever you move inside the border, you cause the wheel to spin. Similarly, you can use this function to cause the steering wheel to morph into a miniature Ferris wheel—or into something else.

The drawbacks of REND386 include its lack of texture-mapping and its limited support for object interaction. Rend386 suffers from visibility errors (these "hidden-surface" problems result in the user sometimes seeing through objects to the objects behind them), and occasional accuracy errors.

Most importantly, REND386 doesn't provide a built-in modeler or tools to help you create complex objects or assemble a world. All this means that nonprogrammers can't do much with it.

Those of you who want to master REND386 should consider subscribing to the garage VR newsletter *PCVR,* which runs a regular column called "Working with REND386." The complete guide to running REND386, written by Bernie Roehl, Dave Stampe, and John Eagen, is the hefty book *Virtual Reality Creations* (Waite Group Press, 1993). This volume comes with a floppy disk containing REND386 (version 5.0) executable (no source code), 21 sample worlds, more than 100 sample objects for including in your own worlds, and a cardboard viewer with fresnel lenses for stereoscopic viewing.

Dave Stampe and Bernie Roehl release new versions (and source code) of REND386 with impressive frequency. (Version 6.0 will support new surface types and more I/O devices and networked virtual worlds, it will solve some of those hidden-surface problems, and it will include a conversion utility for objects created in other file formats.) Their provision of source code makes it possible for programmers to adapt the toolkit for new VR-style input and output devices.

For more information about REND386, send e-mail to `broehl@sunee.uwaterloo.ca`.

Macintosh WorldBuilder by Peter Frank Falco

Engine requirements: Macintosh with 68881 math coprocessor, System 7, 2MB free RAM recommended, and 111K hard disk drive space.

Freeware created and copyrighted by Peter Frank Falco (`falcop@rpi.edu`).

Support for VR-style I/O devices? Yes, Power Glove and Logitech 6DOF Mouse/Head-Tracker.

Support for stereo images? Yes.

Comments: Designed for programmers. Object creation requires the ability to write your own routines and integrate them into applications.

Source: FTP from `ftp.apple.com` in /pub/VR directory.

Consisting of a data file and an application, Macintosh WorldBuilder is a new system built from scratch by Peter Frank Falco, a graduate student at Rensselaer Polytechnic Institute in Troy, New York. Pete released the alpha version of this general-purpose world builder in July of 1993, offering it as freeware so people can provide feedback on what they want and need in low-cost Mac VR.

Mac WorldBuilder essentially is a rough shell for running some simple code. Creating objects requires the ability to write your own code and integrate it into your own applications. To create objects with Mac WorldBuilder, you edit a simple ASCII data file; object creation is based on vector graphics. According to Pete, anyone with elementary math skills can easily create sophisticated objects. He says, "Although I do not do any shading, the clipping algorithm does work, as long as objects are defined correctly."

Although it doesn't include source code or object creation tools, WorldBuilder lets you examine the code used to create and manipulate objects in a virtual world. Mac WorldBuilder requires more RAM than other Mac VR freeware programs, based on the assumption that you'll use it to build large worlds.

When the beta version is completed (soon after this book's publication), Pete says Mac WorldBuilder "will be networkable and will interface with the Power Glove, with two video cards (one for each eye), and with the Logitech 6DOF Mouse/Head-Tracker."

At this stage, Mac WorldBuilder doesn't support the design of interactive, navigable worlds, such as those possible on the Mac running Virtus WalkThrough. Then again, you don't have to pay anything for WorldBuilder. (However, after he completes his thesis, Pete intends to market the software under the company name "Innovative Computer Solutions.")

Please e-mail comments, suggestions, bug reports, and so on to Pete Falco at `falcop@rpi.edu`.

Gossamer by Jon Blossom

Engine requirements: Macintosh (68020 or better), 384K RAM, 534K hard disk drive space.

Freeware created and copyrighted by Jon Blossom (`jonbl@microsoft.com`).

Support for VR-style I/O devices? No. (Support for Power Glove interfaces is planned for Version 2.0.)

Support for stereo images? No.

Comments: Version 1.1 is a programmer's tool that requires the ability to write and integrate routines into applications. Version 2.0 will provide end-user interface.

Source: FTP from `ftp.apple.com` in /pub/VR directory (self-extracting StuffIt archive available for FTP in /pub/VR/source on `ftp.apple.com`).

Similar to REND386, Gossamer is a polygon-based 3D graphics rendering library. It was first uploaded into the public net domain in July of 1993. It is fixed-point (no math coprocessor is required), capable of flat shading and clipping, and supports 1- to 32-bit color (although the simple demonstration that's included is limited to 1- to 8-bit palette-animation displays).

Gossamer's creator is Jon Blossom, who works at Microsoft. (Gossamer is not a Microsoft product, nor is it endorsed or supported by Microsoft.) Jon offers Gossamer to anyone who wants to use it to write programs destined for personal use or the public domain. Commercial applications, including shareware based on Gossamer, must be licensed from Jon.

The package contains the Gossamer library in Symantec's THINK C 5.0 format (Gossamer was compiled with THINK C 5.0), sample source code for the demonstration program, documentation in Microsoft Word 5.1 format, and a "samples" folder of objects that Jon ported from REND386 .PLG files. You load them into the demo using the **File | O**pen menu option.

Jon admits that even though Gossamer's library is "solid," the demo is a bit buggy and slow, "but these are problems we must deal with… and they will be fixed. Gossamer is a 'proof of concept' and a request for suggestions and improvements. I just wanted to get *something* into the hands of Mac VR-heads."

Gossamer doesn't include much documentation for the nonprogrammer. Instead, it provides a brief outline of how the demo works, plus an extensive manual of functions that developers can use in their own graphics programs.

According to Jon, the user interface for the sample VR application included with Gossamer is "a bit under-featured, and there's no way to create new objects interactively. I included the demonstration, with source [code], mainly to show how an application might be written. The demonstration program, although it is sparse, *can* be used by anyone to start playing around. The main thrust is to provide tools for fast polygon rendering that programmers can use to write their own applications. I don't expect the nonprogramming public to be able to use it fluently—*yet*."

Gossamer 1.1 does not support multiple object representations, hierarchical segments, stereoscopic rendering, or spatial partitioning. It's strictly a rendering engine; there is no direct support for 6DOF input devices, although Jon intends to add Power Glove support for the Menelli and/or PGSI interface boxes. His other priorities are to improve the user interface and add direct support for importing REND386 .PLG files. Jon plans to turn the Gossamer demo program into a full-featured VR walkthrough-type program with compatibility for REND386 worlds and objects.

In fact, even Jon hasn't created any major worlds yet, because he's "been too busy just making Gossamer work! But once I get REND386 world compatibility in there, the possibilities are totally wide open."

As of this writing, Jon is in the midst of discussions with Microsoft so he can work on Gossamer without worrying about potential conflicts.

Assuming Microsoft allows its employee to continue working on this outside project, the next version of Gossamer (2.0) will provide a world-building kit. Jon hopes to release 2.0 by 1994. It will remain in the public domain as freeware (and freely distributable for noncommercial applications), available by file transfer from various net sites and from CompuServe.

If you have any questions, comments, or bugs to report, please e-mail Jon Blossom at jonbl@microsoft.com.

VREAM

Engine requirements: PC ('386, DOS 3.3 or later) with VGA graphics, math coprocessor recommended, 4MB free RAM, mouse (3-button mouse recommended), and a joystick. This runs best on a '486/33MHz or better. The Development System requires a 10MB hard drive space.

Retail price: $795 for Development System, $295 for Advanced Runtime System, and $59 for Standard Runtime System.

Support for VR-style I/O devices? Development and Advanced Runtime Systems each support the following: Global Devices 6DOF controller, Mattel Power Glove, Logitech CyberMan, Logitech 6DOF Mouse/Head-Tracker, Maxx foot pedals, Simsalabim Cyberscope, StereoGraphics CrystalEyes, Creative Labs SoundBlaster, Advanced Gravis UltraSound 3D system, and various commercial HMDs. For output to head-mounted displays, VREAM supports the VGA-to-NTSC converter manufactured by ADDA Technologies (Oakland, California, (510) 770-9899).

Standard Runtime System supports keyboard, mouse, and joystick only.

The "fly-through" landscapes (noninteractive) on the next two pages were created with VistaPro by modifying Distance Elevation Model files from the U.S. Geological Survey. Many such DEMs are provided with VistaPro.

The "walk-through" scenes on the next three pages were created with Domark Virtual Reality Studio, versions 1 and 2. The office image represents an interactive world in which various objects react when you click on them. For example, clicking on the drawer causes it to slide open.

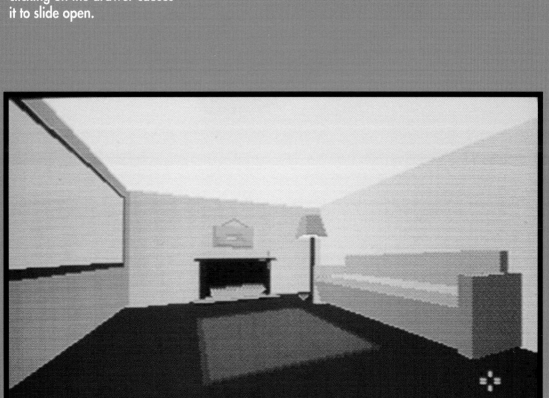

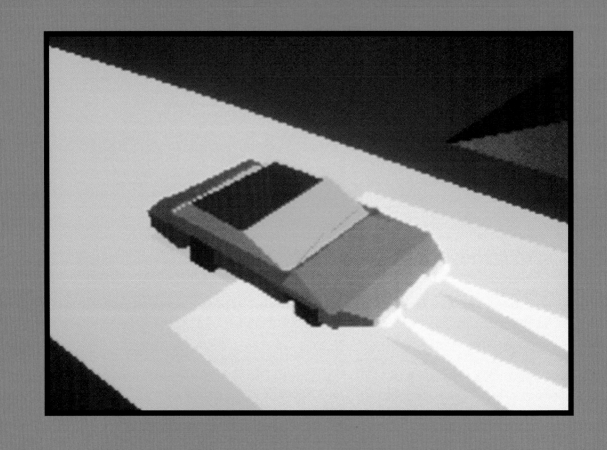

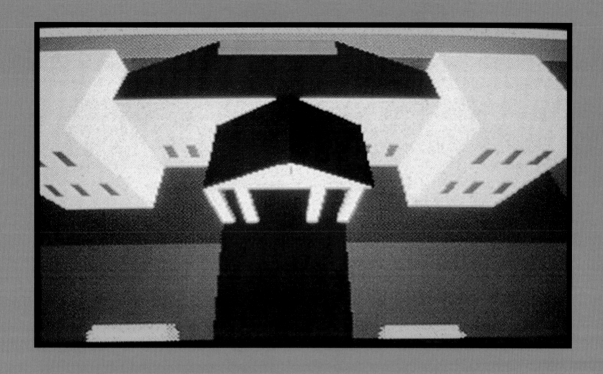

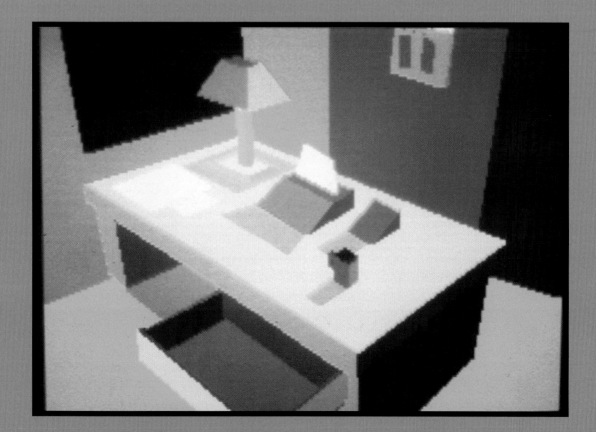

To the left and above: These images show the results in the VREAM Runtime System, in which a Power Glove is used to control the actions of an on-screen hand. (Images courtesy of VREAM, Inc.)

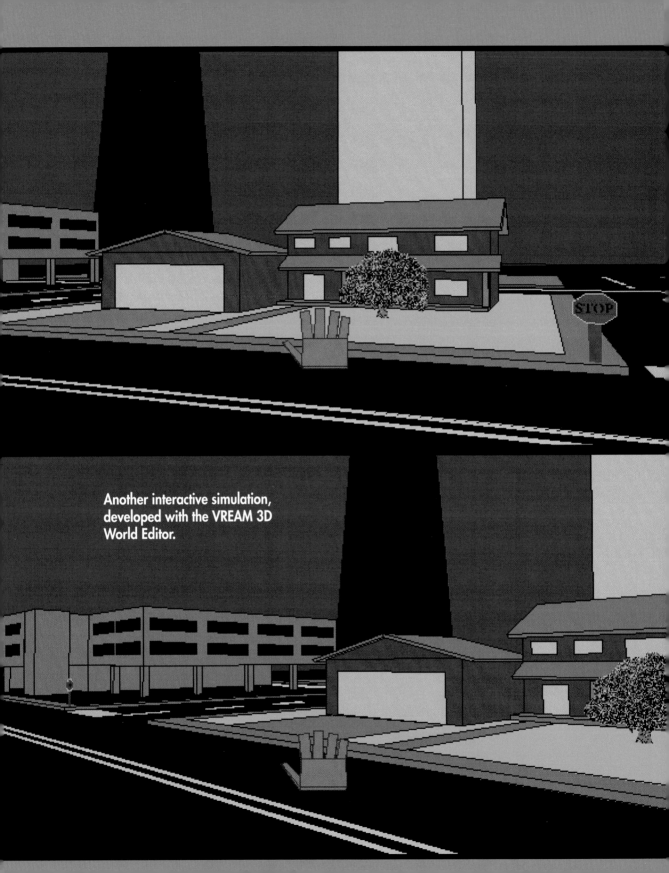

Another interactive simulation, developed with the VREAM 3D World Editor.

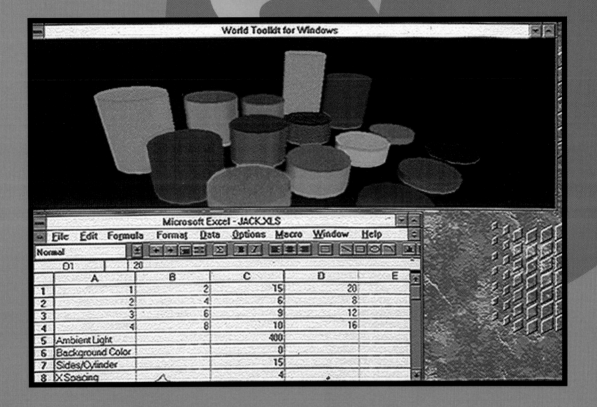

This image shows how an application developed with Sense8's WorldToolKit for Windows can be linked to an Excel spreadsheet. In this example, each spreadsheet cell controls the height of one of the columns in the virtual world. As spreadsheet values change, so do the heights of virtual objects. The participant can fly around this world in real time.

A collection of AutoCAD .DXF files placed inside a virtual world, developed with Sense8's WorldToolKit for Windows to allow real-time exploration. This scene is from an 800-polygon world created by the Visual Systems Lab at the Institute for Simulation and Training in Florida. The model renders at eight frames per second on a '486/66MHz PC.

A scene from an interactive kitchen demo created for British Gas with Sense8's WorldToolKit for Windows. The participant can use the mouse to pick up and move utensils, open drawers and cupboards, and turn on the stove burners. (Images courtesy of Sense8 Corporation)

The scenes on the next five pages show how Mark Reaney, a professor at the University of Kansas, uses Virtus WalkThrough to conceptualize, create, and optimize theater sets. The two images labeled "Rough" reveal his initial set ideas, developed in a virtual world. The "Sketch" images show his subsequent drawings, based on the ideas he generated in VR. The "Final" images are Mark's virtual representations of the completed set designs, which then are realized on the actual stage ("Actual"). These sets graced the university's production of the play *Pink Thunderbird.*

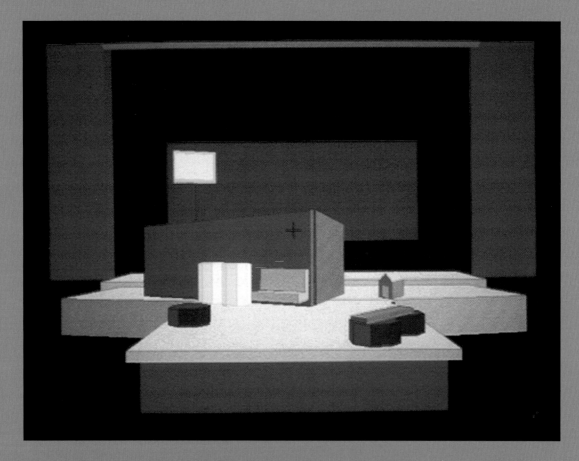

Rough

Sketch

Final

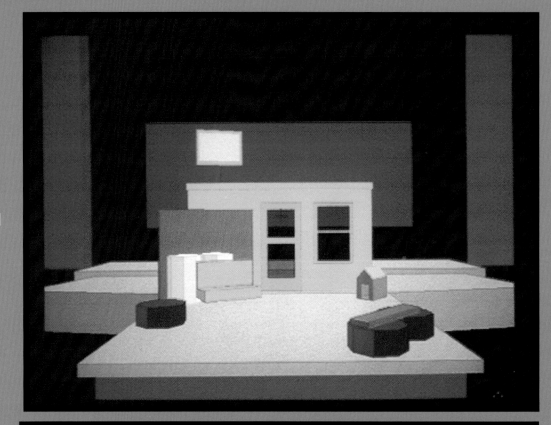

Actual

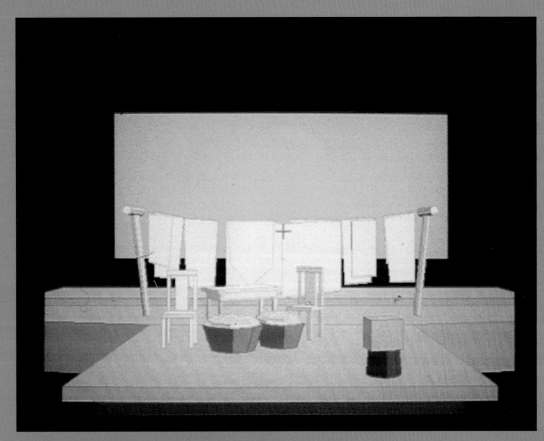

Rough

Sketch

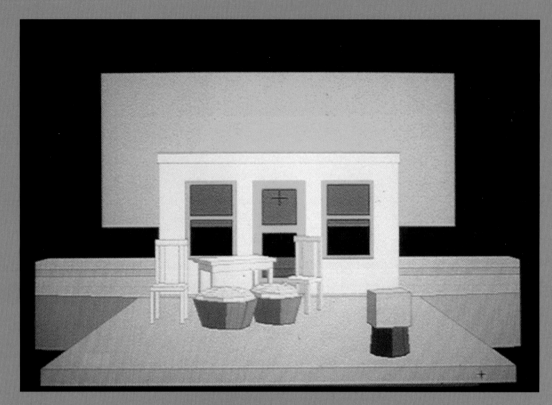

Final

Actual

Support for stereo images? Yes.

Support for interactive sound? Yes.

Comments: Doesn't require programming skills. Basic Runtime System supports desktop VR, and Advanced Runtime System provides support for immersive peripherals.

Source:

> VREAM, Inc.
> 445 W. Erie Street, #3B
> Chicago, IL 60610
> (312) 477-0425

VREAM, Inc. was the first VR software company that didn't demand that you hone your programming chops to build a virtual world. Its products, which also go by the name VREAM (for "virtual dream"), let you create, visit, and interact with real-time virtual worlds, using a mouse and a joystick, as well as more exotic input and output devices. You can "walk" or "fly" to any point in space. You can imbue objects with gravity and elasticity, then grab, toss, or push them, and make them trigger sounds. With VREAM's texture-mapping feature, you can apply a watery finish to your octopus' garden or a marble veneer to your pyramid patch. Figure 7.9 shows a scene created using VREAM.

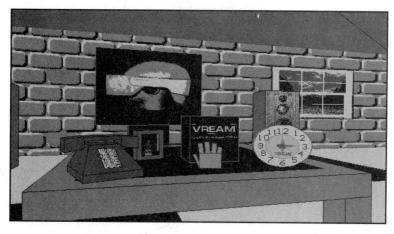

Figure 7.9. *A scene created using VREAM.*

The Development System comprises three modules, one each for modeling, scripting, and runtime.

The modeler, called the 3D World Editor, provides a mouse-driven user interface and a set of tools for drawing 3D objects. (You also can import and export .DXF 3D graphics files and import .PCX bitmap files.) This is the tool with which you define object attributes such as motion, gravity, and sound. You also use it to set up dynamic object links (*conditions* such as touching, grabbing, and moving objects or changing viewpoint, and *responses* such as playing sound files, opening new worlds, or calling external programs). You can assign dynamic links between objects so that user-defined conditions (such as lifting a virtual lever) trigger user-defined responses (such as opening a trap door). With the World Editor, you also define the world's overall parameters, including shading, lighting, and gravity, and define which I/O devices the world will support.

The scripting language also lets you define virtual worlds, in standard text format, using a language based on English.

The runtime system is the business end of the package; it's the part that lets you enter and interact with your finished world. You also can freely distribute your worlds without paying royalties to VREAM, Inc.

While developing a world and its objects, you can switch from the modeler to the runtime system to test your creations, then hop back to the modeler for fine-tuning.

Other than its graphical user interface, some of VREAM's appealing traits include the capability to create, change, save, and delete objects (in real time) while visiting a virtual world. It lets you incorporate pop-up windows, timers, and counters, too.

VREAM's graphics modes support 256-color worlds in 320x240 and 320x200 resolution, and 16-color worlds in 640x350 resolution. The higher-resolution mode is the slowest.

The $795 and $295 VREAM packages come with 122 sample worlds, and the $59 Runtime system comes with 112 sample worlds. These worlds show off VREAM's various features, capabilities, and world-development techniques.

According to the company's head honcho, Edward LaHood, "We get many orders for the Runtime System packages from people who would like to execute VREAM virtual worlds, and from people who buy the $59 Runtime System as a VREAM sampler, which lets them get an idea of the types of functionality which may be included in VREAM worlds."

WorldToolKit for Windows

Engine requirements: PC, '386/'486 (or better), Microsoft Windows 3.1 or higher, and a VGA or S3 display (256-color graphics card minimum). The more RAM, the more texture storage. This does not work with standard 4-bit or 16-color Windows drivers (yet). To develop applications, you need a Microsoft Windows 3.1 development environment with a Windows-based compiler.

Retail price: $795.

Support for VR-style I/O devices? Yes. Power Glove, Advanced Gravis UltraSound 3D sound system, Logitech CyberMan, and others will be added later.

Support for stereo images? No.

Support for interactive sound? Yes. Works with any sound card that supports Microsoft Windows sound development toolkit.

Comments: Heavy-duty programming chops required. Software is upwardly compatible with the award-winning de facto industry standard: WorldToolKit.

Source:

> Sense8
> 1001 Bridgeway, #477
> Sausalito, CA 94965
> (415) 331-6318

Sense8 was founded in 1990 by a couple of hackers who aimed to provide their fellow programmers with relatively affordable, platform-independent, real-time VR tools. Sense8's WorldToolKit for Windows hit the market in the summer of 1993. WTK/Win endows the Windows operating environment with real-time 3D rendering performance. The spawn of a Sense8/Intel Corp. union, WTK/Win is a lower-octane version of Sense8's WorldToolKit, the leading VR fuel for professional-level reality engines.

One word sums up this program's capabilities: powerful. WTK/Win offers real-time display of 3D objects rendered with wireframe, flat-shaded, smooth-shaded, and textured surfaces. It handles 16-bit texture maps in 640x480 16-bit color displays. It also can import data from a concurrently active Windows application—such as an Excel spreadsheet—and display a corresponding data visualization in a virtual world in real time.

To get anywhere with WTK/Win, you must understand DLLs. Essentially, the package is a chunky C library containing more than 400 function calls to "simplify" the process of creating real-time, interactive 3D simulations. It comes with a few complete applications that are compiled and road-ready.

WTK/Win is not a 3D modeling program. Instead, you must create 3D objects with any 3D modeler that generates .DXF or 3DS files. WTK/Win reads these files, then lets you interact with and explore the models in real time. It does, however, contain functions for interactively creating spheres, cubes, cylinders, polygons, and so on. Use these functions to dynamically create shapes within the virtual world.

You can dynamically create and texture-map those polygons using various image data sources. Likewise, you can dynamically create lights or load them in from another file (lights can be updated every frame). You can randomly generate the terrain or load in external files.

After creating the world (or *universe* in WTK jargon) and its objects, you can assign tasks to those objects, link them, attach them to sensors, imbue them with color, texture, and other appearance attributes, and define collision detection between objects and polygons. Then, you define your viewpoints, attaching them to various sensors. Objects and viewpoints can follow predefined paths (which can be dynamically created). WTK/Win also automatically opens new worlds when you pass through a predefined portal.

As is the case with any other rendering package, the performance speed of WTK/Win depends on CPU horsepower and graphics muscle. Sense8 provided Table 7.1, which is based on nonaccelerating engines drawing a 320x240 window at 16 bits-per-pixel image. It shows graphics performance, or polygons rendered per second. (Polygons equals 10x10 pixels, unlit, transformed, quads.)

Table 7.1. Graphics performance (polygons rendered per second).

Engine Configuration	Flat-Shaded	Smooth	Textured
486/25, ISA	3,000	1,800	1,400
486/66, ISA	4,750	3,500	2,300
486/66, VLbus	6,500	4,000	2,500

WTK/Win comes with more than 100 3D models, more than 100 texture maps, and about a dozen demos, which actually rank as complete VR applications that you can use as a starting point for creating your own applications.

For a comprehensive explanation of how WTK/Win approaches the processes involved in building virtual worlds, read *Virtual Reality: Through the New Looking Glass* (Windcrest/McGraw-Hill, 1993) by Ken Pimental and Kevin Teixeria. Ken is the product manager for Sense8.

Creating Stereoscopic Images

The computer screen is a rectangular plane made up of pixels, so we think of the corresponding bits in the frame buffer as *bit planes*. Bit planes often organize video memory so that all the "first bits" of the pixels are consecutive, so are all the "second bits," and so on. A frame buffer holding eight bits for each pixel has eight bit planes.

To display stereoscopic image pairs, you assign some portion of the planes to a second frame buffer. Two frame buffers let the system draw in one set of bit planes while displaying another set. This lets the system switch between two versions of the same picture and update the picture while it's not in view. You do this by allocating an equal number of bit planes to each frame buffer. For example, you could divide the bit planes in an 8-bit frame buffer into two 4-bit buffers. You'll get fewer colors and still enable the display of stereoscopic image pairs.

For 3D viewing of static images, the computer's graphics card should alternate between the two frame buffers at least 30 times per second. For 3D animation, you can achieve this switching process by using two frame buffers (or palette-based animation). That way, you can switch shutters each time the monitor reaches the vertical blanking point, thereby reducing the flicker effect. To handle double-buffered stereoscopic animation, you need four frame buffers: two buffers that are displayed alternately and two buffers to which you're sending images.

On the PC, you need software that can merge the stereo images and drive the shutter glasses interface for cards that support page flipping. REND386 lets you create stereo graphics on ordinary PCs. It configures for the serial or parallel port and nearly any VGA graphics card. Several different programs (available for downloading from the net) can convert 3D Studio, AutoCAD, and other .DXF files for rapid stereoscopic rendering with REND386.

The Houston-based Spectrum Dynamics distributes stereoscopic display hardware and software for the PC (AT compatible or better) with VGA graphics. Targeted for programmers, the PC Stereoscope system—consisting of a $500 stereoscopic card and $350 development software—works with Borland Turbo C 2.0. It provides high-speed graphics functions, animations, and menus for programming from scratch or converting 3D graphics to stereo.

For Macintosh-based stereoscopy, you need a good, high-resolution, 8-bit graphics card so you can divide its output into four 2-bit planes to achieve stereoscopic double-buffering.

Juri Munkki, a garage VR inventor based at Finland's Helsinki University of Technology, divided his Macintosh II screen into four 2-bit planes to run stereo animation with four colors for viewing with LCD glasses. If you want to try stereoscopic animation with a display card that can't support multiple pages (buffers) or CLUTs, Juri suggests you try doing a *bit blit* transfer (a technique used to display moving objects) from the off-screen buffers at the vertical blanking point, then draw using the four off-screen buffers. "Any rate of animation can be achieved as long as there is time left after the blit," Juri writes. "Also, a ±5 volt signal might be enough to run the glasses, but I was informed that ±10V is the right voltage. My interface generates about ±9 volts on the Macintosh serial port." (Juri's source code and documentation can be downloaded from the net; see Chapter 9.)

When you're creating your image pairs, stereoscopy expert Michael Starks of 3DTV suggests placing letters or other marks indicating either R (right) or L (left) in the lower-right corner of the right and left frames, respectively. This way you can ensure that left- and right-eye images don't switch when you're running glasses, a common occurrence. Do not place the letters or graphics at the very top of the screen, however, because sometimes one common byproduct of stereoscopic viewing is distortion at the top of the screen.

On the Amiga, several new rendering programs automatically create a stereoscopic image for viewing with shutter glasses, including Incognito's Optiks, Impulse's TurboSilver SV, and Mindware International's PageRender3D. Or, you can use any Amiga 3D modeling package, such as Byte by Byte's Sculpt 3D or Impulse's Turbo Silver, to create image pairs: first you render one image, then you move the camera angle a short distance (about 2.5 inches apart to approximate the distance between your eyes) and render the second image. Experiment with placing the camera angles parallel with each other, or inclined, to create an "inter-ocular" angle.

VR on CD

If you own a CD-ROM drive, you may want to add a new disc to your collection. A company called Network Cybernetics offers the $129 AI CD-ROM, a disc that works on any personal computer with a CD-ROM drive and standard ISO-9660 driver. The AI CD-ROM contains a large assortment of files and programs related to virtual reality, artificial intelligence, artificial life, robotics, neural networks, simulation, and other futuristic areas.

Revised annually, the disc provides an alternative method of acquiring public-domain programs and text files for those who don't want to hassle with file transfers across the net. Gathered from BBSs, Internet archives, and academic and nongovernmental research sites, the programs run on various PCs and workstations, and include source code and technical notes.

The AI CD-ROM provides an elaborate database of information on the files, including abstracts of each file and (for DOS and OS/2 platforms) an interface for file search-and-retrieval.

VR and simulation programs and files on the AI CD-ROM include REND386 code and demos, demos of VREAM and Dimension SuperScape (a high-end VR world-builder), Power Glove interface code and schematics (including Ron Menelli's code, Macintosh code, and timing diagrams), VR industry conference and corporate/academic research reports, and papers by such VR industry leaders as Bob Jacobson and Randy Walser, plus several VR equipment and resource listings.

For information, contact

Network Cybernetics Corporation
4201 Wingren Road, #202
Irving, TX 75062
(214) 650-2002

PUTTING VR ON THE MAP

Bernie Roehl

KITCHNER/WATERLOO, ONTARIO

PROFILE

4

BERNIE ROEHL:
"Doing VR as a Labor of Love"

Bordered by four Great Lakes on the south and Hudson Bay on the north, Ontario is Canada's province with the most varied landscape: mountainous regions, spectacular lake vistas, rolling farmland, and metropolitan skylines. If you head west from Toronto on 401, after an hour's drive you'll be deep in rural southern Ontario. Here you also will find the twin cities of Kitchener and Waterloo, or "K-W." Swiss German Mennonites from Pennsylvania settled the region in 1800. Its German origins are still evident; K-W's annual Oktoberfest is the largest event of its kind in North America. The beer bash is a treat for the thousands of young people who attend nearby universities, and who provide for an energetic intellectual ambience in interesting juxtaposition to the surrounding religious Amish and Mennonite farming communities. In fact, most of Waterloo's 86,000 residents work for the universities or for high-tech companies spun from the universities; Waterloo is full of software firms founded by alumni.

"From the outset, Dave Stampe and I felt it was important to make REND386 available to people for free, with the source code, because we wanted to see a lot of people developing VR applications. We felt that it was the absence of a free graphics engine that was really keeping people from building virtual worlds."

The wiry, energetic, and charming Bernie Roehl is an exalted member of the garage VR community. With Dave Stampe, he co-created REND386, the popular freeware renderer that lets PC owners build and interact with virtual worlds. A labor of love for Bernie, this accomplishment had no direct bearing on his role as software developer for the University of Waterloo. It did, however, contribute to his subsequent achievements: co-authoring the definitive guide to REND386, *Virtual Reality Creations* (with Dave Stampe and John Eagen) and winning contracts to develop applications for a Calgary company named Virtual Universe. Bernie loves moving at high speed, whether on-screen ('386 PC) or on the road (1990 Nissan Sentra). He's also passionate about theater—not watching it, but performing in it.

Bernie Roehl was born in Montreal, Quebec, Canada on January 9, 1958. He learned to read before he started kindergarten and was reading voraciously by the time he entered West Hill High School in Montreal. He consumed science fiction, mysteries, and books about science and technology—particularly books about computers. Bernie remembers precisely what sparked the latter interest: a model-rocket magazine article about how to program a computer to calculate the trajectory of a flying rocket: "I found it fascinating, but I didn't know anything about computers. So I went to the library, got a book on Fortran, and looked at the programs until I understood how the program worked. Not long after that I bought my first computer, a [Radio Shack] TRS-80, with 48K of RAM and a cassette tape interface.

"Then at school," Bernie continues, "I started doing simple programming projects on an old terminal with a paper tape reader and paper tape punchprinting terminal, no screen, hooked up over a 110-baud modem to a computer at the school board. We could type our programs on paper tape offline, dial in, upload our programs, and get back our answers. I got hooked."

As a teen, Bernie also got hooked on another platform: the stage. Throughout high school, he performed and worked behind-the-scenes as a member of the after-school drama club.

Bernie left Montreal after high school to attend the University of Waterloo. He majored in physics, but continued devoting many extracurricular hours to performing. The theater, Bernie observes, is "an interest that's all-consuming. People who haven't done much theater find it hard to understand how you can spend so much time in rehearsals or workshops, but you really can immerse yourself in it."

In the spring of 1981, Bernie brought home his BS in physics, but bits and bytes interested him more than motion and gravity. By then he had purchased his second computer, an original IBM PC, for $1,800. "For that you didn't get disk drives, not floppies or a hard disk. And for a monitor I used my television with an RF modulator."

Bernie stayed at the University of Waterloo, working for a paycheck instead of a degree. Today, as software developer for the Department of Electrical and Computer Engineering, he oversees general systems programming and works directly with faculty members and graduate students on their own research. He also develops software for research purposes, writing mostly in C.

One of Bernie's programming pursuits—computer animation—coincides with his interest in the theater. It was through his appreciation for animation that he first encountered the topic of virtual reality. "I was looking at the various technologies that take human-movement information and encode it into the computer," Bernie recalls. "Along the way—I don't remember when—I read about the DataSuit [VPL Research's full-body VR input device]. I started reading more about VPL and the DataGlove. I found that even more fascinating than computer animation."

The first time he immersed himself in a virtual world was during a trip to Toronto, where Bernie played W. Industries' Virtuality to experience the alternative reality of the game, Dactyl Nightmare. He immediately drew parallels between virtual reality and theater. "Like VR, theater lets you create an alternative reality, an environment that is different from your real-life environment. And also like VR, theater lets you create another persona for yourself that you can step into."

These days, Bernie creates alternative personas, primarily in improvisational theater groups. He acts in interactive murder mysteries (in which an audience gathers at a restaurant, and, over dinner, characters interact with the audience and involve them in solving the mystery), improvisational comedy (actors request ideas from the audience and create skits on the spot), and competitive "theater sports" (teams of actors compete by improvising skits, their success judged by the audience).

"Improvisational theater is a step closer to VR than conventional theater," Bernie notes, "because it involves interaction with the audience. In both VR and interactive theater, there is a dynamic created among the virtual environment, the performers, and the audience.

"Now what I'd like to see is the ability to enact some theatrical scenario within a virtual environment. You would digitally record the actors' movement and speech, and other visual information, then subsequently render in a graphics engine at higher resolutions. Then you could create a real film of an event that only happened in VR."

Bernie's initial interest in VR brought him to CompuServe, where he could communicate with like-minded people. In 1990, both Dave Stampe (then a computer science undergraduate) and Bernie participated in the same CompuServe computer graphics forum. Bernie eventually noticed that Dave's e-mail address originated from the same University of Waterloo system on which Bernie owned an account. He e-mailed Dave, asking where he was. Dave was sitting in the same building. Bernie invited Dave to stop by his office. They chatted, became friends, and within a couple of weeks began brainstorming VR projects on which they could collaborate. "We both felt that the PC was capable of fast polygon graphics," Bernie says, "and that '386 and '486 PCs with VGA cards were everywhere. We figured we could design a polygon renderer around them."

Thus, REND386 came into existence. Together, Bernie and Dave brainstormed design ideas. Working alone, Bernie would implement the ideas in C, then modem the code to Dave. Dave would refine it offline, then e-mail the results back to Bernie. They went back and forth this way, "iterating the whole design/code/optimize cycle," Bernie says. "In retrospect, we probably would have done things differently in terms of the program's internal structure, although not in any way obvious to the user. That's true of any large project I've ever been involved in. Once you have it running, you look back and say, 'Knowing what I know now, I'd go back and do things differently.'"

Dave and Bernie finished the first version of REND386 in 1991. They created some simple worlds to demonstrate how it worked. Bernie says, "Dave had built a head-mounted display, so he used REND386 to explore and build worlds with his HMD. But we spent most of our effort on development rather than on application. Our goal was to get a wide distribution to a lot of people who were interested in VR so they could have something to use as a building block. Now other people are writing and developing all kinds of worlds with it."

This is possible because Bernie and Dave uploaded REND386 to the University of Waterloo's FTP server on January 30, 1992. They continued to remove glitches and add features, uploading version 2 in April of 1992, version 3 in June of 1992, and version 4 in September of 1992. After the August 1993 publication of their book on REND386, Dave and Bernie uploaded version 5. As of this writing, they're about to release the next upgrade.

The skill required to use REND386, Bernie says, depends on the extent to which a person wants to dive into the rendering and world-building process. "I think of it in terms of four levels of users:

"The first level is for the casually interested people who run the software. They download the executable worlds that other people have built, take a look at them, and use them for demos and hardware interfacing. They don't actually get into world-building. The most complicated skill here is knowing how to download the demo. Running the demo is a piece of cake.

"The second level is for people who are interested in building their own worlds. They actually modify the code that describes the worlds and some of the objects. To build worlds, you need some basic understanding of three-dimensional geometry. You have to know what the x-, y-, and z-axes are, measuring angles and degrees, and so on.

"The third level is for people who are interested in using REND386 to program. They don't necessarily need the source code, they just need a library that they can link with so they can write a program in C.

"The fourth level is for people who run through the guts of REND386 and actually add things to the source code. To do that, you have to be a really good programmer."

One of REND386's winning features is its capability to work "out of the box" with garage VR input and output devices. Support for stereoscopic viewing with Sega shutter glasses is built in; REND386 produces the left-eye and right-eye images that automati-

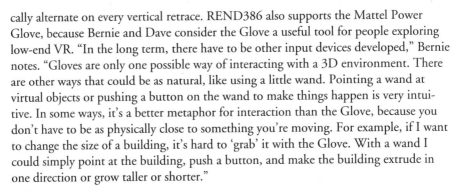

cally alternate on every vertical retrace. REND386 also supports the Mattel Power Glove, because Bernie and Dave consider the Glove a useful tool for people exploring low-end VR. "In the long term, there have to be other input devices developed," Bernie notes. "Gloves are only one possible way of interacting with a 3D environment. There are other ways that could be as natural, like using a little wand. Pointing a wand at virtual objects or pushing a button on the wand to make things happen is very intuitive. In some ways, it's a better metaphor for interaction than the Glove, because you don't have to be as physically close to something you're moving. For example, if I want to change the size of a building, it's hard to 'grab' it with the Glove. With a wand I could simply point at the building, push a button, and make the building extrude in one direction or grow taller or shorter."

As they continue developing REND386, Bernie and Dave will add support for the Global Devices forceball and other devices. Interface device support represents just one area of refinement: "In a future version of REND386, I want to simplify and streamline the interface so it's easier for programmers to work with," Bernie says. "To program with REND386 now, you have to read a lot of the source code. In a future release—probably version 6—we plan to streamline some of that so that any good programmer can sit down and use the library without having to read the source code for the library.

Bernie can't say for sure when version 6 will debut in the public domain, because progress on REND386 occurs at a slower pace now that Dave lives in Toronto (he's working on his Master's degree). That means Dave and Bernie must brainstorm through e-mail. Nonetheless, "we will continue adding functionality to it," Bernie says.

What about making REND386 a tool for nonprogrammers? "I've thought about that. To create really effective worlds with something like VREAM or any other tool for [nonprogrammers], you have to learn the programming language that's built in. The nice thing is you have a learning curve. You can use their software without having to know much [about the built-in programming language]. When you get to a certain level of sophistication, you can use their language to do interesting things. But developing a tool like that would require a great amount of time. I'd have to really think about how to design a language for people to use. The ideal language for doing that kind of thing is C, so I'm inclined to say that when people reach the point where they're pushing the boundaries of what they can do just by creating worlds with a text editor, it's time for them to learn C. That's what the more powerful VR systems use, like Autodesk CDK [Cyberspace Developer's Kit] or Sense8 WorldToolKit."

Yet even those powerful VR systems create worlds that Bernie describes as "ghost towns. There's no one else around. With networking, however, we have the potential to link up people from all over in one virtual world." This is the focus of Bernie's recent work at the university. He and his colleagues are developing a research protocol for sharing virtual worlds over networks. The protocol is called WAVES, for Waterloo Virtual Environment System. Bernie explains, "WAVES lets people using a number of different types of computers, all on the same network, all share the same virtual environment. You could be on an SGi workstation, doing something with texture mapping and multiple light sources, and I could be on a 486 PC seeing a simpler version of the same environment, and you and I could interact at the same time."

Bernie says he'll eventually graft the WAVES protocol onto REND386, and another programmer will graft WAVES onto the world-building software that runs on Silicon Graphics workstations. After that, true to form, Bernie will pour WAVES into the public domain. He wants to make sure it reaches the garage VR enthusiasts, because "most of the really good ideas come from people who are doing VR as a labor of love," Bernie says.

"Low-end VR hobbyists spend long hours learning everything from scratch, keeping in touch with each other to compare notes and share ideas. They build systems from spare parts, wiring up the circuit boards themselves. This approach leads to some very good ideas. Not too many of the really good, innovative ideas are going to come from the big, powerful research groups funded by government or industry. The people who are working in their basements, motivated by curiosity and excitement, will drive the technological innovations in the years ahead."

GVR

Tour Guide's Toolbox

Engine: '386, no-name generic PC, 33 MHz, VGA card, 8MB RAM

Monitor: 13-inch no-name generic

Modem: 2400-baud no-name generic

Primary hardware and software: Logitech 6DOF mouse, Global Devices forceball, REND386, DOS 5.0, NorthCAD 3D modeler and text editor to build worlds, and Borland C++ 3.1

Music to code by: Doesn't listen to music while coding

Total cost of system: Less than $2,000, except for the Logitech mouse, which is on loan from the University of Waterloo

E-mail: broehl@sunee.uwaterloo.ca

Dave Stampe can be reached at dstampe@psych.toronto.edu.

Hacking
for the Trip

CHAPTER
8

Hacking for the Trip

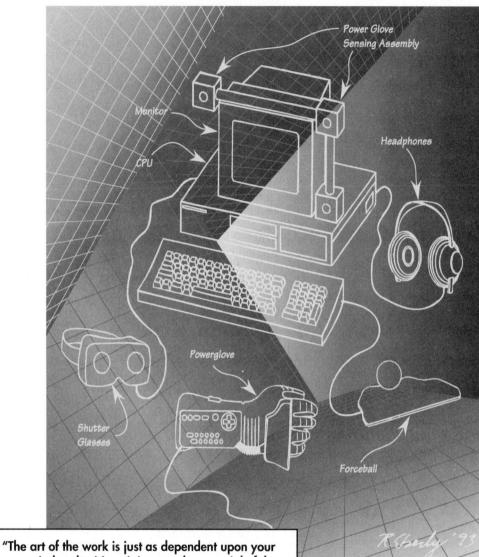

Labels in illustration:
- Power Glove Sensing Assembly
- Monitor
- CPU
- Headphones
- Powerglove
- Shutter Glasses
- Forceball

R. Goody '93

"The art of the work is just as dependent upon your own mind and spirit as it is upon the material of the machine."—Robert Pirsig, *Zen and the Art of Motorcycle Maintenance*

Do you want to hack your own interface box, stereoscopic viewer, head-mounted display, or tracking system? If so, this chapter is your road map. To work on the projects described here, you'll need an understanding of basic electronics. You also must know

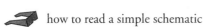 how to read a simple schematic

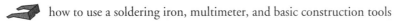 how to use a soldering iron, multimeter, and basic construction tools

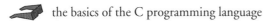 the basics of the C programming language

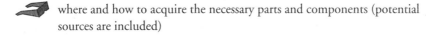 where and how to acquire the necessary parts and components (potential sources are included)

For some of these projects—particularly the Power Glove projects—you also need the programs on this book's disk. It contains sample programs for using the Glove with an IBM (or compatible) PC.

If you're experienced with electronics hobby projects, you know that the best way to construct circuits is to build on perfboard that has solder-ringed holes (sold at Radio Shack and through electronics parts catalogs), using thin, rosin-core solder and a fine-point soldering iron. You also know to *never* solder chips right into the circuit, because if the chip is faulty, your whole circuit is shot. Instead, solder a socket into the circuit, then pop the chip into the socket.

If you consider yourself an electronics novice, but still want to try your hand at one or more of these projects, visit a library and study some basic electronics books. Spend time working on simple electronics project kits, which you can buy at Radio Shack or hobby stores.

Likewise, you can learn the essentials of C programming in a variety of books that are available at libraries or bookstores that carry good selections of computer books. One such book is *Absolute Beginner's Guide to C* (Sams Publishing, 1993).

This series of "how-to" articles, contributed by VR hobbyists and innovators from around the United States, is dedicated to all tenacious tinkerers who thrive on doing-it-yourself.

NOTE

People have used these instructions to successfully assemble interfaces and I/O devices. However, the authors of the instructions, and the publisher of this book, won't accept any responsibility or liability for damage to any computer, input device, output device, or other property that may result from construction or use of these devices. None of the circuits or circuit boards described are warranted by the authors or publishers.

Hacking the Mattel Power Glove

The Power Glove, shown in Figure 8.1, uses a proprietary 7-pin connector that doesn't plug into anything besides a Nintendo game system. Its other nonstandard feature is its communications protocol, a modified, synchronous serial transfer. If a Power Glove is to work with a personal computer, it needs an interface device and software to perform communications protocol emulation.

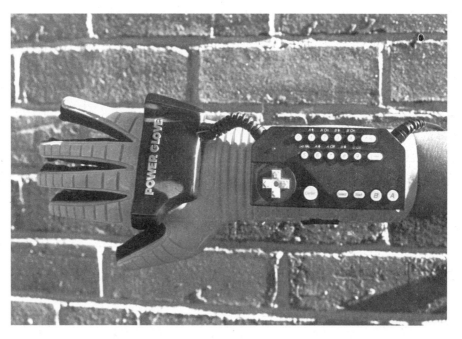

Figure 8.1. *The Power Glove. (Photo by Linda Jacobson)*

The first Glove hackers built their own interfaces by hooking the Glove connector (specifically, the Nintendo connector extending from the sensor assembly) to the appropriate pins on their computers' I/O ports. Then they hacked some code-protocol emulation routines to enable the computer to poll the Glove for input. Because the Glove relies on a 5-volt supply of power, hackers figured out how to route the juice through computer disk connectors, game ports, and keyboard cables (and in the process, a few fried their machines). The more cautious experimenters supplied the Glove with power from a separate 6-12V power adapter through a 7805 regulator IC.

Those homemade interfaces soon found their way into the public domain. Before long, a few entrepreneurs started marketing commercial interfaces. One such device is the Power Glove Serial Interface (PGSI), a project and product of the Student Chapter of the Association for Computing Machinery at the University of Illinois at Champaign-Urbana. The PGSI controls Sega-style shutter glasses in addition to Power Gloves. Enclosed in a small box (1- x 1.5- x 3.35-inch), it incorporates a 40-pin Motorola HC11 embedded microcontroller, support circuitry, and interface connectors to route the chip I/O functions to the Glove. The control program resides in the HC11 processor. The controller determines the state of the chip's pins by reading their values at the appropriate times.

The PGSI connects to any computer equipped with a standard RS232 serial communications port that can handle 9600 bps at no parity and 1 stop bit (9600,N,8,1), as long as the port takes the form of a 25-pin DB-25 connector. Newer IBM PCs and clones provide 9-pin DB-9 connectors, but you can buy adapters from computer stores or from the PGSI group. Newer Macintoshes sport a mini-DIN plug for serial action; again, adapters are sold at computer stores and by the PGSI folks. (For PGSI ordering information, see Chapter 6.)

Just because you can buy such a box (whether the PGSI or the similar VRASP and 3DTV devices) doesn't mean you might not want to build your *own* interface, enjoy the challenges of programming, and learn a lot about the Glove and shutter glasses—or about head-mounted displays, position-trackers, and stereoscopic viewers.

How to Build a Power Glove Interface for the IBM PC's Parallel Port

by Joseph D. Gradecki

© 1992 Gradecki Publishing. Reprinted by permission. All rights reserved.

Among the first sparse sets of instructions posted to various Internet sites were those assembled by Chris Babcock. Chris recommended that hackers build their interfaces with Nintendo game system extender cables (specifically, the Curtis Super Extendo cable, at $7 for two cables). According to Chris, "This makes it easy to also use other Nintendo devices and enables testing the Glove and still being able to exchange a defective Glove [if you bought it new]. (Plus, you get a long cable to the control box)." Today, Chris still uses his Power Glove, but he admits that it isn't a precise input device. For "real work," Chris says, "I use a Mouse Systems 3D mouse (it has a roller on top for z, pitch, and roll)."

About 18 months after Chris posted the Glove interface circuit, Joe Gradecki launched his homebrewer's 'zine, PCVR. In Volume 1, Issue 1, he compiled all the available interface circuit information and elaborated on it. The following is an edited reprint of that article.

One of the first things a VR experimenter should do is to interface the Power Glove to the PC.

System Requirements

(1) PC, of course

(1) Power Glove

(1) Extension cable recommended (you'll be hacking one end of the Power Glove's cable; the extension cable is insurance against a possible accident, and it provides a long cable)

(1) Bidirectional parallel port (I've seen documentation on how to convert a directional parallel port into a bidirectional port, but considering the price of parallel ports today, it's easier and less time-consuming to just buy a bidirectional parallel port card. Different parallel ports use different circuitry and if you try to do a conversion, you might make an unwise adjustment.)

(1) DB-25 male connector (the easiest to use are the ones with crimp pins, although any type will work)

Tools Needed

Wire strippers

Digital multimeter

Soldering iron

Long-nose pliers

Software Needed (Available on this Book's Disk)

IBMPC-HI
GLOVE.C
GLOVE.H
GLOVE.OBJ
GLOVGRAF.C
GLOVGRAF.OBJ
GLOVGRAF.EXE
TEST.C
TEST.OBJ
TEST.EXE
ROUTINES.DOC
MAKEFILE

Values: Measuring Glove Movement

The Power Glove enables four degrees of freedom: x movement, y movement, z movement, and roll. The Glove can register a grip or a flat palm, as well as a press of its keypad button.

The *grip* of each finger (except the pinky) is measured in distinct values, from flat to bend. However, the grip sensors are not sensitive: the only usable values are 0x00 through 0x80 for a flat hand and 0xFF for a full grip.

The *roll* position of the Glove registers values from +0 (when the Glove is palm-side down and horizontal) to +12 (the same position with a full rotation). The Glove's roll sensor also is not sensitive.

For the x-, y-, and z-axes, the Glove's values are relative from a center point of 0,0,0. The values move from 0 in integer increments and decrements.

When the system registers the Glove's horizontal or vertical position, typically a range of values must be used. For the Virtual Hand project described later in this chapter, 0 to 2 is horizontal and ≥3 is vertical.

Wire Functions

First, you must determine exactly which wires in the Power Glove cable connect to the Nintendo connector extending from the sensor assembly.

If you are using the original connector (not the extension cable):

1. Locate the box at the end of the sensor assembly; a short cable should come out of that box.

2. Cut the end of this cable about 1/2-inch from the end connector.

If you are using an extension cable:

1. Connect the end of the extension cable to the end connector that extends from the box at the end of the sensor assembly.

2. Cut off the other end of the extension cable.

3. Strip back about 1.5 inches of the insulation on that end of the cable.

4. Strip off the insulation from each of the wires to expose about 3/4 inches of each wire.

The Connector

The Nintendo connector (extending from the box attached to the sensor assembly) looks like that in Figure 8.2 and is numbered.

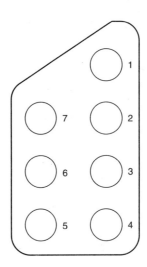

Figure 8.2. *The Nintendo connector.*

I'll refer to these numbers later.

Using the Original Cable

If you are using the original cable, its wire colors should include black, orange, yellow, green, and red (there are two other colors, but you don't need to worry about them now). Each color refers to a particular pin on the connector:

> 1 = Ground = black
> 2 = Clock = orange
> 3 = Latch = yellow
> 4 = Out = green
> 5—not applicable
> 6—not applicable
> 7 = +5 volts = red

If one of these colors is missing or the colors appear wrong, you need to do some detective work. Strip the insulation from the connector and the wires (from which you cut off the other connector), but leave enough of the colored insulation so you'll know which wire you're working with. Now get your multimeter. It should be set to measure resistance. Touch a probe to a wire; then touch each of the pins in the end connector. When the needle or display registers a value, this indicates a relationship between the wire you're touching and the pin that the other probe is touching. Write down the wire color and pin number. Repeat for each color. When finished, you'll have a chart of the relationships between the wires and the pins.

Using the Extension Cable

If you use an extension cable, you must figure out which wire corresponds to which pin on the Nintendo connector. Using your multimeter (set to measure resistance), touch a wire with one probe; then touch the other probe to each of the pins in the Nintendo connector. When the multimeter needle or display registers a value, this indicates a relationship between the wire you're touching (the color) and the pin that's touched by the other probe. Write down the color and pin number. Repeat for each color. When finished, you'll have a chart of the relationships between the wires and the pins.

Now it's time to connect the Glove to the PC.

Connecting the Glove to the PC

Wire the Glove to the parallel port. Here's where you use the DB-25 male connector. Connect each of the Glove's wires to the DB-25 connector as shown in Figure 8.3.

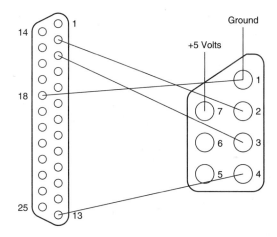

Figure 8.3. *Connecting the Glove's wires.*

The relationship from the DB-25 pins to the Glove sensor connector pins is as follows:

DB-25 Connector	Nintendo Connector
Pin 18 to	Pin 1
Pin 2 to	Pin 2
Pin 3 to	Pin 3
Pin 13 to	Pin 4

Connect Pin 1 on the Glove sensor connector to *ground*.

Connect Pin 7 on the Glove sensor connector to a +5V power source (see the next section for details).

Power Connection

There are three different ways to connect +5V power to the Glove:

1. From the keyboard
2. From an external source
3. From an internal peripheral connector

If you want to be able to move your Glove from one computer to another, you should provide power from the keyboard or an external source.

Connecting the Glove from an external source is probably the safest way to go. But if you don't want to worry about having another power receptacle around for the external source, don't choose that option.

Whatever you choose, be sure that you use only +5 volts wired to Pin 7 (or the associated color), and that the ground pin is wired to Pin 1 (or the associated color).

If you chose to provide power from the keyboard, see Figure 8.4 for the pin-outs. Using both male and female keyboard connectors, you can make a plug that enables the keyboard and the power for the Glove to be connected simultaneously.

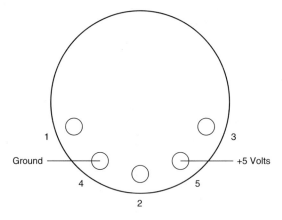

Figure 8.4. *Pin-outs.*

After you connect the power, you are finished interfacing the Glove.

Using the Glove with the PC

After you interface the Glove to the PC, you'll need software to read and request data from the Glove. I've obtained two pieces of interface code for the PC and the Power Glove, which are included on the disk provided with this book (and also printed here).

The code in IBMPC-HIRES and GLOVE is basically the same, but I'll introduce the basics for each. I won't go into details of the timings necessary for strobing the Glove.

TEST Code

Also included are two test programs: TEST and GLOVGRAF. The TEST program displays the values that are continually sent to the PC until you press a key. This is a good program to execute after you interface the Glove to the PC.

GLOVGRAF Code

The GLOVGRAF program displays a box on the PC's screen. The box moves left and right with the Glove. When you move the Glove in the z direction, backward and forward, the box grows larger and smaller.

IBMPC-HI Code

This includes a short main, intended to give an idea of how to use the hires Glove functions provided in the code. It begins by creating an array of length 12 called `buf`:

```
unsigned char buf[12];
```

and a pointer to a structure `glove_data`:

```
glove_data *glov;
```

The structure is declared as

```
typedef struct_glove_data
{
    signed char
dum0,x,y,z,rot,fingers,keys,dum7,dum8,dum9,dumA,dumB;
}
    glove_data;
```

To relate the buffer and the pointer, the statement

```
glov=(glove_data*)buf;
```

is executed. The pointer `glov` now points to a buffer of length 12 and is ready to receive data—and the system is ready to be started. The function call, `Hires();`, puts the Power Glove into high-resolution mode. This system is not interrupt-driven. In order for the PC to receive data from the Glove, it must strobe the Glove. To get data from the Glove, the function `getglove(buf)` is called. Notice that the `glov` variable (previously declared) is never used! However, you can call this function any time you want data from the Glove.

Because of the timings necessary, you need to experiment to gain acceptable readings from the Glove—but the code does work as advertised.

GLOVE Code

This code was obtained from the Internet site sunee.waterloo.edu. It's a conglomerate of code written by different authors, and it wasn't originally developed for the PC or the parallel port. This code includes modes for the Glove's hires and lores modes, as well as the capability to use interrupts. Functions have been added to the code to handle noise from the Glove. You don't need to adjust delay values; that is performed automatically. I've been told that the delay code in IBMPC-HI is somewhat better than this GLOVE code. However, GLOVE is convenient and easy to use.

The GLOVE program has a Glove data structure called glove_data:

```
typedef struct glove_data
{
        signed char x,y,z,rot,fingers,keys;
        unsigned int nmissed; /* number of samples missed */
} glove_data;
```

First, I declared a variable of this type—glov. Next, the appropriate receive mode is set with the glove_init function. The possible modes are HIRES, IHIRES, LORES, and ILORES.

```
glove_init ( HIRES, NULL );
```

Now you can receive data from the Glove. There are two ways to get data, depending on the mode set with the glove_init function. Both methods use the function glove_read. This function is passed the glov variable declared previously.

If interrupts are used during data reception, you don't have to wait for the Glove to reset itself. If interrupts aren't used, you must wait for the Glove.

No Interrupts

Before getting data, you must ask the Glove if it is ready to send data using the glove_ready() function. The function returns 0 for false and 1 for true. If the Glove isn't ready, you must create a delay using the function glove_delay(). A typical receive loop is

```
while ( !glove_ready() ) glove_delay;
glove_read ( &glove );
```

We loop, creating a delay during each iteration, until the Glove is ready to give data. You read data from the Glove when the loop is exited.

Interrupts

If interrupts are enabled, you only need to execute the `glove_read()` function call. It blocks until data is ready.

When you're finished with the Glove, the function `glove_quit()` should be executed to reset the Glove and possible interrupt settings.

The Code in Use

I used the GLOVE code exclusively in my Virtual Hand and Virtual HandShake programs, which are described in the next section. I find that not having to experiment with the timings is quite nice. I move my Glove from several different machines and haven't experienced any problems with this code.

How to Build a Power Glove Interface for the Amiga's Parallel Port

This basic interface data exists in Amiga-savvy VR code sites on the Internet. Reportedly hacked by a programmer named Alan Bland, this interface accesses the Amiga's parallel port directly, without involving the operating system.

This information, along with driver code, also can be found in the file AMIGAHIRES.LZH in the glove-list, among other places.

Refer to Figure 8.2 to identify the correct pins on the Glove's (sensor assembly) Nintendo connector. Then, attach to the Amiga in the following fashion:

Amiga Parallel Port	Nintendo Connector
Pin 18	Pin 1 GND
Pin 2	Pin 2 CLOCK
Pin 3	Pin 3 LATCH
Pin 4	Pin 4 DATA
Pin 14 POWER +5V	Pin 7 +5V

Following are the contents of the controlling data packet (12 bytes):

1.	2.	3.	4.	5.	6.	7.	8.	9.	10.	11.	12.
A0	X	Y	Z	rot	finger	keys	00	00	3F	FF	FF

Hacking for the Trip

Power Glove Trouble-Shooting

Problem:

I built the parallel interface described in the July 1990 *Byte* article, but it doesn't work. When I connect it to my PC, all the LEDs on the Glove light up and stay lit, no matter what I do with the Glove. REND386 just sits there with the screen prompt Waiting for Glove. I'm using the computer keyboard for power. According to my voltmeter, the Glove's getting about 4.75 volts. Is this close enough to 5 volts, or is that the problem? Should I install a driver, or does REND386 do that?

Possible Solutions:

Check your port settings. REND386 might not be looking for the Glove in the right place.

Check your parallel port; there could be a problem with your I/O card.

4.75 volts might not be enough; try a true 5V supply.

Problem:

I'm using the Glove with REND386, and essentially it works, but sometimes the images don't react to Glove motions. What's going on?

Possible Solution:

Make sure you're standing (or sitting) no more than about five feet from the screen; closer is better. You must be a certain distance from the screen before you select objects using the Glove; otherwise, its performance gets glitchy because of ultrasonics bouncing off nearby hard surfaces.

Problem:

I can't get the program GLOVE.C to compile under Turbo C++ for Windows. The link fails. I tried using Borland C version 1.5 and that didn't work either.

Possible Solution:

Your version of GLOVE.C might not be designed for compiling under Windows. A version of the Glove driver is available for Windows and C++. You can find it on CompuServe in the CyberForum and at the anonymous FTP Internet site sunee.uwaterloo.ca.

Problem:

I interfaced my Power Glove to generate clocking signals approximately the same as those specified in the *Byte* article. But the Center function doesn't work. The sensor LEDs either all turn on or all turn off; individual LEDs won't turn on or off based on Glove motion. Is this a clocking problem?

Possible Solution:

The length of the pulse is important (3-8 microseconds). Try varying the pulse. On the Amiga, 7-microsecond pulses work well. It's also important to clock data out of the Glove quickly.

Problem:

My problem isn't described in this section of the book. I can't get the Glove to work right and it's driving me crazy!

Possible Solutions:

Log onto the nets and post a description of your problem in one of the following places:

 The Internet glove-list

 The "garage VR" topic in the WELL's VR conference

 The sci.virtual-worlds on Usenet

 The CyberForum on CompuServe

Chances are, one of the many Power Glove experts on-line will provide some satisfactory answers. Those folks provided almost all the answers to the hypothetical problems just listed!

How to Build a Dual-Glove Interface for the PC's Parallel Port

by Mark Pflaging

This interface was developed by the VR hacker of hackers, Mark Pflaging, vice president of the VR Alliance of Students & Professionals. He too recommends using Nintendo game system extenders, preferably Curtis Super Extendo Cable.

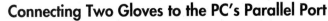

Hacking for the Trip

Connecting Two Gloves to the PC's Parallel Port

Although Mattel never made left-handed Power Gloves, it's possible to build one from the parts of a Power Glove—I've built two "better" Gloves this way. I also changed the code from a right/right system (where two different people use the Gloves) to a left/right system where one person has both hands in Gloves. For that purpose, I sometimes refer to the first Glove as the "Right Glove" and the second Glove as the "Left Glove."

After you build this interface, if you have a hood for your parallel port connector, you can label the two Nintendo cables as "left" and "right" before putting the hood back on.

Following is the pin-out list for wiring the first and second Glove connectors to the parallel port. Note that the first Glove is wired exactly the same as the single-Glove hookup described earlier. If you already have a single-Glove connector, you don't need to disconnect any of the wires already there.

Parallel Port	First Glove
Pin 18 GND	Pin 1
Pin 2 D0	Pin 2
Pin 3 D1	Pin 3
Pin 13 SELECT (input)	Pin 4

Parallel Port	2nd Glove
Pin 18 GND (connect to same pin as first Glove)	Pin 1
Pin 4 D2	Pin 2
Pin 5 D3	Pin 3
Pin 12 PAPER OUT (input)	Pin 4

Alternative connection: It might be possible to wire an identical first Glove connector and connect it to a spare parallel port. The software should detect and use the second Glove as if it were connected to the same parallel port. I haven't tested this, because my PC provides only one parallel port, but it should work.

Power

Connect Pin 7 on the second Glove to any location with +5V. You should be able to use the same power location as the first Glove's. Twice as much current will be drawn. If you're using the keyboard or game port power, there shouldn't be a problem.

The Sensors

Where do you position the second Glove's sensor assembly? It is easiest to simply piggyback the sensors and hold them together with duct tape or similar adhesive. Little Velcro pads might work too. The sensor assemblies should be in close proximity, but make sure they don't block each other.

I used five pieces of tape to securely attach my sensor assemblies to each other, but I'm sure there are other ways.

The following diagram shows the setup of my sensor assemblies:

```
 / — — \                     / — — \
 ¦       ¦===================¦        \
 \ — — /                     \ — + o   ¦
 / — — \             / — — \  ¦o  o  ¦
 ¦       ¦===============¦     \  ¦  o  ¦
 \ — — /             \ — + o   ¦¦o  o  ¦
                     ¦o  o  ¦¦\ — — /
                     ¦   o  ¦  ¦ ¦
                     ¦o  o  ¦  ¦ ¦
                     \ — — /  ¦ ¦
                       ¦¦     ¦ ¦
                       ¦¦     ¦ ¦
                       ¦¦     ¦ ¦
                       ¦¦     ¦ ¦
                       ¦¦     ¦ ¦
                       ¦¦     ¦ ¦
                       ¦¦  / — — \
                       ¦¦  ¦      ¦
                       ¦¦  \ — — /
                     / — — \
                     ¦      ¦
                     \ — — /
```

The Software

I have modified REND386 and its DOS demo and created a new Windows application called Object Glove that uses the Dual-Glove setup. They all access the same driver, which "seeks out" Gloves on three different parallel port addresses, then uses the alternate polling technique for avoiding conflict between the two Gloves. One Glove is polled, then the other Glove is polled, then the first Glove, and so on. In other words, the ultrasonic pulses from one Glove are sensed before the pulses from the second Glove are sent out.

The idea behind Object Glove is to provide people with a simple way of incorporating Power Glove input into their own applications. The demo includes things to do, but I'm the first to admit there aren't any actual useful applications in the demo. There are so many ways to use the Power Glove —too many ways for me to address!

> **NOTE**
>
> To find out how to obtain Object Glove, see Chapter 7. A demo program for Object Glove (filename OBJGLV.EXE) can be obtained from the REND386 directory of the Internet host site `sunee.uwaterloo.ca`. For more information, see Chapter 10.

> **Power Glove Extension Cables**
>
> Need a source? Contact
>
> MCM Electronics
> 650 Congress Park Drive
> Dayton, Ohio 45459
> (800) 543-4330
> Fax: (513) 434-6959
>
> Ask for "Nintendo-Type Joystick Extension Cable," part number #83-0325, $4.75 each. VR hobbyists probably will enjoy the MCM catalog.

How to Create a Virtual Hand

by Joseph D. Gradecki

©1992 Gradecki Publishing. Reprinted by permission. All rights reserved.

The software for the Virtual Hand is on this book's disk; the files you'll need to run are

```
PGHAND1.OBJ
PGHAND1.C
PGHAND1.EXE
```

I interfaced the Power Glove to the PC and then said, "Okay, now what?" At that time, there was no code out in netland that makes the Glove do something, except for the interface box and test code. To get things rolling, there needs to be some software that uses the Power Glove in a somewhat meaningful manner. My first project toward this goal was a "virtual hand."

While I'd like to say that this program's representation of a human hand is excellent, I cannot. Because of the limitations of the PC and my lack of 3D graphics programming experience (which has grown after this experience), the graphics to reproduce the hand are crude and simple, but effective. The graphics could have been better, but I wanted to make sure the movement of the virtual hand was real-time, so when you move the Power Glove up, the virtual hand should move up as fast as the Power Glove. This is true for each axis's movements (*x, y,* and *z*), roll, and grip.

Because of the crude grip values that the Glove registers, the virtual hand has two grip positions: open and closed. I could not receive reliable intermediate values for the grip; therefore, I didn't include these motions.

Graphics

To create a virtual hand, I set up several functions and structures to handle the 3D graphics. I'm documenting my creation of each of the functions and structures here so that others can use them. Other books and magazines explain the basics of 3D graphics.

The first structure details what a point is:

```
struct point
{
        int          x, y, z;
        int          oldx, oldy, oldz;
        int          ax, ay;
        struct point *next;
};
```

The programmer is concerned with the fields x, y, z, and next. The other fields are used by other functions in the system for bookkeeping purposes. x, y, and z are the 3D coordinates of the point. next is the pointer to the next point in a possible linked list of points.

The next structure, called polygon, uses the point structure (previously shown) to form the vertices of a polygon. A polygon can have any number of points. The points should be attached to the polygon in the order that they are to be drawn. Notice that a polygon can consist of two or more points:

```
struct polygon
{
        struct point *points;
        struct polygon *next;
        int            color;
        int            line;
};
```

If the polygon is a line, the field line should be set to 1; otherwise, it's set to 0. The color field is not used at this time. The field point is a linked list of points used (as described previously). next is a pointer to additional polygons. A single polygon can be constructed from more than one polygon.

After you have polygons, you can form objects. The structure object is used for that purpose:

```
struct object
{
        struct polygon *polygons;
        int             number;
};
```

An `object` is just a linked list of polygons. Whenever this object is drawn or erased, the system moves down the list, drawing all polygons that it encounters. The `number` field is used to record the number of polygons that make up this object.

The last major structure is `matrix`:

```
struct matrix
{
        int     m[4][4];
};
```

Each matrix used for transformations or other purposes is declared as structure `matrix`. All matrix locations are integers. Using these structures, you can create any form in the 3D world.

Following in this section are the functions included in the code:

```
void identity ( struct matrix * )
```

This function takes a matrix and initializes it to the three-dimensional identity matrix. There is no return value:

```
void create_view_transformation()
```

This function creates global values that are used when projecting an object on-screen. The values use globally defined constants `rho`, `theta`, and `phi`.

These constants have been defined so that the x-axis is along the horizon of the screen. The y-axis is along the left vertical side of the screen. The z-axis extends in the negative direction into the screen from the bottom-left corner of the screen.

```
struct object * create_object()
```

This function creates an object (allocates memory) and returns a pointer to the object.

```
void release_object ( struct object *obj )
```

This function releases all memory that the passed object has been allocated.

```
struct polygon * add_polygon ( struct objec *obj, int line )
```

This function adds a polygon to the specified object. The polygon is added to the end of the linked list of polygons for this object. If the polygon is a line, `line` should be set to 1; otherwise, it should be set to 0.

```
void add_vertex ( struct polygon *p, int x, int y, int z )
```

This function adds a vertex to the polygon p with the coordinates x, y, and z.

```
void proj ( struct point *p, int *sx, int *sy, struct matrix *mat )
```

This function transforms point p using matrix (mat) and the global transformation values onto the 2D screen. The resulting x and y coordinates are put into the memory locations pointed to by the integer pointers sx and sy. This function has to be called for *every* point to be plotted on-screen.

```
void draw_object ( struct object *obj, struct matrix *mat, int color )
```

This function draws the object (obj) using the matrix (mat) and the color (color). Because you are only using wireframe drawings, the color is the color of the lines that make up the object.

```
void erase_object ( struct object *obj )
```

This function erases the object (obj) using prerecorded values for each point.

```
struct matrix * object_scale ( struct matrix *mat, float scale )
```

This function scales an object equally on all three coordinates by the scaling value (scale) using the matrix (mat). This scaling is applied to the matrix and not to the object directly.

```
struct matrix * object_xrot ( struct matrix *mat, float deg )
```

This function rotates the object about the x-axis by the number of degrees (deg). This rotation is applied to the matrix (mat) and not to the object directly. A pointer is returned to the new matrix.

```
struct matrix * object_yrot ( struct matrix *mat, float deg )
```

This function rotates the object about the y-axis by the number of degrees (deg). This rotation is applied to the matrix (mat) and not to the object directly. A pointer is returned to the new matrix.

```
struct matrix * object_zrot ( struct matrix *mat, float deg )
```

This function rotates the object about the z-axis by the number of degrees (deg). This rotation is applied to the matrix (mat), not to the object directly. A pointer is returned to the new matrix.

```
struct matrix * object_translate ( struct matrix *mat, int transx,
                                    int transy, int transz )
```

This function translates the object by the values transx, transy, and transz. The translation is applied to the matrix (mat), not to the object directly.

The Virtual Hand

My idea was to create a realistic virtual hand that exactly mimics the movements of the Power Glove. I realized I had to accept a trade-off between realism and real-time movements. I opted for real-time movements. As a result, the virtual hand is very simple. It consists of a box for a palm and four stick fingers; there is no thumb.

Using the routines listed here, this virtual hand mimics the movements of the Power Glove in real time. The image is quite realistic, because the hand grows smaller and larger when the Glove is moved in the z direction.

One of the important functions that the Glove performs is the grip. The virtual hand will grip similar to the way the Power Glove does. There is no intermediate movement for the grip because of the lack of sensitivity in the fingers.

Graphics Representation

To represent a three-dimensional space on a two-dimensional screen, several transformations must take place. The x-axis of the space is positioned at the bottom of the screen with 0 at the left corner. The y-axis of the space is positioned at the vertical left of the screen with 0 at the lower-left corner. The z-axis of the space is positioned into the screen starting at the lower-left corner. The z values decrement in a negative direction as you move more into the screen.

The Glove is given a starting location of off-center to the right and in the horizontal position. The system assumes that this is the 0,0,0 coordinates for the Glove.

Three variables are used to remember the previous position of the Glove: `glovex`, `glovey`, and `glovez`. When a movement is returned from the Glove, the values read are compared to the previous location of the Glove. If the values are different, the absolute value of the difference of the Glove is calculated. This value is the amount that the virtual hand will move, according to the values from the Glove. These values are multiplied by an incrementing value to give a more realistic movement of the virtual hand. All three values are applied to the current transformation matrices of the hand.

The Glove is checked for roll and grip; another check is made to see whether the A button has been pressed (to stop the program). If any of these things have happened, the transformation matrices will be updated accordingly. The grip is a different case. In this version of the virtual hand (my first attempt), the actual point values for the fingers are changed instead of the transformation matrices. This tries to solve a positioning problem with the Glove when the fingers are bent.

After all this has taken place, the virtual hand is erased and drawn again. Because I'm working in the VGA screen resolution 640x480, there is only one video page and there is flicker. (This could be solved by using the 320x240 mode with page flipping.)

These functions are performed in a loop until you press the A button on the Glove.

A Better Virtual Hand

In the previous program, the virtual hand was a stick representation. To bend the fingers of this hand, the actual points that make up the finger had to be changed. Here is a description of a true 3D representation of the virtual hand.

The software for the Better Virtual Hand is on the disk included with this book; the files you'll need to run it are

        PGHAND2.OBJ
        PGHAND2.C
        PGHAND2.EXE

Stick Figure

In representing the stick hand, the objects that made up the hand were very primitive. The palm was simply a box, and each finger was made up of three lines and four vertices. The entire hand had 20 vertices. This worked well, except for gripping. In its normal orientation, the hand looked similar to Figure 8.5.

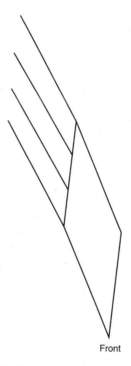

Front

Figure 8.5. Joe Gradecki's stick hand.

When you grip the Power Glove, the virtual finger should move to the left of the hand and form a grip position. Using the normal rotation routines in the graphics code produces a hand like that shown in Figure 8.6. If you grip your right hand, you will see that the first segment of your finger is horizontal (as shown in the virtual hand). The second segment should join the first and be vertical; it is actually 180 degrees from its original position and translated to the end of the first segment. The third segment should join the second and be horizontal—with a move of a 90-degree rotation—and do a translation. You will see from Figure 8.6 that when only the rotation is performed, the segments do not join as they should. If the translations are performed on the joints as well, the segments will join up. These translations are specific to the gripping of the hand. They must be figured out through either trial-and-error, or by using a graph paper and some math.

Figure 8.6. *What happens when the stick hand tries to grip.*

When the translations are performed during the grip, they must be undone when the hand is flexed. If, by some chance, the hand is rolled to a different position, the translations will be wrong. With the second version of the virtual hand, this was solved by keeping a constant record of which position the hand was in, so that specific translations and rotations could be used. The original virtual hand was so "sticky" that it was easier to change the points of the finger object than to perform the rotations and translations.

3D Virtual Hand

The new virtual hand is not a simple object. The palm consists of eight vertices. Each finger has three segments with a total of 16 vertices, for a grand total of 72 vertices. The complexity of the new hand (and my total lack of artistic talent!) makes it impossible to reproduce the hand here. It is still blocky, but it looks more like a hand.

The added complexity of the hand meant that the grip would have to be handled differently. I could no longer simply change the coordinates of the fingers, because they had a total of 64 points. To solve this problem, I learned something new.

Instead of trying to rotate and translate the fingers as a single unit, I broke the fingers down into the three natural segments of a real finger. As the hand is gripped, the segments are rotated, translated, and redrawn from the lower segment to the higher segment. Each of the segments are translated to the origin, rotated to the appropriate degree position, then translated back to their new position. To do this, I used a new function called `mini_proj`. This function returns the new location of a single point. I give a point on the end of the segment that I want to attach to the new segment. The values returned are the translate values that I use for the new segment. For fast reference, the values of the joints are kept in constants.

A Virtual Handshake

by Joseph D. Gradecki

© *1992 Gradecki Publishing. Reprinted by permission. All rights reserved.*

The software for the Virtual Handshake is on the disk included with this book. The files you'll need to run it are

> GLOVE.OBJ
> GLOVE.H
> SHAKE.C
> AXIS.C
> AXIS.EXE

You'll also need two modem-equipped computers—connected through the Internet—and a copy of the public-domain communications software, WATTCP, available from `sunee.uwaterloo.edu`.

After I wrote the virtual hand program, I needed something useful for the virtual hand to do. The VR Handshake was born.

Using two Power Gloves, I wanted to simulate a handshake between two people. The only thing lacking was the communication between two computers. Having built a network parallel-processing environment, I had at my disposal the required network components. As I thought more about the handshake, it occurred to me that the program should be able to interface two people from anywhere in the world—but my networking toolkit was for local use only. What I needed was a TCP/IP package that could send information anywhere in the world.

After looking at several commercial products and determining that they were too expensive, I came upon WATTCP, a public domain TCP/IP package available from `sunee.uwaterloo.edu`. This package is outstanding and works as advertised. With this package, I could accomplish the virtual handshake.

System Requirements

(2) IBM-PC (or compatible) computers connected on the Internet

(2) Power Gloves (one for each computer)

(1) Power Glove-to-PC interface for each computer

The software

Each of the PCs must have an IP address that the local gateway will recognize. The program uses the PC's VGA mode. The Power Glove is accessed through the parallel port.

The software was tested on two local machines on the Internet; everything worked well. Because of the close proximity of the machines, the delay for the remote Glove was minimal.

System Set-Up

I'll start by explaining how to use the program. Each PC must contain a file called WATTCP.CFG in the local directory. The configuration file looks something like this:

```
my_ip=129.72.6.112        ; ip address of this machine
netmask=255.255.0.0       ; netmask for local network
nameserver=129.72.1.2     ; address of a name server
gateway=129.72.3.1        ; address of your gateway
domainslist="uwyo.edu"    ; system extension
```

You need to change each of the values in this file to reflect the addresses of your network. After you do this, you can start the program. One machine serves as host; the other is the caller. The person using the host machine should execute the handshake program by typing shake.

The other person must have the address of the host machine. That person then executes the handshake program by typing shake xxx.xxx.xxx.xxx (with the IP address in place of the xxx's). When a connection is made, the host machine will issue a prompt, hit any key. After you press a key, each machine displays a statement instructing each person to exercise the Glove and press any key.

After both people have pressed keys, two virtual hands appear on each screen. The red hand is the local hand's representation; the blue hand is the remote representation. As each Power Glove moves, the corresponding virtual hand moves. This won't occur in real time unless the machines are located physically close to each other.

Shake

To produce the actual handshake, each of the virtual hands must be equal on the y-axis (vertical) and within an inch of each other on the x-axis (horizontal). The z-axis turned out to be more of a problem; this version of the program ignores it. When the virtual hands are in the right position, both people should grip their Power Gloves. If everything has gone as described, the program will take over and move the virtual hands up and down in a shaking pattern. It may seem childish—but it works!

To end the program, press the Q key. The Internet connection will close automatically.

Operation

The basic operation of the handshake program relies on the virtual hand programs. The graphic manipulation routines are the same. The difference lies in the communication between the remote and local machines.

When the local Power Glove is moved, two things must happen:

1. The virtual hand on the local screen must be moved

2. The remote virtual hand must be moved

The first step involves the standard operations from the virtual-hand programs. To accomplish this second step, a data structure was created and sent to the remote machine. This data structure is called `remote_glove_data`:

```
struct remote_glove_data
        {  int x, y, z, roll, grip, angle, horizontal;
            char ch;
        };
```

When the local Glove is moved, the new x, y, and z values are put into this structure. If the Glove is gripped or rolled, each movement is recorded in the structure. After all the new data about the local Glove is collected, it's sent to the remote machine. A new hand is redrawn on the local and remote machines. The data is sent before the new hand is redrawn; therefore, the remote redraw will occur within a short delay of the local redraw.

The remote machine receives the new data and redraws the remote hand if needed. Because each person sends a large amount of data, the redraws will be slower than when using just the normal virtual hand program alone.

Compiling

To compile the handshake program, you will need the Power Glove code, provided on the disk that comes with this book (GLOVE), and the WATTCP package, which can be acquired from the Internet site `sunee.waterloo.edu`. The WATTCP package includes two library files called WATTCPSM.LIB and WATTCPLG.LIB. Also, there is a header file called TCP.H. The handshake program uses the WATTCPSM.LIB.

The following explanation uses Borland C 2.0. I have not compiled the program using Turbo C or Borland C 3.0. The simplest way to compile the program is to set up a

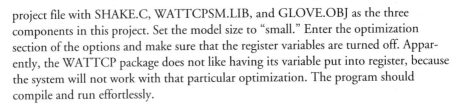

project file with SHAKE.C, WATTCPSM.LIB, and GLOVE.OBJ as the three components in this project. Set the model size to "small." Enter the optimization section of the options and make sure that the register variables are turned off. Apparently, the WATTCP package does not like having its variable put into register, because the system will not work with that particular optimization. The program should compile and run effortlessly.

The handshake code uses various pieces of the virtual hand program. To my knowledge, this is the first piece of useful code for the Power Glove and the PC. I didn't use the earlier version of REND386 initially to write it, because only viewpoint could be moved in the world, not objects.

How to Build a Head-Tracker from a Power Glove

by Douglas W. Faxon

© 1993 Douglas W. Faxon. All rights reserved.

A while back, I discovered that the Power Glove's two ultrasonic emitting devices serve a different purpose. One of them transmits the Glove position signal; that's the emitter on the right when the Glove's on your hand—palm facing away—and the lettering is properly oriented. The emitter on the left deals with orientation (roll data, palm down).

As soon as I learned that Mark Pflaging's Power Glove code could handle dual inputs, I realized that with some modification to Mark's code to use head position data as an invisible "joystick," I could use one of those inputs for head-tracking in a virtual world. I suggested to Mark that the input of Glove #2 could control a cursor on the screen. This cursor would follow the head movements when the emitter device is worn somewhere on the head (such as on a hat). I could set up the screen with invisible "zones" toward the outside edges. When the cursor drifts into the zone on the left side, the screen would begin scrolling to the right and the user's viewpoint would rotate to the left—continuing to do so until his or her head position moves the cursor to the center "dead" zone. This applies to up, down, left, and right directions. Mark's modified code (which can be found in DEMO4B of REND386) even senses distances "near" and "far" so that stepping toward or away from the screen can move the on-screen view closer or farther away.

To make this work, I bought an inexpensive, plastic baseball helmet. Then I took apart a Power Glove, extracted the sensor from the right side, and mounted it on the middle of the edge of the helmet brim. I mounted the guts (the Glove's electronics and control box) on the left side of the helmet. I put aside the left (orientation) sensor as well as the finger bend sensors (for which I plan to find other nefarious uses!).

Not counting the PC and color monitor, the entire system cost just a few dollars to build. The Power Gloves cost $25 apiece and the helmet cost $15. It took about five hours total to assemble the interface adapter for the Power Glove and to hack the Glove for the head-tracker.

Here's how it works: Using Mark Pflaging's Dual-Glove Interface, I connect Glove #1 input to a regular Power Glove for manipulating objects in the virtual environment. When I put on the helmet and Glove, I look straight ahead, "pointing" my head at the center of the screen, and I press the "center" button on the helmet's control panel. This button initializes the helmet position for my head's location in space. To initialize the Glove, I hold my hand flat, pointed forward, palm down, at a comfortable, waist-high position. Then I press the "center" button on the Glove's control panel. Finally, I slowly swing my head toward the left and toward the right to get a feel for the scrolling points.

I use the basic, simple Glove gestures: point to select, clench to grab, and pinch to rotate.

When I show this system to the public—at conferences, for example—I use the baseball helmet. However, an industrial hardhat with a dial-adjustable strap is a better choice, because it fits most people and doesn't make the head all sweaty. A helmet is just one of several mounting options for the head-tracker; the sensor can be mounted to a hat or glasses or safety-pinned to your cheek, if you want!

For our first exhibition of the head-tracker, which took place in the VRASP booth at the 1993 Meckler Virtual Reality Conference, Mark and I disabled the helmet's "up" and "down" rotation functions after the first day. That's because a large percentage of our users were getting lost when they looked up at the sky or down toward the ground and didn't see anything. Disabling that function saved a lot of grief and enabled everybody to have a lot more fun.

I want to thank everyone who contributed to the exhibit's success, especially Mark Pflaging and Vinnie Grier of VRASP, and Bernie Roehl and David Stampe for creating REND386.

Here are the directions for converting a Power Glove into a head-tracker. The head-tracker (see Figure 8.7) is designed to work with Mark Pflaging's Dual-Glove interface and REND386, so you'll need REND386 DEMO4B (see Chapter 7) and Mark's Dual-Glove Parallel Port Interface for the PC (described earlier in this chapter). You'll also need to spend some quality time playing around with REND386 (and thoroughly reading its documentation) before you convert your Power Glove into a head-tracker!

NOTE

This Head-Tracker doesn't work with the PGSI box.

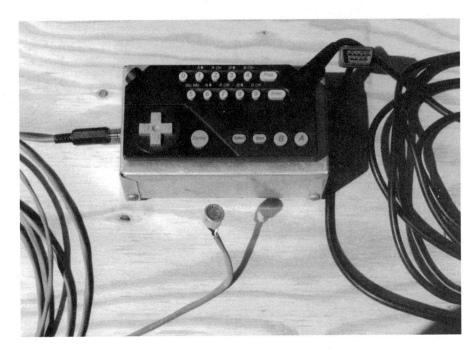

Figure 8.7. Doug Faxon's Head-Tracker. The emitter (foreground) can be attached to a pair of glasses, the brim of a baseball cap, or even the end of your nose. (Photo by Linda Jacobson)

This project is fairly advanced. We recommend that you have prior experience with soldering and circuit construction.

Hardware Required

(1) '386 or '486 PC

(1 minimum) Mattel Power Glove

(1) Dual-Glove parallel port interface for Power Glove and '386/'486 PC. This interface consists of one joystick extension cable, one male DB25 connector, and two Nintendo Super Extendo cables (available at Walmart and other places that sell and/or service Nintendo game systems).

(1) Box on which to mount the Glove electronics. I used a 3x5x2-inch aluminum box, purchased at an electronics parts store. These stores usually sell boxes of various shapes and sizes as enclosures for hobby projects. (You have to drill the holes yourself, a task described in step 12.)

(1) 1/8-inch mini-phono plug

(1) 1/8-inch mini-phono jack

8 to 10 feet of soft, flexible, 2-conductor stranded cable

Assorted washers, standoffs, and tie wraps

Plastic baseball helmet, cap, or eyeglasses

Tools Required

Wire cutters

Wire strippers

Assorted small screwdrivers (such as in a jeweler's set)

Soldering iron

Drill and assorted bits

Razor knife (such as an X-acto blade)

Elmer's glue (or equivalent)

Electrical tape

A little ingenuity

A lot of patience

Hacking the Glove

Every good construction project starts with a bit of destruction!

1. Using a razor knife, carefully cut around the edges of the gray rubber on the Power Glove. Separate the rubber from the underlying fabric (a thin naugahyde substance) without slashing the finger bend sensors underneath. You won't use these sensors in the head-tracker, but you might want to save them for other projects.

2. After you separate the bulky rubber glove from the small fabric glove, flip the Glove upside down. You'll see the screw heads that attach the rubber to the sensor head and the control module (the part with the push buttons). Run some electrical tape around the edge of the control module to hold it together while you remove it from the Glove.

3. Remove the screws and pull the "guts" off the rubber. Carefully pull the bend sensors through the plastic flange that held the sensor head to the Glove.

4. After separating the "guts" from the Glove, discard the Glove remains.

5. Remove the screws from the sensor head, carefully pulling the bend sensors through the hole, and you'll see the underlying circuit board.

6. Remove the screws that hold the circuit board to its plastic cover.

7. You'll see a *piezo beeper* in there. It's a round disk about the size of a quarter with the two wires attached, located in the top plastic cover labelled "Power Glove." Cut the wires off at the circuit board.

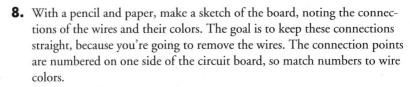

8. With a pencil and paper, make a sketch of the board, noting the connections of the wires and their colors. The goal is to keep these connections straight, because you're going to remove the wires. The connection points are numbered on one side of the circuit board, so match numbers to wire colors.

9. Desolder and remove the finger bend sensors from the board. Tuck them away for a rainy day.

10. Check your drawing to verify its accuracy in identifying the connections. When you're sure it's correct, desolder each wire from the board.

11. Remove the little "flexi" matter from the cable sheath encasing these wires by cutting the upper and lower ribs back at the control box side. Slide this extra plastic off the cable, which is about 1/4-inch. Be careful not to nick into the cable itself, or you may have to resolder new wires to the control board!

12. Mount the control module to the outside of your aluminum box. Before doing so, make sure the position of the box's holes match the position of the module's holes. Here's a match-trick:

    a. Put a neat bubble of Elmer's glue over each hole on the module.

    b. Carefully position the module over the box and press it gently against the surface of the box.

    c. When you lift the module, you will see little dabs of glue that mark the places where you want to drill your holes. Mark these dabs with a pencil.

    d. Wipe the glue out of the module's holes so they don't become permanently plugged.

    Use a drill bit (slightly larger than the shaft of the screws you removed from the module) to drill the holes you just marked.

    Use a 1/4-inch bit to drill a hole in the top-left corner of the top of the box. You'll use this to run the wires through to the inside. You may want to mount the module with a screw or two to get the exact location for this hole.

    Next, drill a hole on one side of the box for the 1/8-inch mini-phono jack (for the sensor output).

    Mount the control module to the box so that the connecting wires stick through the 1/4-inch hole to the inside.

13. Look at the emitter head board. The ultrasonic transducers are the two small cylinders pointing forward with the mesh screen on their front surfaces. You must remove these from the board. Here's how:

    a. Find the plastic that originally housed this circuit board.

b. Orient the board within it properly. If you're looking down on the words "Power Glove," the emitter in the upper-right corner is the one you want.

c. Mark the circuit board with an X where that transducer is connected.

d. Get rid of the plastic.

e. Desolder the sensors and save them.

f. Snip off about six inches of the flexible cable you'll be using for the sensor cord and solder one end to the points you marked with an X for the right-hand transducer.

g. Solder the other end of the flexible cable to your 1/8-inch mini-phono jack.

14. Now for the difficult part: resolder the wires from the control board to the emitter head board inside the box. There's no way to make this easy; it's tight in there! If you have trouble, try extending the wires a bit and soldering outside the box. I ran all new wires between the boards when I made my tracker, but it took much longer and I had enough multicolored bits of wire for the job. If you do it this way, be sure to make a plan of the connection points on the control module, and note that the numbers on that board's points *do not* correspond to the numbers you listed on your emitter board plan.

15. After properly reconnecting all the wires, mount the mini jack to your predrilled hole.

16. Wrap electrical tape around the sensor board to keep it insulated, particularly if your enclosure box is made of metal. If you're using a baseball helmet, tape the box securely to one side of the helmet.

17. You're almost there! Solder one end of the flexible cable to the 1/8-inch phono plug.

18. Solder the other end of the flexible cable to one of the Power Glove emitters.

19. The emitter provides the system with your head-movement cues, so you mount the emitter end of your cable to any item that positions the emitter on your head: the brim of the baseball helmet or cap, for example, or in front of one of the hinges on a pair of glasses (perhaps shutter glasses?). The emitter is small enough to be held in place with an alligator clip.

20. When you have everything wired and mounted, plug the emitter's cable into your interface box and go!

This head-tracker works automatically with Mark's Dual-Glove interface and OBJGLOV.EXE, part of DEMO4B.ZIP. You simply redefine the gestures for movement to reflect changes in the "head-tracking" Glove. The demo, OBJGLV.EXE, includes instructions and sample applications for use with these devices.

When you launch the demo, it looks for the emitter signals from both Gloves. You need to point both Glove and head-tracker at the two Power Glove sensor arrays (which you should have mounted, side by side, as explained both previously and in the TWOGLOVE.DOC documentation). You must be in position as the software launches, because if the sensors don't hear the ultrasonic signals from the emitters, the software will exit, and you'll have to start all over again. After they do register the existence of both Gloves, press the two "center" keys to initialize, as I described earlier.

Your head movements will control an on-screen cursor. The cursor is a thin blue line, barely noticeable, but you see it if you're looking for it. It lets you scroll left, right, up, and down for directional control.

Use the up-arrow key to move forward. Or, you can do a keyboard hack and build your own custom movement controller, such as a forward/backward joystick-type paddle switch. You also can convert a plastic stairclimber exercise machine for this function, like I did (you can mail-order a stairclimber for about $100). There are a lot of possibilities for connecting interfaces based on a keyboard hack, so use your imagination.

Have fun!

How to Build the "Virtual Reality Window": A Low-Cost VR Display

by Mark Reaney

© Copyright 1993 Mark Reaney. All rights reserved.

The Virtual Reality Window (see Figure 8.8) is a simple, inexpensive attachment that fits in front of your computer's monitor. It magnifies the monitor's image so when you look through the VR Window, the image fills your entire field of view. The lens bends light rays in such a way that when you focus your eyes in nearly parallel lines, the resulting image appears to be somewhat distant.

I designed the Virtual Reality Window to help me quickly check the quality of virtual worlds as I constructed them on my computer—without setting up my entire head-mounted display. Unfortunately, unlike a head-mounted display (HMD), the VR Window requires that you keep your head in a fixed position. Fortunately, also unlike an HMD, when used with a high-resolution monitor, the VR Window's picture is extremely sharp and clear. As a result, it works very well as an enhancement for simulator-style computer games.

I have used the Virtual Reality Window on 12-inch, 13-inch, and 14-inch computer monitors with little change in performance.

Figure 8.8. *The Virtual Reality Window. (Photo courtesy of Mark Reaney)*

You can heighten the VR Window's rough, 3D-like distancing effect by manipulation of your virtual world. By overlapping objects, shading them, adding cast shadows, and using a patterned ground plane, you can achieve a convincing 3D illusion.

Hardware Required

Quantity	Part Description	Possible Source
(1)	Flat black matte board	Art supply store
(1)	3 1/2-inch x 5-inch fresnel magnifier	W.T. Rogers Co. #04139 or Edmund Scientific, cat. #C35,936

Quantity	Part Description	Possible Source
(1)	Clear-lens safety goggle (taped to black out the sides)	Eastern Equip. #333
	or	
(1)	Welding goggle (with clear safety lens replacing the dark welding lens)	
(2)	Small angle irons	
(1)	12-inch elastic strap	Fabric store
(2)	1-inch buckles for elastic Tape, glue, small nuts and bolts	Fabric store

Assemble the VR Window by following the instructions (listed in the "About the 'Shroud'" section) and the accompanying construction diagrams.

About the "Shroud"

The "shroud" part of the VR Window blocks out ambient light and keeps the magnifier at the proper distance from the monitor screen. If you use matte board that has only one black side, construct the shroud with the black facing inside.

1. Following the accompanying diagram (see Figure 8.9), cut out the patterns for the sides in one continuous strip.

2. Score and bend the matte board at the corners. This way, you'll only have to join one corner with glue and/or tape. (See Figure 8.9).

3. Cut a notch in the bottom side of the shroud, below the goggles, to allow room for your nose.

4. Cut two slits in each side of the shroud, as shown in Figure 8.9, for the elastic strap.

5. Attach the elastic strap, using a buckle on each side. This strap holds the VR Window to the computer monitor. Buckles make it easy to adjust the fit to suit your monitors.

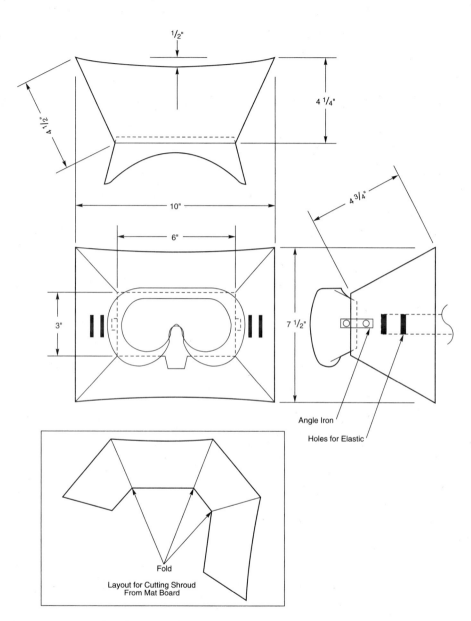

1/2"

4 1/4"

4 1/2"

10"

6"

3"

4 3/4"

7 1/2"

Angle Iron

Holes for Elastic

Fold

Layout for Cutting Shroud
From Mat Board

Figure 8.9. *VR Window plans.*

Building the Goggle

1. The body of the goggles should be opaque. Accomplish this by taping over the sides of a clear plastic safety goggle. Don't spray-paint it, because the chemical that keeps the plastic flexible will prevent the enamel paint from drying! An alternative method is to use a welding goggle. You'll have to discard the dark welding lens and replace it with a clear lens from a safety goggle.

The magnifying lens is made from a 3.5-inch by 5-inch plastic fresnel lens, available through mail order or in most large office-supply or book stores.

2. Using the safety lens as a template, cut the fresnel lens to fit the goggle body, keeping the center of the lens directly between your eyes.

3. To eliminate edge distortion, install the lens into the goggle with the convex side facing the monitor and the smooth side toward your eyes.

4. Use the clear safety lens, too, for added strength. Placing it on the convex side of the lens will help keep that surface free of dust and grime.

5. Attach the goggle to the open end of the shroud, using the two small angle irons. Some experimentation may be needed to determine the distance between goggle and computer monitor that provides the best focus.

How to Use the VR Window

When you place the VR Window on the surface of your monitor and use it to view a virtual world, the view of your virtual world will appear before you and disappear from sight at the edges of the goggles. (See Figure 8.8.) Therefore, take care when building your virtual world not to place important information at the extreme sides of the monitor, or it will be difficult to see.

Take care in setting up the ergonomics of your work space. If you plan to use the VR Window for long periods, raise your monitor to eye level or you'll end up with a sore back from bending!

Currently, there is some debate about the harmful effects of extreme low-frequency electro-magnetic radiation (ELF). Whereas modern computer monitors fall well below government standards, and certainly below the radiation output of other household electrical devices, users still must assess the possible risks for themselves. Remember, your mother told you not to sit too close to the TV!

This research is supported in part by the University of Kansas General Research Fund allocation 3210-X0-0038, and the United States Institute of Theatre Technology's Edward F Cook Endowment Fund.

How to Interface the Sega Shutter Glasses to the Serial Port of the IBM PC

by Joseph D. Gradecki

© 1992 Gradecki Publishing. Reprinted by permission. All rights reserved.

> **NOTE**
>
> The following instructions apply to Sega shutter glasses and the IBM PC, but the interface should work with Toshiba shutter glasses, the serial port of the Amiga computer, and the Macintosh—with the addition of a DIN-to-DB25 modem cable/ adapter. Macintosh owners can download a shutter glasses interface circuit diagram along with a test program from the Internet site `ftp.apple.com`.

For experimenters in VR on the PC, the Internet is the easiest way to find out what other people are doing. Several of their projects involve the use of electronic circuits. I've produced printed circuit boards (PCBs) from those circuits: the Sega glasses interface (which costs less than $25) and Ron Menelli's 68HC11 Power Glove interface (which uses a $50 microprocessor chip).

About the Sega Shutter Glasses

Looking at the glasses, you'll see that they have a pale green lens for the eye ports. The shutter action of the lenses is controlled by three wires. The plug at the end of the connection wire is stereo, thus enabling two hot wires and a ground. Power applied to the appropriate wire will shut a lens over one of the eyes. This lens blocks you from seeing with that eye. When power is alternately applied to the wires, the glasses can be used to view stereoscopic objects displayed on a computer monitor.

Limitations

The first limitation is that you can see the real world with your peripheral vision. This does not create a sense of immersion in the virtual world and can be a real problem when you are in a well-lit room. A heavy black ski mask attached around the outer edge of the glasses will block the light and overcome this limitation.

The second problem is the shutter lens. These lenses supposedly block the eye from seeing the screen. The shutter lenses are not entirely black and you are able to see through them during the shutter operation. I started to get headaches from using the glasses after an extended amount of time.

A third limitation is the computer control. If the computer spends any amount of time doing graphics work, the shutter glasses slow down. This causes many strange reactions to occur in the eyes and brain. The first reaction is a headache. This can be overcome by creating an interrupt routine based on the timer tick of the PC. When a certain number of ticks has passed, a routine is called that flicks the lenses.

Outside these problems, the Sega glasses give you some sense of 3D. I admit it does take some imagination.

Interface Circuit

Here are the schematic, parts list, and PCB layout for the Sega glasses-to-RS232 circuit. This simple circuit (Figure 8.10) has been floating around on the nets for some time. There is no clear reference to the original author, and because the schematic resides in the public domain, I'm using it as a foundation for this "how-to." All parts can be purchased at Radio Shack or a similar electronics components vendor.

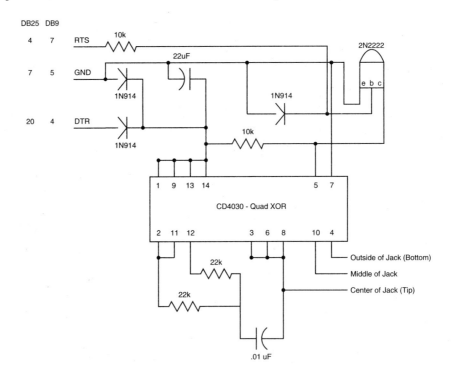

Figure 8.10. *Shutter glasses interface schematic.*

NOTE

For the sake of clarity, two diagrams for the Sega circuit have been included. The schematic in Figure 8.11 was provided by garage VR hacker Mark Koch, who lives in northern California.

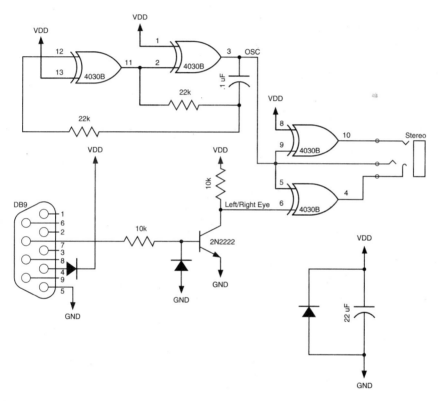

Figure 8.11. *A different look at the interface schematic.*

Parts List

     (1) CD4030 XOR gate IC (do not use the TTL 74LS86 as a replacement)

     (1) 2N2222 transistor

     (2) 22K 1/4-watt 5 percent resistors

     (2) 10K 1/4-watt 5 percent resistors

(1) 0.01 uF ceramic disk capacitor

(1) 22 uF electrolytic capacitor

(3) 1N914 diodes

(1) Stereo 1/4-inch jack

(1) DB25 or DB9 connector

The IC *must* be a CD4030.

For convenience, mount this circuit in a case. See Figure 8.12 for the layout.

The PCB Artwork

The plots are 2:1.

Connecting the Interface

The circuit is quite simple. You connect it to the RS232 serial port of the PC. One of the lens wires connects to the DTR line; the other connects to the RTS line.

To close a lens, the glasses require a voltage change to one of the wires. Because the PC controls these serial port lines, you can easily send a voltage down either of them upon demand. The XOR chip enables only one voltage to be applied to the glasses. According to the XOR truth tables, the only true signal that can be generated is when only one of the input lines is true. If both lines are true, the output is false. The diodes in the circuit restrict the flow of electrons away from the PC, not letting voltage travel back into the serial port.

Software

At first, not much software was available for the PC and the Sega glasses. The software that was originally distributed with the circuit schematic left something to be desired. Then Dave Stampe released a Sega demo for his REND386 package. This demo enables a .PLG object to be seen in stereo. Find REND386 and try out the Banana/ Chess Piece demo .PLG file; it's impressive! Be careful about how far you move the viewpoint back and forth, however, because there are points at which the objects grow farther and farther apart and no longer appear as single entities.

I have written a program, AXIS2.C, that lets objects be created and seen in stereo. First, I'll discuss the serial port interface. The I/O address for COM1 is 0x3FC. If the value of 1 is output to this address, the DTR line is put high and the RTS line is put low. If the value of 3 is output to this address, the DTR line is put low and the RTS line is put high. When the output is alternated between 1 and 3, the glasses begin to shutter. Borland C enables the programming to access I/O ports through the use of the statement `outportb (port,byte)`.

The Top of the Board Looking at the Top

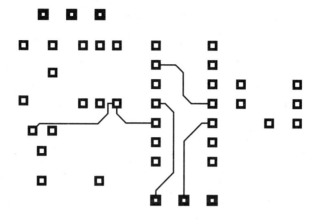

The Bottom of the Board Looking at the Board

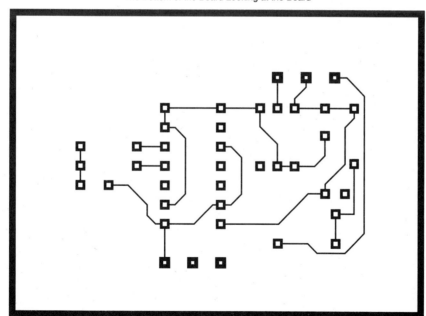

Figure 8.12. *Layout for interface's printed circuit board.*

As explained earlier in this book, the idea behind displaying stereo images on the PC is to display the left eye image and close the right lens of the glasses. As soon as this is accomplished, the right eye image is displayed, and the left lens closes. For true stereoscopic effects, this sequence must occur 60 times each second, enabling each eye to see its appropriate image 30 times each second. To determine when to shut a lens, you can monitor the vertical retrace signal register on the VGA card. The address of this register is 0x3DA. You monitor the eighth bit. When this bit has a value of 1, a retrace has occurred.

Eye Image

One problem encountered is displaying the different left and right eye images on the same monitor. This is solved easily. To display two different images without having to redraw the screens, use two different graphic pages, available with some of the display modes. The display mode 320x200x16/256 on a VGA card with 512K has two different memory areas that can be used to display graphics. These pages are called page 0 and page 1.

Borland C is aware of these different pages and gives two statements to take advantage of them. The first statement, setactivepage(), tells the PC which page to use when graphics commands are given. The second statement, setvisualpage(), tells the PC which page is to be the current frame buffer. When the VGA card begins to paint a new screen, it takes the image data from the currently selected frame buffer. This data can be used to create a program that displays a stereoscopic image.

The algorithm is

```
set the active page to 0
draw the left eye image
set the active page to 1
draw the right eye image

loop
    waitforverticalretrace();
    setvisualpage(0);
    waitforverticalretrace();
    setvisualpage(1);
endloop;
```

The waitforverticalretrace(); procedure is

```
void waitforverticalretrace(void)
{
    static char change = 1;

                while ( inportb(0x3DA) & 8 )
                    while (( inportb(0x3DA) & 8 ) ==0 )
```

```
if ( (change++ & 1 ) == 0)
    outportb(0x3FC,1);
else
    outportb(0x3FC,3);
}
```

NOTE

Credit for this routine goes to Frank Van Der Hulst.

The program following this section displays a simple box in 3D. The box moves in the z direction when you press the F or B keys. By using the previous algorithm and the `waitforverticalretrace` procedure, any image can appear in stereo. Take care when doing graphic draws between the image exchanges. A slow or complex draw causes the lenses to shutter at a slower rate, which causes the view to appear in 2D instead of in stereo.

The Program

The simple test program for the Sega glasses draws a box using the standard Borland line drawing routines. Before a line is drawn, however, the current view transformation is applied to the world coordinates of the box. When the screen x and y coordinates are known, the box is drawn. This creates the image for one eye. To create the image for the other eye, the "eye" (camera) position is moved and new x and y coordinates are obtained. This view can now be displayed as well. Each of the images is put into a different page of the VGA memory space. These pages will be displayed repeatedly, while the shutters on the glasses are changed. If you press the F or B keys, the images will be redrawn into the pages and the sequence starts again.

How to Build a Low-Cost Head-Mounted Display

by Mark Reaney

© Copyright 1993 Mark Reaney. All rights reserved.

Mark Reaney is an associate professor of theater and film at the University of Kansas in Lawrence. He has devised a garage VR system that he uses to facilitate set design for such University Theatre productions as A Streetcar Named Desire.

"Just as an architect uses virtual reality to design a building, a scenographer can use it to design a set. VR is not beyond the reach of the average scenographer," Mark wrote in an article for the theatrical trade magazine Theater Design and Technology. *"Amateur VR*

devotees have found ways to fabricate their own less sophisticated, yet effective, equipment. The system I created cost less than $500. This homebrew virtual reality can be as convincing as more expensive commercial versions for the same reason that the theater is convincing in the illusions it presents."

Mark started using a Macintosh several years ago to sketch sets and costumes. While he was "putzing around with computer models," he ran across some virtual reality software. VR seemed like a logical next step, he says. Over the course of two or three months Mark bought a Power Glove and some used video equipment, which he used to build his own head-mounted display. The total cost of his HMD ran about $200-$250, he reports, "mostly because of frugal shopping at pawn shops."

Using Virtus WalkThrough software, Mark creates sets by designing virtual walls, windows, and props. Then he uses his HMD and Power Glove to "walk around" the sets, checking to see what they look like from above and below, and from the viewpoints of actors and audience. His goal is to create workable set designs.

The system is not without its limitations. The graininess of the HMD's resolution means Mark can't tell the difference between a virtual object that is 20 feet away from one that is 22 feet away. Also, the HMD is somewhat cumbersome.

Mark recently received a $2,000 research endowment grant from the United States Institute for Theatre Technology to further his work in VR. He's using the money to study ways to stage theatrical productions in a virtual world, which necessitates the implementation of networked systems. This relates to one of his future goals: presenting a VR stage production to a helmet-equipped audience.

My HMD is made from two 2.7-inch color liquid crystal display (LCD) television monitors and some homemade optics. The screen resolution is somewhat grainy, but is comparable to that of commercial HMDs. It does provide a good sense of immersion in the virtual world. It can work with any type of computer, provided you also have a video camera or the appropriate RGB-to-NTSC signal converter.

More sophisticated head-mounted displays generate separate stereo images for each eye in order to render a convincing 3D image. However, creating two separate images slows computing time measurably and greatly increases the cost of the interface. Fortunately, a convincing illusion can be created by using the same image for each eye, separating them so that the user's eyes focus in parallel lines. The illusion of depth can be enhanced in the creation of the virtual world by placing objects on a patterned ground plane (a tactic used frequently in computer games).

My system does not include a head-tracker, because this would require a more powerful computer capable of processing information at the speed necessary to create a smooth illusion. If there is a noticeable lag between movements of the user's head and the corresponding change in the view presented in the HMD, a sense of disorientation occurs—in some cases severe enough to cause motion sickness. In a low-cost system,

users can look only in the direction they are traveling. After the user accepts this condition, in this version of reality, the lack of head movement seems natural.

Movement within my virtual set designs is controlled by a Mattel Power Glove. (See Figure 8.13.) The user moves through virtual spaces by motioning with the hand or fingers. I use the Gold Brick Nugget from Transfinite Systems and its accompanying device driver to interface the Glove with my Macintosh. More recently, however, I have become fond of the Gravis Mousestick as a steering device.

Figure 8.13. *A simulation of how Mark Reaney uses his HMD and Power Glove to design theater sets. (Photo courtesy of Mark Reaney)*

The system runs on an accelerated Macintosh LC; the software I use is Virtus Walk-Through. Similar results can be achieved with other types of personal computers and interactive software packages.

The overall effect of the head-mount is rather convincing. As users navigate the virtual scenery, they lean to the side as they go around virtual corners, lean back when they experience unexpected accelerations, and duck their heads under low virtual beams. Because users' perceptions of where they are in the virtual scene do not coincide with their actual physical surroundings, I have them sit in a chair to minimize the danger of falling over or walking into an unseen (real) table.

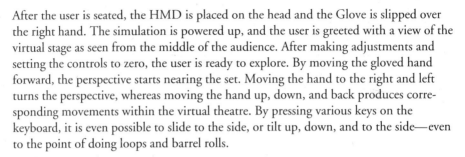

After the user is seated, the HMD is placed on the head and the Glove is slipped over the right hand. The simulation is powered up, and the user is greeted with a view of the virtual stage as seen from the middle of the audience. After making adjustments and setting the controls to zero, the user is ready to explore. By moving the gloved hand forward, the perspective starts nearing the set. Moving the hand to the right and left turns the perspective, whereas moving the hand up, down, and back produces corresponding movements within the virtual theatre. By pressing various keys on the keyboard, it is even possible to slide to the side, or tilt up, down, and to the side—even to the point of doing loops and barrel rolls.

The longer you stay in the virtual environment, the more skillful you become at maneuvering within it. As your perceptions grow accustomed to new parameters, the more realistic the illusions.

This design for a head-mounted display is a prototype. The design did meet and exceed its original four requirements: average performance; low cost; light weight; and ease of use. To operate stereoscopically, the HMD requires two separate NTSC video signals. To operate monoscopically, it requires one split NTSC signal. However, even though there are various sources for video cards and devices that translate a computer's RGB monitor signal into NTSC, I carried out my original experiments simply by aiming a video camera at the computer monitor and sending the camera's signal to the HMD.

Even when operating in monoscopic mode, the parallel focus of the operator's two eyes provides a rough 3D stereo effect. Objects seen through the HMD appear to be positioned roughly 20 feet or more from the viewer. Furthermore, the 3D illusion can be enhanced by careful construction of the virtual world. Shading, casting shadows, overlapping of objects, and patterning a groundplane all provide visual clues that help create a strong 3D effect.

Like most prototypes, this design can be improved. Although obtaining TVs from flea markets and pawn shops let me build the original model for a mere $200, others may find this practice prohibitively time-consuming. *Therefore, don't think of these plans as a definitive source, but as a guide to the basic principles inherent in the construction of an HMD, and as the basis for further invention and innovation.*

This research is supported in part by the University of Kansas General Research Fund allocation 3210-X0-0038, and the United States Institute of Theatre Technology's Edward F. Cook Endowment Fund.

This project is fairly advanced. I recommend that you have prior experience with soldering and circuit construction.

Hardware Required

Quantity	Part Description	Possible Source
(2)	2.7-inch or 3-inch color LCD televisions	Sony FDL-310
(2)	7.5 x 4.5 x 2.25-inch plastic project boxes	Radio Shack #270-224
(1)	Welding goggle (clear safety lens replacing dark welding lens)	Eastern Safety Equip.
	or	
(1)	Clear-lens safety goggle (taped on the sides to black-out the side views)	Eastern Safety Equip. #333
(4)	"Credit card" fresnel magnifiers	W.T. Rogers #04138 or Edmund Scientific cat. #C38,456
(1)	Adjustable headband from welding helmet	Hardware store
(1)	Aluminum yardstick (for the armature)	
(1)	20-conductor ribbon connector	Radio Shack #278-772
(1)	1/16 x 4 x 7-inch sheet of rigid plastic	
(1)	Piece of non-glare Plexiglas	Picture-frame store
	Nuts, angle irons, bolts, and screws, as shown in Figure 8.15	
	Power drill (for drilling mounting holes through yardstick, as shown in Figure 8.14)	
	Elmer's glue or equivalent	
	Soldering iron, screwdrivers	
	(Optional) "Y" adapter to feed one display signal to both TV screens	

Assemble the HMD by following the instructions and the accompanying construction diagrams.

Hacking for the Trip

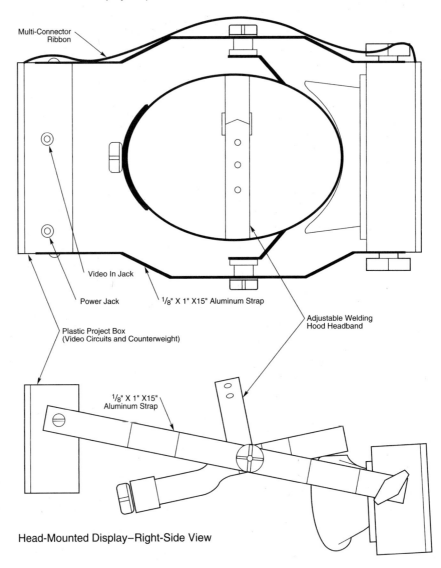

Head-Mounted Display–Top View

Multi-Connector
Ribbon

Video In Jack

Power Jack

1/8" X 1" X15" Aluminum Strap

Plastic Project Box
(Video Circuits and Counterweight)

Adjustable Welding
Hood Headband

1/8" X 1" X15"
Aluminum Strap

Head-Mounted Display–Right-Side View

Figure 8.14. The HMD: top view.

Dealing with the Televisions

The HMD's main components are a pair of 2.7-inch LCD color television screens. LCD screens are preferable to CRTs because of their lack of harmful ELF (extreme low-frequency electro-magnetic radiation) and X-ray emissions. After some experimentation, I chose the Sony FDL 310 model because of its picture quality and the ease with which it can be disassembled and modified. This is an important consideration. With some brands of miniature TVs, it is very difficult to remove the LCD screen and reconnect it within the HMD.

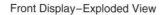

Front Display–Exploded View

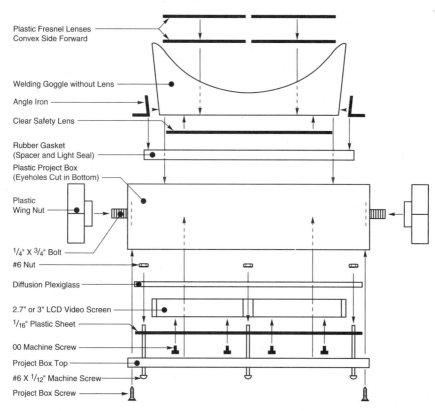

Figure 8.15. The HMD: exploded view.

(In future experiments I plan to use 3-inch LCD video monitors. Intended for use with home video cameras, these screens lack the tuning circuitry of TVs and should prove easier to install.)

In constructing your own HMD, the model of TVs available will demand some flexibility in the configuration. Other options for the screens include 3-inch LCD color TVs, and 2.7- or 3-inch black-and-white displays. Screens less than 2.7 inches will not provide the wide angle of view that is best for achieving VR immersion.

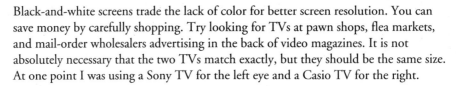

Black-and-white screens trade the lack of color for better screen resolution. You can save money by carefully shopping. Try looking for TVs at pawn shops, flea markets, and mail-order wholesalers advertising in the back of video magazines. It is not absolutely necessary that the two TVs match exactly, but they should be the same size. At one point I was using a Sony TV for the left eye and a Casio TV for the right.

Take these steps to prepare the monitor:

1. Remove the TV screens from their housings.
2. Install the screens in the front-display housing (as shown in Figure 8.15).
3. Attach the LCDs to the thin, rigid plastic sheet, rather than directly to the project box's lid (this will make it easier to fine-tune the assembly later).
4. Move the remaining television circuitry to the rear counterweight housing. Even if you do not move the circuitry to the rear of the HMD, you'll need some type of counterweight to balance the device on the user's head.
5. Connect the ribbon cable so it can carry signals from the TV circuitry to the screens along the side of the HMD. Here's where you'll need to do some fine soldering!
6. As shown in Figure 8.14, the video-in jack is already part of the TVs. I added a Y adapter so that one jack fed both television displays.

Dealing with the Optics

The lens system for the HMD consists mainly of four "credit card" size plastic fresnel lenses. You can buy them at most large office supply or book stores.

1. Position two lenses for each eye by facing the lens' convex side toward the screens and the plano side toward the eye. For easier positioning of the lenses, glue the edges of each pair. See Figure 8.16.

   Because the centers of the LCD screens are farther apart than the average person's eyes, position the fresnel lenses so that their centers also are farther apart—the user's eyes should be aligned with the inner halves of the lenses. Doing this bends the light rays inward toward the user's eyes and ensures that the two separate images from the LCDs will converge. (Experimentation is necessary). The desired effect is that the user's eyes focus nearly parallel to each other to achieve the illusion of greater distance from the image. See the "Optics Diagram" in Figure 8.16.

   Another option is to center the lenses with the user's eyes and converge the two images by adding a wedge prism between each lens and its LCD screen. This is a simple, efficient way to make the two images converge (particularly when using larger LCDs), but it's not cheap; two wedge prisms, such as those found in the Edmund Scientific Catalog (cat. #C30,265), add a cost of about $80 to the project. See the "Alternative Optics" diagram in Figure 8.16.

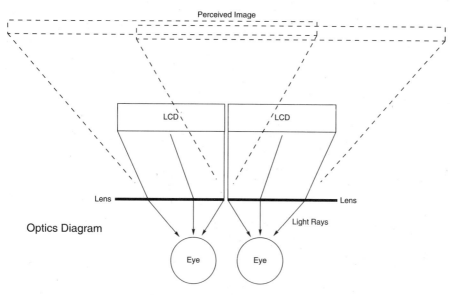

Perceived Image

LCD   LCD

Lens ━━━━━━━━━━━━ Lens

Light Rays

Eye   Eye

NOTE THAT THE EYE IS ALIGNED
WITH THE INNER HALF OF EACH LENS

Optics Diagram

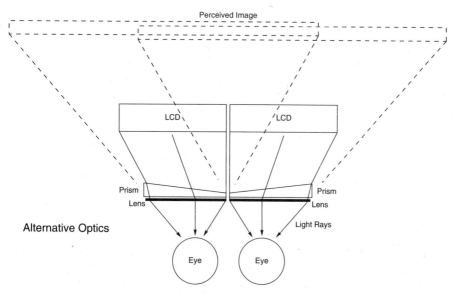

Perceived Image

LCD   LCD

Prism   Prism
Lens   Lens

Light Rays

Eye   Eye

NOTE THAT THE EYE IS CENTERED ON THE LENS
AND WEDGE PRISMS ARE USED TO CONVERGE
THE TWO IMAGES

Alternative Optics

Figure 8.16. Optics diagram.

2. Cut the lens pairs to the size of the welding goggle frames.

3. Insert the cut lenses in the slot that previously held the tinted welding lenses.

4. For added strength, remove a clear lens from the pair of safety goggles and insert it in front of the fresnel magnifiers.

Dealing with Focus

You should position the LCD screens and the magnifying lenses inside the forward housing approximately two inches apart. Depending on the type of TV you use, it may be necessary to experiment with different size boxes for the front housing and various spacers, such as washers or gaskets. I used a 1/4-inch gasket between the goggle and the project box to achieve the proper interval. There is some margin for error, because the image usually is enhanced by being slightly out of focus.

Also, some experimenters claim that angling the LCD screens and lenses slightly farther from the viewer in the center than on either side helps the focus and decreases the problem of converging two separate images.

Dealing with Diffusion

Small color LCDs are designed to use a pointillist effect, relying on the visual blending of small red, blue, and green pixels. This effect is lost when viewed through a magnifying lens. Therefore, it is necessary to reinforce the effect by placing a mildly diffusing material immediately in front of the LCD screens. A piece of non-glare Plexiglas typically used in picture framing produces the best results.

The Assembly

Follow the assembly and mounting diagrams to prepare your head-mounted display for wear. The aluminum strap shown in Figure 8.17 is actually the aluminum yardstick, drilled (and cut, if desired) to serve as the assembly armature.

Powering the HMD

I provided power to my HMD with the power supply that came with the TV (or you can buy an equivalent power supply from Radio Shack). Batteries drain too quickly and are too difficult to change; besides, they add lots of weight.

It's probably even easier to include two separate power jacks—one for each TV—rather than trying to match and split the power requirements of the two together.

Sending the Display Signal

Earlier I mentioned that the video signal can come from an NTSC converter, but I started out by simply aiming a camcorder at the computer screen. More recently, I've used RGB-to-NTSC converters. They have better focus than a camera, but they all seem to suffer from different flicker problems. I mail-ordered a more expensive converter that I hope will do the trick. I'm also looking for a copy of the Macintosh utility program Videosync; I understand it can alter the scan rate of the Mac monitor so that it can be shot "flicker-free" by a video camera.

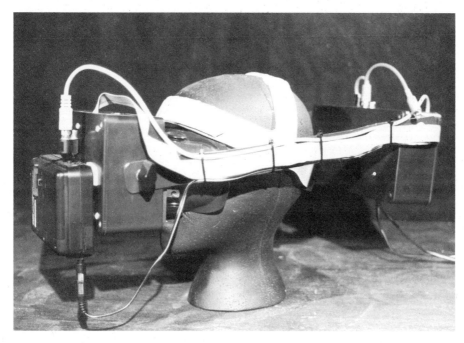

Figure 8.17. *The Finished HMD.*

How to Build a Head-Mounted Display with a Boom Tracking System

by Joseph D. Gradecki

© 1992 Gradecki Publishing. Reprinted by permission. All other rights reserved.

"A VR system is incomplete without a head-mounted display," wrote Joe Gradecki in Volume 1, Issue 3 of PCVR, *his homebrewer's 'zine. "The Sega glasses are fine for a while, but there needs to be more." In Issues 3 through 6, Joe documented his efforts as he built a head-mounted display with a mechanical position-tracking system. This is an updated version of that documentation.*

NOTE

All the programming Joe describes here is written in C on an IBM PC engine. His HMD and tracker, however, work with a Macintosh or Amiga, provided the programs are adapted appropriately.

Homebrew Choices

When researching what it would take to build my own head-mounted display, I came up with five possibilities:

1. Use shutter glasses, but enclose them in a mask so that the outside world does not leak into the field of view. This solution is cheap, but not acceptable. It causes headaches and you can still view the outside world when looking at the computer monitor. Thus, you are not completely immersed in the virtual world—which is very important. If you see parts of the real world, the brain works more than it should and lets you know that you are not a part of the virtual world. But if your budget is severely limited, the glasses will work.

2. Most CGA cards have composite RCA outputs. Because they are NTSC-ready, they can be plugged directly into color LCDs. The cost is around $60 ($30 per card). CGA is limited to four colors, however, which is the main problem with this approach. In addition, most CGA cards have not been built for virtual reality or mainstream graphics use; they're also slow. Another problem is with software: REND386 does not support CGA.

3. You can solve the software problem by using EGA cards. REND386 supports the 320x200x16 EGA mode. An EGA card does not have the composite RCA output; it only has the TTL 9-pin connector. Various magazines have published circuits that convert digital RGB signals to NTSC, using the Motorola MC1377 chip. In the July 1990 issue of *Radio Electronics,* there is a circuit for a digital RGB-to-NTSC converter. This converter enables the CGA/EGA signals to be converted to NTSC.

    I built that circuit, hoping for an inexpensive solution to provide the video to the LCD screens. After several tests using different video cards, the circuit never created a picture that could be used in a VR system. An additional problem when using this option is obtaining EGA cards or VGA cards with digital outputs. Most video card makers no longer manufacture the EGA cards, and most VGA cards do not have EGA connectors.

4. Dave Stampe (coauthor of REND386) gave me several ideas about how to create a head-mounted display using just VGA cards. Apparently, by changing the crystals on the VGA card and reprogramming its internal registers, the card can be "tricked" into generating an NTSC signal. The analog RGB lines are connected directly to the LCD.

   I have not given this option much consideration, because of the following reasons:

   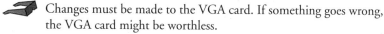 Changes must be made to the VGA card. If something goes wrong, the VGA card might be worthless.

   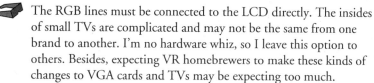 The RGB lines must be connected to the LCD directly. The insides of small TVs are complicated and may not be the same from one brand to another. I'm no hardware whiz, so I leave this option to others. Besides, expecting VR homebrewers to make these kinds of changes to VGA cards and TVs may be expecting too much.

5. A final option uses VGA-to-NTSC video converters. These converters connect to the VGA card, just as a monitor does, through the 15-pin connector using a Y-cable. The other end of the cable connects to the computer monitor. The NTSC output of the converter is an RCA plug. This output connects to a monitor through a composite video input. Additionally, an RF converter can be used and the output can be connected to the antenna input on a TV. The picture will appear on channel 3. If you can hook up a video game system, such as Nintendo, you can assemble a VGA-to-NTSC system.

I chose the fifth option because the HMD project seemed easy to assemble. Also, I am not an electronics engineer and I have little experience working with LCDs and the circuits of the VGA card. Finally, it is a relatively inexpensive way to acquire a low-resolution, low-performance HMD that works well enough to conduct experiments in virtual reality.

I investigated converters that display REND386 in 320x200x16 EGA mode and in 320x200x256 VGA mode. The cost for one converter is approximately $200. For this option, you need two video sources—one for each eye. To accomplish this (in an ideal situation) you would use two 80386 (or better) PCs, two VGA cards, and two converters. That's not what we're doing here, however. I would like to keep the total cost of the HMD under $500. This is a large sum, but it is still a small price to pay for total immersion in virtual worlds—and a far cry from the $6,000+ price tag of most commercial HMDs.

The type of LCDs used in this HMD is one reason for the low resolution/low performance. I use LCDs from Casio Model 470 2.2-inch color LCD televisions, which Casio graciously donated for this project. Of the small televisions I viewed, the Casio TVs produced the best picture quality. The horizontal resolution of its screens is less than 200 pixels.

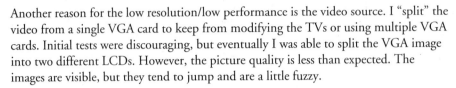

Another reason for the low resolution/low performance is the video source. I "split" the video from a single VGA card to keep from modifying the TVs or using multiple VGA cards. Initial tests were discouraging, but eventually I was able to split the VGA image into two different LCDs. However, the picture quality is less than expected. The images are visible, but they tend to jump and are a little fuzzy.

My intention is to create a head-mounted display for experimentation purposes. *Therefore, I cannot take any responsibility for how other people use this information.*

The Project's Subsystems

My head-mounted display project contains several parts:

1. Video subsystem: LCDs, VGA-to-NTSC converter, connections, and testing.
2. Optical subsystem: the optics that create peripheral vision and convergence.
3. Head-tracking subsystem: the head-tracking part.
4. Hardware subsystem: I simply enclosed the video subsystem and the optics in a bicycle helmet.

System Requirements

(1) PC with VGA card (one PC/VGA combination for monocular output)

(2) LCDs from Casio Model 470 2.2-inch color LCD televisions (@$150)

(1) VGA-to-NTSC converter (such as the PC-Video Converter from Boffin, Ltd.)

(1) Y connector

(2) RF modulators (such as Radio Shack number 15-1273, @$27.95)

(1) RCA 74HC22106 8x8 crosspoint switch chip

(2) 6V power adapters (such as Radio Shack number 273-1655)

(1) Intel 8255-5 microcontroller chip

(1) ADC0804 analog-to-digital converter

(1) CD4051 chip

(3) 1-megaohm potentiometers

[for head-tracker] (1) camera tripod or several 2x4 wooden boards, 1/2-inch wood dowel

(1 sheet) black poster board

(2) small, inexpensive hand mirrors

(2 minimum) full-sheet, plastic page magnifiers

Pegboard

Insulated coaxial cable

Electrical tape, duct tape, glue

Mirror cutter

Assorted screws, nuts, 1/4-inch bolts

Theory of Operation

You must acquire two of everything, because there are two different images to display to the eyes. But this is too much to deal with at the start, so you need a way for a single VGA card to project the different images to the two LCDs.

Do this by using an 8x8 crosspoint switch chip, the 74HC22106, which RCA produced several years ago. Depending on where you obtain this chip, it costs from $5 to $10. The chip's bandwidth handles audio, too, if you need it. The chip acts as a traffic cop. Using a computer control interface, five address lines, this chip directs any of the eight inputs to any of the eight outputs. When you want the VGA card to display the left eye image, the chip switches to enable the signal to go to the left eye. After this is done, the display switches to the right eye. This is the same basic principle as the shutter glasses, but there are two distinct displays for the images.

Figure 8.18 shows the wiring of the HMD video subsystem. The difficult part in designing the video system is with the software. The computer must be able to switch the video output fast enough so that the image to the eye does not appear to fade away after each write.

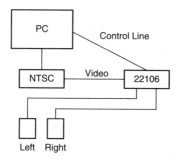

Figure 8.18. *The wiring of the HMD video subsystem.*

NOTE

When I first started this experiment, I thought that providing a stereo image was essential to the operation of an HMD. I have since learned that stereoscopy is just one of many depth cues that can be provided. There are many reasons for using stereo, but the expense to obtain stereo may not be justifiable. Therefore, I now recommend that you do not need the circuit to split the VGA signal (although I will describe it here). You can build your HMD and use a Y-connector on a single PC to generate a monoscopic, or monocular, image and send it to both LCDs. When you have this mono image, you can experiment with stereo. I can say that playing the freeware game Castle Wolfenstein in an HMD is a pretty good experience, even though it is mono.

VGA-to-NTSC

The signals that come out of the VGA cards cannot be used to drive a television. A TV requires a signal based on the NTSC standard. This is an interlaced signal with the red, green, blue, and sync signals combined. One way to achieve this is through a commercial VGA-to-NTSC converter.

There are several converters on the market in both internal (plug-in card) and external (box) form. I chose the PC-Video Converter from Boffin Limited. This card converts CGA, EGA, and VGA screens up to 640x480x16, including the 320x200x256 mode (the mode used by REND386). This converter can accommodate almost all kinds of VGA chips.

This card also includes an AdLib sound generation emulator. Most pieces of software can play music through it. The freeware 3D game, Castle Wolfenstein, recognizes the card and generates a nice sound.

The Boffin PC-Video Converter is an internal card with a Y-connector for the VGA card and VGA monitor. It is connected as shown in Figure 8.19.

Using software provided with the card, any image from the VGA card in the appropriate mode, including text mode, can be displayed on the TV. If the VGA monitor is multi-sync, the image will appear on it as well. Note that the TV must have a composite video input. This type of input is handled with an RCA-type plug.

Using an old Commodore monitor, I tested the output from REND386 and found it to be just as fast and clear as on the VGA monitor. Of course, the image on the VGA monitor is crisper, but the image looked pretty good. It was the first time I wished I had a 52-inch large-screen TV to experience the full potential of REND386.

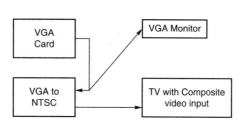

Figure 8.19. Connections.

Hooking up the LCD Video

As mentioned, I'm using 2.2-inch Casio Model 470 color LCDs. These can be purchased at any Target store for about $149. Radio Shack used to sell a small LCD television that seemed identical, but it discontinued the sets.

These TVs are powered by four AA batteries or a power pack. I'm using two 6V adapters from Radio Shack, stock number 273-1655 ($16.95). There might be less expensive ones available, but make sure you match the power requirement of the television with the capacity of the power supply.

The next step is to hook up the video to the LCDs. The TVs have external antenna hookups that accept mini-plugs. This is a VHF input, but the output of the converter card is a composite signal. You'll need another converter. An RF modulator takes a composite video signal and generates a VHF-viewable signal. Here again, I use a Radio Shack product, stock number 15-1273 ($27.95). These modulators take an RCA input and have an F-type connector (similar to a cable TV connector). This cable is terminated with a mini-plug connector. I'm looking for an RF modulator circuit to cut down the cost of purchasing the modulators.

When the system is fired up, the TVs are tuned to either channel 3 or 4, and the image appears. (Boy, is it small!) I used the multicolored Virtual Hand program to generate an image, and the hand was there, rotating on the mini-televisions. Well, so far, so good. The next step is to split the video.

Switcher

For stereoscopic viewing, you need images for both the left and right eyes. You can't feed both eyes the same scene. You need a system that generates, on the LCD, the image that appears on the VGA monitor. Using the 22106 crosspoint switch chip, you'll display both the left and right images on two separate LCDs.

I'll begin with theory. As I mentioned earlier, the 22106 is an 8x8 cross-switch. It provides eight inputs and eight outputs. Any of the inputs can be directed to any of the outputs. What if you use the output of the NTSC converter as the input, and switch this input between two outputs? The first output would be to the left-eye LCD, and

Hacking for the Trip

the second output would be to the right-eye LCD. Just before switching, tell REND386 (or whatever software is executing) to display a different graphics page. Then, you'll achieve something like what's shown in Figure 8.20.

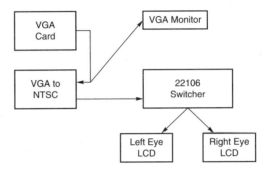

Figure 8.20. *Switching.*

Figure 8.20 doesn't show it, but there are two RF modulators between the switcher and the LCDs. You may be wondering, why not put the RF modulator between the NTSC converter and the switcher? The main reason is that the output of the modulator is a VHF television signal and this signal is sent to the switcher. As you'll see, the switcher is a PC/XT interface card inside the PC. Television signals and the insides of a PC just don't mix. Therefore, you keep the signal composite and there is little distortion. Using insulated coax cable helps cut down on interference and distortion.

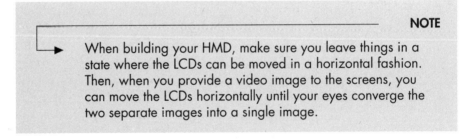

NOTE

When building your HMD, make sure you leave things in a state where the LCDs can be moved in a horizontal fashion. Then, when you provide a video image to the screens, you can move the LCDs horizontally until your eyes converge the two separate images into a single image.

The following section takes a look at the circuit.

Computer Interface

The 22106 chip requires some sort of interface in order to be instructed to open or close a circuit. For simplicity, you build an interface for the IBM PC/XT bus. This interface gives three 8-bit parallel ports for the interface to the 22106 chip, as well as other devices for the future.

The circuit consists of the pin-outs shown in Figure 8.21.

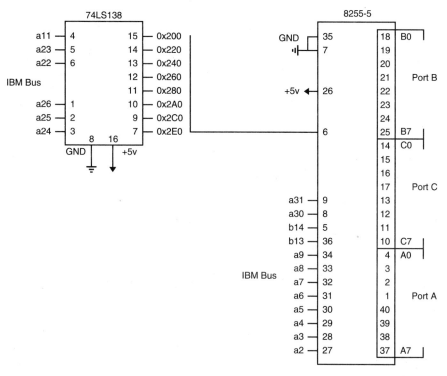

Figure 8.21. *Pin-outs.*

This circuit is loosely based on the circuit from *Radio Electronics* cited in the bibliography at the end of this chapter. Depending on which address line you connect to pin 6 of the 8255-5, the circuit is programmed using that address.

The chip has four address locations (using 0x280 as an example):

> 0x280 = control location
> 0x281 = Port A
> 0x282 = Port B
> 0x283 = Port C

The chip can be programmed to enable each of the ports to be either input or output. The following examples can be assigned to the control location to indicate the status of the ports:

Value	Port A	Port B	Port C
0x80	OUT	OUT	OUT
0x8F	IN	IN	IN

Refer to the Intel data book cited in the bibliography for more values to assign the chip.

After the chip has been programmed for port status, you either read or write to the location of the particular ports. The following C code programs all ports as output and puts the value of 32 to port A:

```
outport ( 0x280, 0x80 );
outport ( 0x281, 0x20 );
```

This is an easy interface circuit. The 8255-5 chip is very versatile. You'll use the ports as address and data lines for the 22106 chip.

The 22106 Circuit

This chip is programmed by

1. Putting a value on the data bus
2. Selecting the chip
3. Determining whether to turn the internal switch on or off
4. Toggling an enable line

The circuit for the 22106 part is shown in Figure 8.22.

For a full explanation of the chip and other uses, check the *Byte* magazine citation in the bibliography.

Combining both of the circuits (shown previously) gives the capability to switch video. Programming the 22106 is a fairly simple task. The value of the internal cross-switch to open or close is applied to port A of the 8255. The 22106 chip is selected by setting port B, line 6 to high. The chip accepts the value on port A by toggling port B, line 7 on, and then off.

To select an internal cross-switch, use the following formula:

```
switch := ( out * 8 ) + in + onoff;
```

To turn the switch on, set the variable onoff to 128.

To turn the switch off, set the variable onoff to 0.

For example, turn the switch to let video run from input 0 to input 1 with the following code:

```
outport ( 0x280, 0x80 );
outport ( 0x281, 0*8+1+128 );
outport ( 0x282, 64 );
outport ( 0x282, 192 );
outport ( 0x282, 64 );
```

This sequence successfully toggles the appropriate cross-switch. To turn the switch off, change the second line to outport (0x281, 0*8+1+0);.

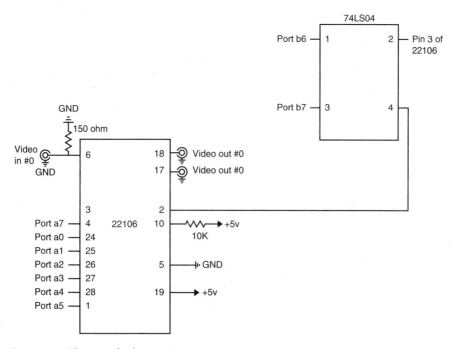

Figure 8.22. *The circuit for the 22106 part.*

The Final Step: Stereoscopy

After carefully extracting the LCDs from their casings, building the circuits, doing the programming, and performing all the other steps, the system still did not work adequately for stereoscopic viewing.

If you build the circuits (previously described) and connect to the LCD through the RF modulators, you get two hard-to-see images on each of the televisions. The fuzziness occurs because the switcher switches in the middle of a sequence of video signals to the LCDs. The LCDs need all of the signal to correctly trace the image on the screens. To compensate for the lost parts of the signal, you must introduce a good signal to each of the LCDs. You can accomplish this through the use of a second PC or a monochrome card. I chose the second (cheaper) option, because the PC enables a second video to coexist with a VGA card if it is monochrome. The monochrome card is necessary to project a blank screen.

Figure 8.23 illustrates the hookup of the entire system.

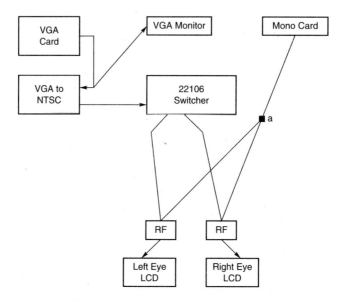

Figure 8.23. *The hookup of the entire system.*

The monochrome card must be programmed to enter graphics mode, display a black screen, and wait until a key is pressed. This provides the good signal to the LCDs. Each of the LCDs receives the good signal. In Figure 8.23, point a is the intersection of the good signals with the LCDs. At this connection, *only* the hot wire should be connected, not the ground. The LCDs use their own ground signals in addition to the hot of the good signal.

This may seem like a kludge, but it works. Another enhancement can be made by using two separate video sources for the black screen. Each source would drive a separate LCD.

I plan to incorporate the RF modulators and two separate video sources into this circuit.

Software

The program SWITCH.PAS on the disk does the following:

1. Sets up graphics pages 0 and 1 with two different images

2. Sets the 8255 chip to all output

3. Clears all internal cross-switches

4. Switches pages and internal switches until Q is pressed

The Head-Tracking Subsystem

For a VR experience to provide a realistic representation of our true world, it must enable you to move and look around. These actions can be considered head-tracking, although moving and looking are different activities. I explored many different forms of available head-tracking for homebrew VR (*PCVR* Volume 1, Issue 5 contains a complete overview) and chose a mechanical head-tracker in the form of a boom system because it cost the least.

A boom head-tracker consists of a series of rods connected together with joints. Each joint has a potentiometer to measure the degree of flex. Figure 8.24 shows a possible setup. The head-tracker is attached to the top of the HMD. As you move around the virtual world, the potentiometers send analog signals to an analog-to-digital convert. The digital information is fed to a computer to calculate your position. The positions of the potentiometers determine the degree of freedom that the computer can detect.

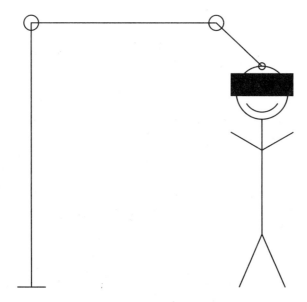

Figure 8.24. *A possible setup.*

The potentiometer at the base of the boom measures the z-axis freedom. The pots at the first and second joints determine the x-axis freedom. There is no direct way to determine the y-axis freedom.

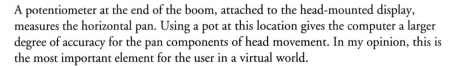

A potentiometer at the end of the boom, attached to the head-mounted display, measures the horizontal pan. Using a pot at this location gives the computer a larger degree of accuracy for the pan components of head movement. In my opinion, this is the most important element for the user in a virtual world.

I don't want to overlook the tilt and roll components. To measure these components, you can use two tilt switches. The switches give the computer three measures each for tilt and roll.

The boom head-tracker restricts you, because it attaches directly to you. However, if it's built correctly, you should experience minimum discomfort. The boom permits instantaneous measurement of your position in 3-space, as well as measurement of the direction in which you're looking.

The boom described here enables tracking of the tilt and pan of your head, and enables updating as fast as the computer can read the interface. The interface is the same circuit used in the head-mounted video subsystem. Simply add an ADC0804 analog-to-digital converter to convert the voltages to a digital form that the computer can read. The overall view of the boom appears in Figure 8.25.

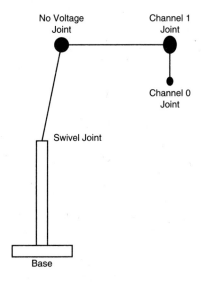

Figure 8.25. *The overall view of the boom.*

Basic Boom Operation

The boom enables four degrees of freedom and measures voltage from two potentiometers to determine the location of your head. (You can add a third potentiometer for a 6DOF system.)

Look at Figure 8.25:

The Channel 1 Joint measures the degree of head tilt.

The Channel 0 Joint measures the degree of pan.

The No Voltage Joint and the Swivel Joint enable the boom to flex when you move your head.

Attached to each Channel Joint is a 1-megaohm potentiometer, which is fed a +5V voltage. Moving your head causes a change in the degree of voltage going through the potentiometer. As long as the voltage of the potentiometers is known when you're looking straight ahead, any decrease or increase in the voltage indicates a head movement. The analog-to-digital converter translates the voltages into digital form for the computer.

Boom Construction

The construction's cost can vary from extremely inexpensive to quite costly. I built the prototype described here for less than $10, including the cost of the electronics. In this section, I'll go over each part of the construction of my low-cost head-tracker.

Base: Construct the boom in a sturdy fashion so you don't feel the interaction of the boom. The base should be about as high as your waist. It should be adjustable so that different people can use the system. One of the simplest bases to use is a camera tripod.

Alternatively, a base can be built out of several 2x4 boards, with an adjustable middle board held in place with a metal pin. See Figure 8.26.

Drill holes in the three pieces of vertical 2x4 wood at regular intervals. If an adjustment is necessary, remove the pin and move the middle 2x4 up or down; then replace the pin. This base can be built for about $3.

Boom Arms: The boom in Figure 8.25 has three arm pieces. The arm attached to the base of the boom was built out of 1/2-inch wood dowel. This dowel is attached to the base using a small hinge. Figure 8.26 shows an example. When using the boom, you stand with your back to the dowel. For a stronger arm, you can use a 3/4-inch dowel or even aluminum mast poles (these are much more expensive, however).

Attach the second arm to the base dowel, then attach the shorter dowel at the end of the boom. These arms are made from 1/4-inch dowels. The main reason for using the dowels in the construction of the boom is their weight. Steel rods are too heavy.

Boom Joints: Figure 8.27 shows the No Voltage Joint between the base dowel and the second arm. This joint should be moveable. Each of the dowels has a small piece of pegboard or other 1/8-inch piece of wood attached to it by two small screws. The pegboard should be mounted on opposite sides of the two different dowels: one on the front of one dowel, and the other on the back of the other dowel. This is done so when you bolt the pegboards together, they are free to move without hitting the dowels.

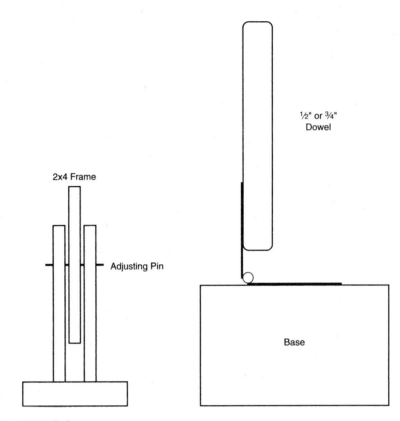

Figure 8.26. *The base.*

1. In the upper part of each pegboard, cut a hole slightly larger than a 1/4-inch bolt. Put together the two pegboard pieces using a 1/4-inch bolt and two nuts. Use the second nut to lock the first nut in place. The bolt should be loose enough to enable the two dowels to act as an elbow joint.

2. When this section of the boom is mounted to the base, the end of the second arm should be free to move forward and backward with little interference.

   Figure 8.28 shows the Channel 1 Joint for the boom. This joint measures the degree of tilt in your head movement.

3. As in the No Voltage Joint, attach two pieces of pegboard on opposite sides of two 1/4-inch dowels.

4. In the upper section of one of the pieces of pegboard, drill a hole large enough for a 1-megaohm potentiometer. (Radio Shack has one for $1.19.) Firmly attach this pot using the provided washer and nut.

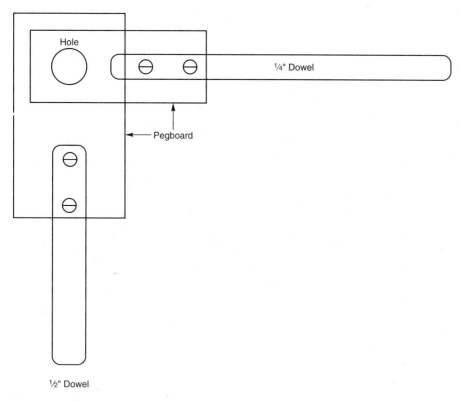

Hole

¼" Dowel

Pegboard

½" Dowel

Figure 8.27. *A boom joint.*

5. In the upper section of the other pegboard, drill a hole slightly smaller than the shaft of the pot.

6. Slide this pegboard over the shaft of the pot. Before attaching the pegboard to the shaft, rotate the pot to the middle of its rotation. The quickest way to determine this point is to use the *calibration method* described later in this section. When you find the middle point, attach the pegboard to the shaft with the shorter dowel placed vertically, as shown in Figure 8.28.

7. You can test the system at this point by hooking up the pot to the ADC circuit and executing the program ADC.PAS on the disk provided with this book. Place the end of the short vertical dowel straight in your hand. Now, move your hand in a forward tilting motion. The numbers for the pot should change. Return your hand to the vertical position. The numbers should be very close to the middle values that were calibrated. Now, move your hand in a backward tilting position. The numbers should change in the opposite direction. The computer uses these numbers to determine your head tilting.

The last joint for the boom is used to measure the degree of head panning. Figure 8.29 shows the construction of the last joint.

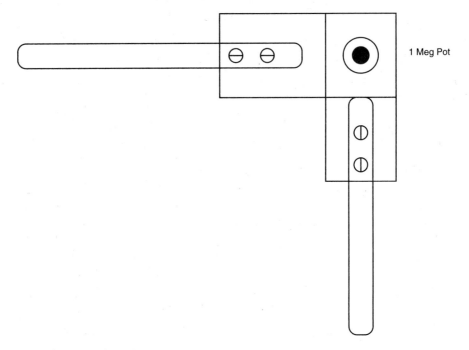

1 Meg Pot

Figure 8.28. The Channel 1 Joint for the boom.

8. Mount a 1-megaohm potentiometer to a small piece of pegboard. Then, mount this pegboard to the top of the HMD; use an elastic band, glue, or electrical tape. Attach the shaft of the potentiometer to the small vertical arm using duct tape or electrical tape. You can test this pot the same way you tested the previous one.

6DOF: To provide for measurement of head roll, you can attach a third potentiometer to the system. However, when I tried this on my system, it didn't work to my satisfaction. Instead of attaching the second arm to the No Voltage Joint, I used a potentiometer as the jointing mechanism (see Figure 8.27). Figure 8.30 shows the design.

As you roll your head from side to side, the pot measures the change in voltage. A problem with this design torque occurs when you move both in a roll and tilt or roll and pan motion at the same time. I've been working on a solution to this problem.

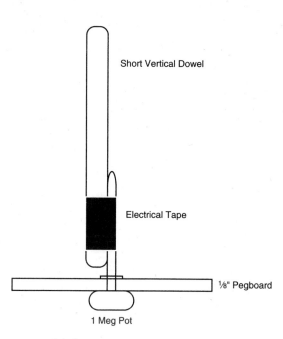

Short Vertical Dowel

Electrical Tape

1⁄8" Pegboard

1 Meg Pot

Figure 8.29. *The construction of the last joint.*

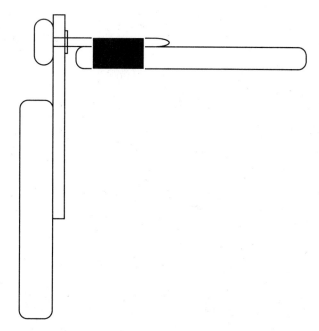

Figure 8.30. *The design.*

Hooking up the Potentiometers

After you finish building the boom apparatus, hook up the potentiometers. The current boom design uses two channels of an 8-channel analog-to-digital circuit. In addition to the two channels, a voltage source is needed for a total of three wires. Each of the potentiometers has three connections; only two are used here.

1. Designate one wire as the voltage source, and mark it as such.
2. Attach this wire to the far-left connector of both potentiometers when you look at them from the back (shaft pointing away from you).
3. Attach a second, different wire to the middle connector of the pot at the very end of the boom. This is Channel 0; designate it as such.
4. Attach a third, different wire to the remaining potentiometer. This is Channel 1; again, mark it as such.

ADC Circuit

Figure 8.31 shows the schematic for the analog-to-digital circuit used for my boom. A total of eight channels is available to use, but the boom uses only two of them (or three, for the optional potentiometer).

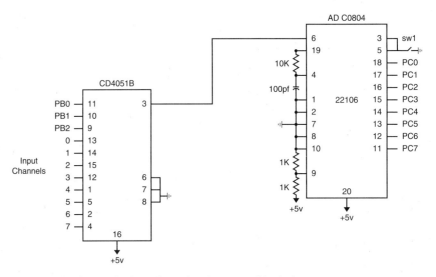

Figure 8.31. *The schematic for the analog-to-digital circuit used for the boom.*

The circuit is fairly simple to build. The eight data lines on the ADC chip are connected to the C port of the 8255-5 interface presented earlier. The three address lines on the CD4051 chip are connected to the first three lines of the B port. Each of the input lines on the CD4051 is selected by setting the correct PB0-PB2 line high. If you want to measure the voltage on line 4, set PB0-PB2 to the value of 4. The ADC chip takes readings from that line.

Switch sw1 resets the ADC. When the circuit is first powered up, this switch should be tripped to enable the ADC to reset itself.

Calibration

To determine the range of a potentiometer, you must calibrate it. The program ADC.PAS is a short program that shows how to use the ADC circuit. This program reads voltages from channels 0 through 2 and reports them on-screen until a key is pressed. When you press a key, the highest and lowest values for each of the channels is shown. These values can be used to determine the middle position of the potentiometers. When attaching the arms of the boom to each other, use this program to move the pot to its middle position.

Software

Programming the ADC circuit is not complicated. I assume you have already built the interface circuit and the circuit (described previously).

The interface circuit resides at I/O location 640 through 643. The first step in using the circuit is to tell the interface that ports A and B are output and that Port C is input.

This is done with the following instruction:

```
outportb ( 643, 137 );
```

After you tell the interface the correct port set up, instruct the CD4051 chip to select an input line with the following instruction:

```
outportb ( 641, x );
```

The value for x depends on the input line number. In this case, just use the actual number of the input line you want to use. After this step, you simply read the ADC chip with the following instruction:

```
value =  inportb ( 642 );
```

If you set up a loop using this instruction, you will find that the values read from the ADC jump around. To solve this problem, introduce a short delay into the read. Before obtaining the value with the instruction above, do a delay of 10 milliseconds:

```
delay ( 10 );
```

This gives the ADC time to produce a correct answer for an input voltage. This becomes especially important when using more than one channel. The following sequence would be read values from two different input channels:

```
outportb ( 641, 0 );
delay ( 10 );
```

```
value = inportb ( 642 );
outportb ( 641, 1 );
delay ( 10 );
value2 = inportb ( 641 );
```

The delays are important, because the ADC will be receiving a different voltage from the new channel. This gives the ADC time to generate the correct value.

REND386 Code

After using the ADC.PAS program for a while, you may feel the need to introduce this head-tracker to REND386. The program HEADTRAC.C is a simple program that reads in a figure file and enables use of the head-tracker. You can test the head-tracker by running this program and the REND386 demo program to see that the keyboard head movements do indeed match those of your new head-tracker.

The HEADTRAC.C program determines head movement in three steps:

1. It determines the position of the potentiometers when you're looking straight ahead. The code that accomplishes this is

```
printf ( "Stand with your hand in an upright forward
        looking position\n" );
printf ( "While I find the position of your head.
        (approx. 6 seconds)\n" );
delay ( 5000 );

outportb ( 641, 0 );
delay ( 10 );
panmiddle = inportb ( 642 );
pancurrent = panmiddle;

outportb ( 641, 1 );
delay ( 10 );
tiltmiddle = inportb ( 642 );
tiltcurrent = tiltmiddle;

printf ( "Thank You!" );
```

The current position of your head for both the tilt and pan motions is kept in the variables `tiltmiddle` and `panmiddle`. These are used as reference points. The current position of the head is kept in the variables `tiltcurrent` and `pancurrent`.

2. After you have the starting position, you can begin to read the position of the head in a regular fashion. I'll introduce code into the main loop of all REND386 programs:

```
outportb ( 641,1 );
delay ( 10 );
value = inportb(642);
if ( abs(value-tiltcurrent) > 5 ) process_tilt(value);

outportb (641,0 );
delay ( 10 );
value = inportb(642);
if ( abs(value-pancurrent) > 5 ) process_pan(value);
```

This code sets the correct input line and delays and reads the port. A test is made of the new value to determine if an acceptable amount of head movement has occurred. If the new position is more than five units in either direction, process the new position; otherwise, throw out the new read. This is done for both potentiometers. If there is acceptable movement, call one of two functions, process_tilt or process_pan.

3. Each of the functions moves the eye position in REND386—according to the value it is given as a parameter. The process_pan function is

```
void process_pan ( unsigned char value )
{
    latitude = (value-panmiddle)*2*65536L;
    polar_compute();
    compute_view_factors ( current_view );
    pancurrent = value;
    redraw = 1;
}
```

The original demo programs for REND386 included a function called polar_compute. This function used latitude and longitude data to determine a new eye position based on the polar coordinate system. Use part of the polar_compute function to create the new eye position. For the pan motion, the global variable latitude is set to twice the angle generated by the current head pan position and the earlier recorded pan middle position. The function polar_compute is called to set the new eye position, and the function compute_view_factors is called to perform the REND386 housecleaning for view positions. Record the new current position; then, indicate that the screen needs to be redrawn.

The same type of function is used for the tilting motion of the head, except that a longitude global variable is used in the polar calculations.

The Optics Subsystem

For the homebrewer, the optics system probably is the most difficult part of constructing an HMD (because of the cost). My experimentation was limited, and I am aware that there are better optics than those I present here. However, the optics built in this article *do* work, and they are not expensive. I assume for this project that the LCDs used in your HMD are those found in the off-the-shelf TVs described earlier.

Background

Why do we need optics? Why can't we just put the LCDs in front of our eyes and see 3D? The answer is two-fold.

First, if you try to put the two Casio 2.2-inch TVs in front of your eyes, you will find that the left eye looks at the right part of one of the TVs and the right eye looks at the left part of the other TV. Ideally, you would like to look at the middle of each screen. You could compensate for the difference in viewing area, but this significantly reduces the field of view.

The second reason is the focusing distance of the eye. To create a true stereoscopic image, a left image must be presented to the left eye only, and a right image must be presented to the right eye only. If the two screens are put in front of both eyes at a distance that they can actually focus on the screens, the eyes will operate as they should by focusing on a single object. Each eye must focus separately on each screen.

If we place the screens close enough to the eyes, we cannot focus on images on the screens. To relieve this situation, we introduce optics. Figure 8.32 shows a reproduction of an early stereoscopic apparatus, taken from the 1932 book *The Principles of Optics* by Hardy and Perrin.

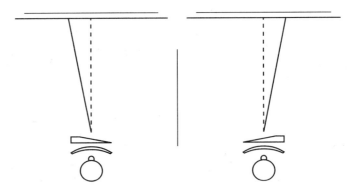

Figure 8.32. *A reproduction of an early stereoscopic apparatus.*

Each eye views a path to its screen; the paths are parallel. The thick horizontal lines represent prisms that enable a larger picture to be viewed. The lens at the bottom of the illustration lets the user's eyes focus correctly on the separate images. The vertical line between the eyes indicates a part of the optics that keeps the images separate.

The optics in most commercial HMDs are produced by a company called LEEP Systems of Waltham, Massachusetts. The LEEP optical system consists of three different lenses per eye. If an image is presented in the correct format for the optics, the optics have a 140-degree *field of view* (FOV). (FOV is the amount of visual space the eye has for viewing objects.) A normal eye has a field of view of 270 degrees. If you look straight ahead, you can see movement up to 90 degrees to the right or left. This is a total of 180 degrees. The eye can move 45 degrees in either direction, so if you look all the way to the right and then sweep all the way to the left, you can see about 270 degrees.

For an HMD, you really should create the total 270 degree FOV. The problem is creating a software system that will display fuzzy images for peripheral vision and creating a LCD screen that is 270 degrees around. The only solution is to settle for a smaller field of view.

Our Optics

Begin the construction of the optics by moving the LCD images so they're presented directly to your eyes. This involves spreading the small TV screens far enough apart in a configuration that still accommodates the power connection. In doing so, notice that both eyes focus on the edge of the TVs. To move the video image to our eyes, we use an old trick we learned as children: viewing through a periscope.

A periscope allows looking around a corner or above something. A simple periscope moves the video from the LCDs to our eyes. Figure 8.33 shows what happens when you look, with one eye, through the periscope, and the LCD image is reflected back at your eye.

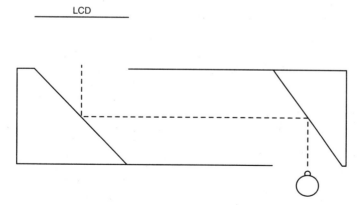

Figure 8.33. *What happens when you look, with one eye, through the periscope.*

Careful construction of the periscope is vital to making the HMD work correctly.

Using a large piece of black poster board, I cut out a five-sided box. The sides of this box are the same length as the height of the LCD screens. I assembled the box with one side overlapping another for strength. Electrical tape holds the box together.

View Openings

The next step is to create an opening for the LCD screen and an opening for your eye to peer through. Cut these openings on opposite ends and sides of the box. Cut the opening for the LCD screen about 1/4-inch from the end of the box, as shown in Figure 8.33. This opening should be large enough for all of the screen to appear.

Cut the eye opening to the height of the box and about 3/4-inch wide.

Mirrors

A periscope operates by bouncing an image off two mirrors positioned as shown in Figure 8.33. You can purchase a small mirror at Walmart for about $1 and a mirror cutter for about $4. This mirror should be large enough for you to cut the four necessary mirror segments (with a little room for mistakes).

1. Cut two segments as tall and slightly longer than your LCD screens. Position the mirrors in the box as shown in Figure 8.33.

2. Mount the mirrors by using two small slits in the box *or* by using electrical tape.

3. When placing the mirrors:

   a. Make sure that the mirrors are perfectly vertical. If either of the mirrors leans to one side or the other, your image will appear to be crooked.

   b. Attach the mirrors so they're at parallel angles to one another.

The easiest way to determine whether you have the mirrors positioned correctly is to simply use the box as a periscope. If you hold the box perfectly horizontal, you should see an image of the screen to your right when you use your right eye. The image also should be perfectly straight. Adjust the mirrors if the image appears to lean, or if you see other parts of your environment.

Lenses

The last part of the optics system construction is to install the lenses. The purpose of the lenses is to enable you to focus on the LCD screens at a reasonable distance.

You can buy your lenses—plastic, full-sheet page magnifiers that cost about $1 each— at Walmart. You need *at least* two of these.

1. When you look at one of the sheets, you'll see a small dot in the middle with many circles emanating from it. Using this dot as a guide, and

keeping it in the middle, cut a square piece of the lens to be slightly larger than your LCD.

2. Mount this lens on the front of the periscope. The dot should be in the middle of the LCD cut-out opening.

Attaching the Optics

1. After you finish one of the periscope optics, build the second one.

2. Attach both periscopes to the LCD screens. With Casio TVs, there is enough plastic border around the screens to allow for a second small box to be constructed over the lens and the LCD. Place the optics about one inch from the LCD screen.

3. Experiment with the placement of the optics until your eyes focus best on the screens.

Enhancements

The preceding setup provides a horizontal FOV of about 75 to 80 degrees. You can extend this FOV by introducing a second lens. Figure 8.34 shows the placement of the second lens.

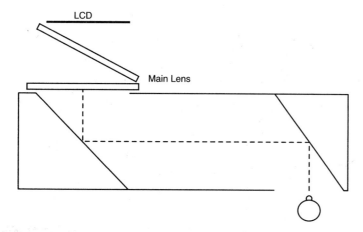

Figure 8.34. *The placement of the second lens.*

The second lens causes the image on the LCD to widen. This increases the FOV by 10 to 20 degrees. However, there is a down side. The images become smudgy and appear somewhat out of focus. Try adjusting the distance between the lenses and the LCD to combat this problem. But it cannot be totally eliminated.

An additional enhancement to the system is the use of right-angle prisms. These prisms bend light by 90 degrees and can be used in place of the mirrors for a slightly better image transfer. The prisms are a bit costly, about $25 each (you can buy them through Edmund Scientific).

Conclusion

The simple head-tracker can be built for less than $10. It works correctly and provides a new level of VR for the experimenter.

The ideal optics for HMDs are LEEP System optics. However, using simple materials, you can create an adequate optic system to provide the necessary level of immersion.

As for the HMD—it *works*. I used it with REND386 and a Pascal test program to build the optics and enclosure. However, if you want to build an HMD, I cannot guarantee your results. The speed of the computer, the type of LCD, and the type of VGA-to-NTSC converter all affect the outcome of the final system.

Bibliography and Sources for Parts

Bek, Robin. "RGB-to-NTSC Converter." *Computer Digest,* December 1989.

Ciarcia, Steve. "Build an Audio-and-Video Multiplexer." *Byte,* February 1986.

Howlett, Eric M. "Wide Angle Orthostereo." SPIE Vol. 1256, Stereoscopic Displays and Applications, 1990.

Intel, *Microprocessor and Peripheral Handbook,* 1989.

"I/O Card." *Radio Electronics,* June 1990.

Motorola Semiconductor technical data, MC1377.

Robinette, Warren and Jannick P. Rolland, "A Computational Model for the Stereoscopic Optics of a Head-Mounted Display." SPIE Vol. 1457, Stereoscopic Displays and Applications II, 1991.

Stampe, Dave. Personal correspondence.

Stevens, Anthony. "PC-to-TV Converter." *Radio Electronics,* October 1991, pp. 33-38.

Voorhees, Mark. "The Home Satellite Weather Center." *Circuit Cellar Ink.* January/February 1988.

Here is the address for Boffin, manufacturer of the $199 PC-Video Converter card:

Boffin Limited
2500 West County Road 42, #5
Burnsville, MN 55337
(612) 894-0595

You can order project supplies, including optics, mirror cutters, prisms, and so forth, from the extensive catalog of

Edmund Scientific Company
101 E. Gloucester Pike
Barrington, NY 08007-1380
(609) 573-6879

You also can try the following catalog:

American Science and Surplus
601 Linden Place
Evanston, IL 60202
(708) 475-8440

PUTTING VR ON THE MAP

Jerry Isdale

PROFILE

5

JERRY ISDALE:
"Developing VR for Personal Growth"

Does anyone walk in Los Angeles? Perhaps only the wide-eyed tourists who clog Hollywood's star-studded sidewalks. L.A. has its topographical ups and downs, but the district that real-estate agents dubbed Marina Del Rey Adjacent is flat land—ideal for bicycling, if not strolling. Indeed, a bike path leads directly to the marina, half a mile away. Here in "Adjacent," the misplaced tourist will find acres of tidy, single-family homes built in the '40s and '50s, clusters of luscious avocado and citrus trees, many hot tubs, and L.A.'s ubiquitous supermarket strip malls.

"I have seen low-cost VR systems do today what the Cray supercomputer couldn't do eight years ago. Commercial clients will not readily accept the quality of current HMDs and REND386, but I firmly believe that there is a *lot* of ground-breaking information design and VR engineering that we can do with lower-end systems."

Jerry Isdale is a programmer who is accomplishing a *lot* with lower-end VR systems. He has modified REND386 to support more 6DOF input devices and uploaded those modifications to the net, along with his paper, "What is Virtual Reality? A Homebrewer's Introduction." As system operator of the CompuServe Cyberforum, Jerry adds to the virtual community's understanding of VR. A gift for conversation and a penchant for detail prompt Jerry to provide long answers to short questions. He waxes poetic about good program design and clean coding technique. Most important to Jerry, however, are his wife Mary Ann and their toddler Eddy, with whom he lives in Marina Del Rey Adjacent in a house that he remodeled. To pay the mortgage, Jerry works for Dreamers Guild,

(Photo by Linda Jacobson)

Inc. as a games programmer. He also takes freelance jobs. In 1993 he programmed a series of multimedia CD-ROMs, the Xiphias "Timetable of History."

Jerry was born on August 17, 1958, and raised in Orange, Connecticut, a town outside New Haven, where he went to Amity High School. As a teenager, photography occupied his spare time. He had a darkroom at home for developing photos he shot at school to earn extra cash. "I was a nerd in the audio-visual department, running around taking pictures," Jerry admits. "I was in the choir, too, because they needed guys in the choir. It was a great way to meet girls."

In senior year, Jerry joined the school's computer club. A single DEC PDP-8 awaited Amity students who cared to decipher its blinking lights, front-panel switches, and paper-tape interface. Jerry did; he learned to program in BASIC and Assembler. The club organized a few group projects, but its members were free to explore computing on their own. Jerry decided to write a BASIC program that would do his calculus homework. "I learned so much about the details of differentiating equations in order to write the program," Jerry recalls, "that I learned it better than if I had just done my homework the normal way."

Jerry graduated from Amity in 1976 and moved to Ithaca, New York, to attend Cornell University. "I was supposed to go for electrical engineering. That's what I thought I wanted to go into. Before freshman year, I went up in the summer and took two classes—introduction to programming and a freshman writing seminar." The programming course affirmed for Jerry his love for computers. Once ensconced in engineering school, he enrolled in every computer science course available to engineering undergraduates. During sophomore year he learned that he would have to wait until senior year to take more comp-sci courses.

By this time Jerry was living the Lambda Chi Alpha fraternity life, "partying big and hard." He balanced the partying and studying with a job at a new Computerland store in Ithaca. "For one of my semesters, I was soldering and wiring up computers and trying to do sales," Jerry says. "I *hated* sales. I couldn't stand having to tell people all the wonderful things these computers could do for them, knowing that they couldn't quite do it."

Jerry felt dissatisfied with Cornell, too. "I failed two classes in successive semesters: statistics and mechanics," he says. "I was not happy. I wasn't able to take any more programming courses, and I really enjoyed programming. I wasn't interested much in electronics design anymore."

In his junior year, Jerry decided to switch schools. He chose the University of Bridgeport in Bridgeport, Connecticut because it offered one of the Northeast's few computer engineering programs. He moved back into his parents' house and commuted to Bridgeport. It was one of the best decisions he'd ever made. "They taught hardware, architecture, programming. I also got involved in a cooperative engineering program and found a terrific job working for a special-purpose computer center at General

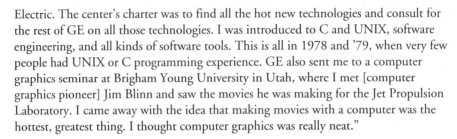

Electric. The center's charter was to find all the hot new technologies and consult for the rest of GE on all those technologies. I was introduced to C and UNIX, software engineering, and all kinds of software tools. This is all in 1978 and '79, when very few people had UNIX or C programming experience. GE also sent me to a computer graphics seminar at Brigham Young University in Utah, where I met [computer graphics pioneer] Jim Blinn and saw the movies he was making for the Jet Propulsion Laboratory. I came away with the idea that making movies with a computer was the hottest, greatest thing. I thought computer graphics was really neat."

Jerry graduated with a BS in computer engineering in December 1980 and set about launching a career. Bypassing the frozen winter roads he would have to drive on the way to work in the Northeast's high-tech corridor, Jerry sought a job in California.

"I became the sales support engineer for a company in Los Angeles called Interactive Systems. They sold UNIX systems," Jerry says. "After about a year, I burned out because I wasn't doing enough programming. At that point, there was a neat little start-up company that had bought our UNIX to do computer graphics. That was Digital Productions in Los Angeles. I went there, initially to work as a programmer."

Again, though, Jerry wasn't given enough chances to hone his programming chops. He moved on to Xerox Electronics Systems in El Segundo, where he provided support for an electronic CAD system and played with one of the early mouse devices and windows systems. It was 1984.

Jerry lasted nine months at Xerox. Bored by the mundane tasks involved in support work, he left to take a job more in line with his interests. He joined Omnibus Computer Graphics on the Paramount Studios movie lot in L.A. "We designed a computer animation system and we were doing animation for film [including Disney features] and television, mostly commercials. I was the toolmaker for the animators, programming the 3D geometry tools that the animators used."

Browsing through a bookstore one day in 1986, Jerry noticed Myron Krueger's book *Artificial Reality.* The title grabbed him. "I read it cover to cover. I loved the idea of artificial reality. But I thought what we really need to do is interactive 3D graphics, not this video stuff."

The concept of artificial reality still brewed in the back of his mind when Jerry decided to go freelance in January 1987. For the next two years he programmed instructional multimedia CD-ROMs before he heard about "encumbered VR, or window-on-the-world VR," he remembers. "I was tired of doing multimedia and I wanted to branch off and start developing something else. I had a CompuServe account and I read [online] about a virtual reality [discussion] section. I started spending time over there and got very involved talking to people about the technology. I was one of the people there who was actually doing computer graphics."

Jerry's first immersive VR experience occurred in 1991 at the California State University Technology and Persons with Disabilities Conference. "I sat in the VPL Research demo area and talked with the people from VPL. I got to stick my head in it there and I thought it was really neat, although very blurry and very slow. A little disappointing—well, very disappointing. I much preferred looking at it on the monitor."

About six months later, Jerry joined the Virtual Reality Special Interest Group in Los Angeles. By the end of 1992, he had discovered REND386 and downloaded it from CompuServe. One of the first REND386 worlds he created "was a world with a ball that shrinks and grows, in response to moving objects, all in random color."

In an effort to document garage VR development efforts and create a FAQ for prospective VR hobbyists, Jerry wrote a report, "What is Virtual Reality?" He uploaded it to one of the CompuServe computer graphics forums in February 1993 and continues to update it regularly.

Jerry also created a public-domain geometry library called "iegeom" for building objects in REND386's .PLG file format. In 1993 he uploaded the library's full source code to the Internet (the site at `sunee.uwaterloo`). He also modified REND386 to add support for the Global Devices forceball. "In the process, I reworked the source code to make it compile easier in Borland C 3.1," Jerry notes. "I also rearranged the source hierarchy to make it more rational, and integrated a Logitech mouse/head-tracker driver that Dave Stampe had written. My version of the code, without Dave's tracker code, is available on CompuServe."

Today Jerry's daydreams transport him into "the networked cyberspace." He is infinitely intrigued by "the idea of navigating the vast information space that is created by the myriad of systems in a multimedia space. Immersion would be nice, but not if you're encumbered by head-mounted display, glove, or cables. Stereoscopy is optional, but motion parallax should be included.

"I would also like to develop a virtual world for personal growth, a world that could be used in a manner similar to guided fantasy," Jerry muses. "Perhaps a virtual tarot world, not for fortune-telling, but for personal insights."

Tour Guide's Toolbox

Engine: '486/33MHz, PC clone, 4MB RAM, 800MB hard drive

Monitor: Color 14-inch SVGA

Modem: 14.4 TwinCom 2400/9600

Primary hardware: Keyboard, Global Devices forceball, Logitech head tracker, two Power Gloves, Sega shutter glasses, Toshiba shutter glasses

Music to code by: "The quiet hum of cooling fans."

Total cost: "When I bought my PC system, it cost about $8,000."

E-mail: `72330.770@compuserve.com` and `isdale@well.sf.ca.us`

NOTE

Jerry's updated version of REND386, version 4—with source, documentation, sample world, serial line-handling functions, and support for the Global Devices forceball—is available via FTP from `sunee.uwaterloo.ca`.

Directory path: `/pub/incoming directory`

Filename: jirend.zip

Jerry's paper "What is Virtual Reality?" is available via FTP from `sunsite.unc.edu`.

Directory path: `/pub/academic/computer-science/virtual-reality/papers`

Filename: whatisvr.txt (or whatisvr.zip)

On the WELL, the paper is located in `~isdale\whatisvr.txt`.

Carpooling

Traveling with Friends on the Data Highways

CHAPTER 9

Carpooling

Traveling with Friends on the Data Highways

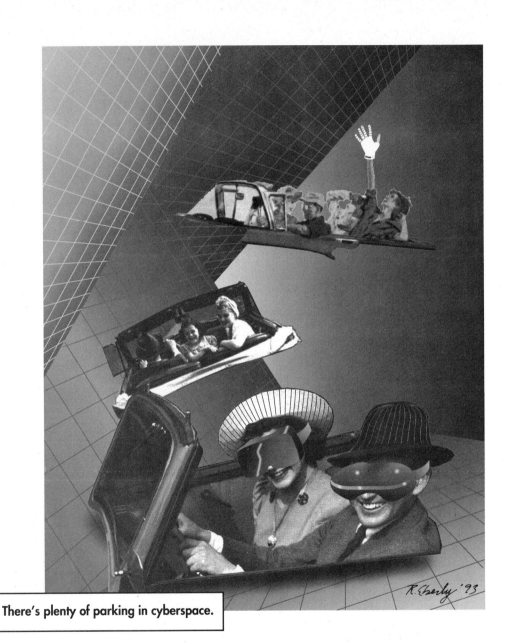

There's plenty of parking in cyberspace.

We are social creatures. Yet when we drive our low-cost reality engines to visit virtual worlds, we usually go solo. That's fun—but even more fun is sharing our experiences and knowledge with fellow travelers. Peaceful solitude is lovely, but after a while, as the song says, "What good is sitting alone in your room?"

Destination: Cyberspace

Cyberspace is a place where electronic information lives. Consider it a virtual environment whose inhabitants consist of data.

Computer-mediated communication occurs in the realm of cyberspace. According to pioneering VR programmer Randy Walser, "Cyberspace gives great power to its audiences and is controlled moment by moment by the people participating in the space."

When a virtual world can be visited by two or more people, it exists in cyberspace. Such an experience, or application, is generally called *networked VR*. Some day, affordable reality engines, interconnected through phone lines over a network, will provide access to multisensory three-dimensional virtual worlds, which large bands of explorers will enter and manipulate, all interacting with the same single, shared environment at one time. Randy Walser calls such multiperson cyberspaces *distributed* (each engine runs a copy of the simulation), whereas single-person cyberspaces are *centralized* (there is only one copy of the simulation).

Thanks to the collaborative process that they naturally engender, such systems will catalyze the creation of larger, richer, more complex, and more interactive virtual worlds than those in existence today. Even more intriguing, these systems will eliminate limits imposed by our bodies—people of different physical abilities will interact on equal levels—and they will eliminate limits imposed by geographical space. Someday, virtual worlds will sustain virtual societies in which people from different cultures will experience real-time, multisensory, and multidimensional group-learning, problem-solving, government, and the ultimate frisbee game.

Reality Check

The establishment of distributed 3D applications on networks of PCs, much less on powerful workstations, presents some thorny technological challenges. Researchers gnaw on them daily. After all, even solo VR is still in the Studebaker days. Before networked VR can enter the home or hit the desktop, we'll need a wide-area network infrastructure and a telecommunications protocol that works long distance over standard phone lines (perhaps one such as ATM—the asynchronous transmission method now being widely adopted and debuting as an AT&T service in 1994). Developers must work out communications modes and methods, tackling traffic delays and routing paths, and such mundane issues as how RAM-hogging 3D graphics will be processed, transmitted, and displayed in real time.

The national Institute of Electrical and Electronics Engineers (IEEE) is supporting such efforts, working toward the promulgation of standards that enable connectivity between dissimilar VR systems. In March 1993, the IEEE approved a set of industry standards (IEEE #1278-1993) that establishes methods for defining the location and motion—even the collision—of 3D graphics objects and the exchange of component objects and related services. You can obtain a copy of this set of standards by calling IEEE at (800) 678-4333.

In the meantime, progress in networked VR is palpable. At industry conferences, VR researchers from educational and corporate facilities have been showing off their networking achievements. They've successfully presented single virtual worlds to a handful of networked UNIX workstations and ordinary PCs. In such systems, each computer operator can view and interact with the same 3D scene. When one operator moves a virtual object in the scene, the other operators see that change, from their perspective, on their computers. The scenes can boast visual complexity, and data carried between computers is compact enough to travel easily over conventional telephone lines.

In 1992, working out of Carnegie-Mellon University, Carl Loeffler, a well-known VR researcher, introduced "Fun House." This immersive VR system featured dynamic, interactive objects within one multiuser environment that were displayed to users (linked by phone line) in the U.S. and Germany. The Fun House world was built with Sense8's WorldToolKit, incorporating MIDI sound effects, dynamic characters, head-mounted displays, and 6DOF input devices. Carl Loeffler continues to update the system and travel around the globe, demonstrating it through live connections between sites in the U.S. and abroad.

In the garage VR domain, one simple implementation of networked VR is the Power Glovin' "Virtual Handshake," invented by Joe Gradecki of *PCVR* (and included on this book's disk). As Joe explains in Profile 2, his efforts to interconnect PC-based virtual worlds over modem led to the development of Mate, the quasi-VR game now sold for $30 by VRontier Worlds of Stoughton, Wisconsin. The Beta version of Mate appeared in June of 1993. It lets two people play chess on a graphically represented board that appears on the screens of two computers, which interconnect with a modem. Mate even supports stereoscopic viewing through shutter glasses (watch out for leaping knights!). Joe and his VRontier Worlds colleagues intend to add texturing and increase the polygon count.

Others interested in low-cost VR aim to achieve similar results with Macintosh computers. Garage VR experimenters want to build a networked VR system so the operators of two or more Macs can share one virtual world. The initial problem here concerns the actual connection between engines; current development efforts involve the creation of custom networking protocols, written in C and using AppleTalk or the standard TCP/IP protocol to communicate between Macs.

Imagine the long-term results: instead of pen pals, we'll have sim pals. We may have to wait a few years for technology that lets us step into a virtual world where we can see, hear, and touch geographically distant friends. But right now, right here, technology exists that lets us use our own little reality engines to get to faraway places and access graphical virtual worlds.

The Information Superhighway

If you want to travel from one city to another, you take an interstate highway. In the digital domain, you take the Internet to travel to data storehouses far and wide. The Internet is an electronic medium, a humongous network that interconnects millions of computers around the world. Travel on the Internet is virtually toll-free. It represents territory that belongs to everyone but is owned by no one.

By directly connecting over a phone line to the Internet, you can send and receive mail and exchange programs and text, graphics, and sound files with other people who use networked systems, anywhere in the world. Most direct connections to the Internet stem from networks established at educational institutions and research centers. That's because the Internet started out as a research program funded by the federal government.

In 1973, the U.S. Advanced Research Projects Agency (ARPA) launched a national program to investigate techniques and technologies for interlinking heterogeneous data networks. The goal was to develop protocols that would support transparent communication between networked computers on multiple linked packet networks. Dubbed the "Internetting Project," this research program resulted in a system of networks known as the Internet. Fruits of the research included a protocol system from which we all benefit today—the TCP/IP Protocol Suite, named after two initial developments: the Transmission Control Protocol and the Internet Protocol.

In the mid-1980s, the U.S. National Science Foundation, U.S. Department of Energy, and National Aeronautics and Space Administration jumped into the "Interfray," providing communications support to connect tens of thousands of additional computers. European agencies joined in at the same time. After 1989, the Internet starting weaving into its fabric support for new communications standards, particularly Open Systems Interconnection (OSI), thus creating a patchwork quilt of protocols.

By the early 1990s, the availability of public domain and commercial implementations of the varied TCP/IP protocols led to the integration of more than 5,000 computer networks in more than 24 countries serving about 315,000 host computers used by as many as *3 million* people.

That's one big no-host party....

If you don't have access to the Internet through work or school, you can make your way there by way of a commercial online service, such as Delphi, that provides a "gateway" to the Internet. This is why you need a modem. In the realm of garage VR, owning a computer without a modem and telecommunications software is like driving a car around a parking lot that has no exit.

Several powerful reasons motivate the garage VR explorer to drive the Internet:

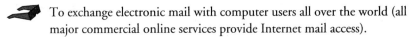

- To exchange electronic mail with computer users all over the world (all major commercial online services provide Internet mail access).

- To transfer files, using the procedure *FTP* (file transfer protocol). With FTP, you can shuttle files and freeware or shareware programs from an Internet site to your personal computer.

- To read USENET newsgroups, a vast collection of ongoing discussion areas, each of which focuses on a particular topic. (USENET, an acronym for User's Network, is a cooperative, decentralized network that's closely related to the Internet.)

- To experience "MUDs," multiuser dungeons (or multiuser dimensions), otherwise known as text-based virtual realities: continuous activities and games in which you participate in real time. In a MUD, you can assume a mysterious or magical persona and interact with others, explore rooms, caverns, castles, and other-worldly spaces, fight monsters, solve puzzles, and create your own rooms and MUDdy items.

- To participate in the "Power On, Dial In, Log On" ritual that connects us to a community.

The following paragraphs provide a compilation of Internet and other online services of special interest to garage VR explorers, including sources for

- Great FAQs (frequently asked question lists: documents that provide newsgroup or mailing-list newcomers with introductory information and resources on the topic at hand)

- Anonymous FTP sites with programs and files related to high-end and garage VR, 3D graphics, and stereoscopy (*anonymous* means you can obtain files from the remote site at no charge by logging in as anonymous, but under restricted access; this isn't a handicap)

- VR-savvy newsgroups and electronic mailing lists

- Commercial online services and bulletin board systems that boast respectable VR conferences

If you learned how to ride a bicycle or drive a car, you can learn to navigate the Internet. The multitudinous acronyms and arcane commands may at first appear intimidating, but you'll get the hang of it. To learn all about FTP and other Internet services, pick up one of the great books that cover the Internet (see Appendix D). Or you can dive right in for an overview by sending e-mail to `mailserver@rtfm.mit.edu` with a body of

```
send usenetnews.answers/internet-services/faq
```

To find out how to read USENET newsgroups, contact your online service's system operator.

Some of the information in the following list was derived from FTP and VR data site lists that appear in the USENET newsgroup sci.virtual-worlds, posted by Bill Cockayne of Apple Computer and Toni Emerson of the Human Interface Technology Lab. Although the net addresses were accurate when this book was published, and most sites stem from stable educational and corporate institutions, keep in mind that net addresses, like normal (snail-mail) addresses, can change over time.

Just the FAQs

Virtual Reality FAQ

Host: `ftp.u.washington.edu`
Directory path: /public/virtual-worlds/therealfaq
Maintained by Mark A. DeLoura (`deloura@cs.unc.edu`)

Power Glove FAQ (Glove-List)

Host: `cogsci.uwo.ca` (129.100.6.10)
Maintained by Eric Townsend (`jet@well.sf.ca.us`)

(This FAQ also is available directly from the glove-list file server. See the glove-list information in the section titled "Electronic Mailing Lists.")

Power Glove Serial Interface (PGSI) FAQ

Host: `ftp.cso.uiuc.edu` (128.174.5.59)
Directory path: /ACM/PGSI
Address: (`pgsi@uiuc.edu`)

Advanced Gravis UltraSound FAQ

Host: `rtfm.mit.edu`
Directory path: pub/usenet/news.answers
Maintained by Dave DeBry (`ddebry@dsd.es.com`)

Carpooling
Traveling with Friends on the Data Highways

Anonymous FTP Sites

General Information

Host: `ftp.u.washington.edu` (140.142.56.1)
Directory path: /public/virtual-worlds
Directory path: /public/hitl
Directory path: /public/virtual-worlds/virtus
Directory path: /public/VirtualReality

Probably the world's best-known VR information base, this site stores, among other goodies, sci.virtual-worlds archives, "TheRealFaq," code for VEOS (Virtual Environment Operating System), and self-running Virtus WalkThrough demos. Be sure to make your way down the directory path: /public/virtualreality/hitl/bibliographies, where the meticulously maintained VR Update (filename vru-vol1rev.txt) lists all recent VR books and articles.

Host: `stein.u.washington.edu` (140.142.56.1)
Directory path: /public/virtual-worlds

Home of sci.virtual-worlds, this is the place to log on to when you can't access `ftp.u.washington.edu` (and vice versa). Check out that FAQ!

Host: `sunee.uwaterloo.ca` (129.97.50.50)
Directory path: /pub
Directory path: /pub/rend386
Directory path: /pub/vr

A requisite stopover for all VR net travelers, this University of Waterloo site overflows with useful files and programs, including Dave Stampe and Bernie Roehl's notorious screen-renderer REND386 and its demos (read the text files first; they explain how to run the demo), a cool 3D wireframe object-viewer (which lets you use your mouse to pivot an object about), quasi-VR demos for 386 PCs, Jerry Isdale's "What Is VR?" article, and the proverbial much, much more. Some of the demos support the Mattel Power Glove and/or LCD shutter glasses. Here are some other directory paths of interest to garage VR types:

pub/amiga (files related to the Commodore Amiga)
pub/glove (files and programs related to Power Glove)
pub/netgame (files related to networked games and VR)
pub/polyblit (Dave Stampe's speedy polygon code for 386 PCs)
pub/raytracers (raytracing graphics packages)
pub/sound (C source for playing sound files on a PC)
pub/vgif (GIF viewer)
Host: `sunsite.unc.edu` (152.2.22.81)
Directory path: /pub/academic/computer-science/virtual-reality

Based at the University of North Carolina, which houses one of the world's leading VR research labs, this site contains academic papers, VR demos, articles, a partial mirror of sci.virtual-worlds and the glove-list, 3D images and software, DOS VR programs, Power Glove software and information, REND386, and other fun stuff.

> Host: `avalon.chinalake.navy.mil` (129.131.31.11).
> Directory path: /pub
> Mirrored on `ftp.kpc.com` (144.52.120.9)
> Directory path: /pub/mirror/avalon

This is a massive data bank for 3D graphic objects archived in various formats, including utilities to convert between formats and documents that explain file formats.

> Host: `wuarchive.wustl.edu` (128.252.135.4)

This Seattle-based site mirrors the sci.virtual-worlds archives. It also contains Power Glove information and a wealth of graphics archives, including source code, in the directory path /graphics.

> Host: `parcftp.xerox.com`
> Directory path: /PUB/MOO/PAPERS

Site of the LambdaMOO MUD (see the section titled "In the MUD"), this Xerox Palo Alto Research Center storehouse contains scads of information on multiuser dungeons/dimensions (MUDs)—also known as text-based virtual realities—and electronic communication in general.

> Host: `ftp.apple.com` (130.43.2.3)
> Directory path: /pub/vr

Direct from Apple Computer headquarters in Cupertino, California, this cyberplace contains information on Macintosh-based VR, news of CAD projects, and a regularly updated list of FTP sites. It's also the home of the Mac VR programs Gossamer and Dr. StrangeGlove.

> Host: `ftp.ipa.fhg.de` (129.233.17.68)
> Directory path: /pub/virtual-reality

Based in Germany, this site contains files describing the work of Fraunhofer Institute for Manufacturing Engineering and Automation (IPA) in Stuttgart—specifically, the Demonstration Centre for VR, founded in 1991.

> Host: `ftp.ncsa.uiuc.edu` (141.142.20.50)
> Directory path: /VR

This relatively new site stores papers and other documentation about VR systems developed at the National Center for Supercomputing Applications (no garage VR here!).

LCD Shutter Glasses Information and Code

> Host: wench.ece.jcu.edu.au
> Directory path: /pub/sega/[320x400|hicolor]
> Host: wuarchive.wustl.edu (128.252.135.4)

These sites contain documentation and code for interfacing Sega shutter glasses with IBM PCs and compatibles.

> Host: vega.hut.fi
> Directory path: /pub/mac/finnish/sega3d

This is the place for source code and documentation for interfacing the Macintosh with Sega LCD shutter glasses. It also provides ASCII and GIF versions of the documentation.

Macintosh VR Information

> Host: ftp.apple.com (130.43.2.3)
> Directory path: /pub/vr
> Maintained by Bill Cockayne (billc@apple.com)

Dip into this treasure chest of Macintosh VR applications, self-extracting archives (Power Glove interface diagrams, programs and compiler for Ron Menelli's 68HC11 Glove interface, a Glove rotation control demo, and lots more). The updated list of FTP sites goes by the filename vr_sites.

News Groups

USENET News Groups: sci.virtual-worlds and sci.virtual-worlds.apps

This inimitable pair of news groups contains the most active, well-known VR discussions, read by more than 15,000 people around the world. They cover developments in the field of virtual worlds technologies (sci.virtual-worlds) and applications (sci.virtual-worlds-apps). Together they serve as an international forum in which regular participants contribute news, insights into technological developments, opinions on scientific and philosophical issues, and discussions of the use of virtual worlds in commercial and social settings. Co-moderators from around the world contribute to both discussions, keeping it topical and "flame-free."

Several FTP sites (listed earlier) "mirror" sci.virtual-worlds, reflecting the daily activities for those who can't directly access the newsgroup.

Excerpts of these newsgroups occasionally appear on CompuServe, GEnie, BIX, and the WELL's VR conference.

Those who can't directly access these newsgroups with the USENET can subscribe to e-mail redistribution lists and receive the complete, daily contents of these newsgroups.

The redistribution lists are named virtu-l for sci.virtual-worlds and vrapp-l for sci.virtual-world.applications. (Traffic is heavy, often more than 30 messages each day.) The lists are managed by Greg Newby, an assistant professor in the graduate school of Library and Information Science at the University of Illinois at Champaign-Urbana.

To join, send e-mail to `listserv@vmd.cso.uiuc.edu` (or to `listserv@uiucvmd` on Bitnet) with a body of

`subscribe virtu-l `*`Your Full Name`*

and/or

`subscribe vrapp-l `*`Your Full Name`*

For example, if your name is Pat Barleycorn, you'd send a message consisting of `subscribe virtu-l Pat Barleycorn`.

If you experience glitches, contact Greg Newby at `gbnewby@uicuvmd.bitnet` or `gbnewby@uiuc.edu`

alt.cyberpunk and alt.cyberpunk.tech

Not for the faint-hearted, these groups often discuss topics that relate to virtual worlds, although VR rarely is the center of attention here.

alt.cyberspace

Check out this news group for lightweight discussion about the present and future of cyberspace.

Electronic Mailing Lists

Like the Internet, these mailing lists are free.

Glove-List

Run by Eric Townsend (`jet@well.sf.ca.us`), the glove-list carries conversation, tips, and news regarding use of the Mattel Power Glove as a computer input device. Subscribers post detailed reports of their trials and tribulations with the five-fingered marvel.

The glove-list operates on an automated `listserv`-type package, which means you subscribe by mailing a message to `listserv@boxer.nas.nasa.gov` with a body of

`subscribe glove-list `*`Your Full Name`*

When you receive a message from the mail server welcoming you to the glove-list, you can ask for an electronic copy of the FAQ by responding with the command

`get glove FAQ`

The glove-list also supports file transfer by e-mail. Eric Townsend does a great job of stocking current versions of Glove-related software and the list archives for distribution through the mail server. To receive a list of available files and programs, send e-mail to listserv@boxer.nas.nasa.gov with a body of

```
get glove README
```

Glove-list files and FTPable programs include

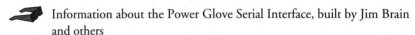 Information about the Power Glove Serial Interface, built by Jim Brain and others

A graph of the Power Glove's timing characteristics

Instructions, schematics, and code for building the Glove interface box designed by Ron Menelli (a Motorola 68HC11-based circuit that duplicates the original AGE box)

REND386, both the demo version and the developer's toolkit

Macintosh and Amiga programs and source code for the Power Glove

REND386 List

For the most up-to-date reports on REND386, new device drivers, new revisions, and so on, join this list by sending e-mail to majordomo@sunee.uwaterloo.ca with a body of

```
subscribe rend386-discuss address
```
or
```
subscribe rend386-announce address
```

where *address* is your e-mail address.

Advanced Gravis UltraSound List

The UltraSound Daily Digest is a mailing list for people who use this sound card. It provides information and banter about PC-based sound applications. To join the list, send e-mail to ultrasound-request@dsd.es.com with a body of

```
subscribe your_full_name
```

The automated server will tell you how to sign up for the mailing list and send along the location of FTP sites associated with the Digest (which receive software updates directly from Advanced Gravis).

Electronic Journal on Virtual Culture

You can subscribe by modem to this relatively new electronic newsletter. Issues are delivered directly to your electronic mailbox. To subscribe, send mail to listserv@kentvm.bitnet, with a body of

```
subscribe EJVC-L Your_Full_Name
```

VR-Savvy Commercial Services

Unlike the Internet and its associated mailing lists and USENET news groups, these online services charge a fee for entry. With a modem and telecommunications software, you can sign on to any service, but first place an old-fashioned telephone call to find out what charges to expect.

America OnLine

The VR discussion on America OnLine is sponsored by Virtus Corporation (makers of WalkThrough). It resides in the Virtus directory. To get there, select Keyword from the Go To menu and type the keyword VIRTUS. Look in the Let's Discuss folder. Alternatively, you can navigate there by way of Departments to Computing and Software to Industry Connection to Virtus Corporation. You need special software to access America OnLine. For America OnLine information, call (800) 227-6364.

BIX

Established and moderated by VR journalist and philosopher Dan Duncan (known as the "poet laureate of cyberspace"), the BIX VR conference can be reached by typing j virtual.world at the system prompt. It also offers academic papers by leading VR researchers and developers, including Bob Jacobson of WorlDesign, Brenda Laurel of Interval Research, William Bricken of the Human Interface Technology Lab, Randy Walser, and others. You can obtain details and rates through your modem. Have your computer dial (800) 695-4882.

CompuServe

The world's largest and oldest online service hosts a dynamic, resource-rich VR conference—Cyberforum, moderated by Jerry Isdale. In addition to ongoing discussions, CompuServe offers many VR demo programs and applications for downloading to your computer. The forum's overall theme is "future computing." Toward that end, it also includes postings and libraries devoted to artificial intelligence and artificial life, networks and computing interfaces, music, film/video, and art. At the system's main ! prompt, type GO CYBERF.

For information about CompuServe, call (800) 848-8199 or (800) 848-8990. (Outside the U.S., call +1-614-457-8650.)

The WELL (Whole Earth 'Lectronic Link)

An active and comprehensive VR conference, including topics on low-cost VR, makes the WELL a destination of choice for garage VR hobbyists (not surprising, considering that the WELL was established by the same mavericks who publish *Whole Earth Review* and the *Whole Earth Catalog*). The VR conference was initiated by *Virtual Reality* author Howard Rheingold and currently is moderated by VR programmer Peter Rothman. VR industrialites from Sense8, Autodesk, WorlDesign, RPI, and Spectrum

Dynamics participate on a regular basis. At the system's OK prompt, type go vr. To jump into the WELL, have your modem dial (415) 332-6106. To speak to a WELL-being, call (415) 332-4335.

Bulletin Board Systems

These BBSs usually charge a minimal entry fee. Factor in the price of the phone call if it's long distance.

> The Amulet
> Based in California
> (310) 453-7705

A collection of public virtual communities (VR conferences attended by people who are building worlds with REND386).

> Diaspar Virtual Reality Network
> Based in California
> (714) 376-1200 (2400 baud)
> (714) 376-1234 (9600 baud)
> Internet: diaspar.com or diaspar@nic.cerf.net

Founded in 1991, Diaspar's 500-600 members include computer and broadcast media professionals, students, educators, authors, artists, lawyers, and others interested in the VR field. Diaspar hosts and archives public online discussions and meetings on various topics; rents "Virtual Networks," online offices for geographically disparate co-workers; and offers a public-domain "Dmodem" protocol to transmit multimedia files. The BBS also publishes and sells online books (sci-fi titles) and intends to set up similar facilities for distributing poetry, music, and graphics images. Other works in progress include development and distribution of low-cost, low-tech stereoscopic viewers and images, and the creation of a library of graphics images and sound modules. The subscription fee is $10 per month. Students receive a discount.

> Toronto Virtual Reality Special Interest Group
> Based in Ontario, Canada
> (416) 631-6625

This active VR club presents meeting information and reports via its BBS.

> Virtual Space Driver
> Based in Maryland
> (301) 424-9133

This BBS features large DOS archives related to things VR.

In the MUD

More and more Internetters are learning about the joys (and addictive qualities) of MUDs (multiuser dungeons/dimensions). MUDs support real-time, textural communication over computer networks. These "dungeons" and "dimensions" are computer-based environments that some folks call "text-based virtual reality."

Truly a virtual community, a MUD comprises a shared database in which participants (called "players") create and engage in varied scenarios and situations, sometimes focused on games and puzzles, and usually whimsical in nature. A MUD is not a virtual world per se because it's text-based (although graphics-based MUDs are in development, and graphical environments characterize the well-established Japanese MUD, "Fujitsu Habitat," created by Lucasfilm in 1985). However, a MUD does present pseudo-spatial surroundings that many people can visit simultaneously, where they can interact and communicate with each other and with the MUD's contents. The environments are player-programmable and extensible: a player can add to and manipulate them. Unlike garage VR development, creating environments and objects (albeit textual) in a MUD is a simple task that demands only imagination and a command of the English language.

MUDs oozed into existence in about 1980 and gained prominence as computer-based recreation in the late 1980s. According to *The New Hacker's Dictionary*, edited by Eric Raymond (MIT Press, 1992), MUDs derive from an artificial intelligence experiment, disguised as a game, that was conducted at the University of Essex in England. Today, MUDs break down into "gaming MUDs" and "social MUDs." The Internet currently houses about 250 known MUDs, each interconnecting between 50 to 100 people at any one time.

MUD specialist Pavel Curtis, a computer scientist at the legendary Xerox Palo Alto Research Center, defines a MUD as "a software program that accepts 'connections' from multiple users across some kind of network (for example, telephone lines or the Internet) and provides to each user access to a shared database of 'rooms,' 'exits,' and other objects. Each user browses and manipulates this database from 'inside' one of those rooms, seeing only those objects that are in the same room and moving from room to room mostly via the exits that connect them…. A MUD user's interface to the database is entirely text-based; all commands are typed in by the users and all feedback is printed as unformatted text…." This is an excerpt from a Xerox PARC paper, "Mudding: Social Phenomena in Text-Based Virtual Reality," by Pavel Curtis, ©1992 Xerox Corp. The following is a typical MUD database interaction:

```
>look
```

```
Corridor
```

```
The corridor from the west continues to the east here, but the way is
blocked by a purple velvet rope stretched across the hall. There are
doorways leading to the north and south.
```

```
You see a sign hanging from the middle of the rope here.

>read sign

This point marks the end of the currently occupied portion of the
house. Guests proceed beyond this point at their own risk. --The
residents

>go east

You step disdainfully over the velvet rope and enter the dusty
darkness of the unused portion of the house.
```

This sounds like a computer adventure game, but "mudding" generally lacks the kind of goals associated with game play. When you participate in a MUD, you don't try to reach some prized end, attain a high score, or compete with opponents. Nonetheless, the experience is a social one; a MUD is visited by more than one person at a time (and sometimes by dozens at a time). They communicate with each other through text messages as they simultaneously browse and interact with the MUD's database and new objects created by players.

A premier U.S. MUD is the Internet-accessible "LambdaMOO," the brainchild of Pavel Curtis. He runs it from his lab at Xerox PARC. Established in October of 1990, LambdaMOO has been visited by more than 3,500 players from a dozen countries. "Based on the names of their network hosts," Pavel writes, "I believe that well over 90 percent of them are affiliated with colleges and universities, mostly as students and, to a lesser extent, mostly undergraduates."

The easiest way to connect to LambdaMOO is the standard *telnet* program (telnet is the name of the protocol that enables remote login to another computer). To access LambdaMOO from an Internet node or gateway, type the command `telnet lambda.parc.xerox.com 8888`.

Those who are interested in learning about developments of a 3D graphical MUD can send e-mail to `3dmud-request@pvv.unit.no` with the subject header

`JOIN yourfullname@yournetworkhost`

(For example, `JOIN FrancesNolan@tree.bklyn.com`.)

For a list of public MUDs that you can access from the Internet, check out the USENET newsgroup rec.games.mud.

See you in cyberspace....

PUTTING VR ON THE MAP

Jay Eric Townsend

PROFILE

6

JAY ERIC TOWNSEND:
"One of Us! One of Us!"

Northern California boasts beautiful vistas, but the view from Highway 101 in Santa Clara Valley isn't one of them. Barring traffic, 101 is still the quickest way to get from San Jose or San Francisco to the city of Mountain View. Here you can buy microchips as easily as you can find fast-food fries and chicken chow mein. Pure Silicon Valley, Mountain View is home to high-technology headquarters, endless strip malls, indistinguishable business parks, and suburban enclaves. Here too are Shoreline Park (a recreation area comprising more than 500 acres of reclaimed bay grounds) and Shoreline Amphitheater (the music playland established in 1986 by the late, great concert impresario Bill Graham). A few miles up the road, you'll find Moffett Field Naval Air Station and National Aeronautics and Space Administration's Ames Research Center, a NASA field laboratory with one of the world's largest wind tunnels. In 1985, Ames researchers launched the Virtual Interface Environment Workstation, the first computer system to combine computer graphics, video imaging, and speech synthesis with 3D audio, a wired glove, and a head-mounted display.

"I'm near-sighted. Pathetically near-sighted. I always wanted a computer screen that could strap to my face so I could work without glasses. I knew about heads-up displays, because my father was in the military; then *Neuromancer* came out in my junior year in high school. Reading that made it all click in my head. But I have no money. Therefore, 'Let's build it ourselves!'"

(Photo by Linda Jacobson)

Eric Townsend may portray himself as a myopic military brat/computer geek, but you wouldn't get that impression upon seeing his shoulder-length ponytail, BMW motor-cycle, ubiquitous skateboard, and the silver stud that pierces his cheek. Eric smiles readily and talks quickly, sprinkling his speech with bits of Cajun French. This transplanted Southerner delights in obscure science fiction, Indian food, parallel computing, cars, and running an electronic mailing list for Power Glove hackers.

Eric was born August 25, 1967 in Fort Benning, Georgia. The Townsend family lived in a series of small towns throughout the South and the Midwest, never far from an Army base. "My mother's a Louisiana dirt farmer going back several generations," Eric says, "and my father grew up in the city but always wanted to be a cowboy. Between the two of them, we always managed to live about 100 miles from civilization."

As precocious as the next future computer scientist, Eric was enrolled at age 10 in a special class at his small kindergarten through 12th grade school. "I was in a program-ming class with high school students. I programmed for three or four years on the school's computers—a bunch of Radio Shack Model 1, Level Twos—before I ever saw a computer game."

Eric attended high school in Leesville, Louisiana. Outside of class, he practiced trumpet for hours a day, listened to jazz, worked at a country-western radio station (KVVP-FM, Country 105), and bought his first car, a 1967 Karman Ghia convertible. By then, he also had bought a Commodore 64. When he was 16, Eric started working for the owner of the local computer store. "He and I both liked to play Dungeons and Dragons, and one day we realized, 'Hey, there are 10,000 GIs next door who like to play D&D, and they drive three hours to the city to a store that sells one or two war games. Geez, we could sell games *here*.'" So they did.

In college, Eric says, he participated in "the infinite degree plan; it took me six years to graduate. I graduated in 1990 or 1991. I changed majors about a half-dozen times. During that time, I was in the National Guard for a while before I got medicaled out. In between semesters, I waited tables, did odd jobs, and worked for a couple of small computer companies. That's when I bought my first UNIX box."

While attending the University of Houston, Eric first experienced computer-mediated communications. "This was in late '85 on a system called RoundTable that ran off a bunch of Radio Shack Model IIIs hardwired together. It was the first multiline chat system that went online that we knew of. I used it to talk to a blind woman and a couple of deaf people who used the systems, which is when I first thought it would be cool to have some strap-on computer monitors with video-enhancing hardware."

After graduating with a journalism degree, Eric worked for the university as a computer systems administrator and as a technical editor. A year later, he moved northwest to join NASA Ames Research Center as a computer systems administrator. When not at Ames, Eric spends a lot of time traveling in cyberspace via the Internet from his home base in Mountain View ("suburban hell," he calls it, taking pride in the fact that the roar of his roommate's Harley annoys the neighbors).

Many VR enthusiasts who hang out in cyberspace know Eric as the originator and administrator of the glove-list, the electronic mailing list that focuses on how people use the Mattel Power Glove as a computer input device. The list seed was sown one summer day in 1991. Eric had been strolling through a shopping mall when he noticed a Nintendo display where someone was playing with the Power Glove. He watched with fascination, deemed the Glove too cool to pass up, and bought one to use with his brother's Nintendo. His brother soon sold the game system. Left with a potentially useless Glove, Eric eyed his Commodore Amiga, then attacked the Glove's circuitry. He decided to connect the Glove to Amiga, then try using the Glove as a 3D input device to move graphical objects around in 3-space on-screen. He experimented with that for a while, with "limited success," he says, considering the "painful slowness" of the Amiga 3000.

A few weeks later, Eric amended his Internet signature file with this message: "If you're interested in Power Gloves and Amigas, drop me a line." Impressed by the flood of enthusiastic responses, he thought, "It's time to start a glove-list." Asked today why he took on this task, he shrugs, "It's not that I had a professional interest in it. I'm doing it for the same reason I once built a couple of engines for Volkswagens: just because it's fun."

Eric started the glove-list in June of 1991 by describing his own attempts to attach the Power Glove to his Amiga. People ate it up, even if they didn't own Amigas. ("The Amiga side of the glove-list fell away instantly because almost everybody has PCs. There are a few Mac people. I'm not really tied to the Amiga anyway, except that I own one and I put a lot of money into buying compilers and software for it.") The glove-list's first few postings, Eric recalls, consisted of such statements as, "'Hi, my name's Bob. I bought a Power Glove. How do I make it work with my PC?' or 'Hi, my name's Bob. I did this to my Power Glove....' I say 'Bob' because invariably everyone was male for the first two years. It's still a rare enough occurrence that I notice when a female name goes by."

Back then, guys were dismantling the Power Glove before they knew its secrets. At that time, no one other than the Glove's developers knew that it could function as anything more than a joystick emulator. Some Glove hackers had read the July 1990 article in the computer magazine *Byte* that described how to attach the Glove to a PC, but that was the extent of their exposure to inside information. "In the early archives of the glove-list," Eric says, "you can read the conversations we had about the possibility that the Glove data was encrypted, and our discussions about the few Glove interface boxes that were sold by AGE [Abrams Gentile Entertainment, the New York company that licensed the glove technology from VPL Research, then licensed it to Mattel]. Then, people learned about hi-res mode but there didn't seem to be a way to get to it. Nintendo wouldn't tell anybody anything about it. Once I called Nintendo, and they could only tell me how to play games. For the longest time, no one would talk."

Eventually, people started talking, primarily on the computer networks. Even the researchers involved in the Glove's design began sharing technical tips, especially after Mattel discontinued production of the Power Glove.

The glove-list continues to provide a forum for folks reporting their Glove hacktivities. At last count, the glove-list was being distributed to 250 subscribers (not counting unknown recipients on redistribution lists, who get what the publishing industry calls "pass-around copies"). Glove-list services now include Eric's archives of glove-list postings, documents covering the Power Glove Serial Interface, a graph of Power Glove timing characteristics, instructions and code for building your own interface box, a copy of REND386, a couple dozen demo programs, source-code files submitted by glove-list subscribers, and a handy new FAQ (frequently asked questions) file.

Most of the free demo software and source code, Eric explains, is created by people who find a new or better way to physically hook Glove to computer and then write software that offers new features. For example, there is the Amiga hi-res code, which moves a small cursor on the screen, based on Glove input. To do anything else with it, however, you need to pulverize and rebuild the code. This problem has been solved by a program called GloveTask, now being distributed. (It doesn't work on all Amigas, of course.) Using the Amiga paradigm of a "port," one can use GloveTask to write code for the Power Glove without knowing much about the Glove's inner workings, Eric says. GloveTask collects information from the Glove, interprets it, and writes it to a named port to which any other program can listen.

Eric recently automated the glove-list to support file requests by e-mail. If someone writes a program (such as Dr. StrangeGlove, the Mac-based Glove controller) and uploads it to an Internet site, Eric copies it onto his machine and transfers it to the glove-list server. That way, people who can't access the Internet but who can send and receive e-mail can obtain such treats as Dr. StrangeGlove. You simply send e-mail to the glove-list and request the desired filename; the glove-list automatically sends that file to your mailbox.

Because Eric owns an Amiga A3000, his most recent enterprise involves writing A3000 code to let the machine work directly with the Power Glove. This necessity of custom coding results from the incompatibility among different Amiga models. "There's a hi-res mode, which is great if you have an Amiga 500 or a 2000," Eric explains, "but the timing's all wrong for a 3000. When you crank up the Glove on the 3000, its sensors are being polled too quickly, and you're hitting it so fast that the Glove takes off to la-la land and locks up." But progress on his new code, he says, is slow. Timing problems are an obstacle, and "it appears that the proto-code everyone uses was written on a machine that was slow enough that the timing issues didn't crop up as much. Actually, I'm considering blowing off the direct Glove/A3000 code. I'll build an interface box instead; I've already ordered the parts. The box has a serial port on one side, a Glove port on the other, and will work with any computer that has a serial port. The A3000 microsecond timing is a pain, and my code would only work on other A3000 machines. I'd have to port *again* for A1400 and A4000 machines!"

Acknowledging the need to deal with incompatible Amiga and Glove setups, Eric also accepts the fact that the Amiga lacks interactive world-building software similar to REND386. Anyway, he'd rather code than switch to PC or adapt REND386 for the Amiga. "There's probably some important assembly deep down inside REND386 that makes it reasonably fast, but the Amiga similarly has really nice hardware that makes it do all sorts of fancy graphics, so you ask yourself, 'Hmm, do I just want to port straight C code [from PC to Amiga] and get slow, clunky graphics on the Amiga, or do I want to do it right?' I'm used to coding everything myself. If I need a renderer, I'm the sort of person who says, 'Well, hell, I'll just take a couple of days to crank out a baby renderer that can throw polygons onto the screen.'"

Eric's next project is experimenting with the Glove and electronic music. "I'm interested in virtual instruments," he says. "I read an article by Jaron Lanier [the VPL Research co-founder who has performed music in virtual worlds], and it occurred to me that maybe I could use the Power Glove to control sound in 3-space. Some people are getting into making sounds move around on stereo speakers as if they're in 3-space, and they're doing it from a homebrew, low-tech, non-mathematical, non-physics perspective, just like the garage VR people. Maybe we can combine what both groups are doing.

"The fact is, if you have money and you want to do immersive VR applications, you go talk to a company like VPL," Eric continues. "If you don't have money, and you just want to play around, the Power Glove's a great way to go. But the Glove is *not* great in terms of technology. It's just cheap, and it's there. Playing with the Glove is like hacking Volkswagens or like owning an old Harley. But you're not going to scratch-build a Glove easily. You can't really build a Harley or a Volkswagen Beetle from scratch; you buy two or three crapped-out ones and you put them together."

Eric ponders his statement. "Apparently, the conductive ink used on the Power Glove fingers is commercially available, although you have to buy 1,000 liters of it or some ridiculous amount. So there's no reason you couldn't make your own Glove. But you probably wouldn't want to. What hopefully will happen is the standardization of interface devices. So, when there are no more Power Gloves around, fine. Make something better. Gloves like that, in terms of commercial use, are dead. When I first played with my Power Glove, I got blisters on the back of my fingers because of the amount of force from the cloth inside. The VPL DataGlove we use at Ames is nicer, but you still want to be able to type and do other things with your hand. Using a glove is like taping a mouse to your hand."

And who wants a mouse taped to their hand? Certainly not our motor-minded pioneer, who compares his aversion for motorcycle helmets and bulky pants to a computer scientist's yen for easy access to data: "I'm annoyed by having to change clothes when I go to and from work. I like being safe, however, so I wear my safety clothes. I am *not* going to take the Glove on and off all day long, nor am I going to put on a special data bracelet or something like that. I want something that's very subtle and not intrusive.

How about micrometer radar, mounted on the desk, that does real-time synthesis of my hand positions? Or cheap trackers that can be embedded in any type of clothing? Or, the interface I'm *really* waiting for is the Lee Press-On Virtual Tracking System!"

Switching back to serious mode, Eric says that the point-sensing technology used in pen-based computers might find an application as an interface to virtual worlds, because such technology is highly accurate and not prohibitively expensive. He also admits that he is intrigued by the Sega VR helmet and the Sega Activator (a large octagonal ring, placed on the floor, that tracks your body movements and translates them to control the on-screen action in Genesis games) and their implications for garage VR.

"We're in the model-one, level-two stage of VR," Eric states, "where people who have far too much time spend it developing tools without having an actual need to use the tools. At the store where I worked, we tried to use a Commodore 64 to keep inventory on 10,000 items. We spent more time recovering from crashes and hacking stuff to make it work than if we'd done inventory by hand on paper. Things with the Power Glove, and the current rash of 3D shutter glasses, are still in that similar proof-of-concept or 'Gee-I'm-bored' stage."

Irked by "people who spend too much time talking about the future," Eric offers his perspective that "at this stage of VR's development, there are too many people who sit around and say, 'Wouldn't it be cool *if.* Won't it be neat *when.*' And none of those people are asking, 'How do we get there?' It's discouraging, because it's the pretty pictures and flashy, futuristic, rigged demos that get all the attention. Whereas the people who are out there hammering out code, making things work, putting it on the shelf, putting it out for FTP for people to use—they get published in *Obscure Journal of Computer Science* from Obscure University.

"I just want computers and computing equipment and information retrieval technology to be transparent," Eric says. "I just want to make tools that make computers easier to use."

Tour Guide's Toolbox

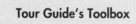

Amiga 3000, 25MHz, 6 megs of RAM

Color 13-inch monitor

50MB hard drive

C compiler (used mostly for utilities and Power Glove development)

IBM PC floppy-disk reader for the Amiga

Power Glove (connected via interface to Amiga's parallel port, "my preferred method of getting to the Glove's hi-res mode")

Joystick and mouse

Stereo speakers

High-speed Telebit Worldblazer modem ("the keen rock-and-roll, kick-butt modem")

Music to code by: "Lately it's been Conlan Nincarrow, German music, traditional Irish music. A lot of old thrash, hardcore, street-core. David Bowie. Art of Noise, Kraftwerk—all the traditional computer geek bands."

Approximate street value: $1,500

E-mail: jet@well.sf.ca.us

Subject: FAQ for Power Glove mailing list

From: J. Eric Townsend (jet@well.sf.ca.us)

INTRODUCTION

The glove-list was established in August 1991 as an informational exchange to help Power Glove hackers.

Its success is due to the hard work and willingness to exchange not only results, but source code, specific information, and general ideas.

Please help this spirit by volunteering information that you discover and code that you write. Testimonials based on work you've done with a Glove would be wonderful.

The glove-list itself runs on an SGi Indigo (old R3000 model) using an automated `listserv` package.

SUBSCRIBING

To subscribe to the list, send e-mail to listserv@boxer.nas.nasa.gov with a body of

```
subscribe glove-list your_full_name
```

Please note:

You are subscribed with the address that you sent the e-mail from.

You can't subscribe an address other than your own. This is considered a security feature, but I haven't gotten around to taking it out.

Your subscription will be handled by software, so any other text you send will be ignored.

If `listserv@boxer.nas.nasa.gov` doesn't respond to your request for subscription, send e-mail to `jet@well.sf.ca.us`.

OPTIONS

If you want to receive the glove-list in digest form, send a message to `listserv@boxer.nas.nasa.gov` with a body of

```
set glove-list mail digest
```

OBTAINING ARCHIVES

There is an e-mail-based archive system with the `listserv`. To obtain the list of current files and a readme, send e-mail to `listserv@boxer.nas.nasa.gov` with a body of

```
get glove README
```

Places to Go

CHAPTER
10

Places to Go

"What we call the beginning is often the end
And to make an end is to make a beginning.
The end is where we start from."
—T.S. Eliot, "Gerontion"

Your garage VR system *works*. With it, you have created a virtual world and its objects from a collection of 3D models. You rendered those objects into images, calculated how they appear from various points of view, and accounted for virtual light sources and the positions of the objects relative to each other. You programmed some of those objects to respond to input data from interface devices. Perhaps you even integrated snippets of audio to enhance the world with sound effects and music.

Nevertheless, the virtual world is primitive. It consists of simple geometric shapes. These images, especially when presented stereoscopically, update only a few times each second. Each time you provide input, there is a brief interlude before the computer provides the corresponding output. The resulting simulation comes nowhere near the caliber of simulations developed by high-end virtual world-builders.

In the garage VR domain, then, the term "virtual reality" does a disservice. If we define reality as the state or quality of being "real," the simulations presented on personal computers can't touch "reality," virtually or otherwise.

Simulating reality is the goal of photorealism. Photorealism in computer graphics is the product of extremely high resolution and millions of colors. Obviously, VR systems based on personal computers can't portray photorealistic images. So let's view garage VR systems with the understanding that we cannot use them to simulate reality, and we *can* call upon our imaginations to supply what our computers can't.

With that in mind, we approach these low-cost systems with the intention of developing interactive simulations and multidimensional visualizations with which we can interact in real time. Within that framework, even the most humble tools provide the means to reach assorted ends.

Things to Do, Places to Go

If you're not ready to tackle the numerous tasks of building custom worlds, a couple of ready-to-wear commercial products will help launch your exploration of virtual space.

PC owners who enjoy chess probably will appreciate Joe Gradecki's game Mate, sold for $30 by VRontier Worlds (Stoughton, Wisconsin). This REND386-based game is played over modem by two opponents; each player must own a copy of the game (or one person can play solo against the computer). Players use the mouse to select, move pieces, and "fly" over the chessboard to view it from any perspective. Mate also supports stereoscopic viewing through shutter glasses.

VR Slingshot is a rudimentary garage VR game for the Commodore Amiga. Priced at $129 and sold by Ixion, Inc. (Seattle, Washington), this flight-simulation game pits two players against each other in one virtual world. Each player uses a different Amiga, and the two computers connect with a modem or a direct link, using modem cable. Players pilot their crafts and try to deplete each other's energy reserves. In solo mode, you play against a computer-generated opponent. Like Mate, VR Slingshot works in

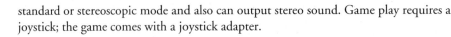

standard or stereoscopic mode and also can output stereo sound. Game play requires a joystick; the game comes with a joystick adapter.

Over the coming months and years, we'll enjoy a wider selection of inexpensive commercial applications for the IBM PC, Apple Macintosh, and Commodore Amiga. Meanwhile, more and more garage VR enthusiasts are designing REND386 worlds and other types of self-running applications and uploading the files into the public domain. You'll be able to obtain these files if you regularly review and selectively download the contents of VR-related FTP sites and online services.

To experience the real challenges and the satisfaction of garage VR, do it yourself. Forewarned is forearmed: you'll experience some frustration with buggy software or crotchety interfaces. You might need to spend a few hours hunting for a misplaced comma in some code or chasing down a loose solder connection. Despite such irksome conditions, you won't be an active consumer of someone else's creativity.

The following paragraphs offer a glimpse of the galaxy of worlds that one can explore in garage VR. I hope the suggestions provided here will inspire you to dream up many more rewarding destinations.

The First Territory to Explore: Your Imagination

Outer space, underwater, rain forest, ancient Greece, or bustling metropolis: what sort of environment tweaks your cerebral cortex? You can build it and explore it with the tools and techniques of garage VR. Experience the spaces you envision in your mental laboratory. Dig into three-dimensional simulations of archaeological sites; visualize relationships and architectural features of structures that no longer (or never did) exist in reality. Transcend real-world physical limitations and soar beyond self-imposed boundaries. Get in touch with the mystery and beauty of your inner nature. Get some of those creative ya-yas out.

Some day, "average" American families will routinely turn to their home entertainment systems to recreate and walk through simulated monuments from overseas, from the past, and from the future. You can do it now.

Develop Applications

The VR industry continues to develop and market virtual-world technologies and tools, but that industry is small. To experience exponential growth, it needs applications to show potential clients and customers what is possible. As *PCVR*'s Joe Gradecki stresses repeatedly, "If you want to get rich in this business, create applications!"

What kinds of applications can we reasonably expect to emerge from the crude garage VR technology? Enterprising entrepreneurs will spin out a multitude of possibilities, a few of which might include those listed in the following sections.

Clip Worlds and Clip Objects for Distribution and Sale

Sometimes, people on the Internet post requests for specific 3D models to use in professional simulations. Investing all their energies in designing simulations, they lack the time to model. If you have an interest in a particular topic, such as animal behavior, cycling, spelunking, music, or kids, consider scanning some of your collected photos and illustrations (scanners are available for rent at computer service bureaus). Use those digitized images as a foundation on which to build custom libraries of texture maps. Use your expertise to model topical 3D objects and build related virtual environments. Save them in a common file format, such as .DXF or .PLG. Upload them to the nets. Send notices about your custom clip catalog to the editors of VR industry newsletters, who have a vested interest in keeping their readers informed of such resources.

"Product Hacking" Services, Information Design, and VR Engineering

Can you visualize complex structures and express abstract ideas? You might offer those talents to coworkers and friends who have ideas for inventions or products but who lack the funds or time to reduce their theories to practice. By integrating the appropriate geometry database with some clever scripting and animation, you can develop a computer simulation of the product or invention and present a "test" of it in the virtual environment it would enhance. By doing so, you can help your associates vividly demonstrate "proof of concept" to secure funding or other support.

Theatrical and Film Set Design

At the University of Kansas in Lawrence, Mark Reaney uses Virtus WalkThrough on his Macintosh-based VR system to design theater sets. As Mark wrote in the Summer 1993 issue of the trade publication *Theater Design and Technology:*

> "You look upon a set that was conceived minutes before. It seems that the stage-left wall needs to be a foot taller and [you] stretch the scenery to the desired height.... You notice that the color of the cyclorama doesn't look the way you imagined, so the paint begins to change from one color to the next until you see one that suits your fancy.... A wave of the hand starts you floating up into the fly loft so you can see how your set will appear in a ground plan.... Exploring a stage set in virtual reality, discovering its spaces one after another as an actor would, going up and down stairs, using its doors, looking through its scrims, is more akin to an actual theatrical experience than viewing a sketch or scale model...."

Community theater groups and university film and television departments might benefit from a similar application of your VR system.

Educational Simulations

In 1991, computer scientists at the University of North Carolina at Chapel Hill used a Macintosh IIci, VPL Research head-mounted display, magnetic position-tracking system, 6DOF mouse, and custom PixelPlanes software to build a virtual world that contained giant protein molecules. The participant could fly inside and among the molecules, seeing them from the perspective of an atom. Also present in the virtual world was *methotrexate,* a drug molecule used in cancer treatment. The participant could fly in and see how the methotrexate acts on the protein molecules.

Learning chemistry is much easier when you can get your hands on a three-dimensional model of a molecule. Teachers relish educational aids that extend students' senses beyond the two dimensions of books, blackboards, filmstrips, and even multimedia computer programs.

If you're an expert in one of the physical or natural sciences, you could play an important supporting role in the theater of education by presenting virtual worlds that spark the intellect.

You could contact the science and math teachers at your local schools and tell them you have something great for show-and-tell. Create a solid-geometry tutorial for math students. Demonstrate the flow of electrical current to budding Faradays. Future medical doctors would gain plenty from an interactive simulation that helps them learn about the blood circulation system: what happens to it when, with the flick of a Power-Gloved finger, you introduce infectious agents and antibiotic drugs? Build a world in which the laws of physics apply. Develop a simple environment that shows how industrial gases trap heat in the atmosphere and trigger the greenhouse effect. Design a world that simulates Isaac Newton's experiments with light.

Any field in which scientific and mathematical laws and theories come into play will benefit from educational simulations. In fact, one VR application developed by a company called Incredible Technologies (of Arlington Heights, Illinois) simulated a billiard game. The simulation showed a cue ball's response to different pool shots. It was demonstrated at "Tomorrow's Realities," a VR exhibition at the 1991 ACM/ SIGGRAPH convention. In the exhibit notes, project manager David Theil wrote, "Since the ball's relative size and mass are easily assumed, all the computer needs to learn is the ball's point of origin, direction, and velocity. This is the function of a gestural interface."

Games and Sports

Dozens of small entrepreneurial concerns yearn to be the next W Industries (makers of the Virtuality immersive game system) or Virtual Worlds Entertainment Center (creators of the simulation VR games BattleTech and Red Planet). Only a few will succeed. Let's hope that those who *do* succeed will have seen beyond the computer- and video-game paradigms of presenting virtual violence and simulated speed as forms of entertainment. Does the world really need more racing car games and air-combat simulations?

Rewards will go to application developers who can bypass the current unimaginative rock 'em, sock 'em, nuke 'em approach to VR gaming and introduce applications characterized by magic, whimsy, and heartfelt adventure. Perhaps you'll be the one to employ the dual-Power Glove interface for a juggling game or to develop sleight-of-Glove magic tricks. Maybe you'll whip up a simple virtual dart game or stage a cyber-contest for the kids on your block to see who can jump onto a virtual floating carousel (and then snatch the virtual brass ring).

New Art Tools and Artworks

The transfer of images into digital form (changing art materials into the equivalent of mathematical formulae) places the fundamental, physical qualities of imagery—shape, color, and lighting—under an artist's precise, predictable control. The inherent excitement arises from the *lack* of predictability about how artists will apply these new materials.

In the realm of garage VR (during the past couple of years), artists have been using Power Gloves to control computer paint and image-processing programs, thereby creating new, kinetic kinds of visual art.

Artists who love music have been using Power Gloves and MIDI software to create and perform unique musical compositions, routing the output of their computer systems to MIDI musical instruments.

Will artists create worlds in which the participant can pound on a virtual piano and let loose a stream of virtual pelicans? Worlds in which the participant can scale murals, adding to the imagery with a flick of the wrist? With a wave of a Power-Gloved hand, might someone conduct a virtual orchestra? With a twist of a forceball, might someone else let loose a virtual spray of luminescent color rays? Will the artist's palette of tomorrow sport virtually silly putty or porky pigments?

Few artistic genres are as wide open for imaginative interpretation and expression as the *cyberarts*.

Introduce Your Colleagues to Virtual Worlds

Professional VR developers are proving that virtual-worlds technologies can and will benefit just about every field of endeavor—sales, manufacturing, engineering, training, service, and support—in just about every industry. Perhaps you labor in an industry or area in which few professionals have experienced the benefits of interactive simulations. Consider developing a virtual world that applies to your field of work. You might be the first on your career block to show your colleagues how VR tools and techniques can contribute to the success of their endeavors.

Places to Go

Share Your Virtual Worlds with Your Community

How many of your friends, relatives, and neighbors know what a computer-generated virtual world really is? Perhaps they have viewed (and been misled by) all the cyber-trendy movies and TV "news" shows, or read some of the dozens of feature articles that claim to report on the status of virtual reality. It behooves all of us who are involved in the VR field to spread the word about the true capabilities of the technology. We can help eliminate false expectations and skepticism, and in doing so, hopefully promote the benefits of this medium.

Plan for the Future

Do you plan to move? Remodel your home? Rearrange the furniture in your room or office? An architectural walk-through provides a great tool for planning ahead, and you don't need to produce stereoscopic images or incorporate 6DOF input devices to wield that tool. Build three-dimensional graphic models of your house or room with furniture and appliances. Put them together in a virtual world. Move it around to your satisfaction. Choose a cabinet surface or a floor texture. Apply different paint colors and wall coverings.

If you're working with Sense8's WorldToolKit for Windows, you can link your 3D model to an Excel spreadsheet and change the height or width of a wall or other object from within Excel and immediately see the corresponding changes in your 3D model.

Prepare for a Career

The VR industry is growing. As new companies take off and existing companies expand, they need more and more people who can build worlds, write device drivers, sell products and/or services, produce documentation, teach others how to use the system, and provide technical maintenance and support. Professionals in the VR field especially appreciate the dedication and foresight characteristic of the self-taught. You can supplement your formal education by working on your own, building, programming, and exploring virtual worlds and garage VR interfaces. (VR companies favor college graduates with degrees in computer science, programming, graphics, communications, and/or electronics and electrical engineering, but they're flexible!)

Then, show off your work at VR workshops and industry conferences. Give 'em the old razzle-dazzle. Describe your accomplishments in letters to the editors of VR newsletters and journals. Submit papers to VR conferences. Volunteer to lead VR world-building workshops at computer trade shows or science fairs.

Extend Human Expression and Communication

This is *really* what the grassroots movement of garage VR is all about: the use of low-cost, versatile computer tools and techniques to join forces with friends—and to make new friends—during the process of collaborating on hardware and software projects. Thanks to the availability of affordable technologies and the ease of modem-based networking, we can teach each other well.

PUTTING VR ON THE MAP

Mark Thomas Pflaging

PROFILE 7

MARK THOMAS PFLAGING:
"The Future of VR Knows No Bounds"

Resting on the Virginia side of the Potomac River is Alexandria, where federal government workers go home to sleep. This affluent urban outpost sits beside I-95 near Washington National Airport. Rush-hour traffic is miserable. Things move smoothly, Old South-style, in "Old Town" Alexandria, which is steeped in almost three centuries of American history and flavored by its Scottish heritage. Robert E. Lee grew up here; George Washington hung out in the Stabler-Leadbeater Apothecary Shop (still open) just a few miles from the White House and within spittin' distance of the Pentagon.

"Virtual reality will invade the world in much the same way as the digital computer. VR is not just a piece of hardware, it's a medium. It's hard for me to imagine an aspect of life that would *not* eventually be related to VR. One day you will think back upon life before VR and wonder how we ever managed without it."

Some garage VR hobbyists wonder how they managed without Mark Pflaging. The vice president of the Virtual Reality Alliance of Students & Professionals (VRASP), Mark is tall, thin, and bespectacled. For a quiet guy, he talks on the phone a lot. He is passionate about music (and, he jokes, about passion) and is as comfortable on skis as he is swimming in the net. When not attending school or working as a researcher, Mark hacks his home VR system. He often pours the results into the Internet for people to siphon into their reality engines. When members of that net-borne community of garage VR talk about their work with the Power Glove, they frequently refer to Mark's accomplishments. Doug Faxon calls him "the god of the Glove."

Mark grew up in Reisterstown, Maryland, a suburb about 10 miles northwest of Baltimore, where he was born on May 9, 1968. As a kid he did regular kid things, except that he studied "too much."

In the summer of 1980, before starting junior high, Mark enrolled in a basic programming course at Loyola College. "I was hooked. I had to have a computer. I got a loan and bought a [Radio Shack] TRS-80 Model 3 for about $1,000. The loan was in my parents' name; it took me years to pay the money back. During junior high, I typed in a lot of programs and wrote some original code. Added more RAM and a floppy disk drive myself. And, of course, I played a lot of games. Believe it or not, there were some really great games for those 'Trash-80s.'"

While at Franklin High School, Mark balanced out his byteworm image by playing in the marching band and competing on the cross-country team. After school, he unloaded boxes of organic produce at his father's health food store or loafed with cronies in the typical suburban hang-out scene. Mark reels off his main adolescent memories: "I listened to the AOR station. I had braces. I never went to any formal dances like the junior or senior prom. I said 'dude' a lot. I got into some trouble now and again. I was really into computers and spent a lot of time programming."

No one was surprised when Mark decided to major in computer engineering at Case Western Reserve University in Cleveland. He graduated with a BS in 1991. Mark did the Greek thing during his college years—joining Phi Kappa Psi—and muses that he was "more of an observer than a participant in a lot of things." He was on scholarship, but he also tutored students at the English department's computer lab, flipped burgers as a short-order cook at the campus bar, and eventually enrolled in a cooperative education program through which he found a job programming "a real-time system to weigh vehicles in motion."

After Mark graduated, he lived for a short time in Romney, West Virginia. Then, U.S. Army Research hired him as a Consortium Research Fellow. Mark decided to continue his formal education at the same time and was accepted to George Washington University in Washington, D.C. In the summer of 1993, he moved from West Virginia to Alexandria, Virginia, closer to work and school. Mark's research relates to the study of psychology, using immersive VR technology. As a full-time student, he takes classes in computer animation and programming.

Mark first learned of virtual reality from a 1990 issue of *Rolling Stone,* which ran a glowing article that covered VPL Research's accomplishments. "I was fascinated, but no one I knew had heard about it, so after a few days the original enchantment wore off," Mark says. "It was not until April of 1992 that a friend invited me to the Springfield [Virginia] mall to play [the Virtuality game] Dactyl Nightmare. Although we both had complaints about the quality of the immersion, we thought it was much better than a traditional video game. Then the same friend gave me a birthday present: a Mattel Power Glove and a disk with PC source code. Although I was thrilled by the Glove, I was disappointed with the software and set out to write my own."

The resulting code is "Object Glove," a set of library functions that C++ programmers can use to interface the Power Glove. Mark sells Object Glove through VRASP and offers a free demo through various Internet sites (see the section titled "Object Glove by Mark Pflaging and VRASP" in Chapter 7). He also has placed his Dual-Glove PC Interface circuit in the public domain. He now leads VRASP Power Glove workshops, where he teaches people how to interface Glove to PC and demonstrates how he transformed a Power Glove into *left*-handed garb.

These days, Mark is building REND386 worlds and exploring uses of object-oriented programming in VR applications. He's tantalized by "the prospect of being part of an 'imaginary' world and being able to escape the 'pressures' of real reality by means of a computer program. Part of this idea is clearly impossible: I already have experienced the discomfort of wanting to get 'out' of virtual reality once I'm in. So VR will probably never be a truly effective means of escaping reality, but regardless, that is the part of VR that I hold dear. I am looking forward to the day when I can travel 'through time' to models of past civilizations."

Of the virtual environments he's designed, Mark's favorite is his Solar System world. "I had originally intended to make a model of the deck of the Starship Enterprise. You know, *Star Trek?*" smiles Mark. "Then I got into the details of creating 3D models and decided to modify my original idea. I had been making a bunch of spheres in an effort to generate the dome over the new Enterprise. I thought if I made the background black and resized the spheres, they could pass for planets! I made the model as realistic as I could, given the constraints, and it turned out very well. There's a lengthy description of Solar System world in the Object Glove archive on the Internet."

These days, Mark fields many inquiries from prospective VR experimenters. His advice to them is, "Everyone expects different things from a VR experience. Sometimes people get so confused by all the potential applications of VR that they forget why they originally liked it. If you can hold on to a unique idea without becoming bewildered, you can make a contribution to the field of VR."

GVR

Tour Guide's Toolbox

Engine: 486/33MHz PC clone, 8MB RAM, 300MB hard drive, Pro Audio Spectrum 16 sound card, CD-ROM drive

Monitor: 20-inch TV with VGA-to-NTSC signal converter (Cardinal Snapplus video card; "Yes, there is a lot of flicker, but I'm used to it.")

Modem: U.S. Robotics Sportster 2400

Primary hardware and software: Two Power Gloves, keyboard with built-in trackball, Advanced Gravis joystick, Toshiba shutter glasses, DOS, Windows, REND386, Borland C++, Virtus WalkThrough for Windows, and "demos of everything in the world"

Total cost: $2,500 to $3,000

Music to code by: Anything techno, industrial, or modern

E-mail: `70233.1552@compuserve.com` and `mtp2@well.sf.ca.us`

VRASP: Let Us "Edutain" You

The Virtual Reality Alliance of Students & Professionals (VRASP) is a national nonprofit organization dedicated to "increasing public knowledge of virtual reality and further the development of VR technology." According to its statement of purpose, "VRASP is acting as a resource bank and a referral network for those seeking information in the VR community. There is a clear need for veracious information to be presented to VR followers and, most particularly, the public. We can be the source people to turn to in order to learn more about VR or be given a book title, academic contact, research laboratory name, and so on, so people can follow up on their own interest. Additionally, we promote our own educationally oriented events as well as those organized by others."

In September of 1992, Mark Pflaging attended a VR industry conference, where he met "a bunch of folks face to face that I had been communicating with electronically. I had originally 'met' most of them through computer art forums on CompuServe. Among them was Karin August, the president of VRASP. I told her I wanted to write for [the VRASP publication] *Pix* and help out any way that I could. Today I am vice president of VRASP, and there is much more to VRASP than just the magazine."

That magazine, *Pix-Elation*, debuted in May of 1992 as a photocopied newsletter notable for lively writing and commentaries on how VR industry leaders look and dress. Now a professionally printed bimonthly 'zine with full-color covers, *Pix* is distributed to select bookstores across the United States. Its articles include transcriptions of discussions and photos from events in the scientific community, interviews with leading researchers and proponents of VR, as well as editorial columns, VR news, feature articles, and a calendar of upcoming VRASP and VR events.

VRASPians live all across the United States. Active members assemble several times a year to staff the VRASP booth at VR industry conventions. They sell issues of *Pix* and various VR-related books, distribute information on VR, and promote and sell VRASP membership. They also exhibit the custom garage VR systems developed by VRASP members (such as Mark's Object Glove applications), including the Literary Gallery, a Power Glove-controlled multimedia application that presents fundamental VR concepts through video clips and sound.

The organization's president, Karin August, lives in the suburbs of New Jersey's Middlesex County. After graduating from college in 1985 with an unlikely double BA in geology and medieval-Renaissance studies, she lived in London for a while, then she returned to the States. She cofounded VRASP primarily to learn more about virtual reality:

"After reading [Howard] Rheingold's book *Virtual Reality* and doing my own research, there was an awful lot that I wanted to know, and there was no way I was going to find it at the local library," Karin recalls. "I could sit and look at the TV set for a decade and not get the information I wanted. I thought I would find out if there are other people like me, but who knew more about the technology. There is power in numbers, and if all of us start actively investigating and researching, we're bound to start digging up stuff."

Karin printed a flyer that asked, "Are you interested in virtual reality?" and posted it around Princeton, New Brunswick, and Highland Park, New Jersey. Enough people responded to encourage her to organize the first VRASP event in March of 1992: a field trip to New York City's Limelight Club, site of a party celebrating the release of the film *Lawnmower Man*. Thereafter, VRASP meetings took place regularly at alternating New Jersey and Manhattan locales: pizza parlors, cafes, university computer centers, even at people's houses. "In the early days we showed videos and came up with the idea of doing a newsletter," Karin says. *Pix-Elation* debuted in May. It featured a report of VRASP's first "big event," a group visit to a presentation on VR at the David Sarnoff Research Center in Princeton, New Jersey.

Today, VRASP membership numbers more than 200. Karin oversees all VRASP activities and serves as publisher of *Pix-Elation*. The editors, writers, and artists who help her produce *Pix* live in New Jersey, Virginia, California, Washington, Texas, and other states.

Because VRASP serves mostly as a meeting ground for younger people who are intrigued by the field but not quite ready for prime-time VR, the organization tends to focus on low-cost technologies and accomplishments. Subsequently, Karin has identified a potentially disturbing trend: "Right now garage VR is serving a very elite market, a highly educated few—perhaps not the most educated, but those who are educated in this niche. As such, [garage VR] remains aloof from the mainstream."

Karin believes that the way VR will reach the mainstream is through consumer-electronics VR, in the form of simulation game systems. "There will be a crossover between people who are using those systems for entertainment purposes and people who are hacking the technology into more interesting, worthwhile applications," she says. "Not that entertainment is not worthwhile; I just think it's been locked into certain male-dominated paradigms that I don't find particularly interesting. That's not to say that I don't like to play a shoot-'em-up game every once in a while."

"Male-dominated paradigm" certainly characterizes the field of VR—as it does every other technological field. Relatively few women drive garage VR engines. People hold different theories on why this is the case. According to Karin, "I've always made an effort to find other women interested in VR and encourage interest on their part. I've been somewhat successful, but I will tell you one thing: Those women who are interested in VR are not as dedicated as the men. They don't stick with it. Some are interested from a technological standpoint, because they are interested in things like CAD, engineering, and data visualization. But perhaps the majority of women are more interested from an artistic standpoint, and they see that right now there simply aren't the VR tools to enable them to fulfill their artistic fantasies. Perhaps that's why they lose interest."

Whether that's true provides grist for hours of debate. Either way, women—including Karin—*and* men agree that VR's greatest appeal to both genders lies in its potential as a medium that can integrate and enhance computing, communications, and the arts. VRASP members tend to focus their VR efforts on those areas.

Karin's long-term vision foresees VRASP as a self-sustaining organization that continues to publish and refine *Pix-Elation* and serves as a networking hub for career and educational opportunities and collaborative DIY projects, through which members can work together to build and distribute virtual worlds and tools. "A lot of people have the interest [in VR development] and don't have all the skills to do it by themselves," Karin remarks. "Certainly none can say, 'I have all the resources.' So it has to be a cooperative effort, and I'd like to encourage that among everybody."

VRASP membership: Annual membership dues are $30 for U.S. residents; all other countries, $40. Dues include a subscription to *Pix-Elation*, regular admission to VRASP "chats," and discounts at VRASP lectures and workshops. Volunteering is strongly encouraged and is rewarded by a "Contributing Member" designation: "This will entitle you to special privileges, such as networking opportunities and the ability to hold office in the organization, as well as public acknowledgment in the newsletter and at conferences."

Contact:
VRASP
PO Box 4139
Highland Park, NJ 08904-4139
(908) 463-8787

The Road Ahead

The Future of Garage VR

CHAPTER 11

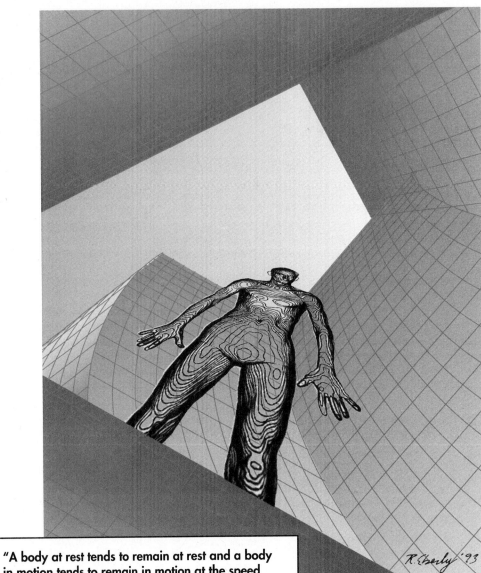

"A body at rest tends to remain at rest and a body in motion tends to remain in motion at the speed and direction in which it is traveling." —Newton's Law of Inertia/Momentum, 1687 (Sir Isaac Newton, 1642-1727)

The Road Ahead
The Future of Garage VR

Earlier in this century, when electronics was the exciting new technology, eager experimenters built radio receivers out of crystal sets. "Nowadays, no one bothers to build their own radio," garage VR developer Mark Pflaging points out, "but lots of people build hi-fi stereo systems from rack components. There has been a shift from building fundamental components to assembling an integrated, refined system. If garage VR is in the 'crystal set' era now, in the future you might see people building home-VR 'theaters' or 'decks' from mass-produced sections or parts."

Before the turn of the century, maybe we *will* be able to bring home VR theater components from Crazy Ned's Electronics Emporium. Or perhaps we'll buy a "home VR kit," a box containing all the materials to transform a personal computer into an interactive simulation development system: a graphics/sound card; software for modeling, rendering, interactive simulation, and 3D sound programming; a 6DOF input device; and maybe even stereoscopic glasses.

Until then, the trend of hijacking and hacking video game and consumer electronic gadgets for garage VR will continue. That's why garage VR enthusiasts eagerly await the Sega VR system. They also wonder what spawn will emerge from the union of workstation developer Silicon Graphics, Inc. and gargantuan games company Nintendo. In August of 1993, the power duo announced Project Reality: plans to develop a 3D, 64-bit, RISC-based Nintendo game machine using proprietary (as yet undisclosed) "Reality Immersion Technology." The system is scheduled to appear in game arcades in 1994. Another version will be sold for home use, for less than $250, in late 1995. Although the companies issued a statement declaring the system's projected high speed, digital audio, and "realistic" graphics capabilities, they said zilch about any immersive, stereoscopic, or 6DOF interfaces that might control the system.

Speaking of interfaces, consider this: right now, simply typing and mousing around for four to six hours can result in eye fatigue, stiff muscles, accumulated stress, and repetitive-strain disorders such as carpal tunnel syndrome. Similar physical ailments afflict those who wear heavy gloves, clumsy head-mounted displays, or "flicker" glasses for even shorter periods of time. Before we can expect home VR or garage VR systems to radically improve our ability to deal with data, communicate, and create and present works of art, the ways we physically interact with them must improve.

They *will* improve. We can count on R&D lab discoveries continuing to trickle down to the domain of garage VR. They'll help us bypass the roadblocks of virtual-world exploration, including those uncomfortable, encumbering "wearable" interfaces, tracking lags, and poor display resolution.

As professional VR developers refine the hardware and software and fill the field of garage VR with better tools, generous garage VR programmers will continue to place their own innovations into the public domain.

Coming Sooner...

More Effective, Less Expensive Output and Input Devices

Manufacturers will continue to homogenize and condense input and output devices for controlling virtual worlds and for displaying those worlds at a smooth, fast rate—with vivid clarity—if not with full stereoscopic splendor.

Some day we'll probably be able to digitize video of any scene and then use it to construct interactive, video-quality, real-time simulations. Video compression problems currently plague the multimedia community, so this won't happen in garage VR any time this century. More likely we'll see a crop of *new and improved, lower-cost shutter glasses* and systems that let groups of people view a single monitor display without flicker.

Visual and audio feedback will soon be complemented by *tactile and force feedback* mechanisms to stimulate the sense of touch in garage VR. Simple contact, pressure, texture, and vibration will come into play. All these sensory stimuli provide for a new channel of communication. They can verify a participant's contact with an object in the virtual world. They can communicate by Braille or Morse code. They can provide cues to signal other types of interactions.

Relatively low-cost input devices already offer limited tactile and force feedback in the form of motor-controlled vibrations (Logitech CyberMan and Global Devices forceball) and programmable resistance (Immersion Probe). VR industry experts predict that glove-like interfaces, 6DOF mice, and forceballs soon will incorporate other skin effectors. For example, a tiny array of metal springs or pins (called *tactors*) recessed into the surface of the interface device could be programmed to push against your fingertip, either individually or in groups. You could program the system to vary the spatial patterns of the active pins or their sequence, force, and frequency. In addition to tactors, tactile and force feedback mechanisms in gloves might take the form of small air pockets or bladders that can be programmed to inflate at appropriate moments.

The implementation of tactile feedback is just beginning. In 1993, the British company W. Industries announced that it was designing a glove with tactile feedback for use in a new Virtuality game system. Other developers are optimizing *touch output* technologies for professional VR applications; we can expect them to wind their way to garage VR.

Likewise, low-cost interfaces will incorporate pressure as an input variable. *Pressure-sensitive input* is a control tactic familiar to MIDI-savvy musicians. Many digital musical instruments feature a capability called pressure-sensitivity (or afterpressure, referring to the electronic keyboard's capability to sense how hard the player is pressing the key). Instead of simply pressing a mouse button, pushing on or squeezing a 6DOF device would let you intuitively signal a command that changes viewpoint position in the x- and y-axes, or select or lift a virtual object. Pressure-sensitivity technology is inexpensive and effective; it's already a capability of the Logitech Space Controller and Global Devices forceball.

Will we see *new, inexpensive wired gloves?* Some people eschew the glove as the way to control virtual worlds. Those who do enjoy the glove must wait and see whether potential glove manufacturers can jump the hurdle of the VPL Research patent regarding the use of the glove as an input device. Hotly contested in discussion, if not in practice, this patent prevents other companies from marketing similar products. Yet we know it is possible to make and produce inexpensive, reasonably effective gloves. The Power Glove proved that. A company could greatly improve upon the Power Glove's performance and still come up with a low-cost device.

The next great step forward in the input/output progression will let you interact with a computer in much the same way that people operated HAL in the movie *2001: A Space Odyssey:* "Open the pod bay door, HAL…." *Speech recognition and synthesis* will let you voice your commands; the computer will obey and perhaps even confirm the action with a verbal response. In the field of VR, speech input is vital in teleoperation and telerobotics applications in which the operator's hands must remain free to perform intricate tasks.

Such speech-recognition capabilities will reach the garage VR workbench. Already, PC owners can equip their computers with simple voice-recognition systems that work under Microsoft Windows. For example, Dragon System's voice recognition technology is built into the Microsoft Windows Sound System, which also offers voice synthesis; it can read back numbers from a spreadsheet, for example. Covox VoiceBlaster software works with any SoundBlaster-compatible card, which is supported by some virtual world-building fuels. These systems don't enable the computer to "understand" and respond to just *anyone's* speech (only the person for whom it was programmed), and they can't handle a slew of different commands or variations on a single command. Then again, they cost less than $300 and portend things to come: affordable, speaker-independent, continuous-speech recognition.

A more expensive ($1,000) voice-recognition system, Listen for Windows, is a developer kit by Verbex Voice Systems of Edison, New Jersey. It includes a circuit card that handles voice-related commands for '286 and '386 PCs. The system answers to commands written with its simple, straightforward programming language. With it, you can develop speech interfaces for various applications. How long will it be before garage VR enthusiasts grab something like this to hack a speech interface for their virtual worlds?

Easier, Friendlier, Unified Software Tools

The creation of an effective, interactive, real-time simulation is an exercise in command-line fascism. It requires working with compiled libraries, mastering the implementation of an *application programming interface* (API). An API is extremely flexible and great for complex simulations, but you have to program in C to use it, and you

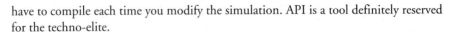

have to compile each time you modify the simulation. API is a tool definitely reserved for the techno-elite.

Other world-building software packages let you use a scripted language akin to the commands understood by Domark's Virtual Reality Studio. In such cases, the simulation instantly incorporates your changes. You can accomplish simple VR feats with nonprogrammer's tools, but VR professionals (programmers) consider them toys, not tools. Future world-building software should support easier and more powerful methods of simulation-creation.

No matter the type of toolkit you use, the experience of building a virtual world is a modular one. If you want to design an interactive simulation to demonstrate motorcycle maintenance, for instance, you need one program to model your three-dimensional motorbike. Then, you have to export the geometry data file to another program in which you determine how fast the wheels should spin, what direction the 'cycle will take when it zooms off, whether the motor rumbles or purrs, and what happens when you twist your forceball or roll your Power Glove to shift gears. You also must load the results into another program module to ignite and experience the simulation.

Eventually, software developers will unify these modules, or at least they'll standardize file formats. This way, more garage VR systems will be able to exchange and import files, similar to the way word-processing systems can exchange text files and import graphics files from a wide range of drawing programs.

Ultimately, object-oriented software with a graphical user interface will make world-building as easy a chore to accomplish as desktop-publishing a newsletter with page-layout software or producing music with sound composition and editing software. *Object-oriented* refers to a highly structured type of programming language that lets you write programs by assembling collections of discrete objects. Graphical object-oriented programming would represent those objects in the form of graphical icons. The ultimate world-building package would let you describe the dynamics of a virtual environment through a simple, intuitive interface to the simulation manager, so you could quickly create and modify simulations (probably not intricate simulations, but good enough to satisfy people who aren't computer programmers).

Industry Standards and Cross-Platform Compatibility

Standards facilitate the interchange of data and the interconnection of hardware and software. By enhancing applications portability and communication between VR systems, standards would support the exchange of resources among different kinds of reality engines. Garage VR experimenters would accomplish much more if REND386 worlds could run on a Macintosh, for example, or if Logitech's 6DOF devices could work with the Amiga.

As mentioned in Chapter 9, the U.S. Institute of Electrical and Electronics Engineers opened the gateway to software standardization with the publication of Application

Protocol Standard No. IEEE-1278-1993. Anyone who is serious about modeling 3D objects for virtual worlds should read this document.

Another standard served as the main topic of a dinner discussion organized by VR experts from Silicon Graphics, Inc., during a May 1993 VR industry conference in San Jose, California. VR industry leaders gathered at a restaurant to discuss position-tracking standards. Their goal was to form a committee to develop a formal, standard API for 6DOF motion trackers.

Participating in the meeting, along with the Silicon Graphics people, were representatives of professional VR manufacturers and service providers, including Ascension Technology and Polhemus (both produce position-tracking systems), Logitech (input devices, position trackers), Evans and Sutherland Simulation Division (workstation-based systems), Fakespace Labs (visual displays), Autodesk (Cyberspace Developer's Kit software), Division (SuperScape software), Sense8 (WorldToolKit software), and New Leaf Associates and WorlDesign (system integrators/application designers).

This group is setting up a rough interface specification and organizing development subcommittees to work out the software API and hardware specs, both of which are required to produce a meaningful standard for motion-tracking.

More Applications

Low-cost, educational, productive, and enjoyable simulation applications for personal computer-based VR systems will hit store shelves and catalog pages. And soon! Let's hope that the entertainment titles don't disguise violence as a form of fun.

...and Later

Neural Input Devices

Alexander Graham Bell, a teacher of the deaf, invented the telephone as a prosthetic device for the hearing-impaired. Today, scientists continue to develop and implement technologies that improve our physiological well-being. Some of those technologies are even implanted directly in the human body. Consider cochlear implants, pacemakers, and hip replacements.

This approach forms the foundation upon which many neuro-hackers build their case for neural input devices. These technoids believe that the ultimate human-machine interface would transmit information directly from the brain. They want to operate the computer by thought input.

To do this, you wouldn't necessarily have to implant a bidirectional parallel port in your skull. Instead, you could venture forth on the neuro-route with a *bio-navigation* system. A bio-navigation system would harness biofeedback processes for use in navigating virtual worlds.

Biofeedback is a technique whereby you learn how to regulate certain body functions, such as heart rate, blood pressure, and brainwave patterns, which normally are involuntary functions. Special monitoring instruments, attached to parts of your body, record changes in these functions. Through these instruments, sensors measure your body's muscular activity, electrical impulses, or other states, and a computer provides visual or auditory representation of the signals.

Until recently, only medical and fitness centers could afford to install biofeedback machines. Some visionary hackers, however, have developed brainwave monitors that work with personal computers.

Software engineer Masahiro Kahata runs a company called Psychic Labs. He spent six years developing the Psychic Labs' Interactive Brainwave Visual Analyzer (IBVA) for the Apple Macintosh. Released in 1990 for $1,000, the IBVA is a simple biofeedback system based on a wireless electroencephalograph, an EEG recorder that can read and store the electrical signals generated by brain activity. The IBVA hardware consists of a wireless, electrode-studded headband (the transmitter) and a small box with an antenna (the receiver) that plugs into the computer's serial port. The electrodes monitor the activity of the left- and right-brain hemispheres. The resulting data is transmitted by radio signal to the receiver, and then on to the computer. The IBVA software crunches the data into the appropriate digital signals. It displays these signals in a colorful 3D graph or on a standard EEG readout, showing activity in the delta, theta, alpha, and beta brainwave frequencies. You don't need to write a single line of code; you just deal with a comprehensive point-and-click interface.

In theory, the IBVA software can use brain signals to communicate with other software, computers, or external equipment, and those signals can travel anywhere that a modem can take them. In practice, several people have routed the IBVA data through MIDI interfaces to control the output of digital musical instruments. Others have employed the system to monitor brainwave activity for meditation training. There aren't any reports (yet) about neuro-hackers using their brain waves to control virtual worlds. Frankly, it's doubtful that the IBVA can translate actual thought processes into input data. (Psychic Labs is located at 280 Park Avenue South, New York, NY 10010; (212) 353-1669.)

Neuro-researcher David Cole runs a nonprofit company, AquaThought, that has introduced a more sophisticated EEG system on a plug-in card for the PC or Macintosh. The IBVA monitors two parts of the brain, and the $2,000 MindSet comes with an *electro-cap* that maps brainwave activity at 16 spots. This performance approaches that which was possible only in clinical lab equipment. (You do, however, need to dab onto your head the same sticky electroconductive gel that hospitals use.) The MindSet software, designed for the "beginning researcher" as well as for the professional neuro-scientist, supports neurological pattern recognition, analysis, and visualization techniques. The system is said to support total computer control. (AquaThought is located at 22321 Susana Avenue, Torrance, CA 90505; (310) 316-4563.)

Over the past two decades, people have used biofeedback to successfully treat disorders such as chronic headaches and back pain. Whether others will employ this technique to control their viewpoint or interaction in a virtual world remains to be seen. What *is* a likely and exciting possibility is that relatively low-cost "desktop EEG" systems will provide many neurologically impaired people with the means to control electronic and mechanical functions (such as room lighting) with a personal computer. Medical researchers have achieved success in this area, testing patients' use of a more expensive and sophisticated EEG-to-computer interface, the BioMuse by BioControl Systems of Palo Alto, California.

For an entertaining, balanced overview of neural interfacing, read Gareth Branwyn's article "The Desire to Be Wired" in the September/October 1993 issue of *Wired* magazine.

The Information Superhighway

Garage VR hobbyists looking for adventure head out on the data highway. Eventually, exit ramps from this highway, now under construction, will direct 3D virtual worlds right into everyone's home.

Mitch Kapor, a computer industry leader and cofounder of the Electronic Frontier Foundation, wrote in the July/August 1993 issue of *Wired*, "Networks that reach into the home will be hybrids of the fiber-optic cable and existing copper wire and coaxial cable used by telephone and cable television companies…[t]o achieve a broadband network capable of delivering high-quality video, voice and data…."

Such a hybrid system would let programming providers pump information over cable into the home. We would view it on a computer screen or a computer-controlled television and interact with the programming by transmitting messages back through a fiber-optic or copper phone line.

No matter how many bit-servings per second a modem can feed to a computer, standard copper phone lines can carry only so much. Fiber-optic cables offer much greater bandwidth; unfortunately, installing fiber-optic cables for every phone customer's home is prohibitively expensive. Coaxial cable—those thick black wires that shuttle TV programming into so many private homes—can handle great big hunks of data. However, few cable companies ever installed bidirectional coaxial cable, which is the kind needed to support interactive simulation transmission.

As a result, telecommunications experts are looking at some new technologies and techniques to support the long-distance, bidirectional transmission of multimedia data over existing wire and cable installations.

ISDN is one relatively new transmission technology that's in the running as a data traffic control system. It works in conjunction with standard phone lines. ISDN stands for *integrated services digital network*, a set of proposed protocols for carrying voice, all kinds of data, facsimile, and video signals across a network. Big companies probably will use it first to transmit live and motion (as opposed to still-frame) video. The Public Utilities Commission has approved the service, but most regional phone companies don't support ISDN because most central switching offices aren't equipped to deliver it. It's also not a high-bandwidth service, the kind needed to transmit virtual worlds.

One solution to the bandwidth problem is *asymmetric digital subscriber line* (ADSL), an experimental broadband p
ipe for pumping data into residential homes. (Broadband refers to the capability of a cable to carry different types of data signals simultaneously.) Through standard copper phone wires, ADSL would support the transmission of video, stereo audio, text, and graphics. ADSL service would work in conjunction with ISDN and with regular telephone service. The regional telephone company U.S. West plans to start ADSL installation and experimentation in the mid- to late-1990s.

Another experimental telecom technology, *asynchronous transfer mode* (ATM), reduces bottlenecks on computer networks and accelerates the transfer of large data files typical of interactive simulations and 3D graphics. This broadband cross-platform/switching technology represents another solution to data traffic jams, but it's a costly one. A PC circuit board for connection to an ATM network costs at least $1,500. Wealthy, data-dependent companies are experimenting with ATM now. Stanford University is trying it out for interactive video lessons. U.S. Sprint plans to set up a nationwide ATM network. Should ATM gain widespread popularity, it could provide a standard format to carry any combination of voice, sound, graphics, or data at sizzling speeds.

Before any of this can happen, obviously, a technical infrastructure must crystalize. The political gridlock—confusion over public and regulatory policies—must clear. When this *does* happen, the super networks initially will deliver movies on demand, interactive multimedia databases, and video conferencing services.

Eventually, those networks also will support *televirtuality:* the telecommunication of shared virtual worlds.

A few forward-thinking companies are preparing to pioneer televirtuality. Kaiser Electro-Optics (a division of the defense contracting firm Kaiser Aerospace and Electronics) united with a new Boulder, Colorado company, VR1 Entertainment, Inc., to bring "virtual reality" programming to the home by way of cable television—through the familiar, high-bandwidth coaxial cable in use today. According to an announcement issued late in 1993, VR1 intends to transmit computer-generated, stereoscopic, 3D virtual worlds over Time Warner's Home Box Office cable channel sometime in 1994. Programming will initiate from Denver, where VR1 owns a satellite uplink. To experience that programming, the customer would need a VR1 decoder box (attached to the cable box), which also would track usage for billing purposes. The customer also would be expected to buy, from VR1, Kaiser's Vision Immersion Module (VIM) Personal Viewer, a lightweight, head-mounted, stereoscopic display that uses color LCDs and offers a 100-degree field of view. This HMD is the offspring of helmets developed for the military. Kaiser now sells the VIM for $10,000 to arcade game developers, but declares that the price will drop dramatically once major production ensues. Meanwhile, VR1 wants to license its VR development software to cable systems and other producers of 3D programming.

Aiming for a similar target, a San Francisco company, RPI Advanced Technology Group, is testing its VR network, ImagiNet. Instead of viewing piped-in worlds on your TV set while wearing a Kaiser helmet, you watch your computer monitor play a simulation game while wearing RPI's lightweight stereoscopic glasses with audio headphones (see Figure 11.1). To connect your computer to ImagiNet, you would need an IBM PC engine ('386 or better), a 2400-baud modem, and a joystick, plus RPI's glasses, network software, and a graphics card. The ImagiNet experience would carry a per-minute cost, in addition to the price of the necessary equipment. Today, RPI's gear goes for about $7,500. The price is high because RPI custom-builds each component. Company representatives imagine it won't be costly for long; they predict the equipment price will drop to about $500 once mass-production begins. However, the company needs a funding source to support such assembly-line VR.

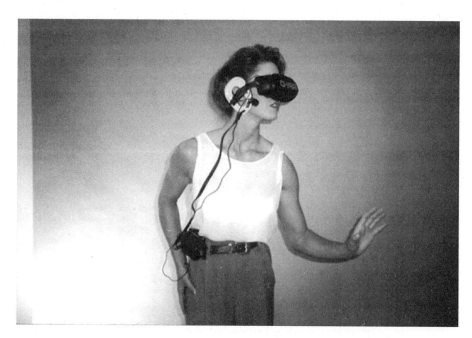

Figure 11.1. *A prototype of the Head-Mount Sensory Interface by RPI Advanced Technology Group: RPI's audio/visual gateway to the networked virtual worlds on ImagiNet. © 1993 RPI, Inc. All rights reserved.*

More televirtuality developers will appear up the road. Working with phone companies, cable TV providers, and computer data networks, they will transmit virtual worlds over long distances by taking advantage of the new telecommunications technologies and techniques.

Now we sit back and wait while the industrialists and corporate executives decide which efforts to support and which technologies will support those efforts. When that happens, "teletechnologies" will take VR out of the garage and bring it into the living room.

Great Applications!

A virtual world populated by inanimate objects is appealing for just so long. We can expect some future applications to feature "intelligent characters," virtual creatures that display their own behaviors. Today's researchers, particularly at Carnegie-Mellon University in Pittsburgh and MIT's Media Lab in Cambridge, devote long hours to nurturing artificial life forms. Intelligent characters know how to move around on their own and respond to simple stimuli that they encounter in the virtual world. A participant's interaction with virtual objects would trigger unexpected reactions from the characters. When this development reaches the desktop, our virtual worlds will support infinitely more engaging experiences.

Few VR experiences are truly engaging today, because contemporary VR represents more technical craft than art form. As the technology's development picks up pace, we'll enjoy increasingly more beautiful, elegant, and effective implementations—in packages that work with our personal computers.

Such implementations will appear if and when commercial applications development is driven by artistic concerns.

Through letters, phone calls, e-mail, and financial support, we can encourage companies to continue supporting low-cost desktop VR and to hire more artists to help develop programs and produce meaningful virtual-world applications at prices that other artists can afford.

Until Tomorrow...

The technologists will continue developing the computer as a practical tool.

The scientists will continue developing the computer as a tool for discovery.

Other folks will continue finding ways to use the computer to enhance their daily experiences, communicate concepts, express emotions, and surpass their physical limitations.

Garage VR can provide all these people with the means to reach their destinations. Come along for the ride!

PUTTING VR ON THE MAP

Jon Lebkowsky and Paco Xander Nathan

PROFILE
8

JON LEBKOWSKY AND PACO XANDER NATHAN:
"Building Community Around a
Fringe Marketplace"

*Superhighway I-35 takes you right into Austin,
which lies between Dallas and San Antonio
about 155 miles northeast of the Mexican
border. Home of the University of Texas, as
well as Texas Instruments and Motorola,
IBM, Apple, and Westinghouse branches,
Austin enjoyed a high-tech industry boom in
the 1980s that attracted tens of thousands to
this liberal enclave in a heavily conservative
state. It's always been a high-tech kind of
place: the first Texan telephone conversation
occurred here in 1924. It's always been
unusual: Austin boasts the nation's largest
underground bat colony. Austin also is
gifted with a vibrant cultural scene,
particularly for music. And Austin is pretty.
That's partly why the Republic of Texas
president Mirabeau Lamar made it the
capital in 1839. Then and now, folks cherish
Austin's lovely surroundings: its soft, rolling
terrain, wooded acreage, and dozens of lakes
spread along the fringes of Texas' Hill Country.*

"'Fringe' is people who are on the edge of
culture, exploring things that are new…people
who love stuff just for their newness, who play with
an idea just because it hasn't been expressed before or
hasn't been expressed very well," says FringeWare's Jon
Lebkowsky. "Also with the fringe, you can create memes,
target the brains of society, and shoot those memes in there.
You start talking on the edges about something, and it can work
its way into the fabric of society."

Many people who perch on the fringed edges of techno-counterculture
know about Jon Lebkowsky and his partner Paco Xander Nathan. Both names

appear regularly as bylines in *Whole Earth Review, Wired, Mondo 2000,* and the technocultist "neurozine" *bOING bOING.* Their primary gig, however, places them at the helm of FringeWare—a mail-order business, electronic mailing list, and quarterly magazine (*Fringe Ware Review*) through which they compile, synthesize, and pump out a stream of ever-eclectic, often profound, and sometimes twisted articles, essays, news, and affordable "fringe-oid" product listings. Through FringeWare channels, Jon and Paco provide a new take on socioeconomics while encouraging a sense of community among fringe artists, inventors, hackers, and others interested in exploring the do-it-yourself angle of digital technology.

Jon, the elder of the two, speaks quietly with a deep Texas drawl. His dark eyes smile from behind black-framed glasses. A programming specialist for the state of Texas and a co-founder of Electronic Frontier Foundation's Austin chapter, Jon lives with his wife Marsha and their baby grandson, Colton. Jon and Paco share many interests: writing, robots, raves, books, music, coffee, good conversation, and challenging the status quo. Both are soft-spoken. Paco, however, reels out his words with a crisp, rapid-fire delivery. A bit shorter and slimmer than Jon, Paco often ties back his long brown hair in a ponytail. A tattoo of the Mobius Strip-like, three-arrowed "recycle" symbol (see Figure P8.1) graces his bicep. A sharp glint brightens his eyes. When he's not writing, traveling to technology conferences, or running FringeWare, Paco works as a programmer, telecommuting to Kansas to a biotechnology firm that studies brain physiology.

Figure P8.1. The "recycle" symbol.

"Our personalities work real well together," Jon says. "What Paco and I have in common is humor. We have a real good time. Rarely do I show him something or he shows me something that we don't get really excited about it. We do come from real different backgrounds, and we may have some philosophical differences, but I think that basically we're philosophically alike."

They also share a talent for articulating their beliefs and experiences. Let's break form (keeping in line with the fringe meme) and let Paco and Jon take turns telling their stories.

Paco: Once upon a Time...

"I was born February 7, 1962 in San Luis Obispo, California. My parents are gone, and I shuffled around a few different families on my way to adulthood. I guess I got some traveling in at a young age. But San Luis was home base until I was 18.

"I got on the nerd track early, because I was always a real sickly kid. I used to have huge fevers, like 107 degrees. I'd turn blue, and they'd have to pack me in ice. I was pretty bright but barely alive, and when I was younger I didn't go to school a whole lot. Instead, I would read all the old Time-Life science books and just get into it while I was pretty much tripping my head off with a high fever. Around the same time I set up a little lab in my basement. I guess the whole DIY thing started right there.

"I grew up in a neighborhood where there weren't too many kids, but those who were there were big and mean. At one point, purely as a survival tactic, I convinced the other kids that they should stop beating the shit out of me because I had plans to build a force-field gun. I had this little clubhouse with little schematics all over the walls, and I would tell them, 'Either leave me alone, or I'll kill you. Or you can join my club.' So they joined my club, and I had them scouring the neighborhood for parabolic mirrors and car batteries and stuff to build this thing. By the time they were old enough and smart enough to know what was going on, I could ride my bike fast enough to get away from them.

"When I was about 10, I discovered computers. At that time, I hated a lot of electrical technology. I had more interest in biology. Around San Luis, there's really cool beaches, and I used to be a real nut about hanging around tide pools. I studied them, took all kinds of elaborate records on salinity and pH. In the basement of the house where I was living at that time, I set up homemade glass cutters and silicon tanks simulating the tide pool environment. I needed some help with it, though. I knew a guy who was studying computer science at Cal Poly in San Luis Obispo, and he took me to the lab there and helped me figure out some stuff using the computers. That's when I started programming. The equipment was Honeywell mainframes and punch tape. The old teletype stuff. They had a CRT at the lab, and they were really proud of that.

"In high school, I was using computers and doing independent study. I tested out of the standard tracks, especially math and science. I also lived for a while with my uncle in L.A., going to summer school at USC. He worked for Seymour Cray, so I got a good dose of computer science at a young age. At one point I went on a summer program to the Naval Academy where they were getting heavily into computer education. I fell in love with the analog computer simulation work they were doing. I think that got a bug in me for cybernetic things. Because cybernetics isn't purely digital—it's biology and real life.

"I wanted to get out of San Luis by the time I was 18. Well, West Point [Military Academy] liked what I was doing and recruited me when I was in high school [where] I was really involved in student government, taking dance classes, and into weight lifting and especially cycling, which I used to do competitively. West Point concentrated on the 'whole person' concept. They gave me a good spiel, and I had a lot of personal reasons for getting the hell out of town.

"West Point's in upstate New York. I went on a visit there and stayed with a guy who was a cadet, and I got to meet the first woman who went to West Point, and it all was intriguing. So I went into the Army. My family life and personal life hadn't been anywhere near like *Ozzie and Harriet*; I was out on my own kind of early, and West Point gave me security and also gave me a lot of potential to stretch my wings.

"At West Point, they put you through a program—well, ostensibly they give you an engineering degree, although they're not accredited and they actually have a very strong liberal arts program. But they want you to be an officer. You also have to be on athletic teams—I was a boxer—and you have to do all the military stuff. So they pretty much own your life. I went in in 1980, and we had Ronald Reagan for a new president. He gave our welcome speech. That set a tone. And then—you know, West Point was sort of into the 18th-century French academy thing, and really heavy-duty into corporal punishment and brainwashing. Tim Leary and I had a good talk about that one; he went to West Point, too. He and I both stayed about two years.

"All the units would have these intense competitions—[in the form of] parades—and you'd have to dress up in combat gear, fully starched and brass, heavy wool, and stuff like that. We'd be out in 90-degree weather, marching with bayonet sticks. You had to stand at attention. People would be falling over on bayonets and passing out all the time. But these competitions between units went on all the time. And you'd be graded at several points along the parade route, and if your unit failed, everyone would be punished.

"At that time they were phasing out mandatory drafting and phasing in computers, and I went into advanced Fortran class and really got into it. The first computers and camcorders were starting to show up there. A friend and I went out with a camcorder, and we took analyses at the parade checkpoints where we had rated poorly. Then we'd run an analysis of variants against the other units to figure out where we needed work. We would videotape that and show it to the unit leaders. So rather than punishing the whole team, they just had to tell a couple of individuals how to correct their motions. Kind of like cybernetic feedback! We were able to win the whole damn competition. It really turned them on their heads. So I got into that kind of stuff when I was at West Point, and that made me some friends and some enemies.

"After two years, the brainwashing thing had been getting to me. We were asked to do a lot of things we didn't want to do. I think I was surfing on New Year's Eve one time in Malibu with my cousins, about ready to go back from leave, and I said, 'Why am I doing this?' So I left West Point.

"It really is a big core of what I'm all about, though. Having to free-climb a rock wall with a guy who's throwing rocks at you from the top while screaming, 'You know that combat is going to be worse!' That can set a tone. Having to run all night while being in charge of the lives of 13 people who all had loaded weapons, being periodically ambushed with artillery simulators and gas grenades until even the big football players were ready to drop. When they went nuts, I had to stop them, and on top of that, carry 35 pounds of radio and keep some semblance of mission, conduct, and order. Things like that stress you to a point where you start to see where your limits are. I really learned a lot about what I was capable of doing.

"If I had gone on a different track, I would probably have had more of an intellectual foundation [in the way I look at situations]. Instead, it's based on immediate analysis of life-and-death scenarios."

Jon: It Was Not a Dark and Stormy Night When…

"I was born in Big Spring, Texas; my birthdate is April 20, 1949. I grew up there, pretty much. My father was a beer wholesaler and later got into the liquor business.

"We moved to Odessa in my senior year and I went to Permian High School. That's oil country. Back then I wrote poetry. I was interested in literature, getting really turned on to James Joyce and Beckett, and I was fascinated by underground movements. That was a scary part of Texas, and I had all this weird stuff coming through the mail; people were probably watching my house! At some point the *Whole Earth Catalog* first appeared; I got blown away by that, and much of my life was shaped directly or indirectly by the *Whole Earth Catalog* and *CoEvolution Quarterly* [now *Whole Earth Review*].

"I went to the University of Texas at Austin. Majored in English. I didn't graduate from the University of Texas, though; I graduated from St. Edwards, which was a smaller university here. I got a degree in English, with a specialization in writing—or *rioting*, I should say! I got married in 1974 to Marsha. We met in college. I already had a son, Robert, when we were married, and we had a daughter, Tana, about a year and a half after we were married.

"Marsha and I were a couple of hippies, basically. I was going to classes, really motivated, thinking I would get my English degree and go to law school. At the same time, I felt real weird about that, because I was also interested in radical stuff. At some point I decided I didn't want to do it anymore, and I started writing. I wrote several short stories and a hunk of what was going to be a novel, none of which impressed me very much. I didn't feel that I had the right experience to write fiction. Around the same time, some guys I knew heard that there were going to be jobs in the Food Stamp program. They went down to apply for a job, and I went with them, and I was the only one who got a job out of it. I was hired, and I became a caseworker for years. That was in 1974.

"So I was working as a caseworker, writing, and listening to a whole lot of rock and roll and jazz. Most of the stuff I was writing was shit; I didn't have my head on straight at all. I was trying to find some kind of community, some sense of being *into* something that I could feel right about, and it just wasn't happening. There were a lot of fragmented communities around Austin; Austin has been sort of aligned with San Francisco in subcultural community development over the years. Head [underground] comics started here and there simultaneously. Anyway, I was on the periphery of a lot of that stuff, including politics. I wrote for the underground newspaper here, just briefly. I skirted the fringes of various movements, everything from politics to environmentalism to New Age bullshit. And nothing was really working for me until I found cyberspace."

Paco Goes to Work

"After leaving West Point I chilled for a couple of weeks, then sent out applications. I had a choice of Stanford [University] or [U.C.] Berkeley, and I decided to go to a little college, California State College at Stanislaus, out by Modesto, in the foothills of Yosemite, to chill out for a semester. I tried to deprogram and become a human again. From there I went to Stanford.

"I started on the math track, then I did a Master's in computer science and put those together. I got both degrees in 1986. I was doing a lot of work there, too. I also studied art formally. I stayed on an extra year at Stanford so I could throw in things like that. Then I started working for NASA Ames. I did flight simulation guidance, graphics programs. It was sort of a precursor to VR. I did a lot of visual representation stuff for NASA—my first virtual worlds. That was in about '86.

"Back when I was at Stanford and NASA, I used to hang out at the user interface seminars at Xerox PARC [Palo Alto Research Center]. My first awareness of virtual reality was at a PARC seminar, somewhere in 1984 or 1985. There were a lot of ideas floating around and interesting people showing up. Like these strange people from a small, unknown company called VPL. The people from VPL gave a presentation on what they called a 'body suit,' and they said that the whole reason for this was because they wanted to play air guitar.

"Then I went to Bell Labs in New Jersey and did a lot of UNIX programming, a lot of comm[unications] work. In 1988, I came to Austin to work for Motorola, doing Mac software, supporting their chip development. They were setting up a neural network venture, and they were involved with a company in Kansas, and I eventually left Motorola and joined that company. That's the biotech firm I work for now, Odin Corporation.

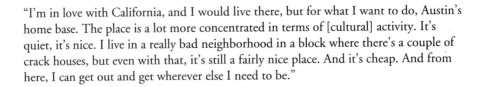

"I'm in love with California, and I would live there, but for what I want to do, Austin's home base. The place is a lot more concentrated in terms of [cultural] activity. It's quiet, it's nice. I live in a really bad neighborhood in a block where there's a couple of crack houses, but even with that, it's still a fairly nice place. And it's cheap. And from here, I can get out and get wherever else I need to be."

Jon Gets Digital

"It's years ago now, probably in the early '80s, when I got my first computer. I had a friend, Chip, who was a computer programmer. He kept telling me that I was a natural for computing; he thought I would make a good programmer and he loaned me a PC, but it just sat around gathering dust. It was a real clunker. It sat in my room staring at me for a long time, and then I'd turn it on and kind of bang around, but I wasn't clear on what its possibilities were. I was mystified. I didn't know what it represented, and that was my first contact [with computers]. I stewed in those juices for a while.

"A couple of years later, though, when I was reading *Whole Earth,* I could see that the people who had kindled my flame for years—the people involved with *CoEvolution Quarterly*—were getting involved with computers. This thing called the WELL appeared, along with the Whole Earth Software Review, and I got excited about that and managed to convince Marsha, who had started working in real-estate work, that we had to buy a PC, that it was a desperate need for her real estate. We got our hands on a PC clone, an XT-compatible, and I started logging into local BBSs. Once I sort of understood the software, I started calling the WELL.

"Anyway, after 10 years as a caseworker, I quit and the deal was that I was going to make my living as a writer. We were having a real estate boom at the time, and Marsha was making good money from that, and also I was finding that I could do document production. I was also doing some technical writing. This was crazy, but I thought I could make a living by tech writing and then on the side I could write the Great American Novel.

"I tried to get into tech writing, but the jobs were hard to get because we went into a recession at about the same time and the economy was bust here. So I did a lot of other kinds of writing. I even wrote resumes and managed a resume office for about 10 months. Then I realized I wanted to learn about magazine and book production. I had worked with people with these elaborate [desktop publishing] systems, and the first thing that struck me was, 'Hey, you could produce a little magazine!'

"So I went to work as a proofreader for a typesetter that did production for major presses like University of Chicago, Addison-Wesley, MIT, and so on. I learned everything I could about the whole production cycle for books. My intention was to print a little magazine.

"Eventually, just to fill the coffers, I thought I'd go back to work for the state and get a paycheck and learn about mundane things like insurance coverage. Real estate was dead in Austin, and Marsha's mother had a stroke and was paralyzed, so we focused on taking care of her and working with the kids as much as we could. We led a care-giver/ social-work life; we were taking care of her mom, and Marsha went back into retail, and I worked two jobs: a typesetter at night and a job with the state by day.

"I was a caseworker but worked up to supervisor pretty fast, and then [the state] implemented a state-of-the-art system for eligibility determination: 450 LANs with eligibility determination software. This huge automation thing. I had gotten pretty adept with the PC, so I evolved into working an automation job with the state. Now that's all I do in my day job: work with this system on software development, specification, and technical support. My title is Programming Specialist, but 'programming' means client self-support services."

Paco Makes a Pact and Meets Jon

"I made a pact with myself when I graduated that I was going to work in the corporate world for about five years, figure out how it was done, then cut out and run my own small business. And sure enough, five years came up, and I had a falling-out with a company. To make a long story short, my technology career was almost over, in a sense, when I started writing.

"I became aware of the DIY VR stuff probably at 2 CyberConf [the second Conference on Cyberspace] in Santa Cruz [California] in the second part of 1991. That's when I started writing. At 2 CyberConf I ran into a lot of people who were interested in following the DIY thing. Immediately after that I got involved with *bOING bOING* [magazine] and [its editors] Mark Fraunfelder and Gareth Branwyn. Mark was the first person to publish me, and Gareth was his right hand.

"Mark kept telling me, 'There's this guy who lives down the street from you, and he's one of our other editors. You ought to get together for coffee.' Jon and I were both running around so much, but finally we slowed down to the point where he and I met and had a lot of coffee and realized how much we liked each other, and since then we've been best friends. That was sometime in February 1992. Jon and I banded together as writers. We're similar in some ways, and very different in others."

Jon Meets VR

"Before I ever heard of virtual reality, I was writing about 'virtual' in an automation context, like working with virtual disks. Then virtual reality came around. It was essentially what I saw in video games. You can make a natural connection between video games and virtual computing, because they both present programmed realities: simulated realities, graphical environments. My first experience with virtual reality was probably a film experience, going to see Cinerama, Omni-Max. The movie *Brainstorm*. That's where I first encountered all that stuff. Of course, I read *Neuromancer* early on, and the concept of data visualization hit me pretty hard, like it did everybody.

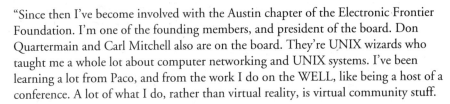

"Since then I've become involved with the Austin chapter of the Electronic Frontier Foundation. I'm one of the founding members, and president of the board. Don Quartermain and Carl Mitchell also are on the board. They're UNIX wizards who taught me a whole lot about computer networking and UNIX systems. I've been learning a lot from Paco, and from the work I do on the WELL, like being a host of a conference. A lot of what I do, rather than virtual reality, is virtual community stuff.

"The thing that I'm most interested in now is MUDs, multiuser systems. Today you use mostly text to describe an environment, but the day will come when you can show those environments graphically. People will be able to go into the environments and build them the way they want to, and create realities that will allow them to expand to whatever they can imagine."

Paco on the Power Glove

"The Power Glove is nifty, but the granularity on it is very coarse, and the Gloves tend to break. They need to be followed up [by a similar controller], and the reason they're not being followed up is because of [patent law] nonsense. Somebody's not using what they have claimed rights to while the [wired glove is] blocked from market use, and I wonder if that's a legitimate use of U.S. patent law. Anybody that really tries to get onto the market is going to have to grapple with the VPL patent. Something's got to give there. There *are* going to be gloves. And if there aren't going to be gloves, then maybe there's going to be—I don't know, *hand* puppets. There's going to be something like that, because we're monkeys and we like using our hands."

Jon on the Power Glove

"We make the Power Glove available [through FringeWare] to people as a tool for further development. I'd like to see the Power Glove come back. A lot of artists would like to use Power Gloves in a sonic or graphical context to try to create, to make art, to experiment. Another reason we make the Power Glove available is the 15-year-old hacker who would like to stumble onto something like that."

Paco on the Future of VR

"I don't really see much of a future in total immersive VR as I do for overlay work [an "overlay" lets you see virtual worlds "superimposed" on top of the physical world; sometimes called "augmented reality," it's used in pilots' heads-up displays]. Let's not focus so much on spending a lot of money on the total immersive stuff, when we can basically throw an LCD image on our eyes. Instead of being constrained, we can use that while we wander around. That can be tricky; it will require a lot of design work. When you put information in a person's face, there will be a whole other level of abstraction in programming, in terms of how to efficiently tailor unconfined virtual and real environments.

"As for input, I'm interested in innovative kinds. I'm a fan of this stuff called FSR [force-sensing resistors], a flexible variable resistor. Force-sense resistors are what they use at McDonald's on their keyboards back in the grease area. That FSR stuff is starting to look a whole lot more like skin.

"People should wake up to the fact that we could get away from joysticks and a lot of really explicit design, and get into some more implicit design. There was a *Star Trek: The Next Generation* episode where they went to a planet and thought it was completely primeval, but in fact the technology was so advanced that it was invisible. That's where my bent is, to get away from putting on goggles and instead have [computer] stuff that's pretty much all around you."

Jon on Linking the Fringe Crowd

"One of our national audiences is teenagers who still have open minds. Teenagers who are in a weird, postmodern scene where everything is sort of disoriented and crazy and they're trying to find ways to make sense of all this weirdness. In every town there's somebody who's just a little bit out of kilter, someone usually fairly bright who's reading weird stuff that nobody else [in their town] knows anything about. Through the net, they find people who think the way they do. And they don't have to leave town to do that. They can go to cyberspace, which is as far away as the modem.

"But when you get plugged into the Internet or BBSs, you start getting exposed to a lot of different realities, and it can be very disorienting for some people. That's why it's even more important for people to find communities. These are some real bright kids...if they get to realize their dreams, they're going to build some really interesting things. High-tech has a lot of greed in it. These kids coming in on their own are not thinking about [money], they're thinking about making a scene. They have a communitarian longing. They want to get connected. It reminds me of the feeling we had in the sixties. The difference was that in the sixties, we couldn't pull people together globally the way we can now, online."

Paco's Approach to Business

"I'm coming from the standpoint of not only 'kill your television,' but 'kill your corporation.' Right now we really have to get smaller and more adaptive, in terms of business activity, to be able to make a living. When [the U.S. economy] had a real strong industrial base, a strong product sector, the people who were in demand were the engineers, who were the former military officers. They were the people who knew how to take technical, physical constraints and solve a problem inexpensively. That's really what engineering is. For the industrial revolution, those people held sway as a sort of marching army. Now we have virtual communities where the only things that we see are symbolic representations of ideas. The engineers are out, in a sense, and the people who will really take over are the ones who can express the ideas, the ones who can deal with the memes."

Jon's Approach to Business

"One thing that struck Paco and me is that people form societies around markets. All the experimentation with socialism and all that crap—its failure was due to the fact that [socialists] didn't acknowledge the market and how the market works. If you see the market system in a basic economic sense as being a foundation of society, you see that the market has certain characteristics. If the market is sick or the market is greedy, then society is going to follow that; it's going to be sick or greedy. If you start healing the market, if you start creating a marketplace that is not greed-based but is more communitarian, more like a street market, where community and service to the community are at the heart of it, then you're taking a step in the direction of healing society."

Paco's Toolbox

GVR

Engine: 386 PC clone; Macintosh IIci ("my main system") with 20MB RAM, 100MB hard disk; Syquest removeable hard drive

Monitor: Apple 15-inch color monitor

Modem: Prometheus

Primary hardware and software: Keyboard, mouse, Power Gloves ("I wouldn't claim to have any permanent system in that regard, because whatever I get goes on the market"), Transfinite Systems' Gold Brick interface ("They include C source if you want to roll your own driver, and they have an X-command, which I use because I do a lot of work with Hyper-Card"), REND386 ("The nice thing is that it's in Turbo C, so you don't have to deal with Microsoft [Windows]")

Music to code by: "Faith No More or some Kate Bush and, of course, a lot of D'Cückoo"

Total cost of system: Approximately $3,500 (including both computers)

E-mail: pacoid@wixer.bga.com and pacoid@well.sf.ca.us

The FringeWare Mission Statement: "Neotribalism in the Global Village"

FringeWare Inc. (FWI) is a commercial enterprise dedicated to community development around a fringe marketplace where the edges of diverse alternative cultures intersect...FringeWare acknowledges the essential importance of trade, but our mission is to create a context for E. F. Schumacher's essay, "Economics as if People Mattered."

We focus on publications, events, and products that we find interesting, fun, and enlightening...we engage in the following business activities:

- Publishing printed and electronic periodicals, including *Fringe Ware Review* and *Unshaved Truths*.

- Moderating an Internet mailing list and providing an automated list server for FWI archives.

- Operating a retail outlet and a mail-order service selling street tech, software, gizmos, DIY supplies, wearable subversive memes, and so on. Our current retail outlet is in our favorite bookstore: Europa Books, 2406 Guadalupe, Austin, Texas.

- Organizing events in cooperation with other New Edge firms and organizations.

We're learning that people can survive quite nicely without huge corporations, huge governments, and huge dogmas pushing their lives. So here's the FringeWare alternative:

Start your own corporation. Trade with other like-minded people throughout the Global Village. Encourage innovation and promote entrepreneurship. Promote fair, cooperative business practices. Emphasize products that facilitate creativity, health, and play. Explore consciousness alternatives. Build community through advanced, available technologies, such as computer networks. Respect and consider the natural environment by promoting sustainable resource use. Have fun, be weird, and make what it takes to survive.

Welcome to the Fringes of art, technology, and society. From here innovation emerges, and here survival—through cooperation and use of the unexpected—*counts*.

Thanks!

Jon Lebkowsky jonl@well.sf.ca.us

Paco Xander Nathan pacoid@wixer.bga.com

About FringeWare Inc.

Do you write code, build electronics, author multimedia? Would you like to buy, sell, or trade some of those funky gadgets in your closet, such as brain toys, Power Gloves, and Pixelvision? Have you been looking for just the right gift for that special cyberpunk or neophile in your life? Would you like to find one of the weirdest "coollections" of technoid gadgets on the planet? *FringeWare Catalog*—both the electronic and paper versions—reviews and sells these kinds of wares.

About the FringeWare Mailing List

The goals of this moderated, interactive mailing list:

- Distribute free copies of our technical reviews
- Exchange DIY source information for developers, enthusiasts, and others
- Publicize upcoming Fringe events
- Hear from the Net, chaotic post-it notes from the /real/ Fringe

To join, send a subscribe message to

fringeware-request@wixer.bga.com

To post a message or join or leave the list, send e-mail to

fringeware@wixer.cactus.org

About *Fringe Ware Review*

As the cyborganic offspring of *Mad* magazine, *CoEvolution Quarterly*, and *The Economist*, the brand new *Fringe Ware Review* offers a quarterly transmission of essays, fiction, comix, interviews, tutorials, and product reviews about "Building Community Around a Fringe Marketplace." Post-corporate info-economic theory, do-it-yourself technology, tutorials and supplies for fringe artists, engineers, and inventors, Internet community, and marginalism in the Global Village: if it's too weird for mainstream press to report and/or mainstream markets to vend, look to *Fringe Ware* as your source.

$3.50 single issue/$12 four-issue subscription, postpaid, in the U.S.; $4.50 single issue/$16 four-issue subscription, postpaid, elsewhere.

Contact:

FringeWare Inc.
PO Box 49921
Austin, TX 78765-9921
(512) 477-1366
E-mail: fringeware@wixer.bga.com

Teenager Builds VR System

Who Says VR Is Expensive?

APPENDIX

A

Teenager Builds VR System
Who Says VR Is Expensive?

© 1993 *CyberEdge Journal.* Reprinted with permission. All other rights reserved.

This interview appeared in the July/August 1993 edition of the VR industry newsletter CyberEdge Journal.

John Lusher II, a 17-year-old high school student from Madisonville, Texas, has built a VR system for less than $1,200. We were fascinated by this and arranged to talk with John at a recent conference in Houston. Here's John's story.

CyberEdge Journal: John, how did you get started in VR?

Lusher: I got started in virtual reality in 1990. I was in geometry class when an idea suddenly came to me: a simulation system with a head-mounted display and a position tracker that changed the user's field of view when he or she moved their head. I didn't know of anything like this system on the market, so I invested over $600 into patent searches and marketing reports. I then started showing my idea to several companies. One said there was a similar idea made by W Industries, called Virtuality. I followed this up and was shocked to find my idea was already in existence. I soon saw an article in the *Houston Chronicle* called "The Next Reality" by Dwight Silverman, and learned there was a virtual reality distributor, Spectrum Dynamics, right here in Houston. I called them to set up an appointment to see what they thought of my ideas.

Mike Zerkus, who is an electrical engineer, found my designs interesting and also told me of the science fairs and how they can benefit people like me. I then came up with the idea, why not build a low-cost virtual reality system?

CEJ: Then what happened?

Lusher: I started working on a system, and succeeded.

CEJ: Describe your system.

Lusher: The first question I had was what the unit would be like. I wanted something small and compact, so I designed the virtual reality system around an office chair that I made from plywood and fiberglass. The system is a compact work station in which a person can design something in the virtual world and then see it, without being tied down with large cables. The chair was the system and it could go anywhere you needed it to go. The next consideration was the computers. I only had $1,200 to spend on the project so I needed something cheap. I used two 8088 XT (10 MHz Turbo) motherboards and installed them in the back of the chair. The motherboards had 640K [RAM], CGA graphics, and I/O cards. The next issue was the sensor and helmet.

CEJ: The head-tracking sensor?

Lusher: Right. The sensor I developed myself using two inclinometers with optoelectronic sensors and a flux-gate digital compass similar to the ones from Radio Shack. The information from the compass was analog so I had to convert to digital form by using an ADC [analog-to-digital converter]. The inclinometers' output was already in digital form so all I needed to do was route this information to an input port. I used a parallel port, LPT-l, for that. I calculate the x-axis by using the sine and cosine outputs from the compass and the inclinometers were already in correct form.

CEJ: What about your HMD?

Lusher: The helmet was made by using two 6" CGA graphic screens from Timeline Inc. LCDs were too expensive, Sharp's running near $600 each. The helmet houses the monitors and the sensor. This was pretty heavy; it weighed near eleven pounds, so the helmet had to be counterweighted. Not great, but what I could do on a budget.

CEJ: How do you navigate in your system?

Lusher: With a multi-directional controller. It's no more than a simple control-pad joystick (NES Advantage) taken apart and a few extras added. The next item was an optoelectronic sensor to detect chair rotation. All the signals are multiplexed and set to LPT-1 with the 3D position sensor. There are several other features, but it basically came down to a slow but complete system for around $1,200. Very good for the money. But I got the Judges Special Award at the Bryan College Station, Texas, regional science fair. I was happy, because I had never competed at a science fair before, and because our school is not interested in engineering and science fairs.

CEJ: What about software, John? What do you see in your system?

Lusher: Basically it just shows a colored, wireframe cube in mid-air. There are some other cubes and triangles inside it. You can walk around it. The joystick lets you move around. You use the stick to choose from the menu, simple things like "left" or "right," then you say "yes" to activate it. It understands eight words.

CEJ: Where did you get the money to build this system?

Lusher: I worked as a surveyor's helper for my dad for a couple of summers. Then when I got this idea I took some of the money—well, most of the money—for the system. My folks like it, though, but my room is still, well, bad. I'm still picking solder out of the carpet.

CEJ: It's all pretty amazing, John. Now what?

Lusher: My future plans are to build more applications in virtual reality, low-cost and full-scale super systems. I plan to attend Texas A&M University, but do not have the money yet, so if someone has a scholarship, give a call. This project ate my bank account. Virtual reality is a growing field that will influence the way we live, just as the television and telephone did. The possibilities are endless.

CEJ: Good luck at school, and congratulations on a fine project. Anything else?

Lusher: Just that I would like to thank the people who made this project a real reality: My parents John and Jan Lusher, my friend Mike Zerkus, and everyone at Spectrum Dynamics.

You can contact John Lusher at Route 1, Box 330L, Madisonville, TX 77864; (409) 348-3432.

Teenager Builds VR System
Who Says VR Is Expensive?

What Is *CyberEdge Journal?*

CyberEdge Journal is the world's leading newsletter of virtual reality, a source of up-to-date information concerning VR news, issues, and technologies. Over 3,000 readers in more than two dozen countries read *CyberEdge Journal.*

Subscribers from around the world include Apple Computer, American Express, Boeing, Daimler Benz, Digital Equipment Corp., Dow Jones & Company, IBM T.J. Watson Research Center, Matsushita Electric Works, MIT, Pacific Telesis, Royal Melbourne Institute of Technology, Silicon Graphics, SRI International, Stanford University, University of Washington, VPL Research, W Industries, Ltd., and Walt Disney Imagineering.

CyberEdge Journal is published six times a year and is delivered by first-class or air mail. A one-year subscription costs $129 (plus $15 for delivery outside North America). A two-year subscription costs $228 (plus $30 for delivery outside North America). VISA and MasterCard are accepted.

The student rate is only $75 per year (plus $15 for delivery outside North America). Ask about bulk rates.

If at any time you decide that *CyberEdge Journal* isn't what you need, you can request a refund for the unused portion of your subscription.

Here's where to write for a sample issue:

CyberEdge Journal
#1 Gate Six Road, Suite G
Sausalito, CA 94965
(415) 331-3343

Fax: (415) 331-3643

E-mail: bdel@well.sf.ca.us or 76217.3074@compuserve.com

How to FTP

Perform an Internet File Transfer

APPENDIX

B

The following instructions show you how to move files (using the *file transfer protocol,* or *FTP*) across the Internet from a remote system to your computer.

These instructions provide the basic commands required to perform an FTP. For more information and power-user tips, refer to one of the Internet books listed in Appendix D, "Information Resources."

The following example shows the acquisition of the IBM PC program REND386 from the popular VR information site, sunee.uwaterloo.ca. This FTP procedure applies to almost all anonymous FTP retrievals. (*Anonymous FTP* provides access to sites in which you don't own an account.)

The FTP command structure is UNIX. After you're logged onto a remote site, you can type help (at the ftp> prompt) to see a list of commands. Type help command for information about a specific command.

Always type instructions or filenames exactly as shown; don't change lowercase to uppercase, or vice versa.

Keep in mind that some program files consume a lot of disk space. You need to verify that the directory on your network service or on your computer's hard disk has sufficient room for those files.

With that in mind, when you issue a get command for a text file and you type "-" (a space and a hyphen, without the quotation marks) after the filename, the system displays the file without copying it to your net account's home directory. (This procedure doesn't work on all systems.) You can open a capture file on your computer to save the file directly to disk. Pause the display by pressing Ctrl-S (^s) and resume with Ctrl-Q (^q).

To avoid network traffic and accelerate file transfer times, the best time to download programs is late at night or in the wee hours of the morning. Remember to take into account the time zone in which the remote system is located. For instance, the sunee site at the University of Waterloo (home of REND386) follows Eastern Standard Time, whereas the Macintosh VR site at ftp.apple.com follows Pacific Standard Time.

Let's give FTP a whirl.

1. Log on to your primary network service.
2. At the system prompt, connect to the desired remote site by typing ftp and the host name or address. For example:

   ftp sunee.uwaterloo.ca

   Or, type the numerical address:

   ftp 129.97.128.196

   This connects you to the site sunee.uwaterloo.ca. If this doesn't work, press Ctrl-C and try again later.

3. When you connect to the site, you receive a prompt that looks something like this:

```
Connected to sunee.uwaterloo.ca.

220 sunee FTP server (Version 5.1 Tue Jun 8 11:57:14 EDT
1993) ready.

Name (sunee.uwaterloo.ca:your_user_id):
```

4. Instead of your name, type

```
anonymous
```

This tells the site that you are logging in anonymously, which gives you restricted access to files.

5. You receive the response

```
331 Guest login ok, send ident as password.

Password:
```

Next, type your full e-mail address:

```
your_userid@your.network.com
```

6. You receive the response and prompt

```
230 Guest login ok, access restrictions apply.

ftp>
```

Now you're logged in and ready to go.

7. Checking out the contents of the top directory is always a good way to start. You can see a list of available subdirectories and text files.

To do this, at the `ftp>` prompt, type

```
ls
```

You receive a response that looks something like this:

```
200 PORT command successful.

150 Opening ASCII mode data connection for file list.

Amiga

nntp

incoming

sound

raytracers

radio

misc

wattcp
```

```
vgif
WHATS_WHAT.README
bicycle
shadows
fractint
glove
vr
polyblit
rend386
netgame
emr
jpeg
mfs
enorgy
```

8. When you first log on to a remote site, the system is in ASCII (text) mode. This site (like most other FTP sites) provides a text file that summarizes what's available and what's new. The sunee site's information file is named WHATS_WHAT.README. Other sites call their information files README, READ_ME, or something similar. If you're visiting a site for the first time, you should read the information file.

   To download or transfer *any* file from the remote system to your computer, type the command get filename. In this case, at the ftp> prompt, type

   ```
   get WHATS_WHAT.README
   ```

9. After you read the file, it's time to get a copy of the program REND386. First, though, you need to move into the rend386 directory. To move into a new directory, type the command cd directoryname. In this case, at the ftp> prompt, type

   ```
   cd rend386
   ```

   You receive a response that looks something like this:

   ```
   250 CWD command successful.
   ftp>
   ```

10. When you enter a subdirectory for the first time—or when you haven't been there for awhile—you should check out the contents. At the ftp> prompt, type

   ```
   ls
   ```

   You receive a response that looks something like this:

```
200 PORT command successful.

150 Opening ASCII mode data connection for file list.

unzip.exe

irit

read.me

floatsrc

old

polyblit

list-archive

demo4.zip

converters

utils

devel4.zip

drkit.zip

plgfiles

applications

226 Transfer complete.

128 bytes received in 0.04 seconds (3.1 Kbytes/s)
```

11. Next, check out the REND386 READ.ME file. At the `ftp>` prompt, type

```
get read.me -
```

(I typed a space and a hyphen after the command so that the text file would scroll without being saved to the home directory.)

Following are the contents of READ.ME:

```
200 PORT command successful.

150 Opening ASCII mode data connection for READ.ME (1781
bytes).

This directory contains Release 4 of Dave Stampe and Bernie
Roehl's fast 3D screen rendering package, REND386.

The package runs only on 386 or 486 based systems (it WILL
NOT WORK on 286s and below!) with VGA displays.

If you're only interested in the demo, just get DEMO4.ZIP;
if you're going to be doing software development with the
package, get DEVEL4.ZIP as well (you need DEMO4.ZIP in
either case).

For development work, you'll need to have Turbo C++ 1.00 or
above, or Borland C. For some modules, you'll also need
```

TASM.

If you want to start writing drivers for other video modes and pointer devices, get the DRKIT.ZIP file as well.

The applications directory contains programs written using the REND386 library.

The converters directory contains several different types of conversion programs that deal with .PLG files.

The floatsrc directory contains source code for a much older, all-C floating-point version of the code. You should probably download and read the READ.ME file in that directory before bothering to retrieve anything else from there.

The irit directory contains a fairly recent version of Gershon Elber's IRIT solid modelling environment. There's a converter to take the output of that package and convert it to .PLG format for use with the rend386 demo.

The plgfiles directory contains objects that people have built.

The polyblit directory contains the source code for an older version of Dave Stampe's polygon blitter routines, as used in REND386.

The utils directory contains utilities that people have written to work with REND386.

For more information about rend386, send mail to broehl@sunee.uwaterloo.ca or dstampe@sunee.uwaterloo.ca (there's also a mailing list... send mail to rend386-request@sunee.uwaterloo.ca to be added to it).

226 Transfer complete.

12. When transferring any program (nontext) files, such as REND386 or graphics demos, you must perform a *binary* transfer. Binary files are files that have been compressed (encoded) to save disk space and transferring time.

Certain files work only with certain computers. Binary files for the IBM PC platform typically use .ZIP as the filename extension. After you download a PC program, you'll probably need to decompress it with a utility such as PKZIP (available on your network) or StuffIt. Many Macintosh programs also are encoded. Decompression utilities are widely available.

Before transferring a program file, you need to issue a command telling the system that you're about to perform a binary transfer. At the `ftp>` prompt, type

`binary`

The computer responds with

`200 Type set to 1`
`ftp>`

13. To transfer a file and download it to your home directory, at the `ftp>` prompt, type

`get filename`

In this case, to obtain the REND386 demo, type

`get demo4.zip`

14. If you want to transfer program files so that you can write new device drivers and use REND386 for software development, at the `ftp>` prompt, type

`devel4.zip`

Typing `mget *.zip` transfers all the files with a .ZIP extension to your home directory. However, the system prompts you to request each file, one by one. Answer yes by typing `Y`.

15. If you don't have a copy of a decompression program for .ZIP files, type

`get unzip.exe`

to retrieve UNZIP.EXE from `sunee.uwaterloo.ca`.

16. Using your telecommunications software, download all the .ZIP and UNZIP.EXE files to your PC.

17. If you want to further explore the `sunee` site by reading other text files, you must command the system to return to text mode. At the `ftp>` prompt, type

`ascii`

18. When you're ready to leave the remote site, type `bye` or `quit`.

19. Back at the ranch—at the DOS prompt, that is—decompress the files by typing

`unzip *.zip`

20. Are you ready to check out the REND386 demo? At the DOS prompt, type

`DEMO`

and you're off!

NOTE

As of this writing, Version 4 of REND386 is available on the network. In September 1993, a comprehensive user's guide to REND386 was published. It was packaged with a DOS disk containing version 5 of REND386. Written by Bernie Roehl, Dave Stampe, and John Eagen, *Virtual Reality Creations* (Waite Group Press, $35) provides everything you need to know about REND386, and then some. You can acquire REND386 by buying the book, but it's good to know how to acquire the program with FTP. Bernie and Dave will continue improving REND386 and uploading future versions to the sunee site.

Vendors of Low-Cost VR Products

APPENDIX C

Input Devices

Advanced Gravis
7400 MacPherson Ave.
Burnaby, British Columbia
Canada V5J 5B6
(800) 663-8558
(604) 431-5020

Global Devices
6630 Arabian Circle
Granite Bay, CA 95661
(916) 791-3533

Immersion Human Interface Corp.
PO Box 8669
Palo Alto, CA 94309
(415) 599-5819
E-mail: immersion@starconn.com

Logitech Inc.
6505 Kaiser Drive
Fremont, CA 94555
(800) 231-7717
(510) 713-4835
BBS/modem: (510) 795-0408; Logitech forum on CompuServe

Multipoint Technology Corporation
319 Littleton Road, #201
Westford, MA 01886
(508) 692-0689

3DTV
PO Box Q
San Rafael, CA 94913-4316
(415) 479-3516

Shutter Glasses, Stereoscopic Equipment, and Supplies

Haitex Resources, Inc.
PO Box 20609
Charleston, SC 29413
(803) 881-7518

MegageM
1903 Adria
Santa Maria, CA 93454
(805) 349-1104

Reel-3D Enterprises, Inc.
PO Box 2368
Culver City, CA 90231
Phone: (310) 837-2368
Fax: (310) 558-1653

Simsalabim Systems, Inc.
PO Box 4446
Berkeley, CA 94704-0446
(510) 528-2021

3DTV
PO Box Q
San Rafael, CA 94913-4316
(415) 479-3516

Sound Cards and Software

Advanced Gravis
7400 MacPherson Ave.
Burnaby, British Columbia
Canada V5J 5B6
(800) 663-8558
(604) 431-5020

Creative Labs
1901 McCarthy Blvd.
Milpitas, CA 95035
(408) 428-6600
BBS/modem: (408) 428-6660

Crystal River Engineering
12350 Wards Ferry Road
Groveland, CA 95321
(209) 962-6382

Focal Point
1402 Pine Ave., #127
Niagara Falls, NY 14301
(416) 963-9188

Software: Graphics and VR

Domark Software
1900 South Norfolk St., #202
San Mateo, CA 94403
(415) 513-8929

Sense8 Corporation
4000 Bridgeway, #101
Sausalito, CA 94965
(415) 331-6318

Virtual Reality Laboratories, Inc.
2341 Ganador Court
San Luis Obispo, CA 94301
(805) 545-8515

Virtus Corporation
117 Edinburgh St., #204
Cary, NC 27511
(919) 467-9700
E-mail: virtus@applelink.apple.com
(Also on America Online)

VREAM, Inc.
2568 North Clark St.
Suite 250
Chicago, IL 60614
(312) 477-0425

VRontier Worlds
809 E. South Street
Stoughton, WI 53589
(608) 873-8523

Miscellaneous

RGB-to-NTSC Converters

Display Tech
936 Detroit Ave, Suite K
Concord, CA 94518
(800) 578-8546
In California: (510) 676-9362

Do-It-Yourself VR Projects

SAI
Dr. Robert Suding
27107 Richmond Hill Road
Conifer, CO 80433
(303) 838-6346

Gold Brick Power Glove/Macintosh Interface

Transfinite Systems, Inc.
PO BOX N, MIT Branch Post Office
Cambridge, MA 02139
(508) 371-7148

Power Glove Serial Interface

UICU Student Chapter of the Association for Computing Machinery
1304 West Springfield, Room 1225
Urbana, IL 61801
E-mail: pgsi@uiuc.edu

Power Glove Interfaces and Software

Virtual Reality Alliance of Students & Professionals
PO Box 4139
Highland Park, NY 08904-4139
E-mail: 70233.1552@compuserve.com

VR Equipment and System Distributors

FringeWare, Inc.
PO Box 49921
Austin, TX 78765
(512) 477-1366
E-mail: fringeware@wixer.bga.com

Spectrum Dynamics
3336 Richmond Avenue, #226
Houston, TX 77098-3022
(713) 520-5020
E-mail: specdyn@well.sf.ca.us

Information Resources

APPENDIX
D

Good Books

This potpourri of reading material covers a wide range of subjects that all pertain, in some way, to the technologies of garage VR and the building of virtual worlds. In this appendix you'll find colorful anthologies, provocative essay collections, balancing perspectives, and entertaining history lessons. Some of the computer books include software on floppy disks (in all cases, for PC DOS).

Advanced IBM PC Graphics by Michael I. Hyman (Brady, 1985).

Artificial Reality II by Myron Krueger (Addison-Wesley, 1991).

Beyond the Third Dimension: Geometry, Computer Graphics and Higher Dimensions by Thomas F. Banchoff (Scientific American Library, 1990).

Computers and The Imagination: Visual Adventures Beyond the Edge by Clifford A. Pickover (St. Martin's Press, 1991).

Cyberarts: Exploring Art and Technology, edited by Linda Jacobson (Miller Freeman, 1992).

Flights of Fantasy: Programming 3D Video Games in Borland C++ by Christopher Lambert (Waite Group Press, 1992). Includes a DOS floppy disk.

Foundations of the Stereoscopic Cinema by Lenny Lipton (Van Nostran Rheinhold, 1982).

Fundamentals of Three-Dimensional Computer Graphics by Alan Watt (Addison-Wesley, 1989).

Hackers: Heroes of the Computer Revolution by Steven Levy (Dell, 1984).

The Internet Companion: A Beginner's Guide to Global Networking by Tracy LaQuey with Jeanne C. Ryer (Addison-Wesley, 1993).

An Introduction to Computer Graphics Concepts: From Pixels to Pictures by Sun Microsystems, Inc. (Addison-Wesley, 1991).

The Media Lab: Inventing The Future at MIT by Stewart Brand (Viking Penguin, 1987).

The Metaphysics of Virtual Reality by Michael Heim (Oxford Press, 1993).

A Natural History of the Senses by Diane Ackerman (Vintage Books, 1991).

Navigating the Internet by Mark Gibbs and Richard Smith (Sams Publishing, 1993).

On Macintosh Programming: Advanced Techniques by Daniel K. Allen (Addison-Wesley, 1990).

On Photography by Susan Sontag (Farrar, Straus & Giroux, 1977).

On the Cutting Edge of Technology, edited by Dean Miller (Sams Publishing, 1993).

Programming in 3 Dimensions: 3-D Graphics, Ray Tracing, and Animation by Christopher D. Watkins and Larry Sharp (M&T Books, 1992).

Ray Tracing Creations by Drew Wells and Chris Young (Waite Group Press, 1993). Includes a DOS floppy disk.

Technopoly: The Surrender of Culture to Technology by Neil Postman (Alfred Knopf, 1992).

Tricks of the Graphics Gurus by Dick Oliver, Scott Anderson, et al (Sams Publishing, 1993).

Using ARexx on the Amiga by Chris Zamara and Nick Sullivan (Abacus, 1992).

Virtual Reality by Howard Rheingold (Simon & Schuster, 1991).

Virtual Reality Creations by Dave Stampe, Bernie Roehl, and John Eagan (Waite Group Press, 1993). Includes a DOS floppy disk and a stereo fresnel viewer.

Virtual Reality: Through the New Looking Glass by Ken Pimental and Kevin Teixeira (Intel/Windcrest/McGraw-Hill, 1993).

The Whole Internet: User's Guide and Catalog by Ed Krol (O'Reilley & Associates, 1992).

Virtual Reality Clubs and User Groups

The following grass-roots groups organize meetings on a regular basis. Neither corporate nor exclusionary (newcomers are welcome), their diverse goals spring from a common desire to create a community and unite people from different backgrounds. Most clubs charge minimal dues, present demonstrations, and experiment with garage VR. Many of these clubs represent the work of volunteers who labor in their spare time to bring VR to the masses. By the time you read this, there might be a VR club in your neighborhood. The following is a list of clubs and groups.

California

Los Angeles VR Interest Group
(310) 545-0369

Redondo Beach Virtual Reality Group
(310) 594-9394

San Francisco VeRGe
(415) 826-4716
E-mail: `avatarp@well.sf.ca.us`

Information Resources

Illinois

Chicago VR Interest Group
(708) 246-0766
E-mail: 71052.1373@compuserve.com

Kentucky

Louisville VR Interest Group
(502) 495-7186

Massachusetts

Cambridge: Boston Computer Society VR Group
(508) 921-6846

New Jersey (national)

VRASP (Virtual Reality Alliance for Students & Professionals)
(908) 463-8787
E-mail: 71033.702@ compuserve. com

Oklahoma

Norman VR Awareness Consortium
(405) 447-3276;
E-mail: gsullivan@aardvark.ucs.uoknor.edu or
gas@well.sf.ca.us

Texas

Houston Cyber Society
(713) 658-3889

Wisconsin

Andrew's VEE-AR Club
624 Jackson St.
Stoughton, WI 53589
E-mail: 70550.2702@compuserve.com

Belgium

Poederlee-Lille
Philippe Van Nedervelde
32-(14)-55-45-31

Canada

Ontario: University of Waterloo VR Group
(519) 888-4870

Toronto VR Special Interest Group
BBS/modem: (416) 631-6626

England

London VR User Group
44-(81)-318-4204

France

Les Virtualistes
90 Avenue de Paris
92320 Chatillon, France
33-(1)-47-35-658

Official Organizations

The following organizations regularly produce conferences, exhibitions, and workshops where you can get your hands on the latest VR gear.

Association of Computing Machinery: Umbrella organization for SigCHI (Special Interest Group on Computer-Human Interaction) and SigGRAPH (Special Interest Group on Computer Graphics), both of which produce annual conferences.

1515 Broadway
New York, NY 10036
(212) 869-7440

Meckler: Producers of virtual reality conferences in New York, California, and London.

11 Ferry Lane West
Westport, CT 06880
(800) 635-5537

SIG Advanced Applications, Inc.: Producers of virtual reality systems conferences in New York.

1562 First Avenue, #286
New York, NY 10028
(212) 717-1318

Technology and Persons with Disabilities: Producers of conferences in northern and southern California.

California State University Northridge
Center on Disabilities
18111 Nordhoff Street, DVSS
Northridge, CA 91330
(818) 885-2578

Information Resources

Virtual Reality Alliance of Students & Professionals

PO Box 4139
Highland Park, NY 08904-4139
E-mail: 70233.1552@compuserve.com

VR Technology Committee of the Institute of Electrical and Electronics Engineers: Producers of the Virtual Reality Annual International Symposium in Seattle, Washington.

5665 Oberlin Drive, #110
San Diego, CA 92121
(619) 453-6222

Glossary

APPENDIX

E

Glossary

accelerator card   A circuit board installed inside a computer to improve the performance of the central processing unit (CPU) or graphics processing.

algorithm   (1)A mathematical term indicating any series of instructions, decisions, and steps used to solve a problem or perform a task. (2)Any catchy saying attributed to President Bill Clinton's vice president.

analog-to-digital conversion   To convert analog data into digital form for input to a computer.

anti-aliasing   The process of removing jagged edges from the sides of virtual objects.

artificial intelligence   The development of programs to enable computers to mimic certain aspects of human intelligence, such as the ability to reason, learn, and solve problems.

artificial reality   Coined by arts scholar Myron Krueger in the mid-1970s to describe his "computer-controlled responsive environments," which took an aesthetic approach to the human/computer interface. "An artificial reality perceives a participant's action in terms of the body's relationship to a graphic world and generates responses that maintain the illusion that his or her actions are taking place within that world."—Myron Krueger, *Artificial Reality II,* Addison-Wesley, 1991.

authoring system   Software that helps developers design interactive applications.

bandwidth   A measurement (typically in Hertz, or cycles per second) that indicates a system's transmission capacity.

BASIC   Beginner's all-purpose symbolic construction code, a high-level computer language designed to simplify the process of programming by using common English words and mathematical symbols.

batch file   A type of file that enables you to execute a series of DOS commands by typing one command. Batch files are text files with the filename extension .BAT. In a batch file, each command is entered on a separate line. When you type the filename, all the commands in that file are executed sequentially.

beta version   A product not yet released to the general public.

bidirectional   Capable of enabling a signal to flow in either one of two directions within a single cable.

binaural   Involving the use of two ears. See *three-dimensional sound.*

bit blit transfer   A technique used to display moving objects, whereby a block of bits representing a portion of an image or scene is moved from one location in the frame buffer to another.

bit plane   A hypothetical, two-dimensional plane in the frame buffer that contains a bit in memory for each pixel on the display.

bitmap   Bitmapped graphics render an image as a pattern of dots. The program records the position of each dot. The bitmap is an array of values in the frame buffer for a certain image.

CAD/CAM   Acronyms for computer-aided design and computer-aided manufacturing. A CAD software program is a precision drawing tool that expedites the design process by providing versatility and automation during initial product or part design and revision processes. CAD programs also offer editing, printing/plotting, and data import/export functions.

CD-ROM   Compact disc read-only memory, a format for storing information digitally on a compact disc. A device that plays a CD-ROM is called a CD-ROM drive, and it connects to a personal computer.

cel   An animation frame.

CGA   Color graphics adapter. A type of circuit board for IBM compatibles that is installed in one of the computer's I/O slots. It can generate up to 25 lines of text with 80 characters on each line, or monochrome graphics with a 640x200 resolution and four-color graphics at 320x200 resolution.

CLUT   Color look-up table (also called *palette*). Refers to the color options in a graphics system, arranged by index number. Used in systems that provide only 8 bits (or less) per pixel.

clock   In digital circuits, the master source of timing information that produces a stream of high-speed pulses that are used to synchronize functions.

collision detection   A property programmed into a simulation that detects when objects come in contact with each other.

command-line interface   A way to control a program through a series of lines of alphanumeric text entered at the keyboard.

compile/compiler   The process (or the software that performs the process) of translating code written in a programming language into the binary format (zeros and ones) that the computer understands.

condition   In computer programming, a statement (such as IF Z = 6) specifying the condition that must be met before a result (event) can occur.

cyber   See *cybernetics*.

cybernation   Cyber(netics) + -ation; coined c. 1961 by D.N. Michael of Peace Research Institute. The use of computers coupled with automatic machinery to control and carry out complex operations, as in manufacturing, or to perform routine, repetitive tasks, as in government and business.

cybernetics   Coined in 1948 by Norbert Wiener; from the Greek *kybernetes,* or "helmsman," + -ics. A science dealing with the comparative study of the operations of complex electronic computers and the human nervous system.

Glossary

cyberspace   A term popularized by science-fiction author William Gibson to describe a shared virtual environment whose inhabitants, objects, and spaces are comprised of data that is visualized, heard, and touched. It is "a consensual hallucination experienced daily by billions of legitimate operators in every nation…a graphic representation of data abstracted from the banks of every computer in the human system."—W. Gibson, *Neuromancer,* Ace Books, 1984.

DataGlove   A gesture-recognition device that enables navigation through a virtual environment and interaction with 3D objects within it. A lycra glove lined with sensors that detect position and send signals to the computer, the DataGlove has fiber-optic cables along its fingers and wrist and an orientation sensor for navigation and virtual object manipulation. DataGlove is a trademark of VPL Research.

deck   The total hardware system, including sensors and effectors, required to run a cyberspatial VR application.

device driver   Software that tells the computer how to communicate with a peripheral device, such as a mouse, printer, CD-ROM drive, or stereoscopic shutter glasses.

digitize   To transform analog information, such as audio or video, into a digital format that can be used by a computer.

directory path   A pathname that begins with \, /, or ::. It tells the system how to find its way to a certain directory, starting at the root directory.

displays   Hardware devices used to represent data in a visual, audible, or tactile form.

DXF   Data exchange format, the common file format used by many CAD and rendering packages.

dynamics   Objects that control actions of objects and interactions between simulated objects.

effector   A device that transmits information (feedback) to the participant. Also called *output peripheral* or *display.*

EGA   Enhanced graphics adapter. A type of IBM PC-compatible adapter that enables you to display relatively high-resolution graphics on a color monitor. It can display up to 43 lines of text with 80 characters on each line, or it can display monochrome or 16-color at up to 640x350 resolution.

8-bit   A measurement of a monitor's capability to display colors. An 8-bit monitor can display 256 colors at once. The greater the number of bits, the higher the quality. This same type of measurement is used to refer to the sampling rate of computer sound cards.

Electronic Frontier Foundation (EFF)   In 1990, Mitchell D. Kapor, founder of Lotus Development Corp., and John Perry Barlow, writer, electronic gadfly, and lyricist for the Grateful Dead, established the EFF to do the following: support and engage in public education on developments in computer-based and telecommunications media; support litigation in the public interest to preserve, protect, and extend First Amendment rights within the realm of computing and telecommunications technology; help the public and policy-makers recognize and understand the opportunities as well as the challenges posed by developments in computing and telecommunications; and encourage and support the development of new software to enable nontechnical users to more easily use their computers to access the growing number of digital communications services. EFF, 1 Cambridge Center, Suite 300, Cambridge, MA 02142; (617) 864-0665; e-mail `eff@well.sf.ca.us`.

electronic mail (e-mail)   A method of exchanging textual messages or other computer data between two or more people when all parties are connected through a computer network.

EMI   Electromagnetic interference. Disturbance in data transmission caused by nearby electromagnetic devices or systems.

enabling technology   Technology that makes another technology possible. "The vacuum tube, for example, was the enabling technology for both radio and television.... Virtual reality based on computers and head-mounted displays has been dreamed of for decades, but had to wait for enabling technologies of electronic miniaturization, computer simulation, and computer graphics to mature in the late 1980s."—Howard Rheingold, *Virtual Reality,* Simon & Schuster, 1991.

entity   An object within the virtual environment.

environment   In VR terms, an inclusive model, or data that can be experienced from the inside.

ethernet   Network protocol for high-speed data transmission, developed at Xerox Palo Alto Research Center.

executable file   A file containing program instructions, as opposed to data created with such an application program. An executable file has the extension .BAT, .COM, or .EXE on DOS systems.

facets   Polygonal faces used to compose shapes in the virtual world.

FAQ   Frequently answered questions file, an introductory document about a particular topic that is addressed by an electronic mailing list, Usenet newsgroup, or Internet discussion site. Pronounced "fak."

fiber-optic cable   Glass or plastic fibers over which modulated light pulses from laser or light-emitting diodes (LEDs) can transmit voice, video, and computer data. Immune to electrical and radio interference, optical fibers carry much more information at a faster rate than traditional metal wires do.

flat-shaded   A method of coloring facets that covers the entire facet with a single shade.

flythrough   See *walkthrough*.

force feedback   See *tactile feedback devices*.

forceball   A 6DOF input device that enables object manipulation or movement of perspective. Its name refers to the fact that you apply force to this trackball-style device to navigate or interact with the virtual world. You push, pull, twist, and squeeze a stationary ball mounted in a box. For example, to move a pointer on-screen, you push the ball in the direction you want the pointer to move.

fractal   Fractal art generation is a computer process that creates complex, repetitive, mathematically defined geometric shapes and patterns that resemble those found in nature.

frame   A single, complete picture in a video recording, film, animation, or simulation.

frame buffer   A temporary storage device that gathers all the data for an image frame from the graphics processor, which runs at a certain rate, before releasing it to the display system, which runs at a different rate.

frame rate   The number of frames per second.

FTP   File transfer protocol. A procedure used to transfer files between systems on the Internet. Also used as a verb indicating the use of that protocol.

geometry   Data that defines a virtual object's physical dimensions and properties.

gesture controller   An input device that translates hand or body movements into computer data.

Gourand shading   A method of coloring facets in which you apply smooth gradations of color over the facet's surface. Compare *flat-shaded*.

granularity   Describes the accuracy of a 3D graphics model (referring to how "grainy" it is).

grok   To understand, usually on a profound level. Coined by Robert A. Heinlein in his science-fiction novel *Stranger in a Strange Land*.

GUI   Graphical user interface. A computer system that supports a GUI enables you to interact with the data visually (by pointing and clicking icons) rather than by typing commands. Pronounced "gooey."

hacker   A person who writes software or who experiments with a computer system's inner workings, typically with devotion and ingenuity.

HMD   Head-mounted display. An output device based on a helmet or goggles containing one or two tiny video monitors (one in front of each eye). Often coupled with audio headphones, the HMD currently is the most popular device for immersing you and letting you experience virtual worlds.

immersive   Characteristic of a computer-mediated experience that involves inclusion or partial immersion (only the hand, for instance) in a virtual world.

input devices   Tools that transfer data into a form recognizable to the computer. Input devices include keyboards, position-trackers, mice, joysticks, forceballs, and wired gloves.

interactive   The capability of a virtual world or object to respond immediately to choices and commands made by the participant.

interface   An interconnection or method of communication between two objects. An interface may be hardware or software.

Internet   See *network*.

ISO-9660   A file structure, approved by the International Standards Organization, that enables multiple types of computers to access the same files from one CD-ROM.

LCD   Liquid crystal display, the device used on digital watches, calculators, and miniature televisions. A liquid crystal is sealed between two pieces of glass and polarizers, then activated by an external source. Electric current toggles the crystal between transparent and opaque.

LED   Light-emitting diode, an optoelectronic device that uses electrical energy to generate light. LEDs are used for numerical displays in electronic test equipment, digital watches, and so on. On the Mattel Power Glove's sensor assembly, red LEDs illuminate to indicate when it senses glove motion.

meme   A term coined by biologist Richard Dawkins that means a cultural or socio-logical concept that is transferred from generation to generation. It comes from the Greek *mnemos,* a remembrance or record. Pronounced "meem."

MIDI   Musical instrument digital interface. A simple computer language that enables digital musical instruments, such as synthesizers, to communicate with computers and with each other. MIDI cables don't carry audio signals; they transmit commands in the form of computer data. Pronounced "middy."

mixing   The process of blending and routing audio signals while controlling their relative volume levels.

modem   A device used to interconnect computers by way of a telephone line so they can exchange data.

MUD   Multiuser dimension (or multiuser dungeon). An Internet-accessible applica-tion that provides text-based "virtual reality" in the form of real-time, group-oriented telecommunications, usually social in nature.

multiplex   To transmit two or more signals simultaneously.

Glossary

network (net)   A system of software and hardware connected in a manner to support data transmission. A local-area network might comprise several dozen computers in one building. A wide-area network might comprise several hundred computers in one region. The Internet is a global network encompassing many thousands of smaller computer networks.

neural network   A mathematical technique of pattern-matching, originally inspired by efforts to simulate the behavior of brain cells.

node   Any device connected to a network. Also, the point where such devices are connected.

NTSC   National Television Standards Commission. Refers to a television's method of displaying images. Used in the U.S. and a few other countries.

object-oriented   In computer graphics, an element that consists of a mathematical formula describing purpose, shape, position, and other attributes. What you see on-screen is a visual representation of the object.

operating system   A master-control computer program that enables other programs, including application programs (such as graphics software) to run.

OS/2   The successor to MS-DOS, this Microsoft operating system runs on 286 and 386 PCs.

overlay   One image placed over another.

palette   See *CLUT*.

parallax   The difference in the viewing angles provided by the line-of-sight path seen by each of your eyes.

parametric shape generation   The technique of generating shapes using mathematical formulae rather than user interaction.

parsing   The process of breaking something into segments.

pitch   Movement with a forward-and-backward rocking motion.

pixel   A contraction of "picture element." The smallest controllable element on a computer display screen. Picture resolution is measured in the number of pixels, usually expressed in horizontal by vertical dimensions. The more pixels per square inch, the sharper and clearer the image.

polygon   A building block of objects in a virtual world. Virtual worlds are constructed of hundreds or thousands of colored polygons. The more polygons a computer display can process and draw per second, the more realistic the virtual world appears. Standard workstation-powered virtual worlds are based on 1,500 to more than 15,000 shaded polygons that render at about 20 fps (frames per second).

port   Physical input or output provided for a connector.

portal   A link between two virtual environments that gives the illusion of a "larger" simulation by enabling a participant to immediately transfer to another part of the virtual world or to an entirely different virtual world.

position tracker   A system that tracks the movements of parts of the body and sends information about position and orientation to the computer for processing. Typically, a position tracker is attached to the head-mounted display, but other hardware sensors, such as wired gloves, joysticks, and 6DOF mice, also provide digital signals generated by the physical actions of the participant in the virtual world.

Power Glove   No longer on the market, this controller for the Nintendo Entertainment System game machine was adapted from VPL's DataGlove and licensed by Abrams/Gentile Entertainment to Mattel. More than a million were sold.

primitives   The fundamental building blocks provided in a computer drawing or modeling program: circles, lines, squares, cubes, polygons, and other simple shapes.

protocol   A set of rules for communicating between computers that determines the way a network manages the flow of information.

psychoacoustics   The branch of psychophysics that explores how people perceive and interpret sound. It's related to *acoustics,* the branch of physics concerned with the properties, production, transmission, and effects of sound. When we talk about a sound's "warmth," "clarity," or "punch," we're speaking subjectively. That's psychoacoustics. When we talk about a sound's intensity or echo, we're speaking objectively. That's acoustics.

QuickTime   The part of the Apple Macintosh System software that enables integration of video, sound, and animation within all applications. Also available for Microsoft Windows 3.1.

RAM   (1)Random access memory—data that can be called up from a computer's internal storage to be read, changed, or erased. A computer with lots of RAM is more powerful and can support faster, more visually complex software. (2)Paul McCartney's first album without the Beatles.

real time   Little or no delay in computer response time, giving the impression of instantaneous response.

reality   (1)The quality or fact of being real. (2)A person or thing that is real—fact. (3)The quality of being true-to-life; fidelity to nature. (4)*Philosophy*—that which is real.

real-time lighting   A technique in which the reality engine recalculates lighting effects and, consequently, the colors of facets, in real time, providing realistic moving light sources.

reflection mapping   See *texture mapping.*

render   To draw an image as it actually appears, rather than in schematic or outline form. The rendering process removes an image's hidden surfaces and jagged edges and defines the image's characteristics, such as color, lighting, and texture.

resolution   The measurement of image sharpness and clarity on a video display, usually measured by the number of pixels per square inch. The higher the resolution, the better the image's quality.

reverb   Short for *reverberation*. A form of continuous echo that gives sound a livelier presence.

RGB   Red, green, blue. Refers to the image-encoding scheme and display output signal used by a computer monitor (mixing red, green, and blue to create colors).

roll   Rotation.

RS232/422   Standards of communication between computers, established by the Electronic Industries Association. I/O devices that connect with RS232 or RS422 cable include mice, modems, and serial printers.

runtime   A self-running program (a data file) that can be loaded and used on a system that doesn't have the application in which the program initially was developed.

scan conversion   The process of changing one signal format to a different format.

scanning   The process of translating traditional images into digital data that can be understood and displayed by a computer.

sensor   An interface device that gathers information from the VR participant. Sometimes, but not always, called *input device*.

server   A computer that provides shared resources, such as data files, to a network.

shutter glasses   (also called *LCD glasses* or *stereoscopic glasses*)Electronically controlled glasses for viewing computer-generated stereoscopic image pairs. Liquid crystal "shutters" are mounted in the lenses of a pair of plastic goggles. The computer controls the electronic shutters, synchronizing them to correspond with alternating left-eye and right-eye versions of an image displayed on the monitor. The shutters open and close so quickly that your brain can't detect the activity. Each eye receives separate image information, but the brain is fooled into thinking that a single, apparently three-dimensional image is being displayed.

signal processing   A digital audio manipulation technique used to change the characteristics of an audio signal (such as pitch). (Audio is the electronic representation of sound.)

simulated object   A virtual-world entity that might have an appearance and/or a behavior. Sometimes called an *object*.

single-pass lighting   A process that calculates the effects of lights in the virtual world once, then assigns the colors to the facets on that basis. That assignment is used from that point on. Compare *real-time lighting.*

six degrees of freedom (6DOF)   A sensor's capability to track movement of spatial position (x-, y-, and z-axes) and orientation (pitch, yaw, and roll).

sound sampling   The process of making and playing back a digital recording (sample) of any type of sound, whether acoustic (a bird song) or electronic (synthesizer output).

sound synthesis   The process of generating, modifying, and producing sound electronically. Sound is assembled (synthesized) from simple waveforms that are altered and combined in various ways.

source (source code)   The lines of code that make up a program. Source code can't be executed directly by the computer; it must be compiled into machine language (binary format).

space   In VR, *space* generally refers to dimensionality. (Not to be confused with *cyberspace.*)

spline   In computer graphics, a curve shape that is defined mathematically by a small number of control points.

sprite   A screen image that can be moved by program or manual control using an input device. Sprites can be characters (such as those in video games), cursor shapes, or patterns.

stereoscopic glasses   A wearable output device used for viewing in stereo to look at computer-generated, 3D graphics that appear to float in front of your eyes.

tactile feedback devices/force feedback devices   Output devices that transmit pressure, force, or vibration to provide the VR participant with the sense of touch. Tactile feedback simulates sensation applied to the skin. Force feedback simulates weight or resistance to motion.

telepresence   (1)The experience of immersion in a remote environment. (2)The remote operation systems that translate human movements into the control of machinery.

texture mapping/reflection mapping   The processes of imbuing a computer graphics image with the appearance of lifelike texture (smooth, rough, rippled, and so on) and light reflections and other characteristics.

TCP/IP   Transmission control protocol/internet protocol. The language that enables computers to communicate on the Internet. This open protocol is nonproprietary; everyone can use it so that their products or systems can connect to the Internet.

torqueball   See *forceball.*

three-dimensional (3D) modeling   Used in computer-aided design and the creation of virtual worlds to geometrically define the shape of an object.

three-dimensional (3D) sound   Reproduced sound that seems to emanate from points in front of, above, below, and to either side of the listener. 3D sound systems can accurately recreate or simulate a binaural recording environment, providing an "acoustic photograph" of sound. 3D sound systems actually trick your brain into *perceiving* the sound as coming from some place other than the speakers or headphones. Thanks to recent advances in computer science, psychoacoustics, and signal processing, 3D sound is possible.

tweening   Short for "in-betweening." Transitional effects between two versions of an animated character performing an action or an object in motion. The tweening function creates a series of frames in which the character or object moves between the first "key frame" and the subsequent action in the last "key frame."

ultrasonics   Frequencies of sound waves above the range audible to human hearing. A form of data transmission used in some types of position-tracking systems.

UNIX   The world's most widely used, general-purpose, multiuser operating system for workstation systems.

vector graphics   Representations of objects, based on complex mathematical formulae.

VEOS   Virtual Environment Operating System, developed at the Human Interface Technology Laboratory at University of Washington in Seattle. The VEOS project was spearheaded by William Bricken, the HIT Lab's principal scientist. The VEOS prototype is "like the glue underneath a VR system [joining] components such as computing platforms, input devices, and software tools," Bricken explains. Initially developed in 1991, the VEOS prototype is written in C for use on UNIX workstations in high-end VR systems. The HIT Lab has released VEOS to the public domain.

VGA   Video graphics array. A type of high-resolution, color display adapter card for IBM compatibles that can display monochrome text and graphics at up to 720x400 resolution, 16-color graphics at up to 640x480 resolution, and 256-color graphics at 320x200 resolution.

video card   A display adapter card that is installed in a computer's option slot. It provides the interface to which you connect the monitor. It also controls the way the monitor displays text and graphics.

VIEW   Virtual interface environment workstation. Developed in 1985 at NASA-Ames Research Center in Mountain View, California, VIEW (for the first time anywhere) combined head-mounted display, VPL DataGlove, speech recognition, 3D audio, computer graphics, and video imaging technology. VIEW was developed to plan space missions.

virtual (reality, community, space, world, environment) According to Webster's, "being such practically or in effect, although not in actual fact or name [a *virtual* impossibility]." IBM started using this word in the late 1960s to refer to any nonphysical link between processes and/or machines, such as "virtual memory," random-access memory simulated using disk drives.

virtual reality (VR) As generally agreed, virtual reality refers to technology that presents data visualizations or simulations in the form of computer-generated and computer-mediated three-dimensional "worlds" or environments that you can "enter," manipulate, and navigate using appropriate input and output devices. Virtual reality is characterized by "immersion" (it feels as if you are "inside" it) and the ability to change your viewpoint and interact with the world and its objects in real time. As such, virtual reality is interactive, and the participant enjoys autonomy, or freedom to move around and manipulate virtual objects at will.

With modern virtual reality, you can see and hear, point and move, pick up things and throw them, and sometimes feel those objects. The popular concept of current VR involves interaction with a computer-generated world with head-mounted goggles, position trackers, wired gloves, and other 6DOF input devices.

Contrary to popular belief, virtual reality and cyberspace are not the same thing. (See *cyberspace.*)

visualization The visual representation of complex or abstract data, usually in the form of a computer graphics model.

walk-through/fly-through A complex, three-dimensional model of a building, structure, or other environment through which you can move your viewpoint as if walking or flying through it. Initially intended for use in architectural CAD applications. In a walkthrough you create a scene or animation for every possible point of view and field of view, then play the scene or animation based on the participant's input. If you climb a tree, for example, you play the animation that moves the point of view from the roots, up the trunk, and into the branches. If you move your input device to look to the left, the animation plays the field of scrolling to the right.

wireframe A 3D graphics image in which lines are used to represent the edges of an object.

yaw To pan. Side-to-side movement around an axis.

Your Garage
VR Fuel Kit

What's on
the Disk

Doug Faxon's Gaynor House

Copy *filename* and bat file to your hard drive. At the DOS prompt, type `gaynor`.

The Gaynor House represents the place at 9947 Gaynor Street in Sepulveda, California, where Doug Faxon lived until he was 13.

When you first launch the Gaynor House demo, you view the house from the perspective of standing on the lawn, facing the front door. (Doug explains that he couldn't include the split-trunk sycamore tree in the front lawn because of the limitations of VR Studio, which permits only 60 objects per scene. In the first Gaynor House scene, even the blue sky ranks as an object.)

In the Gaynor House, interactivity is the ability to navigate: you interact with objects as you walk from one room to another. Doug wrote a simple script that says if you "collide" with a door, which is an object, VR Studio automatically takes you to another Gaynor room.

Individual "rooms" in the Gaynor House include the living room, master bedroom, bathroom with shower, back room, laundry room, garage, and the backyard. In the living room, you'll notice the bar where Doug's father "stashed his booze. And you can see the lamps that were made by my godfather, who's a metal sculptor." Also present is the piano on which Doug pounded out his first solos.

In the office, you'll see his father's little bottle collection.

You'll see the garage where Doug performed many "nefarious experiments with electricity and fire and chemistry." It even has the chalk dispenser next to the garage door, left over from the days when Doug's dad had a pool table.

The backyard features the Faxon family pool and deck. Doug admits that the pool "was very difficult to create, because VR Studio doesn't do round or cylindrical objects. So this pool is made up of about 20 pyramid shapes of varying sizes. First I created a square shape, then I stacked the pyramids sideways around the edges of the square, with the smallest pyramids on the outside. Then I painted the tops of everything blue so the shape of the structure approaches roundness."

If you get lost, press Esc to return to the front lawn.

To exit the program, press Alt-Shift-Esc. This returns you to the DOS prompt.

Doug Faxon's World of Stairs

Copy the *FILENAME* to your hard drive. At the DOS prompt, type `install`. Then, type `escher`.

Type `Runvga Escher.run` on the command line in the directory in which you unzipped this file.

Colliding with doorways (usually indicated by a dark rectangle) usually takes you to a different area. However, in some areas that provide two or more doors, only one of the doors will take you out. If you get lost, press Esc. The Esc key takes you back to your initial position in the World of Stairs. Pressing Shift-Esc causes you to exit from that point back to DOS.

Doug Faxon adds, "This was the first project I created using Domark's Virtual Reality Studio. I spent about 35 hours on it, a labor of love. I hope you enjoy it!"

Commands for Doug Faxon's Worlds

You can use the control buttons Doug provided on the bottom panel or the following keyboard commands:

Key	Command
/	Turn left (pan)
*	Turn right (pan)
P	Look up (pitch)
L	Look down (pitch)
O	Move forward (z-axis)
K	Move backward (z-axis)
U	Make a U turn (z-axis)
N	Make a U turn (z-axis)
H	Move to the left (x-axis)
J	Move to the right (x-axis)
R	Go up (y-axis)
F	Go down (y-axis)
M	Rotate view clockwise (roll)
I	Rotate view counterclockwise (roll)

Virtual Hand Files and Glove Control Software

IBMPC-HI is the new version that works off of timer interrupts on the IBM-PC. It also does auto-calibration of the delay loops.

GLOVE.H contains a number of general-purpose structs, defines, and prototypes for accessing the glove.

GLOVE.C contains the routines for accessing the glove on the PC.

TEST.C contains a very simple demo that just reports, in text mode, the values read from the glove.

GLOVGRAF.C contains a slightly fancier demo that moves a rectangle around the screen as the glove moves.

MAKEFILE is useful for building TEST.EXE and GLOVGRAF.EXE.

Software for Use with DIY-HMD

This file is an auto-execute. Simply type the filename at the DOS prompt and the file will decompress.

Index

Index

</empty>
</void>
</text>

Index

GARAGE VR

GARAGE
VR

Index

GARAGE
V R

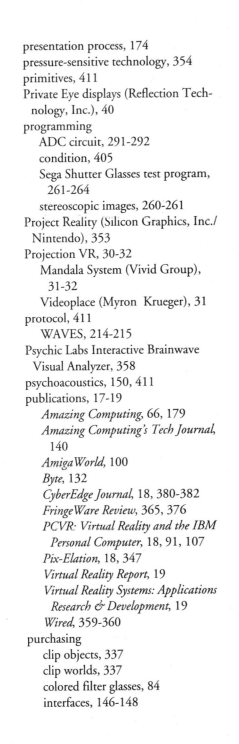

434

Index

GARAGE VR

Index

EXPLORE YOSEMITE
LANDSCAPE MARS
DESIGN A NEW LAKE
RELEASE A RIVER
SHAPE NEW WORLDS
LEARN GEOGRAPHY
PREVIEW A JOURNEY
DEVELOP UNDERSEAS
CREATE NEW FORESTS
STUDY TOPOGRAPHY
CHANGE THE SEASONS
DIRECT THE SUN

AFFORDABLE VIRTUAL REALITY HAS ARRIVED WITH VISTAPRO!

VIRTUAL REALITY

LANDSCAPE GENERATION

SOFTWARE

Mount St. Helens, Washington

Yosemite National Park, California

Inside this book, you'll find a demo copy of Vistapro 3.0, the incredible virtual reality landscape generator based on real-world data obtained from the U.S. Geological Survey and NASA.

Once you've tried our demo of Vistapro 3.0, with its 24-Bit color, 3-D trees, fractal texturing and clouds, we're sure you'll be ready for the real thing! Unlike the demo, the full version of Vistapro 3.0 is loaded with features which allow you to:

● Explore 19 different landscape sets of earth and Mars, (many more available separately!) or explore billions of imaginary fractal places ● Have FULL CONTROL over trees and clouds ● LOAD AND SAVE your creations in a variety of formats (Supports 24-bit BMP, Targa 24, PCX and FLC (Autodesk animation) ● Generate left and right images for 3-D viewing ● Render images larger than 640 x 480 ● Load larger landscapes and multiple contiguous landscapes ● AND MORE!

Mail orders or inquiries to:
2341 Ganador Court, San Luis Obispo, CA 93401
(805) 545-8515 FAX (805) 781-2259
Also available for Amiga. Macintosh available in 1994

ORDER TODAY AND SAVE $60

off the retail price of $129.95!

YES! I want to become a virtual explorer! Please send me Vistapro 3.0 IBM for only $69.95 plus shipping.

Name_____
Address _____
City _____
State/Province _____Zip/PC_____
Country _____Phone _____
☐ VISA ☐ Mastercard # _____
Exp. _____Signature _____

SHIPPING: Please add $5.00 shipping/handling inside the continental U.S. for a total of $74.95. Add $10.00 shipping/ handling outside the continental U.S. for a total of $79.95.

Virtual Reality Laboratories, Inc.   1-800-829-VRLI

Introducing the sequel to the *best-selling VR package:*

Virtual Reality Studio 2.0

Exclusive offer made available only to Virtual Reality Madness readers!

$59.95

Includes:
- Clip art library with color catalog
- Twice as many control commands
- Sound Effects Editor
- Fading and transparent objects
- Flexicubes and spheres
- VCR-style playback function

Call Domark at 415-513-8929 to place your order today!

Offer closes September 1st, 1994

Add to Your Sams Library Today with the Best Books for Programming, Operating Systems, and New Technologies

The easiest way to order is to pick up the phone and call

1-800-428-5331

between 9:00 a.m. and 5:00 p.m. EST.
For faster service please have your credit card available.

ISBN	Quantity	Description of Item	Unit Cost	Total Cost
0-672-30248-9		FractalVision: Put Fractals to Work for You (book/disk)	$39.95	
0-672-30322-1		PC Video Madness! (book/CD)	$39.95	
0-672-30249-7		Multimedia Madness! (book/CD)	$44.95	
0-672-30391-4		Virtual Reality Madness! (book/CD)	$39.95	
0-672-30373-6		On the Cutting Edge of Technology (full color)	$22.95	
0-672-30301-9		Artificial Life Explorer's Kit (book/disk)	$24.95	
0-672-30320-5		Morphing Magic (book/disk)	$29.95	
0-672-30362-0		Navigating the Internet	$24.95	
0-672-30315-9		The Magic of Image Processing (book/disk)	$39.95	
0-672-30308-6		Tricks of the Graphics Gurus (book/disk)	$49.95	
0-672-30376-0		Imaging and Animation for Windows (book/disk)	$34.95	
0-672-30341-8		Absolute Beginner's Guide to C	$16.95	
0-672-30282-9		Absolute Beginner's Guide to Memory Management	$16.95	
0-672-30352-3		Blaster Mastery (book/CD)	$34.95	
❏ 3 ½" Disk		Shipping and Handling: See information below.		
❏ 5 ¼" Disk		TOTAL		

Shipping and Handling: $4.00 for the first book, and $1.75 for each additional book. Floppy disk: add $1.75 for shipping and handling. If you need to have it NOW, we can ship product to you in 24 hours for an additional charge of approximately $18.00, and you will receive your item overnight or in two days. Overseas shipping and handling adds $2.00 per book and $8.00 for up to three disks. Prices subject to change. Call for availability and pricing information on latest editions.

201 W. 103rd Street, Indianapolis, Indiana 46290

1-800-428-5331 — Orders   1-800-835-3202 — FAX   1-800-858-7674 — Customer Service

Book ISBN 0-672-30270-5

Garage Virtual Reality
Disk Information

What's on the Disk

The *Garage Virtual Reality* disk contains the PC version of the award-winning Virtual Reality Studio 1 program, which retails for more than $70. Virtual Reality Studio 1 lets you design your own interactive virtual reality worlds. This is a complete version—*not* a demo! A special on-line version of the complete manual is included.

Plus, you'll find these additional virtual reality files for IBM-Compatible PCs:

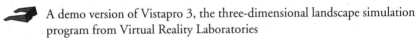

- A demo version of Vistapro 3, the three-dimensional landscape simulation program from Virtual Reality Laboratories
- Source code examples for programming the Power Glove, head-tracking displays, and more
- Executable versions of the sample programs
- Two sample VR worlds

Installing the Disk

You need to run the installation program on the disk to install the software on your hard drive. You'll need at least 2.2 megabytes of free space.

1. At the DOS prompt, type `B:INSTALL` and press Enter if the disk is in drive B; type `A:INSTALL` if the disk is in drive A. The installation program will display an introductory message. Press any key to continue.

2. At the main screen of the installation program, you have the option of changing the drive where the programs will be installed. If you want to change to a drive other than C, press Enter and select from the list of available drives.

3. You also can choose which version of Virtual Reality Studio to install. The default is the VGA version. If you want to select the EGA or Tandy versions, choose `Change the version of Virtual Reality Studio to install` and select the version. It's important that you select only *one* version to install.

4. Choose the `Start Installation` selection. The program will begin installing the files to your hard drive.

5. When the files have been installed, the file GARAGEVR.TXT will be displayed for you to read. It contains information on the software. Press Esc when you're finished reading it.

6. A message will appear when the program is finished. Press any key to exit.

This will install the files for Virtual Reality Studio to a directory named \STUDIO on your hard drive. The demos, source code, and other files will be installed to a directory named \GARAGEVR. For more information on installing the software, read the README.TXT file.